THE
FIRST FABIANS

THE FIRST FABIANS

Norman and Jeanne
MacKenzie

Weidenfeld and Nicolson
London

ACKNOWLEDGMENTS

Anyone who writes on the early Fabians owes a great debt to Dame Margaret Cole, who has not only played a significant part in the Society throughout her long life but has also contributed much in her writings to knowledge of the Fabians and of Sidney and Beatrice Webb in particular. We were greatly helped by surviving members of the families of the first Fabians. Mr. and Mrs. Nicholas Pease, Lady Helen Pease and Dr. Sebastian Pease all provided materials and personal memories of Edward Pease and his contemporaries, especially the Fabian coterie settled around Limpsfield. Mrs. Paul Bland helped with information about Hubert Bland and Edith Nesbit. Mr. R. Walston Chubb did much to increase our knowledge of his father, Percival Chubb, and his associates in founding the Society. Mrs. Olivier Bell, Sir John and Lady Nicholson, Dr. Angela Harris and Dr. Benedict Richards made Olivier family papers available to us. The late Miss May Wallas agreed that we might see and quote from her father's papers.

We appreciate the help given to our enquiries about the involvement of early Fabians in the Society for Psychical Research by Mr. Mostyn Gilbert and Mr. J. Fraser Nicol. Dr. Peter Weiler and Professor Willard Wolfe were kind enough to let us see forthcoming publications in manuscript, Professor Stanley Pierson made most useful suggestions about the location of documents, and Professor Royden Harrison drew our attention to other sources. Miss Doris Ker gave us valuable leads on the early life of Hubert Bland. Mr. T. A. Critchley and Mr. C. H. Rolph directed us to Home Office records on the unemployed disturbances of the Eighties. We particularly thank Mr. George Spater and Professor George Feaver, who read early drafts of this book and made many helpful comments.

We are grateful to the library staff at the University of Sussex, who helped in many ways, and to the other libraries which answered enquiries, provided materials and gave us facilities for research. At the British Library of Political and Economic Science Mr. Geoffrey Allen, Mr. David Bovey and Miss Angela Raspin were unfailingly helpful. We also thank the staff of the British Museum, the Bodleian, the National Library of Scotland, Sheffield University Library, Sheffield Reference Library, the Yale University Library, the Library of Newnham College, Cambridge, the Library of Corpus Christi College, Oxford, the Woolwich Public Library, the Society for Psychical Research and the Fabian Society. We have a special debt to Nuffield College, Oxford, whose library contains the Fabian Papers, and to the University of Illinois, which permitted us to use the Wells Archive there.

We thank all those copyright holders who granted permission to quote published and unpublished material. The British Library of Political and Economic Science gave permission to quote from the Passfield Papers; the Society of Authors acted on behalf of the estate of George Bernard Shaw; and the trustees of the will of Mrs. Bernard Shaw allowed us to quote from her letters. Mr. Nicholas Pease and Mr. R. Walston Chubb released letters written by their respective fathers. Professor G. P. Wells, on behalf of the estate of H. G. Wells, permitted the use of copyright material from the Wells Archive.

There are some individuals to whom we are much indebted. Mr. Ronald Blythe generously shared with us his own research on the early Fabians, and Mr. Tony Godwin encouraged us to undertake the writing of this book. Finally, we thank Mrs. Margaret Ralph, Mrs. Audrey Hunt and Mrs. Netta Burns, who shared the task of typing the manuscript.

In affectionate memory
of TONY GODWIN

CONTENTS

PART FOUR

THE CIVILIZING MISSION

PART FIVE

JUDGMENT DAYS

The authors wish to thank the following sources for permission to reproduce the photographs that appear between pages 224-225: R. Walston Chubb, photograph 2; Pease family papers, photographs 4, 5; Olivier family papers, photograph 7; Radio Times Hulton Picture Library, photographs 10, 11, 12, 16, 19, 21, 25; The Mansell Collection, photographs 17, 18, 22, 24; London School of Economics, photographs 26, 27-A, 27-B, 29; Longmans Publishers, photograph 13.

They saw "no divine part of Christianity," but divinified humanity, or humanised religion, and taught that man was perfectible, but childhood perfect.

—*Lord Acton: Letter to Richard Simpson,*
December 8, 1861

PART ONE

ARDENT
DISCIPLES

❧ 1 ❧
THE NICEST SET
OF PEOPLE

On the evening of 24 October 1883 Edward Pease invited fifteen people
to his comfortable lodgings at 17 Osnaburgh Street, London, close by
Regent's Park, to discuss the formation of a new society. Most of the
group were, like Pease, young provincials adrift in the capital. He himself was twenty-six and had been working for three years in a stockbroker's office. His guests included a couple of junior clerks in the civil
service, a medical student, an architect, some aspiring journalists and half
a dozen ladies of advanced opinions. Some of them he knew already,
acquaintances picked up in London's bohemia; the rest had been suggested by friends as possible sympathizers. None of them had any clear
idea about the purpose of the new society, but there was vague agreement that their lives were unsatisfying and that they needed some common moral purpose.

Pease came to London at a time when the stable Victorian order was
breaking up. Britain's long industrial supremacy was over and the country was beset by economic troubles.[1] Competition from Germany and
the United States was provoking uncertainty and discontent; the trade
slump which started in 1879 made the problem of "unemployment" so
acute in the big cities that the word came into general use for the first
time. In the countryside, where a run of wet summers and imports of

cheap grain from the American prairies had thrown agriculture into a deep depression, things were even worse. Gladstone's Liberal government, swept into office in 1880 on a radical tide, had failed to introduce any significant reforms. Elected as a party of peace, it had become embroiled in military adventures in Afghanistan, Egypt and South Africa. And Ireland was in an uproar under a police terror to keep the nationalist movement under control.

These social stresses were accompanied by severe psychological strains. The new sciences, especially Darwin's evolutionary doctrine, had undermined the Evangelical faith which energized the Victorian middle classes. His demonstration that men were not fallen angels but risen apes confronted even those who accepted his argument with a disconcerting and scarcely tolerable reality. They longed to escape its mortal implications. Since revealed religion was no longer credible, they were driven to seek alternative intellectual systems around which their lives could be structured. For the habit of belief remained, with its constraining emphasis on duty and morality. "There are many about us," W. H. Mallock pointedly remarked in 1878, "though they never confess their pain, and perhaps themselves hardly like to dwell on it, whose hearts are aching for the God they no longer believe in."[2]

The group which came together in Osnaburgh Street was typical of the little clubs and coteries which cropped up all over the country to fill the void. London in these years, Pease recalled, was "full of half-digested ideas." Parlour philosophies were so popular, he said, that it seemed "that we should arise one morning and see the old heaven looking down upon a new earth."[3]

Young men like Pease who were lonely and unable to find a focus for their aspirations were the raw material for such clubs. Pease himself came from a well-to-do and well-connected Quaker family. His grandfather had been an early railway promoter; another Pease had been the first Quaker elected to the House of Commons. The fine Georgian house at Henbury Hill, near Bristol, where Edward Reynolds Pease was born on 23 December 1857 was kept up in considerable style. His father was a self-centred and dilettantish gentleman of means who occupied himself with Liberal politics and Quaker meetings. He believed in the literal truth of the Bible—a fundamentalist conviction which he managed to reconcile with an amateur enthusiasm for the new geology that was doing so much to undermine the religious view of the world and man's place in it. His concern with natural history, indeed, seems to have been the only point of contact with Edward; he was emotionally distant from his children, caring more about the rigours of religious truth than about congenial companionship. His wife was equally aloof. She was a woman, Edward said, whose affection "did not concern itself with the thoughts or doings of her children."

Edward grew up a shy and unimaginative boy who found his pleasure in gardening, reading and carpentry, spending much time with family retainers like his devoted but sharp-tempered nanny, and with local craftsmen. These below-stairs people filled the gap left by his parents and gave life and colour to his childhood. He was educated at home by two tutors. The first was a German who had fled after the collapse of the democratic revolution in 1848. The second, Theodore Neild, came to the Peases when Edward was eleven and coached him until, five years later, he reached university entrance level and his formal education ended. Neild was a man of advanced views, a teetotaller, a passionate Russo phobe and an early supporter of woman suffrage. Although he was an ardent Quaker, his unorthodox opinions stimulated the growing scepticism with which the adolescent Edward regarded established religion and politics.

When Edward was seventeen he went to London to become a clerk to a firm of silk merchants in the China trade, in which his brother-in-law Thomas Hanbury was a senior partner. On his salary of forty pounds a year he lived a modest life; his main recreation was to act as secretary to a small debating society at the Friends' Institute. Thus, he recalled, "began my life-business of being Secretary to everything I was connected with." When advancement required him to accept a posting to China, he was not prepared to go and abruptly threw up his job. He refused an offer from a firm of building merchants because "they wanted a partner who would help them in praying to God for guidance over a doubtful contract, and I was unable to give satisfactory assurances on this point." After a year at home Thomas Hanbury found him a partnership in a small stockbroker's office, where he was soon earning a good income of four hundred pounds a year.

Work among the City jobbers and speculators soon made Pease feel frustrated and morally contaminated. Affronted by the wealth of the Stock Exchange and the squalor of the slums, he began to look for an outlet for what was then called a sense of "social compunction." For a

time he helped the housing reformer Octavia Hill in her work of beau-
tifying old graveyards. His natural shyness made it difficult for him to
make friends, but he found congenial companionship in his cousin Emily
Ford, and with her he went walking, boating, and to the theatre at the
weekend.

It was Emily Ford who carried Pease off one evening in 1881 to one of
the spiritualist seances then the vogue in London. Edward was sceptical
but fascinated. "One sat in darkness singing hymns," he recalled, "till
banjoes banged about the room, and spirit fingers touched one's fore-
head." At one of these sessions Pease met a young clerk in the Post Office
named Frank Podmore, and they soon became close friends. Podmore
was a clergyman's son who, after taking his degree at Oxford, had turned
to spiritualism as a substitute for orthodox Christian belief. By the time
he met Pease his new faith had been shaken by encounters with bogus
mediums and their comic apparatus of tambourines, trumpets, bells, and
ectoplasm spun out of mutton cloth. Yet the twilight world of psychic
phenomena continued to attract him, as it did Pease.

In this same period a group of young dons from Trinity College,
Cambridge, were also turning to psychic research as a substitute for their
lost Evangelical faith. In February 1882 Podmore took Pease to a meeting
at which this group founded the Society for Psychical Research. They
became members of the council of the new organization, which promptly
set about investigating mediums, clairvoyants and hypnotists, with
haunted houses and water-divining thrown in for good measure.[4] Among
those who founded the SPR were Henry Sidgwick, professor of moral
philosophy at Cambridge, Arthur Balfour—later a Conservative prime
minister—and his brother Gerald. As the Society grew it attracted men
as eminent as Gladstone, Tennyson, Ruskin, the physicist Lord Rayleigh
and eight Fellows of the Royal Society.

For a time Pease found an agreeable niche in the SPR as secretary
of its haunted-houses committee, organizing its observers and supervis-
ing their reports. Before long, however, he came to the conclusion that
while there was a strong case for believing in hallucinations, watching
for ghosts "was really foolish," and his enthusiasm cooled.

By the beginning of 1883 Pease was turning to politics. Podmore and
other acquaintances had advanced views. There was, indeed, no clear

dividing line between spiritual discontent and political radicalism in the netherworld of dissent. As Pease made the rounds of the meeting halls his attention was caught by the Democratic Federation, a new party which Henry Myers Hyndman had founded two years earlier. In the summer of 1883 he went to one of its meetings. It was, he wrote to his sister on 19 July 1883, "the oddest little gathering," consisting of "twenty characteristically democratic men with dirty hands and small heads, some of them obviously with very limited wits, and mostly with some sort of foreign accent." All the same, he was carried away by "the spirit of the affair." His strong social conscience and his distaste for the mercenary values of the City had already led him to the conclusion that "a social revolution" was necessary, and the youthful stockbroker impulsively threw in his lot with the little sect that was trying to revive the moribund cause of socialism in England.[5]

Its leader, paradoxically, was also a City man, thoroughly bourgeois in manners and appearance but extreme in his utterances. Hyndman was a financial promoter and journalist from a wealthy Evangelical family who had acquired an odd mixture of radical and imperialist opinions. On a business trip to Utah in 1880 he took along a French edition of Marx's *Capital*. Wrestling with the ideas of Marx among the Mormons, he was seized by the notion that socialism might be the means to national regeneration. His first move was to write an article in January 1881 for the influential *Nineteenth Century* in which he proclaimed "The Dawn of a Revolutionary Epoch." "There must be," he asserted, "a great social reorganisation" to "secure for all the same happiness and enjoyment of life that now belong to the few." He struck up an association with Marx himself and wrote his own gloss on Marxism in his book *England for All*. The next step was the formation of a new party.[6]

Hyndman hoped to profit from the widespread disillusionment with Gladstone's Liberal government, but it was not so easy to rouse the working classes. Few workers had the vote, and those who did clung to the Radical tail of the Liberal Party. Fewer still were organized into trade unions. Though socialism was spreading fast in Germany and France, Karl Marx's name was virtually unknown in the country which he had made his adopted home. Peter Kropotkin, the anarchist prince who had fled from Russia to London, disgustedly noted in 1881 that all the revolutionaries in England could hold a conference in one drawing room.

Hyndman made a cautious beginning: he refrained from mentioning the foreigner Marx when he plagiarized his theories in *England for All*, for fear of evoking a xenophobic reaction. Calling the party the Democratic Federation in the belief that the London Radical clubs might be persuaded to affiliate to it, Hyndman confined its first programme to a restatement of such old Chartist demands as adult suffrage, the payment of members of Parliament (then unsalaried), the abolition of the House of Lords, and the disestablishment of the Church of England. To rally disaffected Radicals he put in the two topical issues of Home Rule for Ireland and nationalization of the land. The manoeuvre was not successful. Before the inaugural meeting on 8 June 1881 most of the moderate sponsors had drifted away, and the Radical clubs kept their distance. Hyndman was inevitably led to the fringes of the political system—to the very poor, who had no votes and were scarcely literate, to European exiles much given to doctrinal squabbles and political intrigue, and to rebellious intellectuals who, by quirks of personality or circumstance, found themselves at odds with society.

Hyndman's one recruit of any standing was William Morris, then at the peak of his reputation as a poet and as a designer whose chintzes and wallpapers were becoming a vogue in middle-class homes. Morris, a temperamental rebel who had been one of the controversial pre-Raphaelites, was in aesthetic revolt against the grubby values of Victorian commercialism and was angry about Gladstone's foreign policy. Hyndman's romantic radicalism appealed to him. By the time Edward Pease stumbled across the Democratic Federation, Morris had become its most attractive spokesman. He was an arresting figure, usually dressed in a blue serge sailor-cut suit which made him look like the purser of a Dutch brig. He had a gruff but informal sincerity which made people like him even when they disagreed with him or felt the sharp end of his temper. Hyndman said that he "impressed upon you the truth and importance of what he was saying, every hair on his head and in his rough shaggy beard appearing to enter into the subject as a living part of himself."[7]

In 1883 the Federation changed its name to the Social Democratic Federation, and its manifesto *Socialism Made Plain* underlined the calls its street-corner speakers were making for the overthrow of the capitalist system. Such heady stuff appealed to middle-class rebels such as Pease, who did not distinguish between revolutionary rhetoric and the actual possibility of making a social revolution. They were, however, put off by the narrow-mindedness and the quarrelsome self-righteousness of Hyndman's supporters. These zealots had a tendency, Pease told his sister, "to whine and to abuse all people who don't agree with them." If society was to be regenerated, he felt, reformers should set a good example by first regenerating themselves. He could not see why they should not "denounce monopoly in wealth, and selfishness in Government" and come out strongly for moral reform at the same time. "We should agitate intellectually," he added in a significant phrase, "scream amongst the educated and the rich. It is for them to abdicate rather than for the poor to seize upon their wealth."[8] Demagogic demands for class war only alienated Pease, and he looked around for more high-minded political associates. The revolution, he decided, must come from above.

Pease believed that a change in personal values should precede reform of the social system. He began to find other educated young men who shared this opinion. It was a part of their Evangelical inheritance that persisted even when they rejected formal religion. One of their regular meeting places was the Cyprus teashop in Paternoster Row, close to the office from which J. C. Foulger published *Modern Thought*, a parish magazine for the unorthodox. From this group there emerged the Progressive Association, founded on 26 November 1882 to promote "the moral awakening which is itself the occasion for all political and social improvement." How such a spiritual revival should be brought about was one of the issues debated at the Sunday-night meetings of the Association in Islington, where its earnest clientele was edified by ethical sermons, political speeches and secular hymns. Its secretary was a medical student named Havelock Ellis, who had renounced Christianity after reading James Hinton's *Life in Nature*, which not only advocated sexual freedom but also offered a mystical doctrine to reconcile the scientific concept of an evolutionary world with divine illumination.[9]

It was Frank Podmore, a keen member of the Association, who introduced Pease to Ellis and to Percival Chubb, a twenty-four-year-old clerk in the civil service. Chubb, a lapsed Anglican alternating between ethical enthusiasms and depression over his own unworthiness and over the dreary worldliness of his poorly paid work at the Local Government Board, had lately focused his hopes on a wandering scholar named Thomas Davidson, whom he had met in the autumn of 1881 at the Aristotelian Society and adopted as a father confessor.[10]

Davidson, the illegitimate son of a Scottish shepherd, was then forty-three.[11] After a frustrated student love affair in Aberdeen, a natural rest-lessness and a passion to discover a satisfying transcendental philosophy combined to drive him to and fro across the world. "You met him, talked to him, were inspired by him," said one of his disciples, "and the next day you found that he had fled"—to Rome, to the site of Troy, to Paris or Boston. Studying all the philosophies, he never found one that satisfied him, but he took instead something from each to weave into his own eclectic idealism. To a philosopher like William James, who had hoped that this "kind of Socrates" might be appointed to Harvard, there was an underlying arrogance rather than curiosity about his intellectualism. "There are men," James wrote, "whose attitude is always that of seeking for truth; and the men who, on the contrary, always believe that they have the root of the matter already in them. Davidson was one of the latter class." The impressionable young men whom Davidson patronized were, on the other hand, captivated by what James called his "inward glory," a charismatic power which made Ellis feel at their first meeting that he was "the most remarkable man, the most intensely alive man, I have ever met."

In the spring of 1882 the itinerant Davidson retreated to Domodossola in the Italian Alps to contemplate the Vita Nuova, or New Life. From there he corresponded with new disciples like Ellis, Chubb, and a misanthropic Radical journalist named William Clarke who shared rooms with Chubb. Clarke, eight years older than Chubb, was the son of a struggling businessman and had gone through Cambridge as a poor non-collegiate student. By the time of his first contact with Davidson he had passed from the fundamentalist beliefs in which he had been brought up, through a conversion to Unitarian doctrine as a student, and then—after a visit to the United States—to a form of Emersonian transcendentalism. By 1882 he was despairingly anxious for some stimulus to help him break free of the psychic paralysis which left him feeling morbid and in-effective.

In June 1882 Clarke wrote to Davidson declaring: "I have hardly a single conviction of any kind left . . . very little knowledge, faith or hope . . . how then can I, of all persons in the world, do anything of the slightest good for mankind?"[12] Davidson gave his followers hope, but he also made them feel guilty and inadequate. Clarke noted his similarity to an Evangelical preacher. "You picture a future for those who don't solve life's problem," he wrote, "as terrible as that of the brimstone gospel for the unconverted sinner."[13]

Chubb too was continually asking Davidson the anxious questions of the Puritan: What must I do to achieve salvation? How can I enter into a state of grace? On 1 April 1882 he told Davidson: "I want to work out in myself the life that should be . . . and to aid in the realization of the Social Utopia." On 25 May Chubb first spoke of his plan for the "founding of a revolutionary organization," a little club which "should be the centre of a general regenerating movement." It began modestly as a "manuscript club" whose members circulated papers on such topics as moral improvement and land reform. They were all, Chubb told Davidson on 7 July, "working for emancipation from their present uncongenial position." One of their daydreams was the creation of a utopian colony in the Lake District. In August Chubb went off to Domodossola to stay with Davidson; he came back full of Davidson's latest enthusiasm for the work of Antonio Rosmini-Serbati, who had founded the lay order of the Brethren of Charity. He was fired by the conception of a brotherhood dedicated to a simple, strenuous, intellectual and communal existence through which its members might find their way to a natural religion.

Through the autumn of 1882, when Davidson visited London and met some of the young men whom Chubb considered potential recruits, Chubb was trying to draft a code of principles for the brotherhood, talking over its possibilities with those of suitable moral tone. What Chubb wanted was men ready to make "a really fresh start, an altogether more vigorous and determined effort to cast off the works of darkness and put on the whole armour of light."[14] Seeing the social problem as essentially one to be tackled by personal redemption rather than by politics, Chubb felt that little was to be expected from the "ardent disciples of George, Marx and the other revolutionary luminaries."[15] There was little point, he said, in trying to build the Ideal City with the present "unmoralized" human material.[16]

When Davidson paid another of his fleeting visits to London in September 1883 Chubb had already brought together the nucleus of a group, and he sought Davidson's endorsement. In his enthusiasm he had collected an odd set of associates. Some of them, like Chubb himself and Havelock Ellis, Chubb's journalistic friend Maurice Adams, Rowland Estcourt and a Congregational clergyman named W. J. Jupp, were romantics who saw the new venture as a spiritual brotherhood. Others, such as Frank Podmore and Pease, saw it as a new kind of radical political club. Chubb had also involved another acquaintance from the Progressive Association, Henry Hyde Champion, who was already an active

associate of Hyndman in the SDF. Champion, a young man from a military family, had recently resigned his commission in the Army as a protest against Gladstone's war in Egypt and, with a capital of two thousand
pounds provided by his father, had joined J. C. Foulger in the Modern
Press to publish unorthodox pamphlets and periodicals; he had a forceful
and ambitious personality with an autocratic habit of command and a
taste for organization. Champion's friend R. P. B. Frost, who had joined
him in agitating among the workless in East London, and James Joynes
and Henry Salt, two young reform-minded masters at Eton, were others
who Chubb thought might be candidates. So was Hubert Bland, a failed
businessman of twenty-eight who spent his leisure energetically attending advanced societies devoted to arts, crafts, literature and politics.

Chubb took the chance of introducing some of these contacts to Davidson before the latter left again for Italy. He roped in as many as he could
for that first meeting on 24 October 1883, for which the hospitable Pease
had offered his rooms in Osnaburgh Street. Chubb brought two friends,
Maurice Adams and Hamilton Pullen, as well as Havelock Ellis. Mrs.
Hinton, the widow of the philosophical surgeon who had influenced
Ellis, came with her sister Miss Haddon; Champion arrived with R. B. P.
Frost and James Joynes. Podmore was there, and Pease had invited two
of his Ford girl cousins. Also present were an architect named Robins
and his wife and daughter.

This assorted company was not quite what Chubb had expected.
Clarke, Bland and some other possible recruits failed to turn up, and
when Chubb arrived he found "a sort of general awkwardness."[17] To get
things going he read from a paper on "The New Life" which Davidson
had already gone over with some of the group before he left. There was
some talk about founding a utopian colony in southern California, which
was quickly squashed by the practically minded Champion. Chubb then
fell back on a plan for a residential commune whose members would
continue to work in their normal jobs but would take part in reformist
propaganda. This too was rejected; the politically minded thought that
it would isolate reformers from ordinary life. Only Chubb and his
friends seemed interested in Davidson's concept of a monastic order. In
the end they settled for an agreement to "form a sort of club . . . , a
place of meeting for discussions, lectures, social gatherings, and so on."

Chubb, worried about the way things were going, held a rump meeting a few days later with Jupp, Adams and Ellis, who agreed that their common impulse was "religious, spiritual, ideal," rather than political. Recognizing that they were in a minority, this group decided to force the issue, "to pitch our note high in unfolding our project . . . , shaming the timid and half-hearted."[18] Chubb and Ellis therefore wrote out a high-minded constitution to present to the next meeting on 7 November.

When they reassembled in Pease's lodgings, however, they had to start all over again. Eight new people had turned up. One of them was Helen Taylor, John Stuart Mill's step-daughter, who was active in the land-reform movement and in the Democratic Federation. Another was Hubert Bland, who had surprised Chubb by asking whether he should attend the meeting in evening dress. The meeting began with a procedural wrangle about the appointment of a chairman. When Pease, as host, was chosen, Chubb thought this was a "misfortune, for Pease, although a very good fellow and most amiable, does not appreciate our design and is not possessed of a strong enthusiasm." The proposed constitution was brushed aside in favour of a compromise proposal that "an association be formed whose ultimate aim shall be the reconstruction of Society in harmony with the highest moral possibilities," and Jupp, Ellis, Champion and Podmore were asked to work out more definite rules. Bitterly disappointed, Chubb concluded that nothing useful had been done and that he and his sympathizers should again try to force a split in what Jupp called "a medley of unmixable elements."[19]

Pease and Chubb both joined the drafting committee when it met at Champion's office on 15 November. Champion, who wavered between what Chubb called "the right mood" and more worldly socialist doctrines, persuaded the others to draft a resolution declaring "that the competitive system has broken down, and that society must be reconstructed in accordance with the highest moral principles." To appease Chubb, Ellis and Jupp, another resolution recognized "the evils and wrongs that must beset men so long as social life is based upon selfishness, rivalry and ignorance" instead of love and wisdom. After Pease and Podmore had objected that to call the society "The New Life" was bumptious and high-flown, it was provisionally agreed to name it "The Fellowship of the New Life." All this made Chubb even more doubtful "whether we can go on as we are." On 17 November he dolefully informed Davidson

that "fellows like Pease and Podmore" were "not of the right fibre." He
felt that "all these agitators" who were affected by socialist ideas were
"losing inwardness, . . . becoming more mundane, . . . in danger of
losing ends in means."

Two factions were clearly emerging, but nothing was settled by the
twenty-nine people who turned up on 23 November. Champion introduced the drafts prepared by the small committee, and amendments began to fly about. The compromise motion was moved by a newcomer,
Frederick Keddell, another clerk from the City, who had been brought
along by Hubert Bland. It asserted that "the competitive system assures
the happiness and comfort of the few, at the expense of the suffering of
the many," and that "society must be reconstructed in such a manner as
to secure the general welfare and happiness." This satisfied those who
wanted the new organization to have a political aim, but those who
thought with Chubb that the spiritual should be the keynote tried unsuc-
cessfully to make a commitment to brotherly love a condition of membership. The argument kept coming back to the conflict between Bland,
Pease and Podmore, who thought they should be "doing something," and
those who shared Chubb's feeling "that there was too much anxiety for
'doing'; our first aim was to 'be' something ourselves." There was even
disagreement about the name for the new society. "The Fellowship of
the New Life" was accepted by a bare majority simply because no one
could suggest a better alternative.[20]

Chubb, supported by Ellis, Clarke and a new ally, Dr. Burns-Gibson,
concluded that they must present an "ultimatum."[21] The wrangling at
earlier meetings had dissipated enthusiasm, and on 7 December attendance had dwindled to fifteen. Burns-Gibson proposed a draft constitution
for the Fellowship which called for "the cultivation of a perfect character in each and all . . . , the subordination of material things to spiritual," and urged simplicity of living, the importance of manual labour,
and a sense of religious communion. Though the discussion was amicable,
a split was now unavoidable. It was decided to put the matter to the vote
at a meeting on 4 January 1884. Podmore, writing to Davidson on 16
December, explained why he and his friends could not accept the Burns-
Gibson draft. At the next meeting, he said, he would propose "to leave
to the subscribers to the new resolution the name 'Fellowship of the New
Life' "; he suggested that a second society be organized "which will not
necessarily be *exclusive* of the Fellowship—on somewhat broader and

more indeterminate lines . . . , it being open to any to belong to both societies."

When Podmore put his plan forward on 4 January 1884 it was indeed "indeterminate." The only indication of the proposed new society's purpose was a slight change in the wording approved on 7 November: Podmore suggested that the members "help on" the reconstruction of society rather than regard this as an ultimate goal. He also proposed that they hold regular discussions and attend the meetings of other organizations to put forward their own views. They were, finally, to "obtain information on all contemporary movements and social needs." To cap these vague intentions Podmore suggested an equally obscure name: the Fabian Society. It derived from a dubious political reference to the Roman general Fabius Cunctator, whose tactics in his campaign against Hannibal were supposedly both cautious and forthright.

Nine people voted to form the new society. Podmore became the secretary, Bland the treasurer, and Frederick Keddell was asked to join them to form the first committee.

Pease, Podmore and Bland found themselves running a society which had come into existence casually. They did not know what to do with it. It was not even clear how far they differed from Chubb, Ellis and the others who had decided to go on with the Fellowship of the New Life. Several Fellowship members, including Chubb and Davidson himself, enrolled as Fabians; several of the Fabian group continued to belong to the Fellowship. For Champion, the only member of the original group with any political experience, nothing useful seemed likely to come out of such woolly discussions and constitution-mongering, and he soon dropped out. There was a general sense that Fabians were sympathetic to the new vogue of socialism, but even that was interpreted so loosely that it could mean support for the Positivist "Religion of Humanity," Secularism, land reform or what Chubb called "the merely materialistic, atheistic, aggressive socialism of the continental stamp"[22] exemplified by Hyndman and the Social Democratic Federation. Bland, his wife and Pease all belonged to the SDF, and Bland persuaded the other Fabians to declare that it was "doing good and useful work" and was "worthy of sympathy and support." Frederick Keddell, writing to Chubb on 18 March, considered the SDF and the Fabians as "fellow-workers and not rivals," though he thought "our more moderate and prudent programme will gain us the support of many of their members."[23]

There was as yet no programme, only a state of mind. At first the Fabians seemed to be little more than yet another congenial debating club, meeting on alternate Fridays to discuss the Condition of England and what might be done about it. "The talks after the Fabian meetings are very jolly," Edith Bland wrote to a friend in February. "I do think the Fabians are quite the nicest set of people I ever knew." All she could say about the Society's purposes was that it aimed "to improve the social system—or rather to spread its news as to the possible improvement of the said SS." She reported that there were "two distinct elements in the F.S., the practical and the visionary—the first being the strongest—but a perpetual warfare goes on between the parties which gives to the Fabian an excitement which it might otherwise lack."[24]

There was indeed more excitement outside the Society than within it. Hyndman had started a fire-eating weekly paper, *Justice*, in January 1884 with a gift of three hundred pounds from the poet Edward Carpenter. He and the staff sold it down Fleet Street and the Strand,[25] "Morris in his soft hat and blue suit, Champion, Frost and Joynes in the morning garments of the well-to-do, several workingmen comrades, and I myself wearing the new frock-coat in which Shaw said I was born, with a tall hat and good gloves, all earnestly engaged in selling a penny Socialist paper during the busiest time of the day in London's busiest thoroughfare." Harry Champion had also launched a monthly journal called *To-Day*, intended to serve the new socialist movement as Foulger's *Modern Thought* had provided a platform for the Progressive Association. And while the Fabians held their genteel causeries at Pease's rooms the SDF men were busy in the streets, holding meetings at dock and factory gates and in the parks, trying to organize the unemployed into militant demonstrations. Hyndman had a regular audience at Hyde Park; "I laughed a little at myself," he recalled, "standing there in the full rig-out of the well-to-do fashionable, holding forth to these manifest degenerates on the curse of capitalism and the glories of the coming time."

The Fabians were young, earnest political novices who had no contacts with working-class life and no experience of agitation. In March they did send a speaker down to a large meeting of unemployed in Manchester, but they were more interested in ideas than in action. Willing to listen to Hyndman, Morris or Carpenter, anarchists, land nationalizers or moral reformers, they were open-minded and uncommitted. As Keddell told Chubb, they believed it wise to avoid any "definite statement . . .

until we understand more clearly how far we all go together in the direction of Socialism." Early in March they agreed to start publishing their views in a modest way. "Some pamphlets which are in course of preparation," Keddell informed the impatient Chubb, "will no doubt help us towards a definition of our position."[26] The first of these, amateurish and theoretical, asked the central question which troubled the conscience of the reforming middle class in late-Victorian England. It was called *Why Are the Many Poor?*

2

THE DOWNSTART

"This meeting was made memorable by the first appearance of Bernard Shaw," he himself later wrote as an insertion in the Fabian Society minutes for 10 May 1884. It was a characteristic gesture, but there was truth in it. He at once brought a lively good humour to that intense little group. In 1884 Shaw was an impecunious youth of twenty-seven trying to scratch a living on the margins of journalism. He turned up at political and literary gatherings, one of his associates said, looking like a fairly respectable plasterer, his cuffs trimmed with scissors, his black coat green with age, his boots shabby and cracked, and his tall hat worn back to front because the brim was broken. The effect of his odd appearance, intensified by his angular figure and a reddish beard that made him resemble a pantomime demon, was offset by his sardonic wit, the engaging Irish brogue which softened his voice, and an overt pride which saved him from being a pathetic scarecrow. Even in London's bohemia, where unconventional dress and behaviour were the mode, Shaw was an odd man out.

When Shaw fell in with the Fabians he had been in London for eight years, but he was still living from hand to mouth with no prospects or recognition of his talents.[1] Though he had put his native Dublin behind him, he carried into his adult years a style of life which had been shaped by an eccentric and disorganized family. He was born on 26 July 1856 at 3 Synge Street, a shabby little house on Dublin's south side, at a time when his father was pulling the family into ruin by his amiable fecklessness, his incompetent management of his grain business, and his habit of consoling himself with the bottle.

His father, Shaw said, was "a Downstart" from a Protestant family, "a gentleman without a gentleman's means . . . and so only a penniless snob" who clung to the shreds of his gentility and was guiltily ashamed of his poverty and his dipsomania. Ostracized by his relatives, this Micawber-like man had little to mark him off from the Catholic poor but a pride in the family connections who disowned him—a state of social isolation that Shaw later described as "poverty at its most damnable."[2] For Irish Protestantism, Shaw said, was not so much a religion as "a side in political faction . . . a conviction that Roman Catholics are socially inferior persons, who will go to hell when they die, and leave Heaven in the exclusive possession of ladies and gentlemen."[3] As the Shaws slipped down the scale of shabbiness, they seemed to be on the way to purgatory while they lived. They had fallen from Protestant grace into a limbo where they subsisted between the rulers and the ruled. All Shaw's childhood was pervaded by a sense of exclusion from the elite which dominated Irish society.

George Carr Shaw's defence against resentment was ironic humour and indifference towards his wife and children. Lucinda Elizabeth Shaw, however, reacted against the disasters by rebellion. She became, Shaw said, "a Bohemian anarchist with lady-like habits."[4] Brought up in an authoritarian home, she exchanged the misery of childhood oppression for the aggravation of marriage to an unassertive middle-aged alcoholic. These experiences made her hard, emotionally numb and frigid to the point where she had a horror of being touched. She had no respect for her husband and ignored him as best she could. Her attitude towards her children was equally casual and distant. George Bernard, called "Sonny," and his elder sisters, Lucy and Agnes, were brought up haphazardly by cheap servants, taking their meals in the kitchen and left much to themselves in their graceless and ill-managed home. Even the bleak religion in which Bessie Shaw had grown up was put away by the time her son was ten, since she found more pleasure in communing with the spirits at seances, often taking Sonny with her to visit mediums.

As Bessie Shaw broke with the conventions, she found compensa-

tion in her musical talents. Gifted with a fine mezzosoprano voice, she
acquired both a teacher and a companion in the person of George John
Vandaleur Lee, part impresario and part charlatan. Lee, who mounted
operas and oratorios in which Bessie Shaw appeared, had more than a
dash of vanity. He was given to quirks of humour and was faddish about
fresh air and brown bread. As Lee needed rooms for teaching and the
Shaws were glad of help with the rent, they set up a joint establishment
at 1 Hatch Street—a peculiar *ménage à trois*. Though there were rumours that Lee and Bessie Shaw were lovers, even that he was Shaw's
natural father, Shaw dismissed such ideas with the remark that any man
who could have seduced his mother "could have seduced the wooden
virgin at Nuremberg." All the same, Lee became in effect the head of
the household. His arrival distracted Bessie Shaw and accelerated the dis-
integration of normal family relationships; it also transformed the dreary
home of the Shaws into an anteroom of the stage and the platform.

The young Shaw profited musically from his mother's association
with Lee, but her new interests increased the family's isolation from the
Protestant middle class to which it nominally belonged. For Lee was a
Catholic, and he and Bessie Shaw performed in Catholic churches and
associated with Catholics socially; Lee, moreover, had Shaw transferred
from the Wesleyan Connexional School to the Central Model Boys
School, where he was mortified to find himself among Catholic children
and thus "a boy with whom no Protestant gentleman would speak or
play." It was this social ostracism that the young Shaw felt keenly,
rather than the different religious environment; he had already rejected
established religion when he was still young. Brought up on the Bible
and forced to attend depressing Protestant services before his mother
adopted spiritualism and Lee, he had turned to the literary classics by
the time he was an adolescent; what remained of that early indoctrina-
tion was a frame of Puritan attitudes and an abiding sense of shame and
loss at his exclusion from the Protestant pale.

All through his youth Shaw thus felt a miserable misfit, and he
found his early experiences so distressing that in adult life he could not
bear to speak of them. His father's failure was peculiarly painful; the
discovery that George Carr Shaw was a drinker, he said, shattered his
illusions. "I have never believed in anything since," he remarked in middle life; "then the scoffer began." The contrast between his father's professed good intentions and his inability to live up to them seemed a

paradox of hypocrisy rather than of weakness, provoking scorn rather than compassion, and teaching Shaw to expose rather than to understand human foibles. His mother's failure was different in kind. Her dedication to her musical career and her indifference to her husband and children set a model for his own career and stunted his capacity for love. And from Lee, his "complementary father," he acquired a derisive humour as a protection from emotion and humiliation. Later in life he called his whole youth his "fiasco," comparing it to the experience of the blacking factory which seared Charles Dickens; it was, he said, "a devil of a childhood, rich only in dreams, frightful and loveless in realities."[5]

At fifteen Shaw gave up formal education and became a clerk for a land agent, work which he did mechanically but competently. The only overt sign of reaction to the boredom of his employment, and to the pressures which had been threatening to break up the Shaw family since 1866, was the onset of depressive headaches which afflicted him at intervals late into life. The family finally fell apart in 1872, when Lee decided to seek his fortune in London. Less than a month after his departure, Bessie Shaw and her daughters followed him, leaving her husband and son to shift for themselves. For the next three years Shaw led an unrewarding life in Dublin until, in April 1876, he threw up his job and set off to join his mother.

He arrived at a bad moment. His sister Agnes had just died of tuberculosis. His other sister, Lucy, beginning a stage career, resented his presence in the house, regarding him as a parasite. And his mother, busy with her own affairs, seemed to consider the provision of a room and board for her son the limit of her maternal obligations. Shaw had no idea what to do in London. He had been poor long enough to have little need for cash, to be accustomed to shabby clothes and skimpy meals. Except for a few evenings when he played the piano to assist Lee, he had no occasion to go into middle-class society; socially inexperienced, he was so fearful of gaucherie that he bought and memorized a book of etiquette. Some days he simply lazed in bed, indulging in attacks of hypochondria and depression. He was always restless, and for three years he mooned about London, filling in his time at such free entertainments as the National Gallery and band concerts in the parks. In April 1879 he finally found work with the Edison Telephone Company, at a pound a week, as a canvasser whose task it was to persuade householders to allow the company to run telephone wires across their property.

When the company merged with the rival Bell Telephones he found an excuse to resign.

The summer of 1880, when men were being laid off in large numbers, was an unhopeful time to look for work. Shaw made matters worse for himself because he had no serious intention of finding a post. "I dodged every opening instinctively," he wrote; "I was an incorrigible Unemployable." While he was working for Edison he had begun to draft a novel which described his own life in London as an aimless clerk itchy with the promptings of unrealized talent. "I was driven to write because I could do nothing else," he said.[6] Training himself to write five pages every day, Shaw let the plotless novel *Immaturity* sprawl to two hundred thousand words before he despatched it to Chapman and Hall. Sent to George Meredith for a reader's report, the manuscript received a laconic "No," the first of the fifty-odd rejections which Shaw's novels were given over the next five years.

He was not daunted when the brown paper parcels came back from the publishers without encouragement; the hope of financial reward was not the motive which drove him. As he toiled at four more novels—*The Irrational Knot, Love Among the Artists, Cashel Byron's Profession* and *The Unsocial Socialist*—he was trying out his developing conception of a bohemian hero quite different from the stock figures of the late-Victorian novel. Argumentative, perversely satirical, these books served Shaw as a dress rehearsal for his own role in life: part clown, part preacher, whose wit was a defence against humiliation and whose intellect was to put the world to rights. "Be a tramp or a millionaire," he wrote twenty years later, "it matters little which: what does matter is being a poor relation of the rich; and that is the very devil. Fortunately that sort of poverty can be cured by simply shaking off its ideas."[7] This belief that a new identity could be acquired by cerebral effort was a view of human psychology which was shared by many of his contemporaries. By a mental somersault, those who felt damned, worthless and cast out by the world could in turn become a new elect, with a new faith that made them morally superior to the society which had rejected them.

The search for such a faith sustained Shaw through all his adversities and through the apparently purposeless days he spent prowling about London. In December 1880 the Shaws moved to lodgings at 37 Fitzroy Street, within walking distance of the British Museum. Shaw now began to spend much of his time in the reading room of the Museum, browsing and writing. It served as his university. It had, as Shaw remarked, great advantages for an impoverished writer—communal heating, lavatory accommodation, electric light, a comfortable seat, unlimited books, and ink and blotting paper all for nothing. In the evenings he attended free lectures on any subject that caught his fancy, or turned up at literary and debating societies where the discussion ranged from Darwinism to the status of women and the virtues of the vegetarian diet he had just adopted. This was a great time for talk, when words seemed the key to power; Shaw realized that if he was to be effective he must overcome his innate shyness and learn to talk well, acquiring the technique of debating even if he was not yet certain what he had to say. He took lessons in French and elocution from Richard Deck, an anarchist refugee from the Paris Commune, who also introduced him to Proudhon's doctrine that property was theft and that those who lived without working were either thieves or beggars.

During the autumn of 1879 Shaw met James Lecky, a civil servant who shared his interest in music and speech and introduced him to phonetics. Early in 1880 Lecky took him along to a meeting of the Zetetical Society, founded a year before as a junior version of the older and more prestigious Dialectical Society. This group was influenced by the liberal ideas of John Stuart Mill and committed to discussing "all matters affecting the interests of the human race; hence no topic theological or otherwise, discussed with decorum, is excluded from its programme." Its aims were more imposing than its membership, which consisted largely of young men who wanted intellectual exercise. By 1881 Shaw found himself on its committee, along with a young clerk in the civil service named Sidney Webb. Among the talks given that winter was one by Shaw attacking capital punishment, and another by Webb on "Heredity as a Factor in Psychology and Ethics."

Such gatherings made up Shaw's social life. At first even political occasions embarrassed him, and he forced himself to speak by submitting his name at question periods. "I had an air of impudence," he recalled, "but was really an arrant coward, nervous and self-conscious to a heartbreaking degree. I suffered agonies that no one suspected."[8] He was also drawn into a cluster of literary clubs—each named for a poet such as Shakespeare, Browning, Shelley and Chaucer—run by Frederick James Furnivall, a barrister and amateur philologist, who daily received his coterie in the A.B.C. café across from the British Museum.[9] Among the short-haired women and long-haired men who joined Furnivall for tea, cakes and talk about their spiritual aspirations Shaw began to create a framework of odd acquaintants. They ran the gamut of personal, political and social eccentricity. There were Secularists, food and dress faddists, atheists, Malthusians, freethinkers, evolutionists, Positivists, the first disciples of Ibsen, land reformers, and sympathizers with the Irish peasantry. Shaw had found a milieu in which there was a surfeit of intellectual stimulation, but he sampled all these offerings promiscuously.

He was suffering from an unduly protracted adolescence. He could not break through his inhibitions and commit himself intellectually or emotionally. He clung tenaciously to his independence, "the frightful self-sufficiency," he said, which "stemmed from the fact that nobody cared for me particularly."[10] He continued to live at home, in an apartment at 36 Osnaburgh Street to which he and his mother had moved in April 1882, and to hunt for employment in a desultory manner. He applied for a post copying manuscripts, but got only as far as telling his potential employer how to write novels.

In the summer of 1881 Shaw began an inconclusive flirtation with a young woman named Alice Lockett, who was training to be a nurse. She was sufficiently attracted to arrange for music lessons with Bessie Shaw as an excuse for meeting her son regularly. She found him as indecisive in seeking love as he was in seeking work. Always shying away from personal intimacy, Shaw would blow hot when they were apart and cold when they met, teasing her into needless lovers' quarrels. He much preferred to carry on his dalliance through the protective screen of written words—a situation in which he retained the advantage. "You are a novice at letter-writing," he informed her on one occasion. "I am a novice at love-making, you an expert. Let us then improve ourselves by practice. Write to me, and I will make love to you—to relieve the enormous solitude which I carry about with me."[11]

On the evening of 5 September 1882 Shaw wandered into a meeting promoted by the Land Nationalization Society in the Memorial Hall in Farringdon Street. He then regarded himself as "an independent radical," but he had no settled political convictions. He was simply attracted, in politics as in literature, music, drama and philosophy, by anything that was opposed to the accepted values of the Victorian middle class. For once, however, his attention was seized by the speaker, the American journalist Henry George, who was stumping the British Isles declaiming with religious fervour that the greed of the landlords was the cause of poverty.[12] As an Irishman, who had worked for five years in the office of a land agent, Shaw was ripe for George's message. It was addressed directly to issues which he understood, the intertwined problems of Ireland and the land which were then dominating British politics.

Ireland was almost in a state of siege, garrisoned by more police and soldiers than Britain needed to govern the whole of India. The depression in agriculture meant that the peasants were unable to pay their rents; and their distress found political expression in the Irish Land League and the nationalist party led by Charles Parnell. The landlords, mostly English Protestants, reacted by wholesale evictions—over ten thousand in 1880—and the Irish in turn retaliated with boycott, riots and murder. Gladstone, straddling an issue that was soon to disrupt his party, tried to please everyone. He needed the parliamentary support of Parnell and the Irish members; to them he offered the policy of Home Rule which was anathema to some of his own colleagues. He sought to placate the peasantry by a Land Bill designed to create a class of land-owning peasants at the expense of the landlords. And, to mollify the law-and-order faction on both sides of the Irish Sea, on 1 February 1881 Parliament passed a Coercion Act which enabled the authorities in Dublin to suspend habeas corpus and imprison agitators without trial. For the next year things went from bad to worse, deteriorating into a muted guerrilla war and political assassinations.

Radical opinion in Britain was roused as much by coercion in Ireland as by the growing campaign against landlordism at home. Almost all those who were drawn into the socialist revival of the early Eighties made their first break with the conventional parties during this agitation. Ireland made them disillusioned with the Liberals, and the Tories were tainted by the curse of landlordism. The Liberal Party, however, had not yet broken apart on the Irish question, and demagogic attacks on the great landowners helped to hold its ramshackle structure together. It was not so much a party as an alliance of interests. Led by Whig aristocrats, it was backed by Nonconformist industrialists who fervently believed in free trade and unfettered competition, and it was dependent

for much of its vote on shopkeepers and Radical workingmen. Though
the balance of the British economy had shifted to industry from agriculture, and though the problems of poverty and unemployment were
becoming even more pressing in the towns than in the country, the landlord rather than the capitalist still seemed the natural enemy of progress.
Liberals might differ about Ireland, but they could unite in attacking
such rural magnates as the Duke of Northumberland, who owned
160,000 acres in one county alone, enjoyed a rent roll of over £100,000
and was able to spend over £32,000 in one year on his household expenses. And they could make a dramatic contrast between such privilege and the living conditions of the poor, searingly exposed in a series
of newspaper articles from 1880 onwards.

"Whilst we have been building our churches and solacing ourselves
with our religion and dreaming that the millennium was coming," cried
a Congregational clergyman in *The Bitter Cry of Outcast London*,
"the poor have been growing poorer, the wretched more miserable, and
the immoral more corrupt. . . . THIS TERRIBLE FLOOD OF SIN AND MISERY
IS GAINING UPON US." When this pamphlet was published in 1883, it carried the stench of the slums into thousands of middle-class homes. The
authors, indeed, felt *"compelled to tone down everything . . . or the
ears and eyes of our readers would have been insufferably outraged"* by
the truth about life in the "pestilential human rookeries" inhabited by
men, women and children who toiled fourteen hours or more a day for
a few shillings, lived in vermin-infested squalor and died of the rampaging diseases of poverty. More than one Londoner in three lived in families huddled six to a room; more than one in eight died in the workhouse.

What could explain this situation, and how might it be changed?
Henry George produced an answer to both questions that was stagger-
ingly simple and immensely persuasive. Land was the source of all
wealth, and all inequalities were caused by the fact that a few men
monopolized the birthright of the people. Impose a single tax on the
value of the land and, in the process of expropriating the landlords,
sufficient revenue would be produced to pay for all the reasonable needs
of society. George, who had seen the parcelling out of the American
West to railway interests and land speculators, had asked himself why
the United States should have achieved so much progress and yet have
produced so much poverty. "When some men take to themselves more
than their share," he concluded, "others must get less than their share."

George had been evangelizing his own country for a decade when he completed his most influential tract, *Progress and Poverty*, but he was still unknown in Britain. When he crossed the Atlantic in the late autumn of 1881 to report the troubles in Ireland for the New York *Irish World*, his first contacts were with the Democratic Federation. Though George also met Herbert Spencer, Joseph Chamberlain and John Bright, he made little impact; certainly there was nothing about him to suggest that he was about to transform the radical politics of Britain. What brought him to public notice was a police blunder when he went back to Ireland in August 1882. He took with him James Joynes, who had undertaken to write some descriptive pieces on the Irish troubles for *The Times*. At Loughrea, a small town in Galway which was packed with police and soldiers, the two men were arrested as suspected Fenian organizers. Joynes was indignant, and it was his shocked report in *The Times* of 4 September which brought George sudden notoriety, led to the resignation of Joynes from Eton, and created a packed audience for the meeting at the Memorial Hall.

From that meeting Shaw carried away a copy of the cheap edition of *Progress and Poverty* which had come out in England in December 1881. As he read it he realized that the clue to what was wrong with society was not to be found in the theoretical disputes which preoccupied the debating societies but in the social system itself. "It flashed on me then for the first time," he remembered, "that the conflict between Religion and Science . . . the overthrow of the Bible, the higher education of women, Mill on Liberty, and all the rest of the storm that raged about Darwin, Tyndall, Huxley, Spencer and the rest, on which I had brought myself up intellectually, was a mere middle-class business. . . . The importance of the economic basis had dawned on me."[13]

As Shaw's interest was caught by the agitation of Henry George, he began to meet the politically minded young men who in April 1883 set up the Land Reform Union and published its struggling journal, the *Christian Socialist*. Despite his scorn for the "middle-class business" and his recognition that he was in revolt against bourgeois society, almost all his new associates came from what he called "the professional and penniless younger sons classes." The Union's secretary was Henry Hyde Champion. With J. L. Joynes came Henry Salt, who had married Joynes's sister Kate. Salt too resigned from Eton in protest against working with "cannibals in cap and gown," deciding to devote his life to

vegetarian and humanitarian causes, and opting for the Simple Life on
a hundred pounds a year. Stewart Headlam, the radically minded curate
who could not obtain a living because of his unorthodox views on
dancing, the stage and political reform, brought in members of the
Guild of St. Matthew, a small society of Anglicans concerned with social problems that he had founded in 1877.

Shaw also turned up at one of the meetings of the Social Democratic Federation. There, he said, "I found Mr Hyndman in the chair
and I saw at once . . . that there was a movement behind his silk hat,
his beard, and his plausible delivery."[14] Shaw was attracted by the SDF
and was for a time a "candidate member." He attended at least one
meeting of its council, and Chubb thought of him as one of its leading
men. Yet he was put off, deciding that Hyndman's vision of proletarian
revolt was a sentimental illusion. Hyndman himself, for all his talents,
Shaw considered the worst of leaders. Shaw also shared a common reaction against the zealotry of the Federation, already "noted for its cranks,
the disquieting celebrity of its individual members, its open intolerance
and want of intellectual discipline."[15]

When Shaw spoke at one meeting on the virtues of George's policy
he was told to go away and read Marx. So he did. Through the autumn
of 1883 he worked away in the British Museum at the French version
of the first volume of *Capital*, taking in political economy from Ricardo,
Adam Smith and Mill along the way. The effect of Marx was overwhelming: Shaw felt that he had discovered what was wrong with the
world and why he was so miserable in it. George had shown him that
bourgeois society as a whole was a thieves' kitchen, driving home the
point with fierce moral denunciations that exactly caught the tone of
Shaw's own resentment. The real secret of Marx's fascination, he recalled later, "was his appeal to an unnamed and unrecognized passion:
the hatred in the more generous souls among the respectable and educated section for the middle-class institutions that had starved, thwarted,
misled and corrupted them spiritually from their cradles."[16]

Shaw was captivated by Marx's dialectic. It showed him how, by
turning capitalist society inside out, he could attack it with its own logic
and on its own assumptions. He had stumbled on the device whereby all
his critical ideas could be expressed as paradoxes.[17] It also put an end to
his own miserable sense of exclusion. The propertied classes—his own
rich and condescending relatives writ large—were not, after all, his

superiors but his moral inferiors. Conventional morality was based upon hypocrisy and fraud; the truly moral person was the revolutionary who rejected the bourgeois values. "I became a speaker with a gospel," Shaw declared.[18] He was soon testifying to his new enthusiasm by speaking at SDF meetings, and he started a novel designed as "a gigantic grapple with the whole social problem."[19]

The Unsocial Socialist was the first English work of fiction to be directly influenced by Marx. It was little more than a series of didactic speeches—a bargee orates on the law of wages, a shepherd declaims on Malthus, and the hero delivers summaries of *Capital* and *The Communist Manifesto* to his bemused wife—but while these monologues were scarcely the stuff of fiction, they showed how Shaw as a propagandist was already developing a style and a paradoxical humour that put him in a different class from the other Federation speakers with their jargon-ridden stump speeches.

Shaw now considered himself a socialist. Although he was searching for a congenial political home, it was more by accident than conscious choice that he fell in with the Fabians.

In the early months of 1884 the Society still had no more than twenty members, who had so far met on eight alternate Friday evenings at Pease's lodgings. They had talked about the public lecture given in January by Henry George and spent several inconclusive sessions to decide in what respects they differed from the Federation. The only practical decision they had taken was to print two thousand copies of the four-page pamphlet *Why Are the Many Poor?* This tract, discussed sentence by sentence by the whole group and revised by Bland and Keddell, was drafted by W. L. Phillips, a house painter who had been influenced by reading Auguste Comte and by his experience of helping runaway slaves in the United States. Phillips, for years the only worker recruited by the Fabians, had produced an unsophisticated tirade against rich idlers and a demand for the workers to "shake off their blind faith in the Commercial god Competition, and realise the responsibility of their unused powers." Below the title, however, was a motto which was in sharp contrast to the apocalyptic tone of the text. Frank Podmore, pursuing the line of pseudo-history which had led him to endow the Society with its classical name, invented a text to justify it: "For the right moment you must wait, as Fabius did most patiently when warring against Hannibal, though many censured his delays; but when the time comes you must strike hard, as Fabius did, or your waiting will be in vain, and fruitless."

The notion of waiting was a good deal more appropriate to the handful of young Fabians than was the prospect of striking hard. Thomas Davidson had impressed on his acolytes the importance of preparing oneself with patience for a new life. The problem was how to fuse moral regeneration with social change. William Clarke, for example, joined the Fellowship of the New Life and did not formally attach himself to the Fabians for another two years. Writing to his friend the American journalist Henry Demarest Lloyd in January 1884, he declared: "I don't see how you are to solve the social problem except—to some extent—on Socialist lines";[20] but a year later he wrote to Davidson that he had decided that socialism was "really all wrong." "It ignores ethics, and would transform society into mechanism . . . controlled by ignorance and selfishness. Even William Morris, fine and noble man as he is, never rises beyond the plane of the material: he says that misery is due to deprivation of material wealth, and to want of opportunity for pleasure. That is not so, if there is any truth in the doctrine of a spiritual order with which we must be in right relations."[21]

Many of those who attended the early Fabian meetings were as ambivalent as Clarke. They certainly had no inclination to join the evangelizing SDF speakers at the streetcorners or to arouse the unemployed for demonstrations. They were put off, undoubtedly, by the Marxist ideologues, who, Clarke wrote to Davidson on 13 January 1884, were "actively irreligious" and seemed "to desire revolution quite as much for the sake of overthrowing ethics and the spiritual side of things as for the sake of improving the material condition of the people."[22]

If the Fabians were to survive, they needed to find an identity. If Shaw was to find an identity he needed a stage on which he could dramatize himself. The coincidence of interest was decisive. He was recruited by Hubert Bland, who talked to him about the Society in the *Christian Socialist* offices on 4 May 1884 and next day sent him a copy of *Why Are the Many Poor?* with an invitation to attend a Fabian meeting.[23] (On 5 September Shaw formally enrolled.) He immediately began to dominate the little group. On 16 May he delivered his first talk, making a set of seventeen propositions which the meeting agreed should be pub-

lished as the first Fabian manifesto.[24] The document bristled with
Shavian epigrams. Wealth cannot be enjoyed without dishonour or
forgone without misery. Private ownership has divided society into
hostile classes, "with large appetites and no dinners at one extreme and
large dinners and no appetites at the other." Competition "has the effect
of rendering adulteration, dishonest dealing and inhumanity compulsory," and its defects can be rectified only by the state itself becoming a
producer. There followed some of Shaw's own hobbyhorses. The state
should compete with parents in providing happy homes for children, "so
that every child may have a refuge from the tyranny and neglect of its
natural custodians." The sexes should have equal rights, since men "no
longer need special political privileges to protect them against women."
There was a hint of equal incomes. A final clause, which made Edward
Pease feel very uneasy, suggested that the Society was by no means
committed to constitutional methods. "We had rather face a Civil War,"
the manifesto concluded, "than such another century of suffering as the
present one has been." In a thousand words Shaw had given the Society
a new start. The document was more witty and elegant than anything
the socialist movement had yet produced; it was also different in kind.

Shaw's shift from the Social Democratic Federation to the Fabians
came at a significant moment. Like Morris and some other SDF leaders,
he was finding Hyndman tiresome and his clique quarrelsome. On 24
October Shaw wrote with only a dash of satire to his friend Andreas
Scheu, an emigré Communist, that he feared that Hyndman's vision of
the revolutionary future was "a Committee of Public Safety composed
of the Executive Council of the S.D.F." Morris and some of his associates broke away from the SDF to found the Socialist League; Shaw
opted for the Fabians. They were educated, intellectually tolerant and
middle-class; they had no fantasy about leading the militant workers to
the barricades. Shaw's hero in *The Unsocial Socialist* had declared that
the proletariat was a useless tool for the would-be revolutionary: the
world could be changed only by those who had superior brains and organizing skills. That line of argument went down well with the Fabians.
Shaw was so pleased by their response that within a few weeks he was
urging middle-class socialists to join the Fabians to save the movement
from "a mob of desperate sufferers abandoned to the leadership of ex-
asperated sentimentalists and fanatical theorists."

By the autumn of 1884 Shaw had at last found an occupation—as a socialist propagandist. There was no money in it. He never took fees for his lectures, though he spent much effort on preparing them.[25] Champion did not pay him a penny for *The Unsocial Socialist*, which was running as a serial in *To-Day*, and offered him only five pounds to produce an English edition of Laurence Gronlund's *The Co-operative Commonwealth*, a utopian book which had a substantial impact on the socialists of the Eighties. He was acquiring instead a good deal of experience and some reputation. The Fabian Society was the right milieu in which to exercise his repertoire of talents.

❧ 3 ❧

BOHEMIANS

At a meeting at the South Place Institute in May 1884 Shaw defended socialism against the criticisms of the Secularist leader Charles Bradlaugh and provokingly announced that he himself was nothing but "a loafer." Annie Besant, Bradlaugh's closest associate, was in the audience. Though she was already familiar with Shaw's debating tricks, she was "fairly astounded at the audacious confession that he led so shameful a life."[1] Shaw's ironic manner and her lack of humour had trapped her into misunderstanding him. She soon found "that he gave time and earnest work to the spreading of Socialism . . . and that a 'loafer' was only his amiable way of describing himself because he did not carry a hod." Shaw, in fact, had the kind of dedication which appealed to her. Despite his "passion for representing himself as a scoundrel," he might well have the makings of a saint.

This discovery began one of Annie Besant's conversions to a new faith—this time from a crusade against God to a campaign against Mammon. For in each of the spiritual crises which punctuated her anguished pilgrimage through life—from her Evangelical childhood through free thought and socialism to leadership of the esoteric cult of Theosophy—a change of mind was associated with a change of heart. Conversion was personified in an attachment to a new male idol, preferably a man

who seemed a victim of hostile circumstances and was forced to vindi-
cate himself against great odds. Though she was herself a magnetic personality, a powerful orator, an able journalist and author, and an effective organizer, her temperament seemed to demand a masculine partner
whom she could both admire and patronize, a focus for powerful emotions which required all the elements of a marriage except sexual intimacy. Shaw, with similar predilections, was a natural candidate for
such a relationship.

Annie Besant's long search for an engrossing but celibate affection
had started when she was a girl. Her childhood had been loveless. Her
father had died in 1852, when she was five, and her mother had sent her
off to be raised by a benevolent but rigorously Evangelical spinster who
made it her vocation to bring up impoverished girls of good family.
Before she was fourteen Annie had developed a sense of persecution
which in later years led to feuds with her associates and litigation with
her enemies. She was able, well read and personally attractive, but misery made her morbid to the point of religious hysteria. As a girl she
saw herself in her daydreams as "a great religious leader" preaching a
new faith, and she sought to mortify her sinful flesh by fasting and flag-
ellation. Her spiritual aspirations led her to the idea of becoming a nun,
then to the Oxford Movement and the mysticism and sensual imagery
of High Church ritual, and then to marriage to a dominating clergyman.

Frank Besant, looking for a wife who would suit a country rectory,
saw her religious fervour and missed the emotional pressures behind it.
The marriage was disastrous from the beginning. Annie was twenty, innocent, and frightened by its clumsy consummation by an unimaginative
husband. She craved an intellectual stimulus which could appease her
religious scepticism. When she created a scandal by refusing to take the
sacrament, Frank Besant turned her out of her home. Her last act before
leaving was to deliver a speech to the empty church pews, discovering
then her gift of oratory.

With only a small allowance from her husband, she tried to support herself, her daughter and her mother by needlework. She was
embittered and depressed. "The Church established by law," she wrote,
"transformed me into an unbeliever and an antagonist," and she was
soon writing free-thought pamphlets. She was a natural evangelist. Shaw
described her as a woman of swift decisions, "who came into a movement with a bound, and was preaching the new faith before the astonished spectators had the least suspicion that the old one was shaken."

In London Annie found a temporary home with the Unitarian preacher Moncure Conway. Many of his friends were freethinkers, and his South Place Chapel was a forum for cults and heresies in London in the Seventies.[2] It was through him that Annie, who had just enrolled in the active National Secular Society, met Charles Bradlaugh, its leader. Bradlaugh was forty and fast making a national reputation as a militant atheist and a popular educator. As soon as Annie met him she succumbed to his charisma and began to write for his *National Reformer*. She made her first public speech on 25 August 1874, on "The Political Status of Women," and before long she had become so popular as an orator that she could successfully stand in for Bradlaugh himself. At his Hall of Science, the London Secularists' centre, she led the lay services, which were an inverted form of revivalist religion, and wrote her own *Secular Song and Hymn Book* for such occasions. Her repertoire of subjects grew steadily as she followed Bradlaugh on the main issues of the day— abolition of the House of Lords, the rich perquisites of bishops, flogging and capital punishment, Home Rule for Ireland. Within a year she had become vice-president of the National Secular Society and Bradlaugh's trusted deputy.[3]

They made a striking pair when they appeared at meetings as a double act. Annie was small, with rich brown hair and a delicate oval face, and with a radiant energy. Bradlaugh was handsome, with an imposing presence and a talent for resounding oratory. Though they were soon living as neighbours in St. John's Wood and were commonly slandered for their irregular relationship, they were companions rather than lovers. Both of them had been seared by marriage, Annie being bound to her vindictive husband and Bradlaugh to a wife who was a dipsomaniac. Their partnership was one of the curiously intimate "mystic betrothals" —common enough in revivalist sects—in which passion was transmuted into evangelistic fervour.

This fascination with celibacy, however, was not accompanied by prudery. Both Annie and Bradlaugh were provokingly outspoken on matters which were taboo for polite Victorians, notably on "Malthusianism," or birth control, as a means whereby the working class could improve its living conditions. In 1877, when they were prosecuted for republishing *The Fruits of Philosophy, or The Private Companion of Young Married People*, they made a courageous and sensational defence of contraception. Among those who volunteered to assist their campaign by distributing the book was Shaw, who was horrified by their trial. Annie's speech before the Lord Chief Justice, running to forty thousand words, was the first of her writings on population control to achieve a wide circulation. They managed to stay out of gaol, but the case and its aftermath made Annie a public martyr.

By 1880, the National Secular Society had over six thousand members and Bradlaugh had begun his long struggle to be seated as a member of Parliament for Northampton. Elected as a Radical, he was refused his seat on the grounds that an atheist could not take the oath, and he had to win four elections before the House of Commons finally admitted him. Annie loyally supported him through these battles, but her emotions had shifted to a new protégé who was fast making a name for himself among the Secularists. "Our mistress Liberty has won this new Knight," she declared in the *National Reformer* on 17 August 1879, describing Dr. Edward Aveling as a man with artistic charm, scholarship, and "a brilliancy of brain I have not seen surpassed." Other people did not share Annie's enthusiasm for Aveling. William Morris's daughter May thought him "a little lizard of a man," and Hyndman felt that nobody could be "as bad as Aveling looks."[4] He soon acquired an unsavoury reputation; according to Shaw, "as a borrower of money and a swindler and seducer of women his record was unimpeachable."[5] Born in 1849, the son of a well-known Congregational minister in Hackney, Aveling had studied medicine and science.[6] He had married a childhood friend in 1872 and then abandoned her after running through her dowry, supporting himself by teaching anatomy at London Hospital. He had lost his religious faith in 1877, after his mother's sudden death, and become an enthusiastic Darwinian. His conversion to free thought led to his dismissal from the hospital in 1882, but he scratched a living by giving popular-science lectures and by writing for the *National Reformer*, *Progress* and Annie's own journal, *Our Corner*.

For a couple of years Annie, Bradlaugh and Aveling worked closely together as "the Trinity" which controlled the National Secular Society, but by the end of 1882 Aveling began to drift away. He was becoming more interested in politics, and in November he was elected to the London School Board with the help of the Democratic Federation. This attraction to socialist ideas, which ran counter to the radical individualism of Bradlaugh, was a source of strain, not least because the agitation of the Federation was beginning to wean away a significant number of Secularists. It was also, for Annie, a more personal matter, because Aveling's roving eye had settled on the attractive and talented youngest daughter of Karl Marx.

Aveling's patronage of Eleanor Marx did not immediately arouse Annie's jealousy, even when he began to publish articles by her in *Progress* and *The Freethinker*, which he edited for a time. But as he gave his energies to the Federation and spent evenings with Eleanor indulging their common passion for the theatre—he as a would-be dramatist, she as an aspiring actress—Annie felt betrayed. The game of pull devil, pull baker, with Aveling torn between old and new female companions, went on all through the early part of 1884. The strain began to tell on Annie, who fell ill of congestion of the lungs. Realizing that she was fighting a losing battle, by the late summer she had written off Aveling and taken up another young Secular propagandist, John MacKinnon Robertson. What had decided the matter was Eleanor Marx's agreement in June 1884 to set up a free union with Aveling.[7]

When Eleanor Marx met Aveling she was still recovering from a severe breakdown. One of the symptoms had been anorexia nervosa, which started some time before her father's death in the spring of 1883. The Marx home had not been happy, for it was the scene of hidden marital problems and was afflicted by penury. Eleanor would have preferred to escape into her theatrical ambitions instead of inheriting a public role as the political heiress of the revolutionary prophet. Aveling encouraged both her longing for the stage and her involvement in the socialist movement. Though he was pathologically coldhearted and lacked any moral sense, Eleanor was fascinated by him.

Eleanor's name and the patronage of Friedrich Engels were enough to make the Avelings politically respectable, even to comrades who knew he was a sponger: the Social Democratic Federation was full of odd characters who tolerated personal weaknesses more than doctrinal differences. The Avelings, moreover, were accepted in London's literary bohemia; Eleanor was part of Furnivall's set and had become friendly with Shaw. On 21 November 1884, just before the Avelings and Morris broke with Hyndman to form the Socialist League,[8] Shaw joined them in organizing an Arts Evening in Bloomsbury for SDF members at which the Avelings performed a one-act play called *In Honour Bound*—an odd title for a play written by Aveling, but, according to Marx's housekeeper, it was "more or less their own history."

A common interest in the theatre was, in fact, a stronger link between Shaw and the Avelings than their socialist politics. During the next two years Shaw took part in several amateur performances got up for socialist meetings. The Avelings were enthusiasts for Ibsen: Eleanor, like many women struggling to find themselves, identified with Nora in *A Doll's House*. The play was performed in London at the Prince's Theatre in 1884 in a bowdlerized version by Henry Arthur Jones which ended in reconciliation and happiness, but Eleanor hoped to see the original text produced and she aspired to play Nora herself. In the early months of 1885 Eleanor, who had brought Ibsen to Shaw's notice, frequently discussed the project with him. On 2 June she wrote asking him to play the blackmailing Krogstad. Despite Shaw's encouragement it was not until 15 January 1886 that the reading of the play came off, with May Morris taking the part of Mrs. Linde, Eleanor that of Nora, and Shaw as Krogstad.

The activities of such enthusiasts provided a setting in which Shaw could explore the relationship between the avant-garde theatre and advanced politics. One of Aveling's associates in the Secularist movement was William Archer, a young Scotsman who was the dramatic critic of *The World* and a close friend of Henry Salt, and he arranged for Shaw to contribute articles on music to the newly founded *Dramatic Review* and to write on books for the *Pall Mall Gazette*. For the first time Shaw earned a little money. Though paid journalism "put a stop to my life's work" of writing novels, the income was welcome. In April 1885 his father died, disregarded by his family. "Telegram just received," Shaw wrote to a friend, "to say that the governor has left the universe on rather particular business and set me up as 'An Orphan.'" When he found that he was to inherit a hundred pounds on an insurance policy he went out and bought "the first new garment I have had for years."

The suit he purchased for five pounds fifteen did nothing to diminish the oddity of his appearance, for Shaw had been introduced by Andreas Scheu to the faddish notions of the clothing reformer Dr. Jaeger. The material, natural undyed wool stockinette, and the design were spectacularly eccentric. With his red hair and beige suiting, an acquaintance remarked, Shaw looked like "a forked radish in a worsted bifurcated stocking."[9]

Shaw was at last beginning to organize his life into a more coherent pattern, and the change affected his personal relationships as well as his political and professional activities. The lingering flirtation with Alice Lockett died away in the spring of 1885, and on 26 July he wrote in the diary he had begun to keep that on that day "begins an intimacy with a lady of our acquaintance."[10] This, he added, "was my first connection of the kind. I was an absolute novice. I did not take the initiative in the matter."

Jenny Patterson was an accomplished but sharp-tempered widow of some means who was at least ten years older than Shaw. She was one of his mother's pupils, a family friend and a frequent visitor to the household. She was attracted to Shaw. He was willing enough to tease with philandering innuendoes, but when she responded he retreated. The normal role of the sexes in courtship was reversed, Shaw playing the coquette and the woman assuming the role of the passionate lover.

His seduction by Jenny Patterson was swift by comparison with the lingering and unconsummated relationship with Alice Lockett. The climax came after only three weeks of tittivation. On 4 July Shaw visited Jenny and stayed until the small hours, noting, "Vein of conversation decidedly gallant." Six days later he walked home with her: "Supper, music, and curious conversation, and a declaration of passion. Left at 3. *Virgo intacta* still." In the next three weeks his behaviour was a strange mixture of casualness and fascination, as if he were fluttering around a flame. On 25 July he met Jenny with his mother. "Took Jenny home about 11 p.m. and stayed there until 3 o'clock on my 29th birthday which I celebrated by a new experience. Was watched by an old woman next door, whose evil interpretation of the lateness of my departure greatly alarmed us."

The laconic entries continued throughout the autumn, coolly recording the intermittent progress of the affair. "To J.P. to eat and make love until 1.20," Shaw wrote on 5 August. When Jenny became emotionally possessive and jealous of other friends he noted with detachment that he had "replied to J.P.'s angry and plaintive letter." He would not surrender his independence, nor would he break off the relationship, turning up at Jenny's house at odd hours when the impulse took him. On 31 December 1885 he went "to see the New Year in with J.P., but she was in bed: lights were out. So I stayed on the other side of the Square and watched the Colliers and others come out on their doorsteps to see the New Year in." He seems to have been kept up to the mark by a combination of vanity and loneliness, for he was already tiring of Jenny's ardent attentions. "Revulsion" is the one-word entry early in January,

though when he arrived a few days afterwards and found Jenny entertaining another admirer he could not forbear to tease him. "He was bent
on seduction and we tried which should outstay the other. Eventually
he had to go for his train." By this time Shaw was seeking to disentangle
himself from the lady. In May he wrote a firm letter saying that henceforth their relations must be merely platonic. Jenny hurried round in a
distracted state. "There was a scene," Shaw wrote on 12 May 1886, "and
much pathetic kissing and petting after which she went away compara-
tively happy."

Jenny's hold on Shaw was strong enough to keep him hovering about
her for years after he had first resolved to be done with her. She had
broken through the fastidiousness which had kept him a virgin so long,
but her reward was to see Shaw released to become a philanderer, especially with women who were unlikely to make physical demands upon
him. During 1885 he began to spend his evenings with women who were
content to have his company to talk or play piano duets. Hubert Bland's
wife, Edith, explained his attraction to a friend in Australia. "He is a
very clever writer and speaker," she wrote, "the greatest flatterer (of
men, women and children impartially) I ever met, is horribly untrustworthy and repeats everything he hears, and does not always stick to
the truth, and is *very plain* like a long corpse with a dead white face—
sandy sleek hair and a loathsome small straggly beard, and yet is one of
the most fascinating men I ever met."[11] He had a similar effect on other
women who welcomed his platonic flatteries and his stimulating conversation. In the course of 1885 he fell into the habit of dropping in on
them without notice. He was still a restless prowler, punctilious about
his political and professional engagements, but casual in his social
activities.

Most of Shaw's friends, themselves bohemian in their habits, easily
accepted his unpredictable behaviour. Jenny might be jealous of the time
he spent with other women, but Shaw's reputation was that of an agreeable and intellectual philanderer, not of a roving seducer. He had a
marked preference, indeed, for three-cornered friendships which resembled the odd arrangement in his own home in Dublin between his
father, his mother and Vandaleur Lee. He often went out to Hampstead
to play the piano and sing with Charlotte Wilson, the anarchist wife of
a City stockbroker and a fellow member of the Fabian executive. About
once a week he called on the Avelings or walked to Hammersmith to
see May Morris at Kelmscott House, and when he had time and money

he ran down to Surrey to visit the Salts or to Blackheath to spend time with the Blands. In each case the attachment was primarily to a woman, but without causing offence to the man concerned. In almost all these friendships, moreover, there was an element of sexual oddity. Aveling and Bland were womanizers, and both Eleanor Marx and Edith Bland found Shaw's interest a compensation for the infidelities they suffered. May Morris, whose primary attachment was to her famous father, did not find men sexually attractive. And Kate Salt, living in a companionate marriage, was explicitly lesbian; the only man for whom she cared intensely, apart from Shaw, was the homosexual poet, socialist and Simple Lifer Edward Carpenter.

Shaw's coquettish attitude to women inhibited him from forming an exclusive relationship with any one of them, yet spurred him to seek for some aspect of his ideal in each. What they had in common was forcefulness, an almost masculine quality of assertion which penetrated his shyness and offset his temperamental laziness. This need to be carried along by a woman with a strong personality attracted him to Annie Besant. "During this year," he noted as he began his diary in 1886, "my work at the Fabian brought me much into contact with Mrs Besant and towards the end of this year this intimacy became of a very close & personal sort, without, however, going further than a friendship."

Their friendship began slowly, for it was nine months after Annie had attacked this "loafer" that they were formally introduced. During that time she had been moving away from Bradlaugh's individualism to a more radical attitude to social problems. She was now widely known as a controversial propagandist. In the ten years since she had thrown in her lot with Bradlaugh she had published fifty-one books and pamphlets, nineteen on religious subjects, a dozen on science and another score on politics and social reform. With these, and with her speeches and articles, she had built up a substantial following among the Radical artisans and autodidacts who trailed behind Bradlaugh's irreverent crusade. Through the Secularist papers, her own sixpenny monthly *Our Corner*, and the publishing firm she ran in partnership with Bradlaugh she also had access to a well-run publicity machine. She was a formidable asset to any movement, especially one that was still in so formative a phase as socialism was in the mid-Eighties.

All through 1884, in the wake of a public debate on socialism between Bradlaugh and Hyndman which was a debating triumph for the Secularist but began the slide of his supporters to socialism, Annie remained publicly loyal to her old friend's principles. She did not wish to hurt his feelings at the height of his struggle for his parliamentary seat. It was, therefore, a severe shock when she turned up at a meeting of the Dialectical Society on 21 January 1885 and dramatically revealed her change of mind. Shaw, who was there to speak on socialism, recalled the occasion.

> I was warned on all hands that she had come down to destroy me, and that from the moment she rose to speak my cause was lost. I resigned myself to my fate, and pleaded my cause as best I could. When the discussion began everyone waited for Mrs Besant to lead the opposition. She did not rise; and at last the opposition was undertaken by another man. When he had finished, Mrs Besant, to the astonishment of the meeting, got up and utterly demolished him. There was nothing left for me to do but gasp and triumph under her shield. At the end she asked me to nominate her for election to the Fabian Society, and invited me to dine with her.[12]

The incident eventually bore fruit for Shaw: in April *Our Corner* began to carry *The Irrational Knot* as a serial, which ran for the next two years. With Harry Champion running *Cashel Byron's Profession* simultaneously in *To-Day*, Shaw felt encouraged, especially since Annie paid him five shillings a page for the instalments of the novel and extended what Shaw called her "singular habit" of paying contributors to cover his articles and a column of art criticism as well.

There was no question of Annie following Aveling into the Socialist League, although she admired Morris, because she would have been at uncomfortably close quarters with the Avelings. Hyndman's "bitter and very unjust antagonism to Mr. Bradlaugh" was itself enough to keep her out of the Social Democratic Federation. The Fabians were the only possibility, and their emphasis on moral values made them naturally congenial to her. On 19 June 1885 she was elected to membership and early in July *Justice* reported that "Mrs Besant made her first speech as a member of a Society avowedly Socialist, and at once made the Fabians feel how much they have already been strengthened by her accession." At that time the Society had a mere forty members and had scarcely engaged in any noticeable activity. Annie Besant was the first person of any public reputation to join it, and to her it probably seemed no more significant than the Friends of Russia, which she had founded that August. What Shaw called her "Russophile party"—at whose formation he and Pease were present—in fact attracted more notables than the Fabians, including the distinguished exiles Prince Kropotkin and Sergius Stepniak, who had fled Russia after his sensational assassination of the head of the Tsarist security police.[13]

Annie began to attend Fabian meetings regularly and was elected to the Society's executive early in 1886, but it was not until the end of that year, after she had acquired as much influence as Shaw over the Society's affairs, that Shaw started to see her regularly. Once again a masterful woman was enticing him into a fascinating but embarrassing intimacy.

By then, however, Shaw was no longer a novice; he had finished his apprenticeship. Immaturity and the experience of love among the artists lay behind him, and he was about to begin his career as the successful unsocial socialist.

❧ 4 ❧
ACQUAINTANCES
IN TROUBLE

"Quite the cleverest thing I ever did in my life," Shaw said, "was to force my friendship on Webb, to extort his, and to keep it." He was taken with Sidney Webb at first sight when they met at the Zetetical Society in 1880. Webb was then "a young man of about twenty-one, rather below middle height, with small hands and feet, and a profile that suggested an improvement on Napoleon the Third." Shaw recalled that at their first meeting Webb "knew all about the subject of debate; knew more than the lecturer; knew more than anybody present; had read everything that had been written on the subject; and remembered all the facts that bore on it. He used notes, ticked them off one by one, threw them away, and finished with a coolness and clearness that, to me in my then trembling state, seemed miraculous. This young man was the ablest man in England."[1]

Sidney Webb was born in Cranbourne Street, London, just off the Charing Cross Road, on 13 July 1859. His family came from the genteel fringe of the lower middle class. His paternal grandfather had kept the inn in the Kentish village of Petham; his mother was an orphan brought up modestly by aunts in Essex. She had been able to borrow enough money from a relative to set up a hairdressing business which provided most of the family income, since Sidney's father was an accountant who earned only small and irregular fees from doing the books of local shop-keepers. She was the dominant figure in the Webb household; full of energy, with a strong sense of purpose, she wanted to do her best for her two sons, Charles and Sidney, and she ensured that they had a decent education to fit them for the world. Webb's father was frail in health and spent more than half his time on politics, avidly reading news-papers, following parliamentary debates and serving unpaid on the local vestry and as a Poor Law guardian. A Radical in his opinions, he was a keen supporter of John Stuart Mill when he ran for Westminster in 1865. His wife's enthusiasm ran in a more religious direction. She was a devout Evangelical, and Sidney remembered how she took the boys and their sister Ada from one church to another in search of eloquent preachers who did not offend her Low Church feelings by excessive ritual. It was a household without much comfort. The house was cramped and ugly, and the Webbs kept largely to themselves; Mr. Webb felt isolated from his class by his superior intellectual tastes. But the home was full of argu-ment and interest in public affairs. What it lacked, Sidney wrote in 1885 after a visit to the cathedral close at Salisbury, was calm. It was "a *happy* family," he recalled, but "we have always been in the thick of the fight, and I feel that one of the great influences I have missed is this peace, which I have never known."[2]

As a boy Sidney was something of a loner, and much of his pleasure came from wandering through London's squares and alleys. He once said that it could take him an hour to walk down Fleet Street because he was so absorbed in reading the newspapers displayed in the windows. At school his ability to read quickly and his astonishing memory soon marked him out as a scholar. His mother sent him to a middle-class day school in St. Martin's Lane. She then took the unusual step of despatching both her sons to a school in Switzerland where they were to learn French and prepare for careers as commercial clerks. After three months the boys were shipped off to Wismar, a small town near Hamburg, where they lived for almost two years in the house of a Lutheran clergyman. By then Sidney was seventeen, and he returned to London to join a colo-nial broker's office in the City.

Work did not interrupt his studies and he spent his evenings at the City of London College, where he won first-class passes and prizes in French, German and commercial subjects.[3] He went on to the Birkbeck Institute and by 1885 he calculated that he had won £450 in prizes and awards. He was clearly a phenomenon. Disliking the commercialism of the City, he moved into the civil service through the Inland Revenue, but in 1882 he passed the competitive examination for the upper division and was appointed first to the War Office and then to the Colonial Office. In 1883 he was awarded the Whewell scholarship in international law at Trinity College, Cambridge, but he could not take it up without losing his civil-service appointment. His attitude to his work was ambivalent. On the one hand he saw the service, like his father's idol John Stuart Mill, as a proper place for a man of public spirit who also wanted leisure to study and think. On the other hand he felt the decision was cautious rather than ambitious and regretted that his passion for "wanting at each step to see my whole life in advance" had led to the "Impasse du Bureau des Colonies" instead of the "Avenue directe à Mondésir."[4] Yet the underlying ambition remained: Sidney not only had talent but had dreams of changing society. And so, with an eye to a possible change of occupation, he consoled himself by working on an external law degree at London University in 1884, passing brilliantly two years later.

At the Colonial Office Webb was promoted to the responsible post of resident clerk, sharing this duty with Sydney Olivier, who had beaten him out of first place at the qualifying examination. They became friends despite differences of temperament and background. Webb was painstaking, shy and gauche, with a Cockney accent; Olivier was impulsive, dominating and stylishly handsome. When Shaw first met Olivier at the Land Reform Union in 1883 he was struck by this "extraordinarily attractive figure . . . handsome and strongly sexed, looking like a Spanish grandee in any sort of clothes, however unconventional . . . he was a law unto himself, and never dreamed of considering other people's feelings, nor could conceive their sensitiveness on points that were to him trivial."[5]

Olivier was born in Colchester on 16 April 1859. He came from a good family of Huguenot descent with a tradition of eccentricity and rebellion. He was the second of the eight children of the Reverend Arnold Olivier, an Anglican of stern dedication whom he described as "a somewhat bitter religious bigot." Olivier reacted against his father and had to struggle to discover his own set of values. "I have never

settled in my mind," he wrote in 1885, "whether it is worse for a child
nowadays for its parents to be too 'religious' or 'irreligious.' I know in
my own case that the never having *really* the same standards of right
and wrong as my parents . . . has not been good . . . and I should
have been better under equally moral but secular parents."[6] Such feelings, latent during his years at Tonbridge School, became troublesome
when he went to Corpus Christi College, Oxford.

At Oxford Olivier formed a close and significant friendship with
a fellow student, Graham Wallas, then in his second year.[7] Wallas, born
on 31 May 1858, was also the son of a clergyman, an energetic Evangelical with the orthodox belief in hell-fire and damnation to be expiated by piety and good works. Graham, the eldest son of nine children,
was a good but unhappy child, and although he became a talented classical scholar at Shrewsbury School he disliked his life there and kept
himself aloof from his associates. By the end of his first year at Oxford,
after an acute spiritual crisis, he abandoned his faith, turning instead to
the new evolutionary science and to aggressive Secularism. Though
Wallas now drew his ideas from Aristotle, Darwin and Bentham rather
than from Holy Writ, he retained his father's strong moral sense and
dedication to service. Wallas was a kindly man but something of a prig,
willing to make a martyr of himself for principle. His search for the
springs of goodness in human nature understandably affected the impressionable Olivier.

It was Wallas who introduced Olivier to the ideas of Samuel Butler,
whose notion of purposive psychic evolution seemed a preferable alternative to the Darwinian lottery of natural selection. Olivier had already
read Herbert Spencer and Darwin, but had been troubled by the inability of Darwinism to explain the growth of spiritual values or such arts
as music. From Butler Olivier took "a tenable conception of evolution"
and "an inveterate mental habit of seeing people's faults as diseases." This
conception of human frailty, which Butler made the central theme of his
fable *Erewhon*, converted Olivier "to a belief in the reform of social
conditions as a palliative for original sin."[8]

It was an unsettling state of mind for a youth brought up to be a
gentleman and to expect service from others. Olivier now found himself
in conflict with his Church and his class, and troubled about the contrast between privilege and poverty. When his family pressed him to become a barrister he refused because "I disliked what appeared to me the

practice of professional insincerity involved in pleading cases." Without much money to back him, and brought up to regard any moneymaking occupation as socially unsuitable, he used his great abilities to secure a place in the public service. He entered the Colonial Office in the spring of 1882.

His appointment left him a good deal of freedom, for the work was not exacting and the Colonial Office imposed no constraints on the political or other interests of its senior clerks. Olivier had time to follow Webb in studying for law examinations. He became involved in settlement work at Toynbee Hall in the East End, taking lodgings in the slums of Whitechapel; he taught a Latin class at the Working Men's College; and he was an active member of the committee of the Land Reform Union and one of the team which put out the *Christian Socialist*.

Webb was more cautious. Though he was giving lectures about reform in the early Eighties, his main emphasis was on moral improvement, and his politics were not significantly different from the run-of-the-mill London Radicalism in which he had been brought up. It was only in August 1883 that Shaw persuaded him to join the Land Reform Union, and even then Sidney paid his half-crown subscription with the proviso that he was not committed to land nationalization.[9] As late as the spring of 1884 he declared, "I am, I am sorry to say, no believer in state socialism, the impossibility of which I need not even attempt to demonstrate." He was, he added, "a sincerely orthodox believer in Political Economy."[10] He was also interested in the Positivist theories of Auguste Comte, to which he had come from a study of Herbert Spencer and T. H. Huxley's gloss on the evolutionary ideas of Darwin; and Olivier's enthusiasm for Comte—stimulated by a spell as tutor to the son of the leading Positivist, Henry Crompton—greatly influenced his fellow clerk. "Whether one considers Comte's ideal Capitalist system or a Socialist system of industry as ultimately the most desirable," Olivier wrote on 28 October 1883, "it does appear to me that a great advance in the direction of Socialism must be the next move."[11] For the next two years Sidney Webb slowly moved in that direction.

Positivism had a strong appeal for lapsed Evangelicals. T. H. Huxley ridiculed it as "Catholicism without Christianity," for Comte's Religion of Humanity involved elaborate rituals. Yet the central theme of

Comte's teaching, which transferred the idea of service to God to a self-subordinating service to man, had an impact which went far beyond the Positivist sect. The Positivists were not socialists. Well aware of the inequities of Victorian society, they thought it could be made more efficient and morally acceptable if capitalists could be persuaded to change their ways. Comte envisaged a highly organized industrial system which would be ruled by "Priests of Humanity," an elite of unselfish businessmen and high-minded administrators inspired by the forces of spiritual evolution. This sense of social duty, which would make the wealthy the trustees rather than the exploiters of society, led the Positivists into conflict with industrialists who obdurately refused to be saved or to accept their notion of a controlled social order. Progress could not be achieved by grasping individualists or by the competition of the market, as the Liberal captains of industry insisted; the public good must be sought constantly and deliberately by those who understood that society could be changed only by changing the hearts of men. Such beliefs had led Positivists such as Frederic Harrison and E. S. Beesly to help the struggling trade unions in the Seventies, and to support the idea that workingmen should send their own representatives to the House of Commons.

By the beginning of the Eighties, the Positivist movement itself was on the wane, but it left its mark on the young middle-class reformers who were drifting towards socialism. The Marxist journalist Belfort Bax made the quip that Positivists believed in the moralization of capitalism whereas socialists thought this was simply the moralization of brigandage. Yet the legacy of Positivism remained, giving weight to the early Fabian belief that moral reform should be the prelude to social change. In January 1884, in a letter objecting to the Marxism of the SDF, Olivier wrote of "the inevitable evils of a socialist system, organised without as thorough a revolution in morality as would suffice to obviate the ills of the capitalist system."[12] Sidney Webb made the same point in a talk to the Argosy Society in 1884, which he repeated in March 1885 as his first address to the Fabian Society. "The improvement in public morality needed to make socialism viable was so great," he suggested, that it would be "easier to moralise the capitalist than to expropriate him."

The idea of moral reform rather than a separate political party of reformers had led the Positivists to believe that more good might be done by working through existing organizations than by opposing them—an attitude which led the veteran reformer G. J. Holyoake to describe the

Positivists as political cuckoos who laid their eggs in other people's nests. Before long the same was to be said of the Fabians, who adopted the same tactics. And from the Positivists the Fabians also inherited Frederic Harrison's belief that serious reformers must be willing to discard demagogic rhetoric and grind away at the details of industrial organization and social legislation.

As Olivier and Webb worked through their political apprenticeship, it was Positivism which served them as the transitional stage between reformist Liberalism and socialism. In October 1886, ten months after Sidney Webb became a socialist, he wrote a letter to Pease which clearly revealed the way in which he had translated the Positivist legacy into Fabian terms.

> . . . nothing in England is done without the consent of a small intellectual yet practical class in London not 2000 in number. We alone could get at that class, & we shall give up that work if we compete with the SDF.
>
> The social organisation is a very complicated machine, and as each item of it is endowed with nerve tissue highly sensitive to pain, I am much afraid of tinkering with it. I know, indeed, that *every* change, even for good, causes immense pain . . . what I try to do is make people think . . . I don't believe ten per cent of us are fit for a Socialist state yet.
>
> I doubt the wisdom of a separate Socialist party in Parliament except as a means of propaganda. We, like the homeopathists & the old radicals, shall win without being acknowledged victors, by permeation of others.[13]

Webb and Olivier lived an earnest and modest existence in a London, where the sight and smell of poverty was an everyday reminder of the miseries that lay beneath the comfort of the middle classes. They felt a personal duty, even with their restricted means, to raise the poor from those lower depths—as if the sin of social advantage could be expiated only through service. They shared the views that Arnold Toynbee put dramatically in a lecture published in November 1883, in which he told the pauper masses: "We have neglected you . . . wronged you . . . sinned against you grievously . . . if you will forgive us . . . we will devote our lives to your service."[14]

In the autumn of 1884 Graham Wallas, for whom such feelings of ascetic obligation were the ruling passion of his life, was appointed classics master at Highgate School in north London and took up his friendship with Olivier and Webb. He had first met Webb in 1882 when he called one evening at Downing Street to see Olivier and found Webb on duty. "Almost at once," Webb recalled, "with Wallas's characteristic gift of intellectual intimacy, I found myself engaged in a game of chess, and simultaneously discussing the state of the nation."[15] By the early months of 1885 this oddly assorted trio—they soon became known among Fabians as "the Three Musketeers," with Shaw casting himself in the role of D'Artagnan—were sharing their pleasures and troubles as well as their political interests.

They were already mixing with Fabians, though Webb and Olivier did not enroll until 1 May 1885—with Wallas delaying another year. For they were in the group which met regularly at the house of Charlotte Wilson on the northern edge of Hampstead Heath. This forceful young bluestocking from Girton, married to a stockbroker, felt the need to demonstrate her socialist opinions by opting for the Simple Life in a comfortably converted farmhouse furnished in the current vogue of arts and crafts. With the novelist Emma Brooke acting as secretary, she started what she called the Karl Marx Club (though it later assumed the more innocuous name of Hampstead Historic Society) and invited a very mixed group of reformers to read Marx together. The initial meeting was chaired by the committed Marxist Belfort Bax, who had gone with Morris when the Socialist League broke with Hyndman; Joynes, John Burns and other avowed Marxists occasionally attended. Most of those who came, however, were ignorant of Marx. Pease, Clarke, Webb, Olivier, Shaw and Wallas turned up regularly, usually walking out to Hampstead and back late at night talking so furiously that they attracted the attention of passersby.

Shaw missed the first meeting, at the end of October 1884, when Charlotte Wilson read a paper on the first chapter of *Capital;* and Webb wrote to him on 4 November, "Unless some utterly unscrupulous socialist dialectician like yourself turns up there, we shall have discarded *Le Capital* within a month."[16] Much the same happened at the following meetings. Five years later Shaw jokingly recalled that "a young lady used to read out *Capital* in French to us until we began to quarrel, which usually occurred before she had gone on long enough to make us feel seriously fatigued."[17]

At first Shaw took on the defence of Marx at the monthly meetings, as he had already done in a controversy—published in *To-Day* in the winter of 1884–85—with the Unitarian minister and economist Philip Wicksteed.[18] Yet as the hard arguments went on, with Webb attacking Marx as methodologically unsound and Olivier asserting that Marx neglected noneconomic values, Shaw decided that the Marxist theory of surplus value was untenable. Wicksteed's attack on *Capital*, based on the new theory of marginal utility advanced by W. S. Jevons, had shaken Shaw, and his doubts were intensified by his experience in yet another group (later to become the British Economic Association) which met regularly in Hampstead at the house of the stockbroker Henry R. Beeton. Sidney Webb was another member of that group; like Shaw, he too came to believe that Jevons offered a better explanation of the causes of inequality than Marx.

Before long the Hampstead Historic Society had moved on from Marx to wider issues of socialist theory and practice, serving as a seminar in which the most able members of the Fabian Society put themselves through a stiff course of study and worked out their conceptions of capitalist society and the best ways of changing it. The programme for the winter 1887–88 included papers by Webb, Wallas, Shaw, Podmore, Olivier and Charlotte Wilson on the development of society between 1600 and the emergence of the utopian socialists, the Chartists and the Positivists in the early part of the nineteenth century. A year later, meeting fortnightly, this inner group of Fabians were looking at the problems of the Poor Law, the women's movement, trade unionism and cooperation; the Hampstead discussions were, in effect, the private view of positions taken publicly in the normal Fabian sessions. Shaw summed up their drift in an article in the *National Reformer* in October 1887. "Read Jevons and the rest for your economics," he wrote; "read Marx for the history of their working in the past and the conditions of their application in the present. And never mind the metaphysics."

These intense, private discussions, carefully prepared and rigorously argued, were the seedbed of Fabian attitudes and policies; though little information about them survives, it is clear that it was this sustained intellectual encounter which began to make the Fabians a coherent group, providing a core of leaders who fully understood each other and had learned to express themselves succinctly and forcibly. But the arguments also spilled over into their ordinary lives. They wrote to each other at length about their opinions as well as confiding some of their personal hopes and disappointments. Sydney Olivier had another confidante, Margaret Cox, a pretty but self-effacing girl who was the sister of his old school friend Harold Cox. They were married in May 1885. Although Olivier maintained his enthusiasm for the Fabians—he succeeded Frederick Keddell as their secretary—Margaret found them intimidating. Their intellectual virtuosity made her feel inferior. She preferred the company of people like Henry and Kate Salt, who were now pursuing the Simple Life at a cottage at Tilford in Surrey. The tie was strengthened when Margaret's sister married the brother of Edward Carpenter, so much admired by the Salts. In 1885 her brother Harold also went down to Tilford to engage in honest if unrewarding toil on a patch of barren land near the Salts' cottage. It was, according to G. Lowes Dickinson, who joined Cox in this attempt to start a cooperative farm, "desperate from the first." This arcadian idyll was soon shattered by reality. Dickinson went off to an academic career; Cox departed to teach mathematics in India, returning to become a Liberal MP. The Salts stayed on, attracting visitors more by their amiability and gentle culture than by their spartan hospitality.[19]

Sidney Webb, without the companionship of Olivier, turned more to Wallas and Shaw. Wallas was in trouble: he was forced to leave Highgate School because he refused as a matter of principle to take Communion in the school chapel. "You are . . . in fashion in being in low spirits," Sidney wrote to him on 2 July 1885 when Wallas had sought his advice about an alternative career. "It seems to me that my acquaintances all round are in trouble. (Only Olivier excepted—he is most unreasonably & inhumanly happy, I know). Some who have money are sick about other things. Some are sick about money."[20]

Sidney himself was sick about something other than money. He was, he told Shaw on 5 August, suffering from the misery of a frustrated infatuation and facing the "bitter & overwhelming reality" of disappointment in love.[21] Believing that happiness was unattainable, he feared that "a logical deduction" from this state "would be 1) Alcohol; 2) Opium; 3) Suicide." He was racked all summer by this experience, which touched on his innate depression. "I have had no *impulse* to suicide," he

wrote to Wallas on 17 August, though "the thought has never been totally absent from my mind for years." When the girl, Annie Adams,
jilted him for the young Liberal barrister Corrie Grant, Sidney begged
Wallas "to bear with me whatever I may do as I feel very desolate indeed. Why *did* God put such a thing into life." The affair had, moreover, affected his outlook: "it is faith-destroying. I am distinctly *more*
atheistic than before, and I am afraid also more unsettled as to the ethical
standard and its application."[22]

The Fabian Society offered an outlet for his pent-up energies, and
he was spending an evening a week teaching Shaw German by reading
through the second volume of *Capital*. German was then very much the
vogue among intellectual radicals. German idealist philosophy appealed
greatly to them; so did the romantic culture of the German university
towns and the efficiency of the German educational system. While
Webb tutored Shaw, Wallas went to Germany for the summer to learn
the language. Webb decided to join him there. "I have no repose of
mind," he wrote to Wallas when telling him of his plan, "but a self-
devouring activity, which is very restless and impatient."[23] Steady application to work could sustain him even when he could find no joy or
hope or faith in life.

The journey to Germany proved helpful. He and Wallas stayed in
Weimar with a woman who had lost her husband in the war with
Austria. It was this widow, Webb recalled six years later, who taught
him an essential lesson: "It is wicked to be faithful to a dead or shattered
idol—you must live, and therefore must forget."[24] He was also helped by
reading Edward Bellamy's novel *Dr. Heidenhoff's Process*, in which the
doctor's ideas on "cerebral hygiene" (a technique similar to psycho-
analysis) suggested that tormenting thoughts could be eliminated from
one's consciousness. In Bellamy's story the process was used to alleviate
the oppression of religious anxiety, but Webb found it so helpful in his
own troubles that he learnt long passages by heart. He concluded that
a man should adopt a pragmatic attitude to social problems, subordinating personal to communal interests. By the time he returned from
Germany he was already emerging from his despair, but he did not find
it easy to regain his momentum. On 20 November he reported to Wallas
that he had "settled down to a very dead level of life" without hope or
fear. "I am much as I was 18 months ago, plus experience and several
memories, and a certain unrest, and minus some of my youth and
hope."[25]

Edward Pease was also restless. He had made up his mind that he did not want to spend the rest of his life "running after rich men" as a stockbroker. His decision to leave the City was made easier by the fact that he had inherited £3,000 from his father and had saved about £750 of his own earnings; this capital ensured him an annual income of £200. He took classes to improve his hobby of carpentry, and looked around for a suitable opening "to identify myself, for a time at any rate, with the manual labour class." The influence of Henry George and the ethical simplicities preached by Edward Carpenter combined to create an ideal of a return to the land, or at least of the redeeming power of physical work. It was particularly appealing to middle-class reformers who were not dependent on toil for their subsistence. "Simplification," Pease said, "was in the air: one regarded manual work as the real thing, and middle-class occupations as artificial."[26] When he failed to get taken on as a craftsman by William Morris, Pease went off in 1886 to join a cooperative furnishing workshop in Newcastle-on-Tyne. It was a tottering enterprise, nominally a cooperative but actually privately owned, which was kept afloat in part by loans from Pease that took half his capital and were repaid only in later years. He enjoyed the work and his trade-union activities; he also lost his illusions about the English worker. "I think I can say positively," he remembered, "that I never met a shop-mate, even in the Co-operative shop where one expected better things, who took the remotest interest in politics or socialism, or trade unionism or Co-operation. They *were* interested in racing . . . they were simply bread-winners."

The ascetic high-mindedness of this group of Fabians was complemented by the bohemian style of Hubert and Edith Bland, whose home in south London became a meeting place for Fabians whose socialism was an expression of aesthetic revolt against the ugliness and moral conventions of Victorian society. At one pole, in Hampstead, there was an academic study circle; at the other, in Lee, there were parties, charades, musical evenings, enthusiasm for the arts-and-crafts movement, and advanced ideas in the theatre. It was not a hard-and-fast division: the Oliviers and Shaw mixed socially with both groups.

The Bland home was a disorganized ménage, but Shaw's experience of domestic eccentricity enabled him to play a steadying role whenever they ran into a crisis.[27] Bland liked to give the impression that he came from a good family that had come down in the world. In fact his grandfather was a house painter and plumber. His father, who described him-

self as a gentleman, had done well enough in business to give his three
sons and daughter a moderately comfortable middle-class home in Woolwich and a decent schooling. Hubert's youth, spent in the shadow of the
great military barracks, was dominated by the martial and patriotic sentiments which he retained even when he became a socialist. In this respect
he was far more like Henry Hyndman and Harry Champion—a kind of
Tory socialist—than his fellow Fabians who came from Liberal and anti-
imperialist families. He would have liked to be an army officer himself,
but his father's death when he was still a youth put paid to that ex-
pensive hope.

By the time he met Edith Nesbit he had set himself up in business.
After he was ruined by an absconding partner he could not find an occupation which was both genteel and remunerative. All the same, he
continued to give himself the airs of a gentleman, dressing up to the part
in top hat and monocle and taking a high moral tone in public. This was
in marked contrast to his disorderly private life; he had a compulsion
for sexual adventure which had already led him into several entangle-
ments before he met Edith Nesbit.

Edith succumbed to his charm at an early age. She was the youngest
of the six children of John Nesbit, who ran an Agricultural, Chemical
and Scientific Academy in Lambeth. He died when Edith was four, and,
though her resourceful mother ran the Academy for another five years,
the family slipped down the social scale. Edith was put out to live with
a family in France and was educated in an Ursuline convent and in a
boarding school in Germany. She was something of a tomboy, fey by
disposition, talented but at a loss what to make of her life. She met Hubert in 1877, when she was nineteen. They were married on 22 April
1880 when she was seven months pregnant. Bland had lost his money
and they had to scrape to make ends meet. Edith kept them going by
selling odd pieces of writing, colouring Christmas cards and doing paid
recitations. Even after Shaw had assisted Bland into journalism it was
Edith's writing that really supported the household and underwrote
their lively entertaining.

Money was not the only source of their marital problems. At Fabian
meetings it was the flamboyant Edith who appeared the more eccentric,
for she gave herself all the airs of an "advanced" woman, cutting her
hair short, dressing—on Shaw's prompting—in "healthy" woollen clothing, rolling her own cigarettes and smoking them in a long holder.

When crossed in argument she was prone to throw fainting fits, a performance that became a familiar turn at Fabian discussions. It was, however, the outwardly conventional Hubert who was the cause of the trouble. His moral homilies and overt rectitude were a façade which concealed the fact that he was an assiduous philanderer. His inability to break off a relationship led him into bizarre sexual adventures. It was three years after their marriage that Edith discovered he was still engaged to a woman who had borne his child. Recognizing that he could not bear inflicting pain, she not only forgave him but made friends with the woman. It was thereafter accepted that when Hubert was found out Edith would tidy up the mess.

Early in their marriage Edith befriended Alice Hoatson, a manuscript reader on *Sylvia's Home Journal*, which printed Edith's first stories. The girl became part of the Bland circle in 1885. She was the assistant secretary of the Fabians, and the Blands took her in as a companion help to their two children. There the unassertive Alice Hoatson remained, "Mouse" to Edith's "Cat" in the family nicknames. In 1885 Edith's son Fabian was born. In 1886 Edith had a stillborn child, and her loss was sharpened by the fact that Alice Hoatson gave birth to a daughter, Rosamund. Edith generously adopted the child as her own; it was another six months before she realized that Hubert was the father.

It was to Shaw she took her troubles. He still had the jealous Jenny Patterson on his hands; he was getting into deep water with Annie Besant; and Edith worked on his sympathy as if to draw him into another intrigue. She was attracted to him and was bitterly resentful at the way in which Hubert had manipulated her into a *ménage à trois*. Shaw, fascinated and sympathetic, met Edith two or three times a week for confidential chats at the British Museum or in nearby cafés. He often escorted her home after a meeting, but became alarmed when she pressed her attentions on him. "Mrs Bland . . . would not be denied coming here to tea," he noted in September 1886. In the following May he wrote: "She went away after an unpleasant scene caused by my telling her I wished her to go as I was afraid that a visit to me would compromise her."

Shaw was eventually driven to deal with Annie Besant in much the same way. They became increasingly close in the course of 1886. He went regularly to her house on Monday evenings for the piano duets which were frequently part of his romantic routine. By Christmas he was seeing her or writing to her almost daily. The intimacy with Annie, began his 1887 diary, "reached in January a point at which it threatened to become a vulgar intrigue, chiefly through my fault," and he claimed, "I roused myself in time and avoided this." Years after, he attributed the breach to "the apparently heartless levity with which I spoke, and acted in matters which were deeply serious." Annie Besant, Shaw later recalled, drew up a formal contract of the terms on which she was prepared to live with him. This to him was a trap, "worse than all the vows of all the churches on earth," ten times worse than any legal marriage. Jenny Patterson was making scenes about his association with Annie and followed them about. Shaw declared that he would meet Mrs. Besant only in public to avoid scenes with both women. When Annie requested the return of her letters and poems, Jenny got wind of the exchange, broke into Shaw's room and read the letters that had come back to him. Shaw decided to end the matter by burning all the evidence. "Reading over my letters before destroying them," he noted, "rather disgusted me with the trifling of the last two years about women."

The first Fabians hung together in a casual way because they found the Society a congenial club for talking things over with their contemporaries. They all had other interests, and none of them took the Society more seriously than they did competing organizations to which they belonged. The Society, choosy about its members, grew very slowly in 1885 and 1886: two years after it was founded its membership was only sixty-seven and its income was thirty-five pounds and nineteen shillings. A year later Webb complained to Pease that the Society was in debt; "the difficulty is that only about 10 members do any work to speak of, *in connection with the Society*."[28]

The Fabian minutes in these first years convey a sense of isolation from the excitements of the political world. In the course of 1885 and 1886 the members listened to such talks as "Industrial Villages," "How Can We Nationalise Accumulated Wealth?," by Annie Besant, "Private Property," by Edward Carpenter, "The Economics of a Positivist Community," by Sidney Webb—who then stated for the first time that he was a socialist, being no longer "sure that the capitalist can be moralised"[29]—and a characteristic talk by Graham Wallas on "Personal Duty under the Present System." Though there were occasional discussions of such topical issues as a strike of coal miners in Yorkshire and the struggle against police attempts to suppress street meetings in the East End, the Society was little more than another middle-class talking shop. Shaw, familiar with the contumacious meetings of other socialist sects, gave a droll impression of its genteel aimlessness. When Carpenter spoke on "Private Property" on New Year's Day 1886, he wrote in the minute book:

> Awfully dull meeting. Wilson yawning like anything—No wonder! Infernal draught from the window, Coffin fidgeting—putting coals on the fire, distributing ipecacuanha lozenges, & so on. Miss Coffin sitting on the landing, evidently bored. . . . Something making a frightful noise like the winding of a rusty clock. Mrs Bland suspected of doing it with the handle of her fan. Wish she wouldn't. Two or three meetings like this could finish up any society.[30]

Marxists, Socialist Leaguers and anarchists passionately believed in a cause. The early Fabians, on the other hand, were unsure what they believed; despite the clash of temperaments, they were tolerant of differences to the point of indecision. Their open-mindedness was, however, an unusual asset at a time when hair-splitting over doctrine was a destructive characteristic of sects like the SDF and the Socialist League. Morris said despairingly that his main task was one of "keeping the peace among people of different temperament, people eager and impetuous, but possessing a positive genius for misunderstanding each other."[31] The Society was saved from such splits and personal animosities, enabling it to act as a forum in which rival theories could comfortably be debated, because no one expected argument to lead to action. It offered a platform to anyone against the existing system: Morris was as welcome as Annie Besant, Carpenter's advocacy of the Simple Life was received as equably as Webb's suggestion that the mission of middle-class socialists was to "enforce" social duty on recalcitrant capitalists.

They were little more, in Sidney Webb's phrase, than "a mere group of friends meeting to discuss their own intellectual difficulties." They were so far from possessing a collective opinion that when a committee was set up to draft a tract called *Government Organisation of Unemployed Labour*, dealing with the thousands of workless men in London, the members insisted that it be signed by its two authors, Frank

Podmore and Webb, and not by the Society—a precedent which was followed for most of its later publications. The fact that there was no orthodoxy was the secret of the Society's appeal. Its undemanding tolerance left room to explore new ideas and relationships. The members fell into the Society having, so to speak, fallen out of society. The apparently aimless search for an identity for the Fabian Society coincided with their own attempts to find adult identities.

❧ 5 ❧

ENGLAND, ARISE!

In 1880 Gladstone triumphantly led the Liberals back to power, but he was unable to cope with the problems which, he said, "rushed upon us like a flood."[1] During the next five years his government was dragged into foreign adventures; it drifted into the excesses of coercion in Ireland; and it was incapable of finding an answer to the depression in agriculture and trade. It was, moreover, a government that was divided against itself. By 1885 Britain was an industrial nation in which questions of social reform were becoming as important as the political reforms for which the Liberals had stood for half a century.[2] On those questions it was becoming increasingly difficult to hold together a party which included manufacturers and workingmen, Whig aristocrats and Radical agitators, Nonconformist shopkeepers and trade unionists. Each attempt to conciliate one faction antagonized another—and even when compromises were patched up on domestic policy the Irish issue created new and bitter divisions.

The stresses on the Liberal alliance were intensified by the Reform Act which Joseph Chamberlain introduced in 1884. It enlarged the electorate from three to five million, giving half of all adult men the right to vote. It abolished the double-member constituency—a device which had enabled the Liberals to straddle by running a Whig and a Radical in uneasy partnership—and it increased the number of seats in Ireland. Coming after the introduction of the secret ballot in 1872 and the Corrupt Practices Act of 1883, it created a mass electorate at a time when new political allegiances were being formed. A year later, after months of dissension within the Cabinet on Irish policy, the Liberal government was defeated in the House of Commons by a combination of Tory and Irish nationalist votes. Gladstone resigned and Lord Salisbury formed a caretaker administration of Conservatives. As the election approached, Gladstone decided to make his last throw. In Chamberlain's words, he "found salvation and plumped for Home Rule" for Ireland as a way of "avoiding divisions in the party between Radicals and Whigs and ensuring Parnell's support."

The emergence of the Liberals as the largest party in 1885, with 335 seats, was an apparent success. It was actually the prelude to a catastrophe which put the Conservatives into office for most of the next two decades. For the Tories had come back with 249 seats and Parnell led 86 Irish members pledged to Home Rule, thus producing a dead heat if he supported Salisbury. To win those vital Irish votes Gladstone committed himself to Home Rule—and split his party in the process. Chamberlain and a significant group of his Radical associates would not accept the dissolution of the union with Ireland, and these "Unionists" joined with dissident Whigs to oppose Home Rule. When Chamberlain resigned on this issue in March 1886 Gladstone's administration was doomed. The remaining Radicals thought his Irish policies too tender to the landlords; the landlords would not tolerate Home Rule; the Irish thought the measure too timorous; and the middle class feared the breakup of orderly government. In June, in an unprecedented defection, 93 Liberals went into the lobby with the Tories to defeat Gladstone. In the ensuing election the Tories and their Liberal Unionist allies came back with a majority of 116 over Gladstone and Parnell.

"It has been a year of shock and strain," Gladstone said when it was all over. As a comment on the year which broke the mould of Victorian politics that was an understatement. When the pieces were reassembled Britain had a three-party system, a Parliament whose procedures had to be altered to accommodate Irish disruption, and a Liberal opposition which could not agree upon a policy. The new Conservative government under Lord Salisbury was clearly identified with loyalty to the Crown, expansion of the Empire, the protection of property, the mainte-

nance of British supremacy in Ireland at any cost and sufficient concessions in social policy to appease the masses at home.

The shock wave went right through the system as Chamberlain's
desertion deprived the Radicals of their most effective leader. He had
gone into the election of 1885 with his own advanced programme of
land reform, housing reform and stiffer taxation on the rich. A year later
he was the means of putting in power an administration which was
clearly for the classes against the masses. The parliamentary battle had
been played out against the background of a grim winter, fog-bound,
and bitterly cold, in which the suffering of the poor drove them onto
the streets in protest and processions of unemployed from the East End
frightened respectable householders with the bogey of revolution. The
aged Tennyson, taking a last pessimistic view of his age, cried, "Chaos,
Cosmos! Cosmos, Chaos! who can tell how all will end!" and asked,
"When was age so cramm'd with menace? madness? written, spoken
lies?"[3]

The old order was crumbling, but no group offered an effective policy
for progress. The focus of opposition was the Radical wing of the Liberal Party; few Radicals, however, went much further than the programme which Chamberlain had put forward in 1885 or a desire to increase their influence within the Liberal Party and to elect a few more
sympathizers to Parliament. They were loosely organized in the Radical
clubs. There were over two hundred of these in London in the middle
Eighties, with a nominal membership of twenty-five thousand, and probably as many more in the rest of the country. At best they controlled
about a fifth of the Liberal vote and claimed the same proportion of Liberal seats in the House of Commons. Most of these Radicals were artisans
and shopkeepers, with a sprinkling of middle-class activists, and though
they favoured measures to assist the working classes they were not sympathetic to proposals to create a new party committed to the independent representation of labour. In any case, the franchise was still heavily
loaded in favour of the propertied classes; and workingmen candidates
found almost insuperable difficulties in meeting their election costs or,
since MP's were unpaid, supporting themselves if they were elected.

For the small socialist sects, the problems of parliamentary action
were not only practical but ideological. They were so weak and so poor

that it would have been merely a gesture to nominate candidates. In 1885 the Social Democratic Federation had at most 700 members; the Socialist League had no more than 150. They had, moreover, little use for what William Morris called the shams of the parliamentary game. As socialists they had broken with bourgeois society; as sectarians they were often more hostile to Radical "compromisers" than to the Liberal or Tory leaders. Hubert Bland remarked that the first reaction on becoming a socialist was "to shut oneself up as it were in a little mansion of one's own and with a few eclectic friends to think scornfully of the world outside."[4]

This sense of belonging to the same cause held the socialists together against the outside world even though their movement was broken into factions—Marxists, Christian Socialists, Anarchists, Fabians, Simple Lifers and Land Reformers. Despite their differences on niceties of doctrine and tactics, they attended each other's meetings, exchanged speakers, read their little journals and held joint demonstrations. When, for instance, the police tried to clamp down on free speech in Dod Street, Whitechapel, a traditional "speaker's corner" for Radicals and socialists, everyone rallied round. After some arrests on 20 September 1886 volunteers were asked to speak in turn. Morris was taken up, but released. The following week there was a crowd of thirty thousand. One of the volunteers was Shaw, who found the prospect of imprisonment "anything but agreeable," telling a friend that he was "in a state of terror about this East End business" which might put him in gaol for a month.[5] When he spoke—with Hyndman and Aveling, who delayed the meeting by a quarrel about which of them should have the honour of being arrested first—no charge was made. Before long the police were forced to let the meetings continue unmolested.

There was such an overlap of opinions that it was hard to know what anyone believed, especially as the disagreements often seemed to be more personal than political. But significant differences were beginning to emerge, and they were argued out in the little papers which served as rallying points. The Fabians had no journal of their own and they placed their articles where they could. The SDF had *Justice*, extravagant in its language, at times openly insurrectionary in tone, which preached a Marxist doctrine of class war. When Morris broke with Hyndman he financed *Commonweal* for the Socialist League. His influence reached beyond its narrow circle of readers, for his writing and speeches were the common property of the socialists. Disliking all government and dreaming of a utopia which owed more to the aesthetics of Ruskin than to the economics of Marx, Morris was a propagandist for ideals rather than action: the coming of socialism, he continually insisted, must be prefaced by the making of socialists. *Commonweal* gradually became the focus for those who put principles before politics. The anarchists themselves, divided into individualist and communist factions, had their own fly-sheets, the most important being *Freedom*, which Charlotte Wilson produced under the patronage of the emigré Russian Prince Peter Kropotkin. Annie Besant kept *Our Corner* going as her personal property, though part of it was devoted to Fabian business. *To-Day*, with somewhat stronger theoretical pretensions, kept open house under Champion and Bland, publishing articles from Marxists, Ethical Socialists, Positivists and supporters of Morris, and catering to the mixed intellectual clientele from which the Fabians drew their support. From 1886, Thomas Bolam's paper *The Practical Socialist* served as a forum for the moderate socialists, shading away through land reformers to utilitarian followers of Mill and the fringes of the Radical movement.

What, then, was socialism? What means should be employed to abolish capitalism and establish a new society? And what would that new society be like? On none of these three vital questions was there any agreement. Should one take to the streets like Hyndman, to the stump like Morris, to the fields like Carpenter, to the anarchist commune, the producer cooperative or the self-improving idealism of the Fellowship of the New Life? Or should one follow the Avelings, who, coached by Engels, were arguing for a labour party modelled on the European social democrats? Or perhaps the way forward lay through the capture of the Radicals for more advanced policies, using and trying to change the Liberal Party in the process?

The Fabians had no settled view of any of these questions. Their own emotional poverty had led them to ally themselves with those who were materially impoverished. They took their membership in the intellectual proletariat for granted, but they still had to decide on a political and economic policy that made intellectual sense. Shaw was temperamentally inclined to the revolutionaries. Bland took the SDF seriously, feeling moved by "the confident appeal of Marxism," but he opposed Hyndman's insurrectionary romanticism as strongly as he detested Radicals and Nonconformists. Annie Besant was emotionally disposed towards the Ethical Socialists but thought the SDF more concerned with practical politics. Charlotte Wilson was a declared anarchist. Olivier was drawn to the Simple Lifers and the moral improvers. Webb and Wallas wanted to cooperate with the London Radicals, to which they both belonged. The leading members of the Society, in short, had decided nothing about its future by the summer of 1886. It was clearly time to do so if the Fabians were to survive as anything more than a congenial debating club.

The events which led the Fabians to define their political role began with the controversial decision of the SDF to run candidates in the general election at Hampstead and Kennington. The money to pay for these contests came secretly from Tory sources in the hope that the SDF would draw off Radical votes—though one candidate received thirty-two votes and the other only twenty-seven. Everyone was upset. Radicals were outraged by this resort to "Tory Gold." The Socialist League condemned the SDF for "trafficking with the honour" of the movement, and the Fabians denounced the move as a calculated disgrace—a criticism which forced the Society's first secretary, the SDF member Frederick Keddell, to resign in protest. The consequent vacancy on the Fabian executive was filled by Sidney Webb. It was Shaw, however, who saw beyond the moral indignation to the political point. This "disaster," he insisted later, demonstrated the weakness of the socialists, exposed the tactical incompetence of the SDF and played into the hands of the insurrectionists and anarchists who had all along been opposed to political action.[6]

The lesson was not lost on the Fabians. They rebuked the SDF and set aside £110 to promote the cooperation of all progressive associations. Two weeks later John Burns defended the SDF case for revolutionary measures. Annie Besant retorted scornfully: "What is your revolutionary strength in London; may we not gauge it by your fifty votes or so . . . bought and paid for with Tory Gold?" Foreshadowing for the first time the characteristic policies of the Fabian Society, she insisted that society was to be reformed "by a slow process of evolution, not by revolution and bloodshed. It is you revolutionaries," she retorted to Burns, "who stem and block the evolutionary process."[7]

It was the provocative bluster of the SDF speakers that the middle-class Fabians found most disturbing; even Shaw felt that the SDF leaders were carrying demagogy to dangerous lengths among the unemployed. There were loose talk about dynamite and rumours that Hyndman's lieutenant Harry Quelch was training SDF volunteers in military drill in his back yard. On 11 February 1886 Shaw wrote in the *Pall Mall Gazette* that the workless were "as great a nuisance to socialists as to themselves. Angry as they are, they do not want a revolution: they want a job." Hyndman and Burns may have had dreams of leading a mob of desperate Londoners to the seizure of power, but the Fabians were increasingly sceptical. Bland talked of "this silly bull-at-gate business of a few men,"[8] and though he thought some kind of armed struggle might eventually be necessary, he took the same line as Shaw. The unemployed, he wrote, were "*not* the people to make a political revolution or even to carry a great reform. The revolt of the empty stomach ends at the baker's shop."[9]

The February riot in Trafalgar Square was the second event which drove the Fabians to distinguish themselves from the militants. During the unemployed marches that winter the SDF created a machine which could mobilize up to twenty thousand demonstrators, but its activities were concentrated on the East End. It had run into competition there with another group, led by renegade trade unionists and backed with Tory funds, which was trying to whip up support for "Fair Trade"—the slogan of the protectionists, who blamed the economic crisis on Liberal free-trade policies. When the Fair Traders proposed to hold a rally in Trafalgar Square on Monday 8 February, the SDF decided to swamp it with their own followers.

Sir Edmund Henderson, in charge of the Metropolitan Police, was warned that the rival meetings in the square might lead to trouble, but he sent only sixty-six men.[10] Most of the reserves of 563 constables were placed to the south and east of the square, controlling the routes by which the demonstrators came in and providing cover against a possible march on the Commons. After John Burns, H. M. Hyndman, and Champion had delivered inflammatory speeches from the plinth of Nelson's Column, scuffling broke out and the surging crowd got out of hand, breaking through the thin cordon of police on the west side of the square and into Pall Mall—the centre of London's clubland. Hyndman had recently been expelled from his own club for his socialist views, and

in his speech he went out of his way to contrast the misery of the unemployed with the comfort of the smart clubs. The marchers, thus
primed, reacted angrily when they were jeered as they carried the red
flag past the clubs. Picking up stones in Waterloo Place, they broke windows, and before long the situation was out of hand: rioting and looting
spread up to Piccadilly as the police lost control.

Police incompetence left the West End open to an orgy of violence
and aroused old fears that London might see a repetition of the Paris
Commune. It was, the Queen complained to Gladstone three days later,
a "monstrous riot . . . a momentary triumph for socialism and a disgrace to the capital." The mild Henderson was dismissed, his post being
given to the fire-eating Sir Charles Warren, a former army officer whom
the *Pall Mall Gazette* described as "a belated Ironside." "Society, saved,
came out of its hiding place," Shaw said afterwards, "rallying to a government that had frightened it out of its senses with an imaginary
revolution."[11]

Within days, sterner measures against the socialists were being
planned—and thousands of pounds swelled the Lord Mayor's relief fund
for the unemployed. Almost two months later, Hyndman, Burns and
Champion were tried together at the Old Bailey for seditious conspiracy; they defended themselves vigorously, and were acquitted on a
technicality.

The Fabians were anxious to disclaim any association with the riot,
and they managed to plant mollifying descriptions of the Society in a
number of newspapers. One report ridiculed the idea that it was "a
slumbering volcano of revolution" and insisted that it was "as harmless
an institution as any Young Men's Debating Society in the rural provinces."[12] And the *Morning Post*, on 25 March, carried a long report on a
typical Fabian meeting in "a well-appointed and fashionably-situated
mansion," where the reporter was shown up to the drawing-room by
"the blue-coated, gold-buttoned manservant of the Socialist host." Such
decorum was a long way from the East End hovels, the looted bread
shops and the dock at the Old Bailey.

The newspapers that took the trouble to find out anything about
the Fabians were always surprised to find them so genteel, that they
were essentially idealists rather than agitators, who believed that socialism was more a matter of justice for the poor than envy of the rich. Edward Pease, writing on "Ethical Socialism," insisted that socialism was

inevitable and that the main question was whether one worked hope-
fully for it or opposed its coming:

> If we prepare the way before it, and receive it gladly, it will come
> to us peaceably and as a welcome friend. If, on the other hand, we
> harden our hearts, and close the gates of our minds against the truth,
> it will come upon us none the less, but as a destroying angel, with
> fire, and bloodshed and confusion. On us, of the upper and middle
> classes, rests the burden of this choice.[13]

The Fabians were the only socialist group in which such opinions
could be voiced without evoking sarcastic jeers. They believed deeply
in the "civilizing mission" of the middle class; indeed, they doubted
whether the workers were likely ever to be the gravediggers of the
old society. They therefore took care to admit only those who they
could be sure would accept their assumptions. On 19 February 1886 it
was agreed that local groups could be formed where there was sufficient
support—though the members were careful to insist that such bodies
should be distinct from *the* Fabian Society. And in April, after electing
the new executive of Besant, Podmore, Shaw, Webb and Charlotte Wilson, with Pease as secretary and Bland as treasurer, they laid down careful rules about admission. The Fabians did not welcome everyone who
was willing to pay a subscription. Each applicant had to have two sponsors; the executive had a right to a blackball, and candidates had to serve
a period of probation, attending meetings as guests before being elected.
   Procedures, however, were a simple matter compared to decisions
on policy. When Tract 4 attempted to explain *What Socialism Is*, its authors had to confess that English socialism was "not yet definite enough
in point of policy to be classified." The best they could do was to suggest that the "conscious growth of social feeling" might avert a class
war, and that socialism might eventually divide into two parties, "a Collectivist party supporting a strong central administration, and a counter-
balancing Anarchist party defending individual initiative against that
administration." The distinction was, interestingly enough, summarized
as "the conflict of the uneradicable Tory and Whig instincts in human
nature."
   It was Annie Besant who, with Bland's support, consistently took
the initiative in trying to get the Fabians into practical politics. The idea
of local societies came from her; so did the notion of bringing all "pro-

gressive associations" together in a conference planned for mid-June at the South Place Chapel. It was a motley group. The SDF decided to boycott the occasion, but fifty-three societies sent representatives. Apart from members of the London Radical clubs and Secular societies, there were delegates from the Socialist League, Headlam's Guild of St. Matthew, the Kropotkin wing of the anarchists, a scattering of socialists from the provinces and some land reformers. Shaw later claimed that all the conference proved was that "we had nothing immediately practical to impart to the Radicals and that they had nothing to impart to us." The Fabians, however, had intended only an exchange of views. The roster of speakers, indeed, was familiar. Among those delivering the eighteen papers were Morris, Aveling, Webb, Carpenter, Annie Besant and Stewart Headlam.

This aimless and amiable meeting did not satisfy Annie Besant or Bland, who wrote disparagingly about the Socialist Leaguers who wanted to go off "with two sticks of brimstone and a box of matches to make a little hell of their own." In September Annie induced her colleagues to call another meeting, at Anderton's Hotel in the Strand, to which "all Socialist bodies in London" were invited to discuss her motion that it was "advisable that Socialists should organise themselves as a political party for the purpose of transferring into the hands of the whole working community full control over the soil and the means of production, as well as over the production and distribution of wealth." For once the Fabians found themselves making common cause with the SDF, whose representatives took a similar line against the anarchists and other antiparliamentarians such as Morris. It was Morris himself who put up an amendment which stated the case against party politics. The first duty of socialists, Morris claimed, was

> to educate the people to understand what their present position is and what the future might be, and to keep the principle of Socialism steadily before them, and whereas no Parliamentary party can exist without compromise and concession, which would hinder that education and obscure those principles, it would be a false step for Socialists to attempt to take part in a Parliamentary contest.[14]

Annie Besant's motion was carried by forty-seven votes to nineteen, after a noisy debate. Shaw said the "unseemly heat" was generated by an anarchist tinsmith who had drunk too much, but the uproar so upset the manager of the hotel that the Fabians were summarily told to hold their meetings elsewhere in future. On Sydney Olivier's initiative, arrangements were soon made to meet in Willis's Rooms, a well-appointed rendezvous with silver candelabra and liveried footmen, used by many learned societies; the esoteric name of the Fabians probably conveyed respectability.

Annie Besant had won her debating point. The Fabians had earlier drawn the line against the commotions promoted by the SDF; they now declared against the utopian "impossibilism" of the anarchists. Yet it was easier to deal with such issues in principle than to carry them out in practice. The Fabian moderates needed SDF support to vote down Morris and his followers, and there was still sufficient sympathy in the Society for Socialist Leaguers and anarchists to prevent the Society plumping for conversion into a political party. There was resistance, too, from the Hampstead group against the strong line that Annie Besant and Bland were taking. Shaw certainly objected, and Webb had little sympathy for anything that smacked of a separate socialist party. "I am not a man of action," Webb told Pease on 24 October, adding that he regarded "collectivist Socialism (as apart from mere socialistic radicalism) as a mere academic ideal like Plato's republic, which wants a lot of thinking about before one could vote for its adoption en bloc."

Annie, however, was not deterred, making yet another attempt to carry the Fabians for what was then called "possibilism." On 5 November 1886 she proposed that those Fabians in favour of parliamentary action should form a separate body to be called the Fabian Parliamentary League. Once again Bland was her main ally. He had just published an article in *The Practical Socialist* calling for a socialist party which could attract the "well-fed and educated workers" and promote constructive legislation. Webb, temperamentally against impulsive decisions and anxious for compromise, told Pease: "It is only with great difficulty that we have been able to hit on a modus vivendi which enables Mrs Wilson to remain. . . . I don't want a secession. I think we are doing good work in talking these things over by ourselves, & in attracting one bourgeois after another."[15] The formation of the League was the only way he could see to avoid a disruptive vote.

The new organization had a short life. A year later the anarchist issue had ceased to trouble the Society, and the Parliamentary League was transformed into the Political Committee. It had done little more than issue a single manifesto in February 1887, noting the progress of parliamentary socialists in other countries and insisting that English socialists should follow their lead. Graham Wallas, who had taken responsibility for the League, presciently extended the word "parliamentary" to include municipal and educational work.

The Fabians still preferred to talk, settling for the discussion of papers and gatherings in private houses. Annie Besant and Shaw were the only prominent members who regularly went about debating and speaking. Although Shaw was bumptiously claiming that the Fabian lectures were "famous throughout the world," the Society was actually in the doldrums. It was not, as he also observed, a favourable time "for drawing-room Socialism and scientific politics." The publication of Sidney Webb's first penny compendium of *Facts for Socialists*, which he put together at Shaw's suggestion, was a small event to set against unemployed marches or the ideological euphoria of the Socialist League. There was, however, something symbolic about this quiet statement of facts against such a noisy background. At a moment when the Fabians could easily have been swept away by any of the more turbulent factions around them, Webb was tenaciously working to keep the Society calm and to preserve its independence.

For this reason he felt that it must redefine its purposes, and a drafting committee was set up to prepare a new "Basis." This document, produced in June 1887, was to be used for the next thirty years as the test for admission to the Society.[16] By comparison with the fiery proclamations of other socialist groups it was uninspiring. It asserted, "The Fabian Society consists of Socialists," and then defined socialism in terms so woolly—avoiding the touchy question about the means of achieving it—that William Morris, Charlotte Wilson, Shaw, Webb, Besant, Bland and Wallas could all subscribe without any qualms of conscience. The crucial clause stated that they wanted "the spread of socialist opinions" and suggested that this could be achieved "by the general dissemination of knowledge as to the relation between the individual and Society in its economic, ethical and political aspects." By devising this catch-all constitution, Webb ingeniously ensured that the Society would remain a forum for free discussion without being torn apart by doctrinal disputes. He also made it clear that its primary aim was research and education, rather than action.

Sidney Webb was not against direct political activity; he simply felt that the Society had a different role to play and that its members should be free to join any political organization that appealed to them. Eventually, perhaps, a socialist party might emerge, but in the meantime the task of socialist intellectuals was to prepare themselves for that day. Writing to Wallas on 14 June 1887, Webb advised him to study for the bar. "It qualifies you," he urged, "for several things which might come your way, in after life, when we all get into power."[17]

As part of that preparation several of the Fabians took an active part that summer in the Charing Cross Parliament, a mock legislature which enabled them to enjoy the charade of forming a socialist government. On 15 July Champion was chosen as its prime minister, with Webb as chancellor of the exchequer, Annie Besant as home secretary, Bland as foreign secretary, Shaw as president of the Local Government Board, Wallas as president of the Board of Trade, and Olivier as colonial secretary. For the first time the leading Fabians felt, if only vicariously, what it was like to take office and present their ideas in the form of draft legislation.

While the Fabians debated, the unemployed demonstrated. At the end of the winter the unemployed had become so accustomed to parading about the streets that demonstrations developed spontaneously, without any SDF initiative, in London and in some provincial cities. This mood of rebellion was not matched by any definite strategy. Morris, in his diary for 3 March, noted the "weak side" of the SDF tactics: "they must always be getting up some fresh excitement, or else making the thing stale and at last ridiculous; so that they are rather in the position of a hard-pressed manager of a theatre—what are they to do next?" The same thought struck Champion, who felt that there should be either an attempt to bring all the socialist sects together on an agreed policy or some last-ditch effort to bring matters to a head—possibly by taking all the unemployed to Trafalgar Square and occupying it until something happened.[18] This, Shaw remarked sarcastically, was "perhaps the best available attempt at a revolution possible under the circumstances."

Champion had a good tactical sense, but his autocratic personality made it difficult for him to carry other people with him or persuade them to trust him. He had the reputation of an intriguer, and his career was a series of false starts in potentially sensible directions. He was, moreover, prone to seek help in discreditable quarters. He had been behind the "Tory Gold" fiasco, and on other occasions his willingness to use "tainted" money and to propose covert approaches to influential Tory friends outraged his comrades. In the summer of 1887 he devised a plan for reshuffling the socialist movement, and he put it forward to a private meeting with representatives of the Socialist League and the Fabians. At first it seemed a reasonable scheme.[19] In June 1887 Bland wrote an article in *To-Day*—in which he was closely associated with Champion—calling for a new organization "free from any but immediately practicable proposals, and quite absolved from the insane delusion that changes come about in England in any other way than by the ballot box." Champion hoped to pull many of the SDF members away from Hyndman and persuade Morris to bring in the less extreme elements of the Socialist League. Edward Pease, who had come down from Newcastle for the talks, felt that the Fabians would be able to endorse a joint manifesto which kept off divisive theoretical matters and concentrated on immediate issues. Yet Champion soon wrecked his own venture, forcing a premature showdown with Hyndman and leaving the SDF in pique. When Pease heard what had happened he decided that they had been pawns in an ambitious intrigue. Champion's intention, he concluded, "was to capture the S.D.F., and then tell the others that they could come in if they liked, under his command." At the same time, differences between Hyndman and John Burns had reached a point where the SDF no longer knew what it wanted or where it was leading the unemployed. The demonstrations had become a matter of habit rather than of policy.

There were other distractions that summer as the festivities organized to celebrate the Queen's Golden Jubilee year got under way. In vivid contrast to the disorder that had become normal in London's streets, the procession to Westminster Abbey on 20 June included three kings, and lesser princes and potentates from all over the world. With the memory of Fenian bombing attacks in central London still fresh, and with the revolutionary rhetoric of Burns and others providing a perpetual reminder that the lower depths might at any moment erupt, there were fears of violence behind the pageantry. Sidney Webb, spending a holiday in Norway with Charlotte Wilson and her husband, wrote to Graham Wallas: "Mrs W. startled us all on Jubilee day by saying quite calmly that she hoped the Queen would only get well shaken and not killed!"[20]

Once the Jubilee circus was over, the question of bread was raised again. Champion's idea of permanent demonstrations in Trafalgar Square was being realized spontaneously. On 22 October Sir Charles Warren wrote to the Home Secretary: "We have in the last month been in greater danger from the disorganized attacks on property by the rough and criminal elements than we have been in London for many years past. . . . The language used by the speakers at the various meetings has been more frank and open in recommending the poorer classes to help themselves from the wealth of the affluent."[21] Three days later he was complaining that he needed two thousand police on duty every day to control the processions, which had been going on daily for over a fortnight; he asked permission "to take such measures as I consider necessary." The government, with fresh disorders and new coercive policies to keep its attention on Ireland, was unwilling to give him his chance to treat London workmen like Irish peasants.

It was actually an Irish issue—the one theme which always united the Radicals and the socialists—that led to the showdown Warren wanted. By the end of October the daily clashes had convinced him there was a real threat to public order, and the complaints of shopkeepers whose trade was spoiled by the troubles had begun to tell on the authorities. Though Warren was reminded that he must keep within the law, he managed by Tuesday 8 November to get an order closing Trafalgar Square to any further meetings—a decision which seemed a fresh provocation to the advocates of free speech. The largest demonstration yet planned had been called for Sunday 13 November and this time its sponsors were the London Radical clubs, which had been infuriated by the arrest and ill-treatment of an Irish MP, William O'Brien. On the Saturday evening there was a joint meeting of the Radical and socialist leaders at which the decision was taken to defy Warren and move on Trafalgar Square next day with four converging columns.

Warren's plan was simple. The first police cordons were to break up the demonstrations with baton charges before they could reach the square. Any groups that managed to break through were to be kept out of the square itself by nearly two thousand police, drawn up four deep on the vulnerable south and east sides and two deep elsewhere. Four squadrons of cavalry were in reserve, and four hundred soldiers with live ammunition were posted at the nearby St. George's Barracks. The police, in an ugly mood, knew what Warren expected of them. Before the demonstrators had forced the bridges over the Thames twenty-six injured had already been carried off to St. Thomas' Hospital. Shaw spoke at Clerkenwell Green, where another procession started, this one including Morris and Annie Besant. It was brutally attacked as it moved through Holborn to the square. Shaw, who had been full of misgivings about the wisdom as well as the legality of the whole affair, was disgusted. Writing to William Morris four days later, he scornfully reported: "you should have seen that high-hearted host run. Running hardly expresses our collective action. We *skedaddled*. . . . it was the most abjectly disgraceful defeat ever suffered by a band of heroes outnumbering their foes a thousand to one." He eventually managed to work his way past the police to the square, looking for Annie, from whom he had become separated in his flight. About five o'clock, when the fighting was reaching its peak in the square, he went home for his tea.

By midafternoon enough of the disorganized crowd had reached the square to worry Warren, who called for cavalry at three o'clock and brought in the Foot Guards an hour later when he feared the police would be overwhelmed by the pressure. There was no leadership for the demonstrators, who were simply carried in waves up to the police lines, where they were clubbed or ridden down. Annie Besant, in a frenzy of excitement, tried to organize a primitive defence line of wagons, but like everything else on that chaotic afternoon the attempt was swamped in in the confusion. Even John Burns and the eccentric socialist MP Cunninghame-Graham, both well known to the police, could do nothing more than chain themselves to the railings of Morley's Hotel and wave the red flag until they were arrested. By six o'clock the battered demonstrators had taken enough and began to disperse; the cavalry returned to their barracks, and the soldiers marched away without a shot being fired. Henry Salt, pacifically observing the turmoil, had his watch stolen by a pickpocket and ruefully regretted that he could not protest against the behaviour of the police and then call them in to recover his private property. The tragicomedy of "Bloody Sunday" was over. With the dispersing crowd went the revolutionary illusions of the past two years. Sir Charles Warren had made his point, and it was not lost on the Fabians.

Only Annie Besant wanted to continue the fight. She had already organized a Socialist Defence Association for the victims of police brutality, and her first reaction was to arrange bail and legal defence for the many demonstrators who had been arrested. The riot had aroused her old desire to play the heroine, and her predisposition to martyrdom—the only way, Shaw said acidly, to "become famous without ability"—led her to make an impassioned demand for a return to Trafalgar Square to fight the free-speech campaign to a bitter end. Though Annie was defeated, feeling still ran high enough to launch an abortive rally in the square on the following Sunday, when a bystander named Alfred Linnell was so badly beaten by the police that he died. The socialists now had a martyr. William Morris wrote his "Death Song" for Linnell's huge funeral procession. And Sir Charles Warren had twenty thousand special constables sworn in as an insurance policy.

"It all comes," Shaw wrote in his sardonic footnote to the affair, "from people trying to live down to fiction instead of up to fact."[22]

✌ 6 ✌

STUMP AND
INKPOT

In a few hours on a Sunday afternoon Sir Charles Warren had brutally shattered the dream of an English revolution. The socialist leaders could not even capture Trafalgar Square.[1] Some, like Morris and Shaw, were quick to see that insurrectionary talk and unemployed riots were leading nowhere. Others tried to recover the initiative. Annie Besant was one who refused to admit that she was beaten. The eccentric Radical journalist W. T. Stead, then editing the *Pall Mall Gazette*, had for the moment become her new leading man. With him she formed the Law and Liberty League, an authoritarian organization more suited to a conspiracy than to normal political agitation. It came to little; the shock of Bloody Sunday had diverted too many people away from revolutionary heroics.[2]

Within weeks Annie had shifted the emphasis of *The Link*, the new paper she had founded to back the Law and Liberty League, from the struggle against the police to "the Temporal Salvation of the World" and was proposing "a New Church dedicated to the Service of Man." Her religious fervour, even when it found secular outlets, was always at fever pitch, and in her reaction against the failure of the free-speech movement she was casting about for a new crusade. Her talent for organization turned to the plight of the unskilled workers who had no one to speak out against long hours, low pay and appalling working conditions. Harry Champion had decided that the unskilled were a more promising field for agitation than the unemployed and Herbert Burrows, one of the SDF leaders, took the same line. It was he who persuaded Annie to work with him in a campaign to expose sweating and exploitation.

The Link had a regular feature called "The Lion's Mouth" which "posted" employers who treated their workers harshly. One of these reports, in June 1888, prompted Annie to go down to the East End to talk to some of the girls employed at the match factory owned by Bryant and May. The girls, who worked fourteen hours a day for a wage of less than five shillings a week, suffered from chemical poisoning and miserable conditions. Annie reported what she learned under the banner heading "White Slavery in London" and followed this exposure with a passionate appeal to the company's shareholders to repudiate the means whereby their profits were earned. Did they know, she cried passionately, "that girls are used to carry boxes on their heads until the hair is rubbed off and the young heads are bald at fifteen years of age? Country clergymen with shares in Bryant and May's, draw down on your knee your fifteen year old daughter; pass your hand tenderly over the silky clustering curls, rejoice in the dainty beauty of the thick, shiny tresses . . ." Annie distributed copies of *The Link* and gave roses to the girls. With the *Star,* Stead's *Pall Mall Gazette* and the *Echo* behind her, as well as the Secularist and socialist papers, she organized a series of meetings on the Mile End Waste. The girls, undeterred by the company's proposal to bring in new girls from Glasgow or move the factory elsewhere, stood firm and struck.[9]

Annie, Burrows and other SDF members managed the organization. They secured tremendous publicity for the strike, and sympathizers rallied round with money and help. At the strike headquarters in Mile End, Sydney Olivier and Stewart Headlam did some of the clerical work; Bland, Wallas and Shaw acted as cashiers, taking the money down once a week to dole out strike pay. After a strike lasting less than three weeks, the match girls went back to work with improved conditions.

The strike taught Annie Besant and Burrows the need to organize as well as agitate, and they went on to form a Matchmaker's Union, with Annie as its secretary. The new organization, which had over six hundred members, was large by London standards; only three unions had more than two thousand members. Annie had shown that the poorest and most exploited workers could be mobilized and that significant public feeling could be rallied behind them.

Annie was now over forty, plumper, with silver streaks in her hair, and she dressed in short skirts and heavy boots as she went about the industrial districts. In the next few months she and Burrows were involved in strikes by chainmakers at Cradley Heath, near Birmingham, by furriers, capmakers, tailors, tramwaymen and house painters. The strike of the match girls had caught the dry tinder of men and women who had previously seen no hope of improving their lot.

There was no central organization which planned this campaign, only an informal association of individuals who turned away from doctrinal arguments and drawing-room debates towards working-class realities, but this change of direction owed a good deal to the Avelings. Engels too had been urging socialists to organize the working class. It was Champion, however, who struck out most clearly in a new direction. He saw great possibilities in the Labour Electoral Association, recently created by the Trades Union Congress with the aim of putting up independent candidates to support labour issues. In 1888, to support this move, he founded *The Labour Elector,* which linked the campaign for the eight-hour day with the need for a labour party—a position which led him naturally to support the pioneer candidature of Keir Hardie at the Mid-Lanark by-election in 1888. For Hardie, a self-educated Scots miner who had become a union organizer, was now beginning his campaign to put workingmen into Parliament.

The Fabians felt no need to take part in what Shaw called "the revengeful growling over the defeat at the Square," because they had never had hopes of a victory from such encounters. Violence had been so discredited that Shaw considered this was the moment when "the way was clear at last for Fabianism" by the cultivation of middle-class reformers. Stewart Headlam was soon calling on the Society's members to take the Fabian message out to more "drawing-room" gatherings. There were plans to promote the Society in Oxford and Cambridge. "Our favourite sport," Shaw recalled of this period, "was inviting politicians and economists to lecture to us, and then falling on them with all our erudition and debating skill, and making them wish they had never been born."[4] It was done with a mixture of banter and moral earnestness which Shaw claimed was the salvation of the Society "from the gushing enthusiasts who mistake their own emotions for public movements."[5] It led to lively debates and enabled the Fabians to hit hard intellectually without giving or taking offence. But it also gave the Society a reputation of not being entirely serious and irritated those who felt excluded by the Fabian penchant for family jokes and allusions. These, however, helped to bind the Fabians together—a form of recognition which in other Socialist groups was provided by theoretical jargon and political clichés.

At the annual meeting in April 1888 the new executive was elected, consisting of Besant, Bland, Clarke, Olivier, Shaw, Wallas and Webb, a group which reflected the balance of attitudes within the Society. Annie Besant and Bland spoke for the opposition, strongly inclined to direct political action. Clarke soon fell away from the inner clique: he had a special antipathy to Shaw, although Shaw charitably gave him covert help in his career as a journalist. Olivier, Shaw, Wallas, and Webb had already learned to work as a team in the years of argument at Hampstead; they were now the dominant figures in the Society. Of the group which had launched the Fabians four years earlier only Bland and Clarke remained on the executive. Chubb went to live in America in June 1889; there he turned to his own conception of the spiritual life, joined the Ethical Culture movement and taught English in its school. Keddell dropped out also and went to live in the Middle East. SDF members like Joynes and Frost soon gave up their membership. Frank Podmore, who had named the Society and given it its motto, became more heavily committed to the Society for Psychical Research.

The first task of the new executive was to give the Society the sense of unity which had hitherto been lacking from its fortnightly meetings, at which speakers were simply invited to talk on topics of special concern or current interest. It was now decided that the autumn programme should be a set of prepared talks in which each member of the executive would deal with one aspect of socialism—a series which would provide the Society with a prospectus for its future work of education and propaganda. Webb was to prepare the first on the historical background, Shaw was to deal with economics, Olivier with morals, Clarke with capitalist industry, Wallas with property under socialism, Besant with socialist production, and Bland with the immediate political prospects. The fact that the lecturers were bound to differ in their approach caused no concern. Their only commitment so far was to constitutional socialism; they now had to define what that meant and how it was to be achieved.

Edward Pease had temporarily fallen away from the group because he was still working in the furniture cooperative at Newcastle. He kept in touch with London friends, however, and did what he could to advance socialist ideas and develop trade unions in the northeast. In 1886 he became interested in Marjorie Davidson, a Scots schoolteacher of twenty-four who had taken up with the London Fabians and attended some meetings of the Hampstead Historic Society. She was a tall, forceful girl, a Perthshire clergyman's daughter who was struggling to shake off the constraints of the manse. She and Pease corresponded for a time and then she visited him in Newcastle. They became engaged at Christmas 1887, in Edinburgh. Pease enjoyed his stay in the North, but he was still unsettled and making no headway towards a career. Miss Davidson was also anxious to return to the South to improve her teaching qualifications. Webb too was still in a restless and unhappy state of mind, overworking to the point where he felt the need for extended leave from the Colonial Office. He and Pease decided to take a trip to America; Pease had an idea that he might even settle there. They set off at the beginning of September 1888. At the same time Miss Davidson started work at Cheltenham Ladies College.

Pease went down through Ireland to join Webb on board the *City of New York* at Queenstown. He told Sidney about his engagement, but it was received with mixed feelings. Sidney was pleased, but he was also jealous. When he wrote to congratulate Marjorie Davidson he told her: "an old wound, which still embitters me, was torn open, and bled, as it bleeds now while I write these words." Pease's obvious happiness and his continuous talk about his fiancee made Sidney feel "left out." He was now nearly thirty and he asked why, when he was "passable, honest, sincere, and not obviously hateful or repulsive," he could not easily "catch on" to "congenial spirits."[6]

They had planned a busy visit, taking with them over a hundred letters of introduction to people ranging from the Governor General of Canada to the Chicago anarchists, and intended to swing up to Canada and down to Washington. They were not greatly impressed by what they saw and thought little of the social reformers they met: "there is very little for us to learn there," Webb commented disparagingly. New York, he wrote to Wallas, was a "ramshackle" place, "new buildings high & gorgeous, but all else mean & untidy, pavements *worse* than a small German town, tel. poles undressed & unpainted pine stems, . . . weather reduces us to pulp."[7] In Boston he was better pleased, thinking much of the Massachusetts Institute of Technology and reporting to Wallas that Harvard was "quite the most ideal 'academe' " that he had seen; "Oxford & Cambridge are grossly materialist, industrial in comparison."[8] Pease did not care for Washington, which "we found a dreary place, extraordinarily mean in buildings, tho' laid out magnificently."

When Webb left for home early in December Pease stayed on, hoping to find work as a cabinetmaker, but he was sacked from his first job in an hour, "a most humiliating experience," he recalled "with shudders."[9]

The Fabian habit of debate was not confined to the search for a new social morality. Fabians were just as concerned to find the right personal morality. When Marjorie Davidson became engaged to Pease she told Shaw: "We want to know what is the right thing to do & then to know how to do it. All suggestions from the elect are thankfully received."[10] Sidney Webb gave his views. He was afraid that she might "do the socialist cause *harm* by marrying one of its most useful members" unless she ensured "that Pease plus Davidson = *more* than Davidson and Pease, not, as is usual, much less." Explaining his own theory of life, he revealingly remarked that he felt at every moment that he was "acting as a member of a Committee & for that Committee—in some affairs a committee of my own family merely, in others a committee as wide as the Aryan race. But I aspire never to act alone, or for myself." Marriage, therefore, should be a partnership: "let the partners, in every detail, act in & for the partnership—except in such spheres as they may severally act in and for larger committees."[11]

In January 1889 Marjorie Davidson raised the problem again. "We want to know what is the ideal Socialist home—I don't think we ought to have servants but that is an open question," she told Shaw.[12] This time Sidney Olivier weighed in with advice. If Marjorie Davidson were to work as a teacher it would be impossible for her to "do all the house-

work and cooking." Letting the landlady's servant help was an evasion
which did not solve the moral dilemma. "The most wholesome and satisfactory solution in such cases," Olivier declared, "is that the work
should be done by unmarried relations." Failing that, one should search
for "the most congenial kind of assistant available in the proletariat. . . .
One can only approach to equal cooperation in the household so long as
there is inequality in society."[13] The Oliviers themselves made an uneasy
experiment in equality by insisting that the servants eat at the family
table.

Friends were putting pressure on Pease to return to England and
settle down. Olivier in particular, pressed by his increasing responsibilities, wanted Pease back to relieve him as secretary of the Society by the
middle of 1889. Pease was soon on the ship, and he and Marjorie Davidson were married in Gateshead near Newcastle, with Webb as a witness,
before they returned to London.[14] Pease still had trouble finding a job.
He hoped to work at his trade, but he was sacked from his first job after
a week. After he had spent three months at a cabinetmaker's in Red Lion
Square making drawing-room knickknacks, the Fabians decided to take
him on as their first employee, at fifty pounds a year. Some Fabians objected to paying a member for his services, because of both cost and
principle. To get round these difficulties Webb pitched in with another
fifty pounds to cover Pease's nominal services as his personal secretary.
It was a good investment. Pease served the Society well, despite his
crusty manner. He had all kinds of solid qualities and was scrupulously
honest and methodical, with a strong streak of phlegmatic common
sense.

Shaw was also having trouble in earning a living. "For the present I
am tied, neck and heels, to stump and inkpot," he told T. P. O'Connor,
the Irish Home Ruler, on 16 September 1888. He had toiled for years in
a hand-to-mouth manner, writing articles for a pittance and accepting
every speaking engagement he could manage. "For years past every
Sunday evening of mine has been spent on some more or less squalid
platform, lecturing, lecturing, lecturing and lecturing," he wrote in
June 1889.[15] Apart from miscellany pieces that he wrote for the *Pall
Mall Gazette*, he was contributing art criticism to *The World*, the most
fashionable London weekly—clumping round the galleries in strong
shooting boots to save costly repairs—but his earnings from *The World*
amounted to only £40 in 1887. In January 1888 H. W. Massingham, assistant editor of *The Star*, which T. P. O'Connor had just launched as a

Radical evening paper, hired Shaw to write leading articles at a salary of £125 a year. "I was given a column to myself precisely as I might have been given a padded room in an asylum," he recalled.[16] Within three weeks of his appointment he wrote, "I must give myself the sack," since O'Connor disliked his intemperate prose and had refused to publish an attack on the Radical politician John Morley.

It was, however, a short-lived separation, for O'Connor called him back to contribute what Shaw called a column on music "coloured by occasional allusions to that art." Writing under the pseudonym "Corno di Bassetto," Shaw let himself go. He knew more about music than about art, and his confidence in his own judgment fused with his talent for invective to produce a most remarkable chronicle—"a mixture of triviality, vulgarity, farce and tomfoolery with criticism." Conscientious to a degree, Shaw went to everything from band concerts at the Crystal Palace to solo recitals and the opera. He believed that the true critic "is a man who becomes your personal enemy on the sole provocation of a bad performance, and will only be appeased by a good performance." He spared no one. In a typical passage he objected to the Bach Choir dragging "its way from interval to interval and counting one, two, three, four, for dear life." Audiences too were savaged. After a piano recital Shaw wrote that "when every possible excuse is made for the people who coughed, it remains a matter for regret that the attendants did not remove them to Piccadilly, and treat their ailment there by gently passing a warm steamroller over their chests."

Whether Shaw was writing music criticism, political articles or Fabian lectures, his style was the same combination of serious comment and jocose, disarming insults. This posture of the crusader against humbug was the key to his appeal as a speaker and a journalist. As he was genuinely kind in personal relationships, Shaw's intellectual arrogance was commonly dismissed as no more than a debating device. It was in fact fundamental to his character: the unconscious assertion of virtue by the man who knows the way to salvation. It was also a means of compensating for being an outsider. When Shaw supported Whistler, or took up Wagner, or championed Ibsen, it was not simply because he had an eye for novelty. He singled out the artists who shocked and defied conventional taste as possible harbingers of a new moral order. His cultural enthusiasms sprang from the same compulsions as his socialist propaganda. The inkpot and the stump served similar ends.

It was a wearing and financially unrewarding life, but Shaw was concerned to make his own impact, not money. In the whole of 1888 he earned only £150, and things were not much better in the first months of 1889. The strain showed in headaches, fits of lassitude, trembling hands and attacks of nausea, but he kept his miseries to himself. His associates merely marvelled at the jesting manner through which he sought relief. By 1890 "the ubiquitous Mr Shaw," as *The Star* called him, was becoming a well-known personality, going about London in his strange garb of a one-piece yellow Jaeger suit, wide-brimmed hat, red scarf, gloves and umbrella. His habits were eccentric, but he could not go all the way with friends such as Salt and Carpenter in the Simple Life. The sandals which Carpenter was now making were soon abandoned by Shaw on the practical grounds that they made his feet sore. He was resolute, however, in his devotion to a vegetarian diet, warning intending hosts of his idiosyncrasies:

> I do not smoke, though I am not intolerant of that deplorable habit in others. I do not eat meat nor drink alcohol. Tea I also bar, and coffee. My three meals are, Breakfast—cocoa and porridge; Dinner—the usual fare, with a penn'orth of stewed Indian corn, haricot beans or what not in place of the cow; and "Tea"—cocoa and brown bread, or eggs.

All he needed for his Sunday dinner, he added, was "brown bread & cheese, with a glass of milk & an apple."[17]

This spartan fare did not curb his restless energy. There was something compulsive about the pace at which he lived, mixing politics, social life and journalism, as if time had to be filled with activity. He moved about constantly and kept late hours. After a day at the British Museum, a gallery and a concert, he would write his reviews and then sit up talking till the small hours. "With Wallas & Massingham to Headlam's arguing about religion till 1 a.m.," was a typical diary note in the summer of 1888. One evening in February 1889 he went with Massingham to spend the night with Belfort Bax at Croydon, and table rapping was suggested. "I cheated from the first," Shaw confessed. "As soon as Massingham detected me he became my accomplice & we caused the spirits to rap out long stories, lift the table into the air, & finally drink tumblers of whisky & water to the complete bewilderment of Bax. . . . I have not laughed so much for years. At breakfast we explained to Bax how we had deceived him."[18]

Sometimes he visited friends in the country like the Salts. Although they were living at "a hole called Tilford," he was always happy at the Salts'. "We never talked politics but gossiped endlessly about our friends and everything else." Eventually the Salts moved to a cottage at Crockham Hill near Westerham in Kent, and this pleasant area of wooded hills within convenient distance of London soon attracted other Fabians. Emma Brooke went down to nearby Froghole. The Oliviers took a summer cottage at Limpsfield, a village on the North Downs which epitomized rural England with its blacksmith's forge and the windmill at the corner of the common. Margaret Olivier remembered that "besides the beauty of the Chart woods and the commons there was the scent of it all, the smell of fir trees and of the mossy soil—and there was the view over the Weald."[19] The Oliviers now had two daughters—they named their second child Brunhild after the heroine in Morris' romantic saga *Sigurd the Volsung*. Sydney, a great admirer of Morris, would read his work aloud to Margaret in the evenings. A third daughter was born in November 1889, and the country suited their family life so well that two years later they converted a pair of cottages into a permanent home called Champions. *191086*

Before long Olivier was joined by another Fabian commuter. When the Peases wanted to settle down and raise a family they took a converted oasthouse within walking distance of the Oliviers. For the remainder of his working life Edward went up to the Fabian office every day from the country. Up a nearby lane, the Russian Nihilist Sergius Stepniak—a close friend of the Fabian set—had a cottage; further into the woods the Garnetts built a house. Edward Garnett, the publisher's reader who encouraged many new authors at the end of the century, was married to Constance Black, the translator of Russian novels and plays. Her sister Clementina was another active Fabian, who served for a time on the Society's executive.

It was a close-knit community of radicals and writers, and it soon acquired such a reputation that one family had to buy its house through an intermediary because the landowner was uneasy about the influx of rebellious eccentrics into what came to be nicknamed "Dostoievsky Corner." In the early Nineties they had enough support for a slate of candidates led by Olivier to sweep the board at the elections for the parish council; for many years thereafter Marjorie Pease was a dominant figure in local politics.

When the Oliviers converted their cottages in 1891 some of the work was done by W. L. Phillips, the Fabian craftsman "in the lath & plaster line," as Shaw put it. One feature of the house was a long play-room used for charades and amateur dramatics. There were many visi-tors. Olivier, like Salt, was a keen naturalist, and Shaw sometimes went down for the day to walk in the unspoilt countryside with its long views over the Weald.

Shaw enjoyed the jolly Fabian domesticity at Limpsfield as much as the eccentricities of the Bland household. In 1889 the Blands moved to a larger but still modest house at Lee. Hubert had begun to make a career as a journalist, writing regularly for the *Daily Chronicle* and the Manchester *Sunday Chronicle*. Shaw wrote to him sympathetically in November 1889, saying that it was "a devil of a fight to acquire the power to do what you like and to get fed and clothed for doing it." Bland's flight from the conventional was still a source of stress. Edith was bringing up Alice Hoatson's daughter Rosamund as her own so faithfully that the child always called her true mother "Auntie," but the *ménage à trois* provoked constant tension. Shaw was familiar with the domestic dramas, the rows at mealtimes and the slamming of doors. "Scenes as usual," he noted in his diary after one visit. But there was al-ways a lively atmosphere, and when the Blands were not quarrelling they were excellent hosts. They liked entertaining admirers and acting as patrons to young writers, and visitors such as Shaw helped to divert them from their domestic worries.

Shaw gradually became the common denominator of a number of relationships. For all his eccentricity he was a faithful friend. Sarcastic, even brutal in controversy, outside the ring of debate he was considerate, generous and willing to put himself out for others. People who met each other only at meetings or were at odds with each other socially or politi-cally welcomed Shaw as he flitted among them, carrying gossip, ideas and arrangements which fertilized a whole movement.

Shaw was the only prominent Fabian who kept up close relations with Morris. Whenever attempts were made to bring the SDF, the So-cialist League and the Fabians together it was Shaw who was the Fabian representative. Despite Morris' distaste for Fabians "as a species," he could get on with Shaw. By the late Eighties Morris was disillusioned with all the socialist organizations. The Avelings had left him to found a splinter group of their own in Bloomsbury, while the League and *Com-monweal* fell into the hands of anarchists who were advocating violence.

Several members of the League became involved in bomb plots and were sent to jail, and *Commonweal* was suppressed.

Though Morris often addressed the Fabian Society, he never belonged to it. He thought the Fabians were bureaucratic collectivists without any desire to create what he called "the Society of Equals." The kind of reforms they advocated, he argued, were nothing more than "schemes for substituting business-like administration in the interests of the public for the old Whig muddle." Morris thought that Webb and his colleagues mistook "quasi-socialist machinery" for socialism—the benefits it brought might be of temporary value, but they would do nothing towards "educating the people into *direct* Socialism."[20]

When Morris withdrew from the League, he set up a coterie of his own called the Hammersmith Socialist Society, which held regular meetings in a converted stable at his house on the Thames at Hammersmith Mall. For a few years these Sunday-night gatherings at Hammersmith were a unique experience for socialists—a congenial, almost conspiratorial atmosphere dominated by the patriarchal figure of Morris. He was only fifty-six in 1890, but he looked ten years older, and his political disappointment intensified his gruffy intemperance. He had a habit, when annoyed, of pulling single hairs violently from his moustache and growling, "Damned fool!" Yet he was unaffected, comradely and accessible. "No man I have ever known was so well loved," W. B. Yeats recalled in his autobiography. "He was looked up to as to some worshipped mediaeval king. . . . People loved him as children are loved . . . I soon discovered his spontaneity and joy and made him my chief of men."

Shaw was similarly drawn to this dreamer of the Middle Ages, admiring the dedicated seriousness with which Morris took both his art and his socialism. They made an odd pair, complementing each other in their idiosyncrasies. Both were gregarious, but Shaw attracted the admiration of women rather than of men. Morris was dependent on his clique of followers. Shaw prided himself on his independence and preferred to go his own way. Morris was a man of emotions, impulsive and volatile, while Shaw believed that his actions derived from intellectual logic. Yet, despite the difference in their styles, their assumptions were broadly the same. Both had a millenarian streak, desiring the destruction of the capitalist order; and both expressed their imaginative alternatives through art and literature. Morris believed that industrial society was ugly, Shaw that it was immoral, and both of them had the Puritan faith

that men, by an act of will, could find salvation. Both, too, were uto-
pians, without a historical sense or the utilitarian belief in orderly and
rational progress: what lay between mankind and the New Jerusalem
was moral inadequacy, and hope therefore lay in conversion.

Shaw himself lived without grace or comfort, but he appreciated
Morris' style of life. There was, he said, "an extraordinary discrimina-
tion at work in this magical house" in Hammersmith, and "I, the most
irreverent of mankind, felt its magic instantly and deeply." It was a composed essay on the dictum of Morris that a house should contain nothing
that the owner did not believe to be beautiful or know to be useful—in
itself a standing criticism of the Victorian taste for rooms cluttered with
ornate furniture and bric-a-brac. There was, Shaw recalled, "an oriental
carpet so lovely that it would have been a sin to walk on it; consequently
it was not on the floor but on the wall and half across the ceiling." Even
the meals were part of the composition. To refuse Morris' wine or the
viands of Jane Morris was, Shaw added, "like walking on the great carpet with muddy boots."[21]

Morris brought his workmen friends and scruffy socialists into the
house, much to the disapproval of his lovely aloof wife. Jane Morris was
an aesthete whose real milieu was with her close friend Dante Gabriel
Rossetti and the Pre-Raphaelites. She spoke little, Shaw recalled; "in fact,
she was the silentest woman I have ever met. She did not take much notice of anybody, and none whatever of Morris, who talked all the time."
It was a compelling but cold household, dominated by the vigorous rest-
lessness of Morris, yet permeated by the emotional chill of his rejecting
wife.

Shaw often spoke at the Sunday meetings and he became a frequent
visitor at Kelmscott House. He had known Morris' younger daughter
May for some time as a Fabian and an active meeting-goer, and in the
course of his visits to Hammersmith he strengthened the friendship. In
her way she was as odd as Shaw. She had something of her mother's
austere rejection of sensuality and something of her father's artistic
talent. Shaw, comfortable with women who mingled romantic coolness
with admiration for his intellectual gifts, enjoyed an unspoken flirtation
with her. "One Sunday evening," he wrote, "after lecturing and supping,
I was on the threshold of the Hammersmith house when I turned to
make my farewell, and at this moment she came from the dining-room
into the hall. I looked at her, rejoicing in her lovely dress and lovely self,

and she looked at me very carefully and quite deliberately made a gesture of consent with her eyes. I was immediately conscious that a Mystic Betrothal was registered in heaven."[22] Shaw was content with such an understanding, and so was May Morris, who became engaged to Harry Sparling, a thin unassertive man known to his comrades in the Socialist League as "the gas-pipe." A three-cornered relationship suited them all.

Shaw, however, could give May Morris only a part of his attentions. There was still the desultory relationship with Jenny Patterson, but it brought no joy or satisfaction. She seemed an object more for Shaw's cruel teasing than for affection, and he almost deliberately provoked her into fits of rage and jealousy. His diary records frequent meetings where Jenny "raged" or "parted in high dudgeon" or "flung a book at my head." But he was unmoved. "Women are nothing to me. This heart is a rock," he wrote in January 1890; "they will make grindstones for diamonds out of it when I am dead."[23]

7
ANGELS ON OUR SIDE

Bloody Sunday taught the Fabians a lesson, and the great dock strike of 1889 gave them an opportunity. The years of propaganda through public meetings and unemployed demonstrations had begun to produce results. While the working classes had not been converted to socialism, they had at least acquired a group of energetic leaders; as trade improved at the end of the Eighties the workers who had been neglected by the restrictive skilled unions began to assert themselves. The strike of the match girls was only one sign of a change. Amateurs like Annie Besant and Burrows showed what could be done. Professionals like Tom Mann and John Burns now took the same message to other unskilled and exploited trades. Mann, an engineer in his early thirties, had joined Burns in the SDF in Battersea in 1885 and had become a free-lance union organizer. He and Burns were typical of this new generation of labour leaders, self-educated men with a strong sense of class consciousness, organizers rather than ideologues, temperamental rebels for whom socialism was more a matter of emotion than of intellect.

The Fabians thought Burns a blustering demagogue and held him in part responsible for the fiasco of Bloody Sunday; they were also antagonized by his conceit and his jealousy of rivals—traits which made it difficult for him to work with others and led by the summer of 1889 to

a rupture with Hyndman and his resignation from the SDF. When he
went to Paris in July 1889 to attend one of the two rival international
socialist congresses staged to celebrate the centenary of the fall of the
Bastille, he gibed at his British comrades. As an active member of the
Amalgamated Society of Engineers he was there, he said, "not as a bogus
delegate representing twenty or thirty half-grown youths, but as the
chosen spokesman of fifty-seven thousand skilled artisans combined in
the strongest trade union in the world."[1] Hyndman called him "the best
stump-orator I have ever heard."[2] Everyone knew him. He turned up at
Fabian meetings, at demonstrations for the eight-hour day, and spent
himself rising before dawn to walk half across London to speak at dock
and factory gates before he himself went to work.

Burns was then thirty-one, and he had lived a hard life. He was the
sixteenth child of a poor family brought up by an illiterate mother who
took in washing. He started work at ten as a page boy; then he was employed as a potboy before earning enough to pay for his apprenticeship
as an engineer. He picked up a political education along the way, partly
from Victor Delahaye, a refugee from the Paris Commune who befriended him, partly in the temperance and Secular movements. In
1878 he was arrested after speaking on Clapham Common. He spent a
year working as an engineer in West Africa, reading Adam Smith, Mill
and other economists. He was good at his trade—in 1881 he drove the
first electric tramcar to be demonstrated at the Crystal Palace—and a
keen trade unionist, but he was soon devoting himself to politics. "When
he first came among us, early in 1884," Hyndman said, "he was as ignorant and as rough a specimen of the English working man as I have
ever encountered." Within a year he was on the SDF executive. He was
looking for a suitable base for his political ambitions but could do no
more than campaign against the stodgy conservatives of the Trade
Union Congress and indulge in insurrectionary rhetoric. It was Champion who taught him the importance of linking the day-to-day struggles
of the workers for better conditions with independent political action.

In the spring of 1889 John Burns joined Will Thorne, Eleanor Marx,
Tom Mann and another young organizer named Ben Tillett to form a
union of the gasworkers, and within three months all the gasworkers in
London had been enrolled.[3] It was a triumphant campaign in which all
the men's demands were met without a strike; they had been working
a twelve-hour shift under unhealthy conditions at near-starvation wages.

It was also the first real success of a new kind of trade unionism, which enrolled thousands of men without asking for more than their solidarity and a subscription of twopence a week. Unlike the old craft unions, exclusive and conservative, and more concerned to serve their members with the sickness, unemployment and death benefits of a friendly society than to wage the class war, the National Union of Gasworkers was simply an organization fighting for better wages, shorter hours and improved conditions.[4]

Conditions on the London docks were even worse than those which had driven the gasworkers to organize. Thousands of men, dependent entirely on casual employment, hung around the dock gates, fighting for the chance of work and scavenging the rubbish heaps for food when they were not taken on. Tillett recalled that "coats, flesh, and even ears were torn off . . . mad human rats who saw food in the ticket."[5]

On Monday 14 August 1889 some dockers working on the *Lady Armstrong* thought they were being cheated of a halfpenny an hour and struck.[6] They went to Tillett's tiny union for help, and he called in Tom Mann. John Burns turned up two days later, and as the strike grew in the following week other socialists like Champion, Eleanor Marx and Harry Quelch volunteered their help. This inexperienced strike committee suddenly found itself leading thousands of men in a dispute which closed the port of London. From its headquarters in the Wade's Arms it arranged picket lines, public meetings and above all food tickets for the men and their families, at the same time avoiding the clashes with the police that the dock directors hoped might smash the strike as Warren had dealt with the unemployed two years before.

Burns had learned the lesson of Bloody Sunday, and when he repeated his old tactics of leading huge processions around London he planned them in agreement with the police. He soon caught the public eye as he marched at the head of the daily demonstrations to the rallies at Tower Hill. Behind him came long lines of men, paced by brass bands and carrying their union banners, emblems of their trades, effigies of the dock owners, and poles festooned with the garbage that made meals for the casual labourers. The Army of Labour was at long last on the march; but now there was no talk of revolution. The demand was for justice and for sixpence an hour. On 9 September Burns put the point in memorable epigram. "This, lads," he declared, "is the Lucknow of Labour, and I . . . can see a silver gleam, not of bayonets to be imbued in a brother's blood, but the gleam of the full round orb of the docker's tanner [sixpence]."

Through the rest of a hot August the men held out. There was clearly much public sympathy for them as there had been for the match girls the year before. By the end of the month, however, the strike was on the verge of collapse. The men were tired and hungry, and funds were running out. The choice seemed to lie between surrender and the desperate throw of calling an all-London general strike, when the situation suddenly changed. In an extraordinary gesture of solidarity the Australian unions collected large sums to aid the strike, and, as the funds came in, public opinion backed the strikers. Banks remitted money without charge, the Post Office allowed cables to be sent free, football clubs sent in their gate money, and the Salvation Army donated the profits from *War Cry*. With the help of Cardinal Manning, whose Church had thousands of communicants among the strikers, an arbitration committee was set up. By 16 September the strike was over: the dockers had won their tanner.

They had won much more, indirectly. From their victory a wave of organization rippled out through the whole country, changing the older unions as members poured in, and establishing new unions catering for men and women who had never been organized before. By the end of 1890, over a million and a half workers were represented in the Trades Union Congress, where the balance swung towards the socialists.[7] At the Liverpool congress in 1890, Burns, Mann and their supporters were strong enough to defeat the old guard and to carry a series of resolutions. These, Burns said, "were nothing more nor less than direct appeals to the State and the municipalities of this country to do for the workman what trade unionism, 'old' and 'new,' has proved itself incapable of doing."[8] Though the trade unions had not yet been won for the idea of an independent labour party, the issue was now clearly on the agenda: If the Liberals would not transform themselves into the party of the wage earners, who were at last becoming a majority of the electorate, then the wage earners would soon learn to speak for themselves.[9]

John Burns was one of the first to do so. The "Man with the Red Flag" had emerged as the potential leader of the socialist movement. He had established a strong position at Battersea, where the SDF and the Radicals worked together to send him to the London County Council, which had just come into existence as part of the reform of local government.[10] The Fabians did not put forward any candidates. When Jim Connell, a well-known Radical who later wrote "The Red Flag," asked Shaw in December 1888 to stand for Deptford in the coming County Council elections Shaw explained why no Fabians could offer themselves: "Some of us are civil servants; some have no qualifications; some like myself, have no money."[11] In the following March Shaw was invited to run for Parliament in Battersea, but once again he insisted that he was too poor to be a candidate and success would mean giving up his career as a music critic.[12] The first Fabian electoral success, in fact, was to get Annie Besant, Stewart Headlam and A. W. Jephson on to the London School Board in 1888 with the help of the Radicals.

The Fabians were too few in number and too weak financially to do much in practical politics, and they chose a different role. In the lectures on "The Basis and Prospects of Socialism" that the members of the Fabian executive gave in the autumn of 1888 there were clear signs that they saw the significance of the reforms in local government.[13] The new county councils, Annie Besant argued, "created the machinery without which Socialism was impracticable: units of government which could easily be turned into units of ownership." Shaw made the same point in a talk he gave to the British Association at Bath in September.

The political horizon of the Fabians had so far been limited to the misgoverned capital. They were now beginning to catch up with the changes that had already been tried out in better-governed cities such as Chamberlain's Birmingham. The discovery that socialism might be built on the instalment plan by local councils was so exciting that Annie Besant was carried away by a vision of England ruled by communes which owned factories and farms, provided work for the unemployed, help for the sick and the aged, and ran all the essential public services, from baths to libraries and tramways. Such changes, the Fabians felt, might be easier to accomplish piecemeal than the long haul of winning a majority in Parliament, and easier to manage than ambitious national schemes of common ownership and social welfare.

The Fabians' main role in the first London County Council elections was to issue "Questions to Candidates" in an effort to extract pledges of support for the progressive policies of the London Radicals, who formed the Progressive Party to fight the campaign. Three months after the elections Sidney Webb produced for the Fabians a sixpenny pamphlet called *Facts for Londoners*, which was the most ambitious tract yet issued by the Society. Filled with details about the private and public interests which controlled life in the metropolis, it contained no political novelties; its significance lay in the fact that it made a sharp break with the "revolutionary" attitude of the socialist sects all through the Eighties. With the spread of political democracy, Webb now believed, socialists should try to use the machinery of government for their own ends.

Webb took what Shaw called "this inevitable, but sordid, slow, reluctant, cowardly path to justice" because, as Shaw himself had come to admit, it was the only alternative to an apocalyptic "one great stroke to set Justice on her rightful throne." The experience of the last few years had shown, Shaw argued, that "an army of light is no more to be gathered from the human product of nineteenth century civilisation than grapes are to be gathered from thistles." Now "cautious and gradual change" was necessary, since the transition to socialism could not "be crammed into any Monday afternoon, however sanguinary . . . Demolishing a Bastille with seven prisoners in it is one thing: demolishing one with fourteen million prisoners is quite another."

It was Sidney Webb who brought the Fabians round to this point of view. At the end of the long debate about Marx in the Hampstead meetings Webb was quite sure that he rejected both the Marxist theory of value and the doctrine of a class war. He had, all the same, been impressed by Marx's belief that the laws of motion of modern industrial society were moving it inexorably towards some kind of collectivism. His historic sense, shaped by the evolutionary ideas of Spencer, Comte and Darwin, led him to believe that individualist capitalism would be succeeded by a society in which the state would increasingly control economic and social policy. Since this process would be accompanied by an extension of political democracy and "by the steady growth of social compunction," there was no need to adopt the catastrophic theories of Hyndman or the romantic dreams of Morris, or even to create a separate socialist party based upon the working class. All parties would inevitably move towards collectivism; the difference between them would simply be the speed at which they were prepared to accept that "social arrangements shall be deliberately based on what are essentially Socialist principles." For Webb, as for the other Fabians, the motive of moral regeneration had a vital role to play in bringing about that change. "The

Zeitgeist," he told the Fabians, "is potent; but it does not pass Acts of
Parliament without legislators, or erect municipal libraries without coun-
cillors. . . . It still rests with the individual to resist or promote the social revolution."

Four years after Webb joined the Fabian Society he thus showed,
as Shaw put it, that socialism "could be proposed without forfeiture of
moral credit by a bishop as well as a desperado."[14] That had been the
original intention of Chubb, Pease, Podmore and the other first Fabians,
yet in its early years the Society was distracted by arguments with
Marxists, Morrisites and anarchists—and socialism generally had become
discreditably identified with violent rhetoric and disorders in the streets.
Shaw too had contributed to the uncertainty. He was inclined to favour
desperadoes more than bishops until Bloody Sunday frightened and disillusioned him.

Webb was now the master of Fabian policy. He wrote all three of
the tracts which appeared in 1889 and in the two following years he was
the author of nineteen of the twenty-eight pamphlets in which the Society set out its new doctrine of municipal socialism. Inevitably it was
Webb, self-possessed, persuasive and invariably well briefed with facts
and arguments, who took the lead in the discussions among the executive
members which preceded the 1888 lectures on "The Basis and Prospects
of Socialism."

Shaw was given the tasks of editing the lectures as a book and finding a publisher. The first task was easier than the second. "There is nothing like it in the market," Shaw sadly noted in the middle of November,
"& it is *commercially unproducible*."[15] When no publisher would take it
on, the Fabians reluctantly decided to get the book out for themselves.
May Morris designed the cover, and the socialist artist Walter Crane
contributed a frontispiece. With the addition of Shaw's talk to the
British Association the lectures appeared late in 1889 as *Fabian Essays*.

The delay of several months was helpful, for the political climate
had changed dramatically. In the aftermath of the dock strike there was
a better chance of attracting support for socialist ideas than at any time
since the early Eighties. There was also a dearth of socialist reading
matter. Though rival translations of the first volume of *Capital* were
being prepared, it was still unavailable in English. Recruits to the socialist
movement were nurtured on Ruskin and Carlyle, Secularist tracts, Edward Bellamy's *Looking Backward*, Gronlund's *Co-operative Common-*

wealth and George's *Progress and Poverty*. No one had produced a comprehensive case for reformist socialism based on facts as much as ideology and written specifically for a contemporary audience.

The *Fabian Essays* filled that gap at exactly the right moment. Pease volunteered to distribute the book from his flat in Hyde Park Mansions. Within a month of its appearance at Christmas 1889, he was busy parcelling up dozens of copies a day. The first printing of a thousand volumes, Shaw said, "disappeared like smoke" before the end of January.[16] Selling at six shillings, the book began to bring in a larger income than the Fabians had ever enjoyed, and the sales mounted in their thousands as soon as cheap paper editions were made available.

Pease was delighted with the book. The *Essays*, he proudly claimed twenty-five years later,

> based Socialism, not on the speculations of a German philosopher, but on the obvious evolution of society as we see it around us. It accepted economic science as taught by the accredited British professors; it built up the edifice of Socialism on the foundations of our existing political and social institutions; it proved that Socialism was but the next step in the development of society, rendered inevitable by the changes which followed from the industrial revolution of the eighteenth century.[17]

This was an accurate summary, stripped of the trimmings. At the time, however, the trimmings were important. The authors had taken four years to work themselves round to settled opinions, and they felt it necessary to explain to their readers how they argued the case through from Marx to Jevons and from Positivism to Fabianism. The most turgid part of the argument was the long explanation of the Fabian theory of rent; even Shaw could not make it sparkle for more than a few sentences. This strange amalgam of Ricardo and Henry George, fused with the new doctrine of marginal utility as the source of value, nevertheless served an important if temporary purpose.

The notion that rent was the unearned and unjustified toll that property levied on the whole community had considerable appeal to a generation of reformers who had been reared on agitation about the land and who still found it easier to think of dealing with grasping landlords than with the anonymous rentiers of capitalism. It enabled the Fabians to shift that sentiment from rural to urban issues. Shaw, for instance, started his

case with Adam and argued that private property had been the curse of
mankind since the expulsion from the earthly paradise. It was, he said,
no more than robbery, "unjust from the beginning . . . utterly impossible as a final solution of . . . the problem of adjusting the share of
the worker in the distribution of wealth to the labour incurred by him
in its production." A tax on rents—or, by extension, on profits—was thus
the means of redressing gross inequality. Carried to extremes it would
ultimately recover the land (and other means of production) for the
people. This ingenious combination of a moral argument against selfishness, so attractive to late Victorians, with an economic theory and a political strategy was the essence of Fabianism.

It was not, of course, very different from the ideas Henry George
had preached so effectively that they had become part of the stock in
trade of Radicals and land reformers. That was one of its advantages: it
made the Fabian case both comprehensible and acceptable. The theoretical refinements which Shaw and his colleagues added were intellectually
impressive, but except in one respect they did not do much more than
demonstrate to middle-class socialists that there was a respectable alternative to Marxist economics and its accompanying implications of class
struggle.

The exception was particularly important to Shaw, who had been
influenced by anarchist ideas in the mid-Eighties. In the discussions at the
Hampstead Historic Society he had been struggling to find a way of
shaking off Proudhon as well as Marx, and the theory of rent was his
means of escape. Anarchists, as he explained in his Fabian tract *The Im-
possibilities of Anarchism,*[18] believed that equality had to be achieved
first; the problem of giving workers the fruits of their labour would then
be solved "simply by everybody minding his own business." The theory
of rent showed that this was an illusion. Inequality would immediately
reappear unless there was some machinery of government which would
continually cream off the surplus rents—arising equally from superior
land or skills or brains—and redistribute them again to ensure fair shares
for all. Such a government, Shaw agreed with his fellow Fabians Olivier
and Webb, could not be actuated by the kind of economic motive on
which the Marxist system relied; it would have to be inspired by altruism, imposing the will of more moral members of society upon the
parasitic. It was, indeed, something very like a Positivist state inspired by
a Religion of Humanity and governed by a disinterested élite. Property,

for Shaw, replaced original sin in the Evangelical scheme of things, and the sanctions of the state would have to substitute for those of the Recording Angel.

What Shaw could do brilliantly was to convert such abstract reasoning into vivid phrases that remained in the mind when his juggling with Ricardo's economics was forgotten. "A New York lady," he wrote in a typical passage, "having a nature of exquisite sensibility, orders an elegant rosewood and silver coffin, upholstered in pink satin, for her dead dog. It is made; and meanwhile a live child is prowling barefoot and hunger-stunted in the frozen gutter outside." This sense of ethical revulsion from antisocial and selfish privilege ran through Sydney Olivier's essay, through Wallas' argument that the abolition of private property would mean "a new birth of happiness" for "the five men out of six in England who live by weekly wage," and through Annie Besant's insistence that once all men enjoyed security laziness would be the worst of social crimes and "the longing for wealth will lose its leverage."

The Fabians did not expect consistency from the essayists, and both William Clarke and Hubert Bland deviated from the general line taken by Shaw, Webb, Olivier and Wallas. The evolution of Clarke from a Liberal democrat to a reluctant and pessimistic socialist had been much influenced by his knowledge of American politics, and by his reading of Marx.[19]

When Clarke visited the United States on a lecture tour in 1881 he had been elated to find that the country was "consecrated to simple humanity and that its institutions exist solely for the progress and happiness of the whole people."[20] Three years later he was saddened by the revelations of corruption in the US at the 1884 election and even more by the exposure of Standard Oil and other great corporations by his friend Henry Demarest Lloyd. He told Lloyd in 1884 that he had decided that democracy could not survive without control of private wealth. It was in that frame of mind that he began to study Marx with the Hampstead group.[21] By 1887 he concluded that American politics demonstrated the growing power and evil of capital and that "economic conditions force on a class struggle."[22] He was too depressed to share the hopes of his fellow Fabians that moral regeneration, passionately though he desired it, would save the world. There had to be "a revolution in the physical condition of the 'masses' of our people . . . the necessary antecedent of all mental and physical progress."[23]

Clarke's state of mind, as well as his intellectual convictions, came out clearly in his essay on "The Industrial Basis of Socialism." His colleagues had moved away from Marx; Clarke had come to believe that Marx's "analysis of value and his explanation of the economic development are true in general," a process that would inevitably lead to a "collision between the opposing forces" of capitalism and democracy. Clarke, however, was an observer by nature, not an agitator; he had no sympathy with the socialist sects which actually proposed to wage the class struggle. He desired, like the other Fabians, to mitigate rather than exacerbate that struggle of classes and thus came to much the same practical conclusions by a different route. The growth of monopolies, increasingly directed by a managerial elite, was preparing the way for the state to dispossess the useless rentier, retaining the services merely of "those capitalists who are skilled organisers and administrators."

Hubert Bland was the only one of the essayists who tried to indicate how the transition to a new social order might take place. He had picked up some Marxist ideas—more about political tactics than about theory—from his former associates in the SDF and learned something about practical politics from Champion. From the very first meetings of the Society he argued that the Fabians should be politically active and become the nucleus of a new party rather than a debating club or a pressure group. His presence among the Fabians was largely due to his feeling that "revolutionary heroics" were futile. Until "the capitalist system has worked itself out to its last logical expression," he wrote in his essay, it would be "criminal folly" to talk of the barricades.

Bland, like Clarke, was Marxist enough to believe that eventually the economic cleavage between the propertied and the propertyless would result in a political confrontation. To him the Tories and the Whigs were branches of the same party of property, differing about details, while Radicalism, thriving on demagogy about Home Rule and the land, was simply the "sham socialism" of the "dodgy Liberal." In several cutting asides Bland made it clear that he included Sidney Webb and some of his other Fabian colleagues in these strictures: "although Socialism implies State control," he reminded them, "State control does not imply Socialism." Such optimists had failed to realize that the Radicals could not even get their own moderate programme through Parliament, let alone instalments of socialism. How, then, could one talk of dealing with the entrenched power of capitalism by permeation? There must be a split with the Liberals and "the formation of a definitely Socialist party, i.e. a party pledged to the communalisation of all the means of production and exchange, and prepared to subordinate every other consideration to that one end."

This belief that Radicals were false friends and that socialists would make no effective progress in alliance with them marked Bland off from the other essayists. His Tory antecedents left him with a sharp distaste for any kind of Liberal, and he set himself up as the spokesman for independent socialist politics. In a significant passage in his essay, which was the only one to call for an alignment with the working class, he declared that "the proletariat is even now the only real class," and "the intensifying of the struggle for existence is forcing union and solidarity upon the workers." They would be joined by the intellectual proletariat because the "keenness of competition, making it every year more obviously impossible for those who are born without capital ever to achieve it, will deprive the capitalist class of the support it now receives from educated and cultivated but impecunious young men whose material interest must finally triumph over their class sympathies."

Bland, who had failed at his one attempt to become a small businessman and was now dependent on what he and his wife earned by writing, fitted his own description. Like his fellow Fabians, however, he had an emotional as well as an intellectual reason for rebelling against his class sympathies. He had, he confessed, "a deep discontent, a spiritual unrest" at the "constant presence of a vast mass of human misery."

This feeling of outrage against ever present suffering and squalor was one of the two themes which ran through all the *Essays*. The other, as William Clarke put it, was that "instead of mending and patching a hopeless rotten social order," a truly ethical society "must teach men that it is necessary and possible to bring a new and better order." The lesson instilled by Evangelical parents had been given a secular form. Evolution, or what Webb called the *Zeitgeist*, had taken the place of Providence, yet what Webb described as "blind social forces . . . which went on inexorably working out social salvation" did not relieve men of their moral responsibility. Victorian religion had taught that a belief in God's purposes must be accompanied by an effort to discern and advance them. Socialists who substituted a secular religion for the faith of their youth felt the same compulsion: their task was to achieve the conversion of England—by an effort of will and selfless dedication, to find relief from oppressive guilt in what the Puritans called a state of grace and the first Fabians described as the New Life.

It was this frame of mind that held the Fabians together. It was a bond that transcended differences about economic theory and even political tactics. They had not, in any case, come to the point where it greatly mattered whether they sought to permeate the Liberals, to oppose both bourgeois parties or to found Zion, a dilemma which perennially afflicted reforming sects within the Christian churches and continued to plague their political successors. At this stage in their lives, as the *Essays* clearly showed, they had merely discovered a faith and were ready to bear witness to it. They felt, as Bland neatly said for all of them, that "the angels are on our side."

PART TWO

PRIDE AND
POLITICS

8

LITTLE
BUSY BEE

"I like the man," Beatrice Potter noted in her diary on 14 February 1890 after an evening with Sidney Webb.[1] She had invited him to dinner at the Devonshire House Hotel in Bishopsgate to meet her cousin Mary and Mary's husband Charles Booth, then in the public eye because of his pioneering survey of poverty in London. She appraised Webb as carefully as she did any new and interesting acquaintance. His manner she found unattractive, "his attitudes by no means eloquent—with his thumbs fixed pugnaciously in a far from immaculate waistcoat, with his bulky head thrown back and his little body forward he struts even when he stands . . . with an expression of inexhaustible complacency." Yet she recognized that he had his virtues. "There was," she concluded, "a directness of speech, an open-mindedness, an imaginative warmth which should carry him far." She shrewdly summed him up as something between a London shopkeeper and a German professor.

They had met for the first time early in January in the rooms of another cousin, Margaret Harkness. The meeting had been arranged because Sidney was a possible source of information for the book which Beatrice was then writing about the Co-operative movement.[2] She already knew him by reputation. In October she had read *Fabian Essays* from cover to cover, considering Sidney's contribution "by far the most significant and interesting essay."[3] She told her friend J. C. Gray of the Co-operative Union that he had "the historic sense"; it was also clear that he shared her passion for painstaking research and factual detail. Sidney, for his part, had spotted her distinctive contribution to the first volume of Booth's *Life and Labour of the People in London,* published in the spring of 1889. Beatrice had written sections about sweated labour and the conditions of working women in the East End. Sidney gave a lecture on the book at the Bloomsbury Hall in May 1889, and he commented in *The Star* that "the only contributor with any literary talent" was Miss Potter.

Beatrice Potter was then thirty-two, a tall dignified woman with a strikingly handsome face, nut-brown eyes and sweeping brown hair coiled into a businesslike knot. Her sister Kate described her as "slightly German-looking." Already well established in her career as a social investigator, she seemed a model of the professional woman, unmarried, apparently unemotional, unconventionally willing to mix with all sorts and conditions of men, and able to hold her own in any company. Yet behind her austere manner Beatrice concealed uncertainty about her mission in life, anxiety, and powerful emotions.

Her struggle to establish herself was in curious contrast to the apparent ease of her prosperous Victorian family. Her father, Richard Potter, could have served as a model for the intelligent capitalist whom the Positivists saw as the natural rulers of society. He saw himself, indeed, as a responsible member of the new ruling class. "The central article of his political faith," Beatrice recalled, was "a direct denial of democracy."[4]

The rise of the Potters had been fast. Richard's grandfather had been a farmer and then a shopkeeper in Lancashire. His father made a fortune from cotton spinning and was one of the first Radical industrialists to enter Parliament after the Reform Bill of 1832. Richard's mother, believing that she was of Jewish descent, ran away to pursue her supposed mission of leading the Jews back to Palestine, was overtaken, and was put in an asylum. Richard himself had been sent to public school and university, had lost his money in the 1848 crisis, and had then made another fortune from a timber business in Gloucester and from promoting railway interests abroad. He was travelled, well read, courteous and tolerant. As he grew older he became solidly conservative, yet he loved the cut-and-thrust of argument, and his house was open to intellectuals such as T. H. Huxley and Herbert Spencer, to Radical leaders such as John

Bright, and to churchmen, businessmen and foreign visitors. His daughters were free to read what they liked and to take part in the discussions. He was, Beatrice said, "the only man I ever knew who genuinely believed that women were superior to men."[5]

His wife, Lawrencina Heyworth, however, thought that men were superior to women. She was a talented woman from Lancashire with intellectual ambitions. She lost her mother when she was a child and she came from a family prone to constitutional depression. At one time she wanted to be a novelist; she became instead the efficient and puritanical manager of a large Victorian household.[6] She believed that money should be earned rather than spent, finding more pleasure in advising her husband about his financial affairs than in indulging her family from the profits of his business. The Potter girls were brought up "to feel poor." Beatrice found her mother hard to get along with and constantly compared her unfavourably to her father, who, she said revealingly, was "more of a mother than a father to us." Her mother was emotionally aloof and insensitive: "without tact," Beatrice said. Both parents had the knack of expressing their own anxieties as other people's inadequacies. The impress of their personalities evoked feelings of guilt.

The family grew up at Standish, a country house in Gloucestershire overlooking the river Severn; large and austere, it was more like an institution than a home. Beatrice was born there on 22 January 1858, the eighth of nine daughters. When she was four the Potters' only son was born. Lawrencina now focused her attention on little Dicky, making Beatrice feel jealous and unwanted, feelings which were strengthened when the boy died two years later, for Lawrencina withdrew increasingly into the study of foreign languages and a search for religious consolation. Beatrice felt painfully neglected. "I was neither ill-treated nor oppressed: I was simply ignored."[7] This neglect left its mark in bad temper, resentment, psychosomatic headaches, biliousness, insomnia and even a desperate half-formed intention to chloroform herself. "The loneliness was absolute," she recalled twenty years later.[8] For warmth and comfort she turned to servants—chiefly Martha Jackson, the beloved "Dada" who had come as a nannie and stayed on when the Potter girls grew up. Martha was actually a poor relative from the Lancashire background that the rising Heyworths and Potters had left behind them, though Beatrice was ignorant of this fact until she was twenty-five.

When she was nearing fifteen Beatrice began to keep the diary in

which, with honesty and agony, she was to confide her private thoughts
over the next seventy years. One of its earliest entries, on 23 December
1872, reveals the profound sense of guilt that tormented her over her
yearning for attention and over the stirrings of sexual feelings:

> I am very disgusted with myself, whenever I am in the company
> of any gentleman, I cannot help wishing and doing all I possibly can
> to attract his attention and admiration . . . contriving every possible
> way to make myself more liked and admired than [my] sisters. . . .
> how can I conquer it, for it forwards every bad passion and supresses
> [sic] every good one in my heart. . . . I am *very very* wicked. . . .
> Vanity, all is vanity . . . every night I am miserable.

Beatrice sought comfort in religion, but the conflict between her
spiritual needs and her intellectual convictions made her a sceptic. "It is
a pity I ever went off the path of orthodox religion," she observed in
September 1874, when she was sixteen; "it is a misfortune that I was not
brought up to believe that doubt was a crime. But since I cannot accept
the belief of my church without inward questioning let me try and find
a firm belief of my own, and let me act up to it." The search for such a
faith led her to study, but in her own way and with subjects of her own
choosing. She ranged through the Bible, Plato, Diderot, Voltaire, Arnold, Balzac and Goethe; she investigated heresies and esoteric religions.
She showed every sign of becoming a bluestocking once she had found
solace from her unhappiness in ideas and learned to appease her feelings
of guilt by intense mental activity. As she grew up, her diary entries re-
peatedly extolled the virtue of work against the temptations of the lively
social life that her sisters enjoyed. "How Society bores me," she wrote,
though sometimes she reluctantly admitted that she got a great deal out
of it. She could behave priggishly, going off to Parliament to listen to
Gladstone and Disraeli while her sisters rushed around the season's balls,
but she "came out" like the others, had a fair share of the social round,
travelled abroad and enjoyed clever company.

She was tempted by what she called her "sensual nature" to enjoy a
life of pleasure and even the power that might come from a fashionable
marriage. But she was aware of an inner conflict which she described in
October 1886 as a "free choice between the life of individual work and
the life of womanly love and self-devotion." She thought that her "du-
plex personality," as she noted in December that year, expressed a differ-

ence between her parents. "The sadness and suffering of my early life brought out the *nether* being in me: the despondent, vain, grasping person . . . the phantom of Mother, gloomily religious, affecting asceticism and dominated by superstition . . . under the dominion of this personality my natural vocation and destiny was the convent . . ." The other model was her father, some of whose attributes she saw in herself— "an enthusiast for Truth, regarding Self only as a means to further Truth. Patient, faithful and lighthearted . . . a lover of thought and ready to sacrifice all things to it." If she were a man, "this creature would be free, though not dissolute, in its morals, a lover of women. These feelings would be subordinated to the intellectual and practical interests, but still the strong physical nature upon which the intellectual nature is based would be satisfied." But since she was a woman, unless she fulfilled herself in marriage—"which would mean the destruction of the intellectual being"—her emotions were bound to remain unsatisfied, "finding their only vent in one quality of the phantom companion of the nethermost personality, religious exaltation."

This ambivalence, which brought her almost to collapse in the emotional crisis through which she passed between 1883 and 1887, was a profound and enduring source of difficulty throughout her life. And throughout life her diary was the confidant for the agonies of a struggle which her iron will enabled her to conceal in public. When she went up to London for the 1883 season she was already wrestling with what then seemed a choice between frivolity and self-abnegating purpose: "Shall I give myself up to Society, and make it my aim to succeed therein, or shall I only do so as far as duty calls me? . . . On the whole the balance is in favour of Society." Her dilemma had by then become more acute because her mother had died in 1882 and Beatrice—all her older sisters having married—now became hostess for her father in London and at the Argoed, the attractive mansion overlooking the Wye Valley which Richard Potter kept as a summer and holiday home. Beatrice, he said, was "my little Busy Bee," and she became increasingly indispensable to him as the years went by. Unable to resolve the paradoxes of her temperament, she found herself leading a double life. "I feel like a caged animal bound up by the luxury and comfort and respectability of my position," she wrote. "I can't get a training without neglecting my duty."[9]

In these years of doubt Beatrice turned for sympathy and intellectual support to the elderly social philosopher Herbert Spencer, who ranked almost with Darwin in his influence on Victorian thought. He had been a friend of her parents since the early days of their marriage; he became her personal mentor, guiding her reading, encouraging her belief in her intellectual capacities and setting an example of what she called "intellectual heroism" in his devotion to his evolutionary theory of society. "To the children of the household the philosopher always appeared in the guise of a liberator," she recalled.[10] She read his books *First Principles* and *Social Statics* and learned through him to appreciate the relevance of facts. While she found the scientific method of reasoning valuable, for her it could not be an end in itself. It was in Comte's "Religion of Humanity" that she found the perfect combination of the scientific spirit applied to human purposes. In this way Beatrice found a vocation for herself. "From the flight of emotion away from the service of God to the service of man," she remarked, "and from the current faith in the scientific method, I drew the inference that the most hopeful form of social service was the craft of the social investigator."[11]

In the London season of 1883 Beatrice joined the Charity Organisation Society and went to the Soho slums as one of its visitors; going slumming—what was popularly called "East Ending"—was Christian philanthropy as well as a means of appeasing the guilt of prosperity in the midst of poverty. She was soon convinced that the social workers knew no more than she did about the causes of such distress or about possible means of alleviating it. Feeling that such extreme destitution was not typical, she decided to visit a community of normal manual workers. In November 1883, therefore, she persuaded Martha Jackson to take her to Bacup in Lancashire, her mother's family home; thinly disguised as a "Miss Jones," she went in search of her family's humble origins.

The visit was as decisive in its way as the mental stimulus of Spencer, for Beatrice was captivated by her "gentle cousins" and by the "direct thinking, honest work and warm feeling" she discovered at this "first chance of personal intimacy, on terms of social equality, with a wage-earning family." In exploring the poorer of England's Two Nations she found a sense of security which had always been missing from the nervy, intense life of the Potters and their rich and intellectual friends. "It is curious how completely at home I feel with these people," she said about the solid and straightforward folk of Lancashire. They were not, she realized, "the deserving poor" who were the fit objects of charity: they were self-reliant, and they had learned in their chapels a habit of self-government which they transferred to their trade-union branches and cooperative societies. "That part of the Englishman's nature which has found gratification in religion," Beatrice noted shrewdly, "is now drifting into political life." The visit to Bacup showed her a way forward from philanthropy to social policy; from it she learned "the difference between trying to alleviate poverty and seeking to eliminate its causes."[12]

This experience came at a crucial moment. While she was finding a practical way to sublimate her emotions she was confronted with a relationship which put her self-denial to the test.

One Saturday afternoon late in June 1883 Herbert Spencer gave his annual picnic at St. George's Hill, Weybridge. Among his guests was Joseph Chamberlain, a neighbour of the Potters in Princes Gardens, Kensington, and a Liberal Party colleague of Leonard Courtney, who had recently married Beatrice's sister Kate. Chamberlain was forty-seven, a prosperous Birmingham manufacturer who had turned to Radical politics and, after leading the campaign which had made his city a pioneer of municipal reform, launched himself into national politics as an opponent of the Whig leaders of the Liberal Party. With Sir Charles Dilke he was stumping the country with speeches in favour of free education, rural reform, improved housing, and stiffer taxation on the wealthy. Chamberlain was overtly ambitious, a combative orator who enjoyed forcing an issue rather than seeking compromises, an impressive figure with a good deal of arrogant charm.[13] "I do and I don't like," Beatrice wrote in her diary after their first meeting, and she concluded: "Talking to 'clever' men in society is a snare and a delusion. . . . Much better read their books." But when she met him again at Spencer's picnic and had a long talk she conceded: "his personality interested me." It was not long before he was invited to dinner with the Potters. Beatrice sat next to him and recorded that he was a "curious and interesting character, dominated by intellectual passions, with little self-control but with any amount of purpose."

Chamberlain was a widower, his second wife having died eight years before, and he was one of the most eligible men in London—well-to-do, and clearly destined for office whenever the Liberals returned to power. As leader of the growing Radical wing of his party, he stood to gain immensely from the proposed extension of the franchise and from the discernible trend towards reformist legislation. "My aim in life is to make life pleasanter for the great majority," he told Beatrice. "I do not care in the process if it becomes less pleasant for the well-to-do minority." His interests were precisely those most likely to engage Beatrice's attention, and though she thought him "an enthusiast and a despot" she began to see him frequently. After she had entertained him and his children at the Argoed she realized that her father disliked him and his opinions. But she found that she was in the clutch of feelings which were more powerful than reason or her father's disapproval. She was tense and expectant, feeling during the New Year celebrations "as if I were dancing in a dream towards some precipice." At dinner on the night that Chamberlain arrived "we plunged into essentials and he began to delicately hint his requirements." By the next morning they were on "susceptible terms."

As they walked in the garden next day, however, a dispute over state education broke the charm. "It is a question of authority with women," said Chamberlain; "if you believe in Herbert Spencer you won't believe in me." They fell into a struggle of wills that Beatrice found utterly exhausting. "It pains me to hear my views controverted," Chamberlain told her, beginning a speech that made it clear that he thought women should defer to men. He wanted what he called "intelligent sympathy." Beatrice said to herself, "Servility, Mr. Chamberlain." Chamberlain swept on. "Not a suspicion of feeling did he show towards me," she noted. "He was simply determined to assert his convictions . . . I felt his curious scrutinising eyes noting each movement as if he were anxious to ascertain whether I yielded to his absolute supremacy." Another conversation on the following day failed to clear the air. When he told her that his only domestic trouble was that his sister and daughter were "bitten with the women's rights mania" she challenged him: "You don't allow division of opinion in your household, Mr. Chamberlain?" The most he would concede was, "I can't help people *thinking* differently from me." But, insisted Beatrice, he did not allow the expression of the difference? " 'No,' he said firmly, and that little word ended our intercourse."

Chamberlain, however, was not put off by Beatrice's refusal to acknowledge male supremacy. She was surprised to receive an invitation a few weeks later to stay at Highbury, the lavish red brick home of the Chamberlains in Birmingham. She was predisposed to be critical, finding the house "tasteless" and furnished with an "oppressive richness" which made her "long for a bare floor and a plain deal table." Her visit coincided with a big political meeting in the Town Hall at which the three Birmingham MP's were to speak. Watching from the balcony, Beatrice could see why Chamberlain dominated his supporters.

> As he rose slowly and stood silently before his people, his whole face and form seemed transformed. The crowd became wild with enthusiasm. . . . At the first sound of his voice they became as one man. Into the tones of his voice he threw the warmth and feeling which were lacking in his words, and every thought, every feeling, the slightest intonation of irony and contempt was reflected in the face of the crowd. It might have been a woman listening to the words of her lover.

Such personal magnetism attracted Beatrice against her conscious opinion. It was supported by her admiration for his idealism, the earnest simplicity of his "battle with the powers of evil"—which she contrasted with the "somewhat cynical" political opinions of London society—and by his evident talent for leadership.

Beatrice was obviously torn between a desire to hero-worship the man and a fear of her personality being wholly submerged by him. When he showed her round his orchid house next day she was keenly aware that his approaches did not show "any desire to *please me*," only "an intense desire that I should *think and feel like him*." She was convinced that if she surrendered, "all joy and lightheartedness" would leave her. "I shall be absorbed into the life of a man, whose aims are not my aims, who will refuse me all freedom of thought in my intercourse with him; to whose career I shall have to subordinate all my life, mental and physical." Her relationship with Chamberlain had brought her face to face with her own ambivalence. She was in love with a man whom her reason rejected. "His temperament and his character are intensely attractive to me," she wrote on 22 April 1884, although she realized that marriage to him would mean abandoning both her career and her intellectual independence. She was repelled by his assertive masculinity, but she was also drawn to it because mirrored in him was her own willful nature. Yet she could not mortify her pride. It remained the one means of defending herself against her feelings for Chamberlain; it continually forced her into confrontations with his stubborn inability to unbend. She realized that he did not have the capacity to break through her conflict with genuine love. He was seeking only to acquire her. Every time she asserted her own personality they found themselves in a demoralizing battle of wills. "When I have been absolutely honest with him he has turned away," she recorded. "That is not what he wants and I know it."[14] She concluded that the only honest course would be to break off all relations with him.

During the first months of 1884 Beatrice tried to withdraw from London social life. In April her father gave up Standish and they moved their London base to York House. Beatrice divided her time among care for her father, her studies in economics and philosophy, and her work in the East End. She took over from her sister Kate the role of rent collector in a housing-improvement project run by Octavia Hill. It was arduous work, and she was depressed by the "collective brutality, heaped up together in infectious contact; adding to each other's dirt, physical and moral." Yet the work strengthened her sense of vocation and gave her a feeling that a woman might find a better fate than to be crushed by the masculine domination of Chamberlain. She began to talk about a "ruling caste" of intelligent spinsters. "It will be needful for women with strong natures to remain celibate, so that the special force of womanhood—motherly feeling—may be forced into public work."[15]

Beatrice's effort to sublimate her emotions in social service went on for many anguished months. She tried to protect herself by avoiding Chamberlain, but she was drawn back into tantalizing meetings. In July 1885 he dined with the Potters, and a week later the Courtneys arranged a picnic to bring them together again. "That day will always remain in my memory as the most painful one of my life," Beatrice recalled almost a year afterwards. "The scene under the Burnham beeches, forcing me to tell his fortune—afterwards behaving with marked rudeness and indifference. The great reception given him at the station . . . we all running after him like so many little dogs." Such encounters were clearly distressing to both parties. "The Great Man and I are painfully shy when we are alone," Beatrice wrote to her sister Mary Playne at this time. It was "a state of affairs which seems destined to lead to endless misunderstandings . . . I should think one or the other of us would break off this relationship this autumn by refusing to see more of each other."[16]

She found comfort in the company of Mary Booth and her husband, Charles, who was about to forsake his career in the family shipping line to devote himself to the problem of poverty. On 28 July 1885, after the fiasco at the picnic, Mary sent Beatrice an understanding letter rejoicing that she seemed to have made up her mind. Beatrice, she wrote, "could never be happy with such a man. . . . now that you . . . have given yourself every motive for determining to turn your back on it all, I think you will begin to mend." Mary was too sanguine. Things got worse, not better. In September Beatrice was in despair, confessing to "the old physical longing for the night that knows no morning."[17] She went again to Highbury in the autumn; Chamberlain's sister and daughter tactfully arranged the visit when Chamberlain himself was away campaigning in the general election. After Gladstone, he had become the outstanding politician in Britain, and he was talked about everywhere. Even in his absence his charisma filled the house. It was more than Beatrice could stand. "Will the pain never cease?" she asked herself.

On election day itself, 26 November 1885, Beatrice had to cope with a new misfortune. Her father was struck down with paralysis when he went out to vote; he became a permanent invalid, forced to give up his work and his social life. Beatrice had to abandon her work in the East End, spending the winter with her father in the mild climate of Bournemouth. "Surely my cup is full," she wrote desperately on 19 December. The haunting idea of suicide was never far from her thoughts. In January 1886 she made her will, "in case I should not outlive the year," and in its pathetic hurried clauses inserted the reflection "If Death comes it will be welcome—for life has always been distasteful to me."[18]

There was some consolation for her that month in her first appearance in print. A letter which she had written to the *Pall Mall Gazette*, "A Lady's View of the Unemployed at the East End," was published as a signed article. "A turning point in my life," she wrote on the editor's letter of acceptance.[19] Chamberlain, now in the Cabinet as president of the Board of Trade and grappling with the problem of the workless, read her comments and invited her to come and talk to him about them. She replied from Bournemouth that her knowledge was slight. He pressed her again: "Something *must* be done to make work. The rich must pay to keep the poor alive." "I fail to grasp the principle 'something must be done,' " she replied sharply. "I know no proposals to make, except sternness from the state, and love and self-devotion from individuals. . . . But is it not rather unkind of you to ask me to tell you what I think? . . . It is a ludicrous idea that an ordinary woman should be called upon to review the suggestions of Her Majesty's ablest minister."

Her prickly response stung him into a stiff reply: "I thought we understood each other pretty well. I fear I was mistaken. . . . you are quite wrong in supposing that I under-value the opinion of an intelligent woman . . . though I dislike the flippant self-sufficiency of some female politicians. . . . I hardly know why I defend myself, for I admit that it does not much matter what I think or feel on these subjects. . . . I thank you for writing so fully, and do not expect any further answer." Beatrice, in turn, was wounded. "I was right not to deceive you," she wrote. "I could not lie to the man I loved. But why have worded it so cruelly, why give unnecessary pain? Surely we suffer sufficiently—thank God! that when our own happiness is destroyed, there are others to live for. Do not think I do not consider your decision as *final*."[20]

There had been more pride than real political difference in her objection to Chamberlain's attitude to unemployment, for she was already discussing with Charles Booth his plan to study the poverty-stricken Londoners. He had been provoked to launch his survey by what seemed to him an outrageous claim by Hyndman that a quarter of all wage earners were unable to maintain themselves in a state of reasonable physical health. This, Booth believed, was "sensationalism . . . of the cheapest and most reprehensible order on the part of the Socialist movement." He proposed to use modern statistical techniques to survey the wages and living conditions of Londoners, beginning with the centre of destitution in the East End. Beatrice was fascinated by the project: "just the sort of work I should like to undertake . . . if I were free!" she wrote on 17 April 1886.

She was forced, instead, to spend the summer at the Argoed, caring for her father and her younger sister, Rosy, always poorly and at that time in a hysterical state. The best Beatrice could do was to study economics, and she ground away at Adam Smith, David Ricardo, Karl Marx and Alfred Marshall. She found it hard going, but she was determined to find a link between the way an industrial system worked and the conditions of life of the people. In drafting essays on "The Economic Theory of Karl Marx" and "The Rise and Growth of English Economics" she found relief from her emotional torments. She now considered herself, she remarked on 14 September, "a working woman, who has lived through passion and pain—and come out of it with only a kind of hopeless faith," but two weeks later she confessed that such a life was "weary work for a woman: the brain is worn and the heart unsatisfied—and in those intervals of exhaustion the old craving for love and devotion, given and taken, returns." She went over her diary of the year before and spent "two days castle-building about the great man at Highbury." By the end of the year she claimed that she had "six or seven times . . . refused his overtures made directly or through his family."

During the winter she made an arrangement with her family which released her for a few months from the invalid at the Argoed—the agreement continued after Richard Potter was moved to Box House, near Stroud—and she went up to London to work with Charles Booth on his survey. Assigned an area in dockland, she spent her days talking to the people, interviewing officials and recording social conditions. By March 1887 she was more cheerful: "I am enjoying my life; the old faith in individual work is returning—in the sanctity of moral and intellectual conviction."

The suicidal mood of the previous months was passing, yet she still could not put Chamberlain out of her life. In June 1887 she went up to Birmingham to hear him speak. He was now completely at odds with Gladstone, trying to make his career in the Commons in defiant distinction from his old Liberal colleagues. On a "weak and romantic impulse" she invited him down to visit at the Argoed. When he arrived for a day at the end of July she could not contain herself. "Feeling has over-ridden dignity," she regretfully commented afterwards. In a last attempt to overcome her inhibitions, she broke out with a declaration of love that left Chamberlain embarrassed and confused. This failure was final and harrowing; she at once wrote saying that they should never meet again.[21] Chamberlain, bewildered by her behaviour, wrote back on 3 August to ask: "Did I indeed do wrong in accepting your invitation? If so, forgive me . . . As to the future. Why are we never to see each other again?" He chose his words carefully:

> I like you very much—I respect and esteem you—I enjoy your conversation and society and have often wished that fate had thrown us more together. If you share this feeling—why should we surrender a friendship which ought to be good for both of us? . . . My past life has made me solitary and reserved, but it is hard that I should lose one of the few friends whose just opinions I value. . . . You must decide, and if it is for your own happiness that we should henceforth be strangers, I will make no complaint. . . .

It was possibly his final sentence, in which he assured her that she should not "be ashamed of feelings which are purely womanly and for which I have nothing but gratitude and respect," that provoked Beatrice to the desperate comment she scrawled across Chamberlain's note: "This letter, after I had, in another moment of suicidal misery, told him I cared for him passionately . . . To insist on meeting a woman who had told you she loved you in order to humiliate her further." Two months later Chamberlain sailed for America, where he became engaged to the daughter of the US Secretary of War.

"I have lived through my youth—it is over," Beatrice wrote on 1 November 1887. Marriage to Chamberlain, her sister Kate told her, would have been "a tragedy—a murder of your independent nature." Rationally, Beatrice agreed; emotionally that recognition meant an agonizing and continuous struggle which required all the courage she could muster to come through recurrent fits of despair.

That autumn she had a small reward when the prestigious *Nineteenth Century* published an article by her on "Dock Life" which was based on her contribution to the first volume of Booth's survey. As a result she was invited to speak to a meeting of dock labourers. It was, she wrote, her "first experience of being cheered as a public character." Working with dogged persistency, she agreed with Booth's suggestion that she should now investigate sweated labour. To get a better understanding of the conditions in the East End tailoring trade she disguised herself as a poor seamstress and found a job in a sweater's den as a trouser hand. Called upon to give evidence to a House of Lords committee in May 1888, she nervously exaggerated the time she spent thus disguised, and she was embarrassed by the ensuing publicity. When she wrote up her experiences for the *Nineteenth Century* she suffered agonies of conscience in wondering whether to make a clean breast of this small deception. Yet this adventure began to make a mark for her. The masquerade of a rich society girl as an outcast was romantic enough to attract public attention which Beatrice found embarrassing, but what she had to say was far from conventional. She rejected the common view of the "sweater" as a heartless exploiter grinding the faces of the poor. The sweaters, she pointed out, were in fact middlemen, as much victims of the system as those they employed for long hours at a pittance: the chain of exploitation ran from the top of capitalist society to the bottom.

Her studies of economics and her personal experience were now leading her away from the individualism which she had learned from Herbert Spencer and towards the kind of Radical policies which Chamberlain had advocated. Free competition, she realized, did not lead to freedom and progress but to wage slavery and dreadful poverty. She decided that there must be publicly supported education, opportunities for trade unionists to organize, factory legislation to impose decent conditions of work, and municipal and national efforts to ameliorate the misery of the poor. It was this line of thought which made her wonder whether there might be some alternative to the "dictatorship of the capitalist in industry."

She was now ready to go beyond the limits which Booth had set himself. When he asked her to go on with her research into women's work she decided to strike out for herself into a different field and examine the cooperative movement as a means of bypassing capitalist production and retail trade. Booth tried to dissuade her. The economist Alfred Marshall, urging that she clearly had a gift for enquiring into the state of working women, thought her proposal "pernicious." Beatrice would not be moved, deciding: "I shall stick to my own way of climbing my own little tree." She did not lack sympathy with her own sex, "whether they be struggling young girls, hard-pressed married women or disappointed spinsters," as she had remarked in November 1887. But she felt that she had a "masculine intellect" and that women's problems were much more deeply rooted in the social system than in differences between the sexes. Her distaste for feminist attitudes, indeed, led her in the spring of 1889 to sign a manifesto, organized by the popular novelist Mrs. Humphry Ward, against the political enfranchisement of women. She also preferred the company of men—an attitude inherited from her mother that had hardened into a habit in the years she had acted as hostess for her father to his stimulating friends. Not afraid of breaking the Victorian conventions, she went about alone and took a perverse pleasure in being the only woman at the meetings she attended in the course of her research. "We smoke cigarettes and our conversation becomes more that of business camaraderies," she commented on her evenings with earnest cooperators.

It was, nevertheless, "a grind and no mistake! Six hours a day reading and note-taking from those endless volumes of the *Co-operative News*." She was sustained less by personal satisfaction in her task than by a feeling of mission: as she had told Charles Booth in August 1888, a feeling of "duty to society at large rather than to the individual" was "constantly present" with her. And by losing herself in such work she numbed the nagging feeling of human loss. It was still a miserable struggle. Week by week she recorded her anguish. On 28 February 1889 she wrote: "God help me; and make it not *too* hard for me." On 7 March: "I long every day more for the restfulness of an abiding love—and yet I cannot sacrifice work for which all the horrible suffering of six years has fitted me. . . . I must check those feelings which are the expression of physical instinct craving for satisfaction; but God knows celibacy is as painful to a woman . . . as it is to a man." Later that month she consoled herself with the thought that "future generations may see a woman step out of the ranks as a Saviour of Humanity." In June, halfheartedly courted by a middle-aged economist named Edgeworth, she shamefacedly observed that "relations with men stimulate and excite one's lower nature" and that "that part of a woman's nature dies hard—it is many variations of one chord—*the supreme and instinctive* longing to be a mother." Looking back on 29 July, the anniversary of her final break with Chamberlain, she noted that she would "always consider this day as sacred: a sacrament of pain fitting me for a life of loneliness and work: a memory of deep humiliation." On 17 November she wrote: "I pray earnestly . . . that my life may be a 'living sacrifice' . . . to the work that lies before me. Is it possible for me to live an absolutely religious life without inflation?" Such a phrase could have come from a troubled novice praying for a sure sense of her vocation before taking her vows. Disinterested, determined service was the only way to expunge that self-defeating passion for Chamberlain.

❧ 9 ❧
A YEAR OF LOVE

"I am not sure as to the future of that man," Beatrice reflected after Sidney Webb had spent a Sunday in April 1890 at Box House. "His tiny tadpole body, unhealthy skin, lack of manner, cockney pronunciation, poverty, are all against him."[1] Sidney, better pleased with his visit, wrote to say how much he had gained from "a mentor outside the working circle, a looker-on who sees most of the game." He confided his hopes for the Fabians: "We are constantly seeking chances of translating the crude abstractions of the doctrinaire socialist into the language of practical politics." But he did not know what to do about "such poor creatures" as the Liberal leaders: "I wish their education could be taken in hand in some way that would save the Fabian Society from becoming more & more conceited."

Beatrice had noticed "the conceit of a man who has raised himself out of the most insignificant surroundings into a position of power—how much power no one quite knows," and she found his "self-complacent egotism" both "repulsive and ludicrous . . . A London retail tradesman with the aims of a Napoleon! a queer monstrosity to be justified only by success." All the same, her sympathies were caught. She saw him as "one of a small body of men with whom I may sooner or later throw in my lot for good and all."[2] "It was in my first conversation with you last winter," she wrote to Sidney on 2 May 1890, "that it flashed across my mind that I was, or ought to be a Socialist—if I was true to the conclusions I had already reached . . ."

Both Beatrice and Sidney were in need of a comforting relationship, and they gave each other encouragement. On 16 May she told him bluntly to shut his eyes to what he imagined to be popular opinion and "go straight on collecting information from experts & working it up by the light of socialist principles." She also mentioned that she was off to Glasgow at Whitsun for a Co-operative Congress and suggested that he might like to go along. Sidney did not hesitate. As they travelled up he squatted on a portmanteau while "relays of working-men friends" lay full length at Beatrice's feet, earnestly discussing trade unionism, socialism and cooperation. Sidney, one of their mutual friends remarked to her, "was humbler than I have ever seen him before—quite a different tone."[3]

The reason for Sidney's subdued mood was clear. He had fallen in love with Beatrice, and he impetuously told her so as they walked through the streets of Glasgow. Eager for comradeship but cool to passion, she made it clear to him that such feelings could not be reciprocated. "You understand," she told him frankly, "you promise me to realise that the chances are a hundred to one that nothing follows but friendship."[4] Even that "working compact" made her feel "perplexed and miserable." Still wounded from her encounter with Chamberlain, she insisted that personal happiness must be "an utterly remote thing & I am to that extent 'heartless.' I regard everything from the point of view of making my own and another's life serve the community more effectively." She thought it would be wiser for Sidney to find someone younger who could give him "a life which has not been forced through the fire & forged into a simple instrument for work."

On 30 May Sidney wrote a letter which was the first move in a long campaign to calm and reassure her. "Your letter is full of mistrust," he said, astutely pointing out: "it springs from your generosity to me, your fear lest you do me harm." Yet any harm there might be had been done: "I am through and through yours already." Personal happiness could not be shrugged off. For Beatrice to sacrifice everything to her work, he sharply noted, would not be self-denial but selfishness, "making an idol unto yourself. Your altruism would become an egoism . . . You would have dried up warmheartedness in order to get truth, and you would not even get truth." He begged her "not to crush out feeling. I would rather see another man successful than that this worse thing should happen to you. I cannot think that you will commit this emotional suicide." She asked that this letter *"be the last word of personal feeling"*; the best she could promise was to go on being his inspiration if that made him kinder and more tolerant of suffering humanity. She wanted nothing for herself.

Beatrice was determined to keep Sidney at a distance, but she did not want to drive him away altogether. She wrote to him like an anxious mother. "The general impression seems to be that you are manipulating," she wrote reprovingly while she was away on holiday in Germany. "From that people argue that you are a manipulator & not perfectly sincere—& that, you know & I know to be a false impression as well as a damaging one."[5] Sidney took the criticism of his "egotistical loquacity" in good part and invited other improving comments. He sensed that the only way he could draw Beatrice out of her introspective misery was to emphasize the public possibilities of their private relationship. He argued: "We have the ideas which can deliver the world. You have it in your hands to make me, in the noblest sense, great."[6] Beatrice saw the trap. "Beware how you tread," she replied on 22 June. "You are expecting too much from me—if you do not take care you will frighten me back into acquaintanceship!"

Since Beatrice would not allow a free play of emotions between them, they were forced into a dialogue about moral improvement which enabled them to deal with dangerous topics on an intellectual plane. "You must discourage the love of personal power—it is degrading,"[7] Beatrice declared. Sidney came back with counsels against the disadvantages of withdrawing from the world of action into the world of ideas, citing her adolescent hero Goethe as a cautionary example. "It is much harder to live *in* the world, doing its work, than on the heights of Parnassus or in the convent," he wrote on 29 June. Goethe, in fact, was a "great deserter from the army of humanity," who failed to "recognise what was going on around him . . . It is dangerous to try to be *more* than man, to be 'too bright and good, for human nature's daily food.' " The decay of Goethe's tolerance for his fellow creatures was "a warning not to settle everything too confidently by pure intellect . . . we must recognise instinct and feeling as of some claim as motives."

So he gently coaxed her back to life. They met again that summer when Beatrice returned from Europe and went for a jaunt in Epping

Forest. Sidney astonished her by telling her that he had read all six hundred pages of Alfred Marshall's *Principles of Economics* on the previous evening. Though it was a great book, he remarked, it still left someone the chance of remaking economics. "Who is to do it? Either you must help me to do it; or I must help you."[8] The talk went on into the evening, when they wound up at Toynbee Hall and had dinner with the Radical MP Richard Burdon Haldane and some workingmen, but Sidney had introduced a touch of sentiment while they lay under the trees in the forest by reading Keats and Dante Gabriel Rossetti. He was clearly feeling the strain, for he wrote on the following day to say that Beatrice had been so "angel-good that I had all I could do not to say goodbye in a way which would have broken our concordat."[9] Beatrice, still on her guard against self-indulgence, replied primly: "I am very pleased that you enjoyed your short visit & I trust that after this we shall have straight sailing in friendship without any deviation into sentiment."[10]

At the end of July, Webb and Shaw took off for a cultural expedition to Bavaria. They went first to Bayreuth to hear *Parsifal*, then on to Oberammergau for the Passion Play. The restless Shaw made a dash up the mountainside, "Webb preferring to sit among the trees at the base, writing an article on municipal death duties for *The Speaker*."[11] Shaw as yet knew nothing of Sidney's emotional entanglement; it was this that was concerning Sidney, leaving him little taste for holiday-making. He ardently desired Beatrice but felt that the odds were stacked against him. "I had not realised before," he wrote just before he left Germany, "that you will one day probably be rich. . . . This is one more barrier between us—one more step in that noble self-sacrifice which you must make to pick me up." The prospect looked gloomy. "I do not see how I can go on without you," he pleaded. "Do not desert me now."[12]

When he returned to London there was a tart reply waiting for him: "I ask you, is it delicate or honourable of you to use the relationship of friends which I have granted you as a ground for attack—for a continual & continuous pressing forward of wishes of your own which you know are distasteful to me—& which simply worry & distress and rob me of all the help & strength your friendship might give me?" Beatrice's tone verged on hysteria. Sidney's "abominable letter" could have been prompted by nothing more than an "uncontrolled desire to express

your own feelings, relieve your own mind & gain your own end." Riches
had nothing to do with it, she added, for she had only enough money "to
carry out my everyday life on the plan of greatest efficiency possible to
my very limited ability." Love, she thought, "has in it some element of
self-control and self-sacrifice." The only comfort that she could offer
Sidney was the suggestion that he might read through Marshall's book
with her.[13] He replied in contrition on 11 August: "I will not offend
again. You shall not need to write me another such letter, a terrible
letter."

The manner in which she both encouraged and rejected him confused Sidney, who as yet knew nothing of Beatrice's passion for Chamberlain. She believed that it had been the power of her intellect that had
prevented her from succumbing to that passion; the only way to safe-
guard herself against a repetition of that experience, she felt, was to
block every suggestion that an intellectual relationship might grow into
one of love and genuine intimacy. She had to insist that she was frigid—
the word she normally used was "heartless"—because she feared that she
was not; the more Sidney threatened to arouse her emotional feelings,
the more she felt guilty and the more she retreated to a virginal insistence
on her vocation. She began to write to Sidney like a maiden aunt giving
advice to a promising nephew: "However old your coat may be (and
that is of no importance) *brush it!* Take care of your voice and pronunciation: it is the chief instrument of influence. Don't talk of 'when I am
Prime Minister': it jars on sensitive ears."[14]

All through the summer Sidney was circumspect, writing about his
work and his uncertainty about his prospects. He introduced her to Graham Wallas, who was now employed as a university extension lecturer;
Beatrice summed him up as "a strange, warm-hearted young man, with a
bright intelligence, not much beyond commonplace except in its social
fervour."[15] What did appeal to her was the tie of friendship which knit
the inner group of Fabians together: "it is singularly trustful—you really
care for each other."[16] Sidney was pleased that she liked Wallas, "the
most 'devoted' man I know . . . *too* good-natured," but, while he
praised the Fabian group as "a very pretty piece of intellectual communism," he confessed that he was bothered by the way in which the Society had lately "tended to aggrandise me . . . Now that I have been
pushed into [a] position of leadership, I feel, horribly, the responsibility
of 'living up to it.' "[17]

Sidney still clung tenaciously to Beatrice. At least she took an interest in him. In September they went together to the British Association meeting at Bradford, and she was full of admiration for a "rattling clever speech from S.W." While they were there she felt "the tie stiffening,"[18] and she wrote to him encouragingly about their common interests:

> Let us go forward with this fellowship without thought for the morrow—the form it will take is not in our hands . . . you are too generous & too wise to wish me . . . to *force* a growth which is not natural. It is for you to win that dependence and respect out of which the woman's love arises—you have already won the desire to be helpful—the proverbial Pity which is akin to love—pity used in the largest sense—typical of the Mother's care . . .

Whenever Sidney seemed to falter in his aspirations Beatrice was touched and warmed to him. She encouraged him to keep a diary and to send it to her daily. "You would enable me to feel part & parcel of your life, to watch it & sympathise with it from afar off . . ."[19]

Sidney took up her suggestion. His reply was contained in the first of the red penny notebooks, crammed with his regular round handwriting, which now took the place of ordinary letters. He had never done so much work or been more efficient than in "this glorious summer," he told her; he now decided to write a book on the eight-hour day with Harold Cox as his collaborator. To demonstrate his high spirits he sent her Rossetti's poems, "the first gift I have ventured to make to you."[20]

In June 1890 a retired solicitor named Henry H. Hutchinson from Derby was elected to the Fabian Society. He was an odd, impulsive man. A few weeks after joining he offered to put up two hundred pounds to subsidize Fabian lectures in the provinces. The Fabian executive worked out a scheme for what became known as the "Lancashire campaign." It lasted for five weeks, and about sixty lectures were given by leading Fabians in such towns as Manchester, Oldham, Preston and Liverpool, in a number of Yorkshire communities, and as far as Carlisle. The impact of the *Essays* was thus reinforced by the personal appearance of the authors in places which no socialist speaker had reached before. They were able to "reach the working-men politicians who form the rank and file of the Liberal Associations and Clubs, or the 'well-dressed' Liberals who

vaguely desire social reform, but have been encouraged by their leaders
to avoid all exact thought on the subject."[21] Provincial Fabian groups
now began to spring up all across the North of England.

In September 1890 Sidney went off to do his share of lecturing.
"There can be no doubt that our influence is just now growing fast," he
wrote to Beatrice on 21 September, "& it is important that we should
'keep our heads.' " As he went up through the textile areas of Yorkshire
and Lancashire and swung round to the mining areas of Northumberland
he sensed that the labour movement was entering a new phase: new organizations were springing up in the industrial centres, working not only
for the eight-hour day and trade unionism but also for socialism. And the
people he was meeting were different from the middle-class Fabians.
There were many more workers and Nonconformist radicals. "To play
on these millions of minds," Sidney noted the following day, "to watch
them slowly respond to an unseen stimulus, to guide their aspirations
often without their knowledge—all this, whether in high capacities or
humble, is a big & endless game of chess, of ever extravagant excitement.
Sanctify by altruism & emotion & you get the raw material of the New
Religion."[22]

It was hard work. "I feel it telling on my nerves," he wrote on 24
September, as he described "the irregular life, the perpetual talking to
new people, the constant external stimulus." He found no pleasure in
platform oratory and was glad to get back to the South to go down to
visit Beatrice at Box. "He is certainly extraordinarily improved—and becoming a needful background to my working life—and I the same to
him," she noted on 2 October. Beatrice was certainly unbending towards
Sidney and his Fabian friends. She agreed to meet the inner group at a
party Sidney was planning to give at 4 Park Village East, the house near
Regent's Park to which the Webb family had moved the year before.
Sidney wanted to hold the party before Sydney Olivier left on 17 October for his first overseas post in the colonial service, in British Honduras.
Beatrice in turn showed goodwill by asking Pease and Shaw if they
would go down to Box for Sunday 19 October. Pease had to decline because his wife was giving birth to their first son. Shaw sent a dusty answer. "This is the most unreasonable thing I ever heard of," he wrote to
Beatrice. "Why, I find that it would cost me seventeen shillings for railway travelling alone . . . No: you may reduce the rest of the Fabian to
slavery—they prattle from morning to night about Beatrice Potter in a

way I despise—but if I am to go through my amusing conversational performances for you, you must come up to town: this lion is untameable."[23]

Sidney misconstrued Beatrice's amiable mood and once more pressed
her too hard. There was an embarrassing scene which he described as
"ghastly in its comedy changed to tears."[24] Leaving for another lecture
trip in the North, he assured Beatrice that he would not make the same
mistake again: "I shall have to leave you to propose to me, I believe!" He
sat up most of the night reading Isaiah, and was so upset that he stumbled
haltingly through his speech next day to the local cooperators. The Fabian campaign in the North had lost its zest. It was "entirely virgin soil,
& I *suppose* worth cultivating," he told Beatrice, and he added: "I do not
grudge the time & money: whatever influence the Fabian Society has
gained is due largely to our constant willingness to do small jobs—to be
as cordially eager to convert one man as a hundred . . . I like to think
of ourselves as the 'Society of Jesus' of Socialism—without, I hope, the
mental subjection which Protestants accuse the Jesuits of."

Sidney still hoped that Beatrice would ultimately marry him, and he
insisted that he wanted none of the "vulgar indecencies" that might go
with a public engagement: "When the time comes I should prefer to go
through the barest legal ceremony that convention requires." In the
meantime he wanted affection—"not necessarily the turbulent passion of
first youth, but the more reasonable and durable regard that comes from
real sympathy and cordial trust"—and hope, "a tremendous belief in the
reasonableness of my proposal . . . of the transformation of 1 and 1 into
11." How much easier it would have been, he said bashfully, if she "were
not a person of station & good connection & some wealth: it will not be
very pleasant for me to have to face the things that will be said about me
on this score."[25]

It was now time for Beatrice to put her cards on the table.

> When you spoke to me in Glasgow [she wrote] I did not say, as I
> have said to others, a distinct "no," because I felt that your character
> & circumstances & your work offered me a sphere of usefulness and
> fellowship which I have no right to refuse off-hand. I felt too how
> hard it would be for me to lead a lonely life without becoming too
> hard & nervous & self-willed. On the other hand, you were person-
> ally unattractive to me and I doubted whether I could bring myself
> to submit to a close relationship. Remember that I was desperately in
> love and for six years with another man, and that even now the
> wound is open. . . . Since then I have been trying hard to bring

myself to care for you: some days I have felt the strength and calm which your affection has brought into my life . . . but I do not love you, and until I do I will not be in any way bound . . . When I read your letter this morning, though I had thought previously that probably our friendship would end in marriage, I had another revulsion of feeling—a sort of panic that I would sooner leave life than enter into any promise. . . .

The question of marriage, Beatrice insisted, could not be seriously considered so long as her father still lived. If she were in love, she could perhaps face "the terrible self-questionings of an engagement," but, she added, she was not in love.

> Altogether I feel very very miserable. Try to forgive me any pain I have given you by the thought of my misery. . . . I cannot and will not be engaged to you. . . . Now decide for yourself: if you think I have deceived you or that I demand too much do not write to me again . . . But if you care to wait until the question is a practical one promise me one thing—that we write frankly to each other under the promise that if it leads to nothing we return each other's letters or faithfully destroy them. . . . Dear Sidney—I will try to love you —but don't be impatient. What can I do more? I am doing more than I would for any other man—simply because you are a Socialist and I am a Socialist. That other man I loved but did not believe in. You I believe in but do not love.[26]

Beatrice could not have stated her dilemma more clearly. Sidney sent an understanding reply. "Turn but your face towards me," he appealed, "& love must come—do but give up looking backward."[27] Beatrice could only say depressingly: "I am feeling low & miserable—as if a great burden were laid on me—the burden of unreturned affection."

Her attitude was influenced by her older friends and relatives. "He seemed to me in earnest & genuine," Charles Booth wrote to Beatrice after Sidney had been to dinner, "really possessed with the idea & hope of a better state of things to spring from the advance of democratic socialism." He thought less of Sidney's credentials as a suitor, warning Beatrice: "In that concatenation, I find I don't like him at all & neither Mary nor I can bear to think of you as his wife or of him as your husband. *Don't do it*, I say."[28] There was an equally strong caution from an old friend, Arabella Fisher: "You will get into a position in which you will have to stand very much *alone* both as regards friends and moral support

& you will not have someone to lean upon but someone who in matters
of judgment will be led by you."[29] Such social pressure was only one of
the constraints. She could not tell her father; she knew that he would
have been appalled. Her sisters also disapproved. Yet she could not drive
him away altogether. Though she rejected, he persevered; though she
promised nothing, he hoped.

Work, for both of them, was an anodyne. Sidney had begun to attract attention outside the narrow circle of Fabians: his talks and articles
were always bulging with facts based on careful research. The success of
Fabian Essays, which had already sold over twenty thousand copies and
was still going at a rate of four hundred a week, also helped his reputation. The Liberal Party had asked if it could publish his articles on the
social problems of London as a sixpenny pamphlet. "It will mean a wonderful change on the Liberal programme & way of looking at things," he
optimistically wrote to Beatrice on 14 October. "It is important to make
the provincial Liberal understand that I preach what he has got to accept, that my policy is to be the future Liberal policy." He sent off to
Herbert Gladstone, the old Liberal leader's son who was one of the
party's political managers, a copy of the draft of the Eight Hours Bill
that had been prepared by a group of Fabians, the programme of the
Metropolitan Radical Federation and other papers to influence the Liberal leadership in favour of more radical ideas and of candidates with an
appeal to the working classes. Believing that the socialists could get their
ideas taken up by the Radicals, he wrote in his article *Socialism in England:* "This permeation is apparently destined to continue, and the
avowed Socialist party in England will probably remain a compara-
tively small disintegrating and educational force, never itself exercising
political power, but supplying ideas and principles of social reconstruction to each of the great political parties in turn, as the changing results
of English politics bring them alternately into office."[30]

Sidney's hopes were increased by a fresh crisis in the Liberal Party's
affairs. The Liberals had been losing ground ever since Chamberlain's defection split the party and put the Tories in power, but in London they
had regained the initiative by the Progressives' capture of the County
Council and by the vigorous support of *The Star*. T. P. O'Connor had
built his newspaper up to a circulation of nearly three hundred thousand
by campaigning for housing reform, progressive taxation, free education
and public libraries, shorter hours and better working conditions. Sidney
had played some part in this success, feeding O'Connor with material

and writing editorials for him. It seemed that in London at least there was a real prospect of building up a political base for Radicalism comparable to that which Chamberlain had created ten years earlier in Birmingham. All Webb's political contacts were with the London Radicals, and his pragmatic concern with tactics had made him an advocate of "piecemeal reform" in the Fabian debates over the previous three years.

The Radical initiatives became even more important in the autumn of 1890, when the Parnell case dealt another blow at the Liberals. Parnell was cited as corespondent in the divorce action that Captain O'Shea, one of his lieutenants in the Irish Party, brought against his wife. The hysterical outburst of moral condemnation which followed drove a wedge between the Liberals and the Irish, and divided the Irish amongst themselves when Parnell refused to take Gladstone's advice and resign. The Home Rule issue, which had already cost the Liberals the last election, had now become an even greater liability, and the party badly needed a new domestic programme to distract attention from the Irish question.

Sidney saw this change as an opportunity, but he ran into opposition from those Society members who distrusted the Liberals. The emergence of the New Unionism among the unskilled workers and the growing support for the idea of independent labour representation in local and national politics strengthened those who had been arguing for a new left-wing party. To them, Webb's desire to convert the Society into something like a brains trust for the Radical wing of the Liberals seemed to be mere opportunism, and they said so openly. By the end of the year the Society was divided on the issue of political action, and Webb and Wallas were both sharply criticized for flirting with the Liberals.

The most serious blow to the Society was the defection of Annie Besant on 21 November. She had gone through yet another of her conversions, under the influence of Herbert Burrows, her latest protégé. Burrows was already a convert to Madame Blavatsky's mystical cult of Theosophy. In 1889, when Annie read *The Secret Doctrine* and met Madame Blavatsky, she immediately became a disciple. Shaw was shocked by "this unprepared blow, which meant to me the loss of a powerful colleague and of a friendship which had become part of my daily life," but he thought that "she had after many explorations found her path and come to see the universe and herself in their real perspective."[31] Pease crossed Annie's name off the Fabian list and wrote a note in red ink: "Gone to Theosophy." She had found a new vocation as a priestess.

Though Annie resigned, Bland continued to press her argument for a separate socialist party and found support from Shaw. This led William Clarke, who was rapidly drifting away from the other essayists, to make a bitter attack on Shaw in *The Star* in early December. Shaw was not disposed to smooth over the differences. "Holding our tongues, lest we discover . . . our disunion," he wrote to Wallas on 16 December, would simply leave the field clear for Hyndman. He wrote on the same day to Sydney Olivier in British Honduras that the Society seemed "on the eve of an eruption. The seismological signs indicate that we are spoiling for a fight." Shaw wanted the Fabians to break with the conventional parties: "we must proclaim ourselves not an advanced guard of the Liberal Party, but a definitely Social Democratic Party."[32]

The pressures on Sidney Webb now became more than he could bear. Earlier in 1890 he had begun to map out his career: marriage to Beatrice, the making over of the Fabian Society into an intellectual pressure group for advanced ideas in the Liberal Party, and resignation from the Colonial Office so that he could devote himself to journalism and politics. All three aims seemed feasible, but all three led simply to frustration. In November he caught scarlet fever. The illness struck at his morale, and the tone of his letters to Beatrice sharpened. In his irritation he burnt a bundle of her letters. "You have been good to write to me, but you are always 'hard' on me, and you have contrived to make your letters bitter as well as sweet," he wrote complainingly on 30 November.

Sickness and despair combined to blight his ambitions. "I no longer think it *probable* that I shall leave the civil service," he wrote to Beatrice on 4 December, and he went on to say that he had now relinquished his hopes of marrying her. "I could not in decency ask you to do it." It was, he said, her duty to tell him "if you are *quite* sure that you can never love me, even a little: if you are *quite* sure that no advantage to your own life or mine, or to the Socialist cause, could ever induce you to marry me."

Beatrice gave him the answer he anticipated. "I cried very bitterly over your letter," she replied, saying that she had for a short time allowed his entreaties to lead her away from her better judgment. "I do not love you. All the misery of this relationship arises from this . . . Frankly, I do not believe my nature is capable of love. I came out of that six years agony . . . like a bit of steel . . . I cannot and will never make the stupendous sacrifice of marriage . . . This makes it absolutely necessary that our present relationship should be ended: we must both be absolutely free."[33]

Sidney kept his head in the crisis. "I accept your decision," he answered. "You will not find that I have ceased to love you, but I will cease to regard you as a marriageable person . . . If I adhere to that, do not let us cease to be friends."[34] He turned to Wallas for comfort in these trying weeks; when he went down to Bournemouth to convalesce Wallas went with him. After a few days of walking, reading and loafing he assured Beatrice on 14 December, "I am certainly not unhappy and not in the least 'tearing my hair' or 'pining away,'" and begged her not to withdraw into a lonely retreat from life. "I care for your own life more even than I care for you. . . . Next time I must write only as a friend. But *be* my friend, as you well know how, and I shall learn gradually to cease to regret that you would be no more." When he was back in London, he returned her letters. "He has behaved nobly," she wrote, but she had no second thoughts about her decision. "A year of love, accepted but not given," she noted bleakly in her diary. "The tie that was tightening between me and another I have snapped asunder and I am alone again, facing work and the world."[35]

10

EXIT BEATRICE POTTER

The Fabian Society had been changing while Sidney's attention had been distracted by his courtship. The sudden boom in membership as a result of the *Essays* and the provincial lectures had faced the London leadership with a success which it did not quite know how to handle. Sidney realized that an initiative was needed, and when he and Wallas went to Brighton for the Christmas holidays they drafted a new plan of work. The meetings that autumn, they observed, had not "tended to edification": the Society had "for the moment outgrown in income, reputation and numbers, its organisation for collective work and for the publication of literature."[1]

Early in 1890 the Fabians numbered about 150, of whom only thirty had paid a subscription during the previous nine months. They had spent £32 on printing, £35 on hiring halls for meetings and £40 for postage. A year later the Society had over three hundred members, its tracts and leaflets were rapidly being reprinted—335,000 copies went out in 1891, five times the total distributed since the foundation of the Society—and the income, helped by profits from the *Essays*, jumped to £860. It was also attracting influential figures. Among those who joined in 1891 were Keir Hardie, Joe Burgess—the editor of the *Workman's Times*—the novelist Grant Allen, F. J. Furnivall, H. J. Massingham, Emmeline Pankhurst and her husband, and the new leaders of the unskilled trade unions, Pete Curran, Will Crooks and Ben Tillett.

Fabianism was spreading through the country. The Society kept a close eye on the fourteen groups in the London area, but it could exercise little control over those in the provinces. The Birmingham society, for example, enrolled 100 members in its first eight months; it organized seventeen public lectures with an average attendance of over 200 people, sold 200 copies of the *Essays* and 1,800 tracts, and raised £83. Manchester had done much the same, and new groups were springing up in Bristol, Edinburgh, Bradford, Stockport, Sheffield and a dozen other towns in the North of England. There was even a society in Bombay giving lectures to "educated natives." It was clear that the Fabians were no longer an exclusive debating society: they were suddenly faced with a chance to become a serious political body—a chance which they had not sought and did not wholly comprehend.

One of the first proposals Webb and Wallas made in the plan they drew up at Brighton was assistance for Pease. He was "overweighted with mechanical work," his flat "littered with parcels."[2] An office boy was soon hired at a wage of ten shillings a week, for Pease could not cope. In January 1891, for instance, he wrote over six hundred letters and received as many; he organized nine courses of lectures, apart from ordinary meetings; and he handled all the Society's growing publishing business, including the burdensome task of selling the *Essays*. Before long the Society installed him in its first formal office, at 276 Strand.

The problem which most concerned Webb and Wallas, however, was the influx of members with strong socialist opinions sympathizing with schemes for a new labour party. Something had to be done to prevent the provincial recruits from stampeding the Society against the Liberals, and to hold off the same sort of pressure in London from Bland and other critics. Their remedy, with the ambivalent help of Shaw, who wanted primarily to avoid a split in the Society, was to impose an unimaginative pattern of work on its members. All they could suggest to enthusiasts who were already more inspired with evangelistic fervour for the cause and were moved more by the visions of William Morris than by *Facts for Socialists* was that members of local groups might help prepare new tracts, organize social gatherings, ensure that Fabian publications were noticed in local newspapers, and translate socialist works from French and German. In return the London Fabians would send a lecturer four times a year, circulate proofs of new tracts—on which local societies, unlike the London members, could not vote—and produce the monthly bulletin which became *Fabian News*.

Neither Webb nor Wallas had much idea what should be done beyond keeping the Society running along the familiar and unambitious lines which had been appropriate to its early years. They suggested that it might follow up the lecture series which produced the successful *Essays* with another which would "grapple with the *difficulties* of social reconstruction," arguing that it would be better "to deal imperfectly with a great subject, than to display a facility in 'hunting old trails'"; and Sidney came up with the suggested titles "Law and Government," "State and Industry," "Voluntary Action" and "The Non-Economic Side of Collectivism"—a gesture of recognition for artists like Morris and Crane, and poets such as Carpenter. There were proposals for a new issue of leaflets on practical topics such as public baths, museums and libraries, free schools and meals for schoolchildren, municipal reform, and the enlivening of the dreary English Sunday. They also had the idea of issuing books on socialism and social problems from a central library— the device of circulating book boxes which soon became a mainstay of Fabian educational activity. Yet their doubts about the quality and motives of many of the new members showed through in their conclusions that, despite the need for an expansion of Fabian activity, there was a need for "a new *Purge* of the Society." There was still too much deadwood in it. Sidney Webb had no time for those who were simply joiners. "Webb taught us to work," Wallas later wrote, "and to forget that at Oxford and Cambridge one reserved the afternoon for rest."[3]

In the autumn of 1890 Beatrice talked to Graham Wallas about possible links between the socialists and the Radicals. In December she had a visit from John Morley and R. B. Haldane. Haldane was a rapidly rising young barrister who had been elected to Parliament in the election of 1885 and was now a promising member of the Radical wing of the Liberal Party. He was a well-educated Scot of good family who had an interest in German idealist philosophy and social reform which later earned him the nickname "Schopenhauer." There was much about him that made him congenial to Beatrice: he was rational, painstaking, talented, and fascinated by the manipulations of politics. He had gone through an agonizing struggle to free himself from the rigorous Calvinism of his father, leaving him with a feeling of depressed guilt that was familiar to Beatrice. Along with the political discussion with Beatrice and Wallas at Box, he talked over with her the idea of marriage. She made it clear that she considered marriage akin to self-destruction, telling him, "I cannot bring myself to face an act of *felo-de-se* for a speculation in personal happiness. . . . I am not capable of loving."[4] She had at last realized that it was not Sidney to whom she objected but the fact of marriage itself.

She had not completely broken with Sidney. She wrote at the beginning of 1891 to say that she was coming up to London; she wanted to follow up the ideas she had been exchanging with Wallas and Haldane. "I should like to see you and Mr Wallas so that we might discuss the future together," she wrote.[5] One of the matters on her mind was the possibility of joining the Fabians, and she talked this over with Wallas and Sidney when they dined with her early in January. She found Sidney "in a thoroughly weak miserable state: not strong enough to work—and excited and jealous—more deeply involved than ever." It was, she felt, an unsatisfactory conversation. "Both pressed me to join the Fabians, refused lest it should injure my chances as an investigator—and with a hidden feeling that perhaps it will be impossible for me to continue honourably as S. W.'s friend."[6] She finally compromised by asking that her first annual subscription be entered only over her initials. She expressed her misgivings in a letter to Sidney on 13 January: "I wish I were *absolutely convinced.* . . . My individualist antecedents have still a hold on me."

All Beatrice had achieved by her attempt to terminate her relationship with Sidney was to make them both unhappy and uncertain with each other. She had hesitantly joined the Fabians as a gesture of compensation, but she was determined to keep herself aloof. On her thirty-third birthday she noted: "I feel younger than I have ever done before: except that I feel horribly 'independent,' absolute mistress of myself and my circumstances—uncannily so."[7] She pressed on with her work, gaining in skill and reputation, but her success was soured by doubt. "Oh, how detestable public life is to a woman," she wrote on 7 March, and yet "a sort of fate drags me into it."

Sidney was equally unsure about plunging into politics. He plaintively wrote to Beatrice: "If only I knew what I *ought* to do."[8] He saw the chance of becoming a member of the Progressive Party in the London County Council, perhaps of soon finding a seat in Parliament as a Radical, but the risks worried him: "I distrust my power to earn money. I dislike and shrink from the publicity, the electoral campaign & so on." He told her that for the present he must continue at the Colonial Office and confine his political ambitions to the Fabian Society and the Radical clubs in London.

His hope of using the Radicals as a means of capturing the Liberal Party for advanced policies was not unreasonable. There was a long tradition of Radical cabals and pressure groups within the party and it was conceivable that the Fabian Society might become the nucleus of a group which could shape Liberal policy. For the monied interest among the Liberals had been seriously weakened, while the Radicals had lost their main leaders when Chamberlain defected and Charles Dilke was politically ruined by a divorce case. The party organization was weak, fragmented and vulnerable to penetration by hard-working enthusiasts.

After meetings with Haldane to discuss cooperation he reported to Beatrice that Haldane "confessed to a great change of mind & was prepared to work with us."[9] Sidney had hopes of several of the rising Liberals, such as Arthur Acland, Sydney Buxton, the young barrister Henry Asquith who had defended Cunninghame-Graham after Bloody Sunday, Haldane, who had gone bail for Graham, and Sir Edward Grey, but he was also sceptical. After dining with Grey and his wife he concluded: "they are very nice but he lacks self-confidence & therefore courage. I doubt whether any of these men can lead."[10] He continued to think well of Haldane, whom he saw frequently and on whom he depended as a line of communication to the left wing of the Liberals. It was clear that a general election would come soon and that the Liberals must produce a new platform. Though most of the new members who were coming into the Society sympathized with Bland and the group pressing the Fabians to support an independent labour party, Sidney was determined to prevent the Society committing itself to a position which would weaken the links he was assiduously establishing with the Radicals.

The strain was telling on him and, as the weeks passed, he counted the time since Beatrice had killed his hopes. "Already three months!" he wrote on 3 March. A formal, even cold correspondence passed between them during the winter. When the spring came, Sidney was still in poor health, overworked and suffering severely from fits of jealousy and frustration. Wallas was also unwell with "nerve-fag" and at Easter they went together to the Isle of Wight with the Geologists Association. When Beatrice sent him the proofs of her book on cooperation, he was too tired and dispirited to make a warm response. He told her flatly that he was disappointed. "You have taken too long over it," he wrote bluntly. ". . . The book will not be a *very* great work."[11] He was equally chilling about her idea of writing a book on trade unionism. "It may well be that you are right . . . you will have to justify it by the result. . . . I wish I could have heartily agreed with your idea," was all he could say to encourage her.[12]

It was Beatrice who finally broke the deadlock. Her loneliness, coupled with her recognition of Sidney's intellectual and personal worth, eventually eroded her pride. She dated her change of heart to April 1891, when she went up to London to give some lectures on cooperation. *The Times* asked for an advance summary of her talk and, baffled at the notion of drafting a press release, she asked Sidney to do it for her. Sidney responded with an "admirable statement of my argument, far more lucid than the lecture itself,"[13] for publication in *The Times* the following day. At Whitsun they went to Lincoln for the Co-operative Congress, and in those few days Beatrice came to realize that she could no longer sustain her lonely life. "I cannot tell how things will settle themselves— I think probably in his way," she wrote.[14] It was, even then, "reason and not love that won me." She listed Sidney's virtues, commending his "resolute, patient affection, his honest care for my welfare—helping and correcting me—a growing distrust of a self-absorbed life and the egotism of successful work . . . all these feelings are making for our eventual union—the joining together of our resources—mental and material—to serve together the 'commonwealth.' "[15] Meanwhile, she recognized, nothing could be formally decided while her father lingered through the last months of life; on 20 May she agreed to an engagement on condition that it remain private.

Beatrice was still faced with an inner struggle. She could not admit to herself that personal happiness had much to do with marriage. She had come to the conclusion that she ought to marry Sidney because their union would be useful and productive, not because she felt there would be either pleasure or passion in the match: "it will be an act of renunciation of self and not of indulgence of self."[16] She looked again at the correspondence with Chamberlain, hoping to exorcise the past which "has haunted me day and night . . . Can I be brave and sensible and once and for all vow that I will forgive and forget?"[17] Sidney, for his part, sent reassuring letters, and they made plans for a June holiday in Norway with Wallas and a woman friend.

Before they left London Beatrice's friend Alice Green, who was told in confidence about their engagement, gave a party to further the scheme of bringing the Radicals and the Fabians together. "A queer party," Beatrice afterwards described the evening: the five Radicals, Asquith, Haldane, Grey, Buxton and Acland—all soon to be members of a Liberal Cabinet—and the five Fabians, Webb, Shaw, William Clarke, Massingham, and Olivier, back in England again after his service in British Honduras. Despite the cordial atmosphere, Beatrice felt that the occasion was a failure. Asquith, in her view, was "determined that it *should not go* . . . the machine of the Liberal Party is slow to move."[18]

In Norway Sidney was ecstatic with his happiness and gratitude, reassuring Beatrice about the enormous advantages of "our partnership." She tried to settle to the decision she had made: "The world will wonder. On the face of it it seems an extraordinary end to the once brilliant Beatrice Potter . . . to marry an ugly little man with no social position and less means . . . Our marriage will be based on fellowship—a common faith and a common work. His feeling is the passionate love of an emotional man, mine the growing tenderness of the mother touched with the dependence of the woman on the help of a strong lover."[19]

They had come after a year of equivocation to the bargain which Beatrice had envisaged at the beginning. Now it was sealed she set about organizing Sidney's life, telling him "it is time that you deliberately planned what you intend to be." Sidney asked apprehensively whether she was not expecting too much of him when she said that he must give up the Colonial Office and get more experience of political administration. She was not sure, she told him with her bleak honesty, that he could "become a really big man," but his abilities were at least sufficient "to do first-rate work on the London County Council." Summing up what they might achieve together, she noted: "We are both of us second-rate minds, but we are curiously combined. I am the investigator, and he the executor—and we have a wide and varied experience of men and things between us. We also have an unearned salary. This forms our unique circumstances."[20]

As soon as they were back in London, with Sidney in high spirits and good health, the work began. When he sent Beatrice his photograph, it came back with a reminder of their bargain: "Let me have your head only—it is the head only that I am marrying!"[21] Beatrice had temporarily moved into Herbert Spencer's house in Avenue Road, St. John's Wood, while she started work on her book on trade unionism. Sidney, who resigned from the civil service at the beginning of September, now went up regularly to help her and to join in the discussions with trade-union leaders. "Poor Herbert Spencer," Beatrice wrote, "if he had seen us evening after evening working away together undermining the individualism of the British race—with intervals of human nature."[22] They were happy together and solemnly endowing their liaison with spiritual dedication. Sidney wrote to Haldane on 25 July: "Of course I am awfully happy, but I feel all the responsibility, both that I should not spoil a life which I regard as of high value to the world and that I, too, should not fail to give the fullest possible product in return for my own happiness."[23]

Beatrice went off to Newcastle for the Trades Union Congress, and at the end of September he joined her in the North, where she was drudging at the research in trade-union offices. After two weeks of joint effort Beatrice was able to tell him, "I feel much more confident that our marriage will not interfere with our work."[24] By the end of the year she had come to feel that the relationship could be something more than a working compact. "My engagement," she noted, "was a very deliberate step—now it is an unconscious happiness."[25] Sidney lightheartedly remarked on 3 November, "I can't help it being 'Beauty and the Beast'—if only it is not a case of Titania and Bottom!"

Richard Potter died on New Year's Day 1892. When the funeral was over Beatrice broke the news of the engagement to her family. They took it well. "A letter comes from Beatrice," Kate Courtney wrote in her diary, "which is a great surprise to me and not at first a quite welcome one." When Sidney went round for dinner soon afterwards, Kate found him better than the unflattering accounts she had heard about him. "He was quiet," she wrote, "perhaps shy—but he looks strong and able though not much of a figure of a man, and I hope we may like him. Beatrice seems quietly happy and confident of the future, and she has a softness of expression and manner which looks as if her feelings were engaged."[26] The news was received less sympathetically by Beatrice's friends. The eccentric individualist Auberon Herbert told her sardoni-

cally that she and Sidney would "do a lot of harm and be happy doing
it." When Herbert Spencer learnt that she was to marry a leading socialist he sorrowfully revoked his decision to make Beatrice his literary executor. The response that wounded her most came from the Booths:
they reacted coldly, making it plain that they wished to see neither of
them. "I can never cease to regret it," Beatrice was writing two years
later. "Their friendship was the stay of my life during the real struggle
of it."[27]

Beatrice inherited £16,000 from her father, bringing her capital to
£26,000 in all, enough to yield an income of about a thousand pounds a
year. This, she told Sidney, was "a high salary to get at the start of one's
life," and she hoped that they would use it well.[28] They both felt that
unearned income must be morally justified by using it for the common
good, and that those who lived on rent or interest should maintain the
minimum standard of life needed for respectability and efficiency.

Years before, Sidney had thought out this conclusion, as he explained in a letter in November 1887 to Haldane's aunt, Jane Burdon
Sanderson. She had asked his views on "the proper course of conduct"
for a wealthy person with a social conscience. To refuse to take the
income would be no help to the workers who produced it, he wrote; all
that could be done was to regard oneself as "a steward for the community." Since every fit person had a "duty to labour," the income could
be used to support "unpaid social duty." "Our libraries, our evening
classes, our schools, our poor, our local administration, our political organisation all need help . . . But it must *be* work, i.e. the service must
have some utility to the state, and must be steady and continuous." Personal expenditure should be kept down to essential needs—including
"some art and relaxation"—for "everything beyond is selfish waste." The
owner of capital was "morally responsible for what is being done with
that wealth . . . If you are a railway shareholder . . . take care that
you write letters every month to the directors urging shorter hours &
better wages for the men. *Your* money in the bank is enabling some
army contractor to hire shirtmakers at 6/ per week—with the inevitable
consequences. Your water shares are your instrument of oppression of
the poor whose water supply is cut off or fouled." If, Sidney declared
passionately, "you resent this . . . it seems to me that you should do

what you can to alter the system—i.e. throw your energy and your ability into the cause of Socialism."[29]

These views guided their behaviour from the moment they decided to marry. Beatrice's capital made it possible for Sidney safely to leave the Colonial Office. In November 1891, after tentative approaches from several constituencies, he was asked to run as a Progressive candidate for the London County Council in Deptford, the working-class area in southeast London where Shaw had been asked to stand in 1889. Beatrice immediately offered £100 towards his expenses. Agreeing to take the money, Sidney jokingly remarked that he would then be "the Member for Potter."[30]

Money was also useful in providing help. In January 1892 they took on a young man named Francis Galton as secretary to help Beatrice in her studies of trade unionism and Sidney with his electioneering in Deptford. Galton was a young engraver with a passion for self-improvement and socialist politics. He was impressed by Sidney's political talents. "He seemed to know every move on the board," Galton recalled, "to think of every plan and scheme and to carry out his ideas with such skill and energy that success was inevitable. . . ."[31]

Sidney's decision to become a candidate, however, sharpened the issue within the Fabian Society. "Wallas and I are losing influence because we are suspected of too much attachment to the Liberal Party," he wrote to Beatrice in November, "just at the moment, by the way, when we are becoming less attached to them."[32] Two days after he was selected for Deptford there was a row. "The younger, impatient element in the Society has risen up in rebellion," he reported, "& wants to throw the whole movement entirely in the Labour Party." The pretext for disagreement was "a supposed small action of mine, which I did not do & which has nothing to do with the real issue."[33] A truculent member named J. F. Runciman, who was always suspecting the Society's leaders of backsliding and corrupt self-interest, had taken it into his head that Webb was trying to protect the A.B.C. catering chain from accusations of sweating its employees, and he linked this ludicrous allegation to the more general charge that Webb was "selling us into the hateful bondage of the Liberal Party." Sidney tried to calm things down, writing to Pease to urge that they "keep the Fabian Society, at least, free from the ordinary revolutionary failing of suspecting each other of improper motives for any act of which we do not happen to approve."[34] But, as he told Beatrice at the same time, the uproar suggested that he had "lost the confidence of a certain section of the younger members by entering upon public life as a candidate!" He had been given a bad reception: Hubert Bland and John Burns had "made bitter and malicious speeches on the other side."[35]

Sidney spent most of his energies in the first months of 1892 on making sure of his seat in Deptford. He won handsomely. On 6 March he wrote enthusiastically to Wallas:

> The result was not declared until after 1 a. m. I made a little speech etc. and then was lifted shoulder high by an excited mob, carried downstairs to the imminent risk of scraping the ceilings with my nose, and so out into the road amid a fearful uproar. I picked up Galton and took refuge in a hansom, leaving a howling mob parading New Cross Road. . . . I was *delighted* with the general results else-where. It is simply a gorgeous justification of Fabian electioneering and ought to do something to convince the provincials that our game is the right one. . . . I felt inclined to go round by Cannon Street in order, like Jack Cade, to smite London Stone with my um-brella, and shout into the night, "Now is Mortimer Lord of London." But I went round by the Central Telegraph Office instead![36]

The victory was personally important to Sidney, and the "gorgeous jus-tification" of his tactics was a valuable argument for his point of view in the Society, though the election of six Fabians out of a total of 118 coun-cillors was scarcely a sensational success—especially when they had all been elected on the Progressive ticket, and four other labour men had been returned who had no links with the Fabians.

The Fabians had at last made a practical commitment to the alliance with the Radicals that had been implicit in Webb's attitude for more than ten years. When he produced the London Programme in the au-tumn of 1891 *The Speaker* noted: "Mr Webb writes more as a Radical than as a Fabian and, except on one subject . . . every reform he advo-cates is certainly included in the programme of every Liberal and Radi-cal in London."[37] Part of the Fabians' case, indeed, was the fact that their proposals were not novel: they were seeking to give London municipal progress of the kind already widely accepted in Britain—publicly owned tramways, gas, water and electricity supplies, fair wages for public em-ployees, control of street markets, measures for improved health and housing. All through the Eighties, parliamentary committees and other enquiries had turned out so much detail on the social problems of Britain's towns that there was no dearth of material for reformers. It was upon these sources that Sidney Webb and other Fabians drew heavily for Fabian publications such as *Facts for Londoners*. They saw better government as being as much a matter for informed experts as for political partisans, believing that good evidence would lead to good policies; Webb's own comment on the London Programme was that it set out "to ignore the political differences between Liberals and Conservatives and appeal for the support of all good citizens."[38] What the Fabians did in the period before the 1892 elections was to produce a series of propaganda leaflets, each elaborating a single theme from the London Programme, which were distributed in such numbers that they contributed significantly to the Progressives' victory.

The Fabians, in short, did not "capture" either the Progressives or the London County Council: they simply joined them. The only significant division between the Fabians and the bulk of the Progressives was one of long-term intentions, not of practical issues. For some of the Fabians, at least, reforms were instalments of the general movement of society towards collectivism, while for the Progressives they were simply measures that were desirable on their own merits. In the early Nineties, the left-wing Liberals had no hesitation in accepting allies who were able to conduct effective propaganda and attract votes from workingmen who might otherwise turn towards less amenable socialist groups.

Sidney was delighted by the recognition that came with his success and by the opportunities to use his talents as a committee man to shape up policies for the County Council. "Really this L.C.C. election has gone far to redeem our marriage in the eyes of your family," he cockily reminded Beatrice; "they think I am more of a personage than they supposed."[39] He was invited to meet several members of the family during those months—the Hobhouses, Courtneys, Cripps and Playnes. While he found them pleasant enough, he rather patronizingly dismissed these Potter sisters and their prosperous husbands as decent people who had no awareness of the problem of poverty and lacked "the logic & the intellectual atmosphere" which Beatrice brought to everything. Beatrice, in turn, met his family—his father had died in the previous summer—and sketched "the little mother, frail and shaking with palsy . . . the energetic, warm-hearted plain body of a sister" and "the dingy and crowded little work room with gas fire where Sidney and I sit the evening through."[40]

It was a busy summer, and they were both content at last—"full of love & work & life," Sidney said in May. Beatrice confessed that she had never hoped for such happiness.[41] After the London County Council elections, to give Beatrice a chance to recover from severe influenza, they spent a few days at Arundel in Sussex with Wallas and "the light-hearted Bernard Shaw," as Beatrice called him—a foursome which soon became customary for the country weekends which were a combination of healthy exercise, talk and the correction of books, tracts and articles. In May Sidney was elected as chairman of the Technical Education Committee of the Council. An apparently dull post, as public education began to expand it put him in a key position to influence its development. He was pleased to report to Beatrice that the Liberal magnate Lord Rosebery, the chairman of the Council, "was evidently astonished & rather cast about for an old member" in place of the Fabian parvenu.[42]

The Fabians who believed in permeating the Liberal organization had not found it difficult to make headway in London, and most of them did a respectable stint of lecturing to any club that wanted a speaker. They also had hopes of employing the same tactics in national politics, for in 1889 and 1890 the National Liberal Federation passed resolutions which were very close to the position of the London Radicals. At their New-castle conference in 1891 the Liberals adopted a platform of social re-form, Gladstone delivering a keynote speech which was quite different from his old style. He hinted at limiting hours of work, at providing payment for MP's, even at curbing the powers of the House of Lords. He proposed to make employers liable for accidents to their workers, to disestablish the Church in Wales and Scotland and to set up district and parish councils.

This programme went a long way beyond the traditional *laissez-faire* attitude of the Liberals to social problems. Shaw claimed that it was drafted by Webb and foisted on the Liberals by a manoeuvre in which he played a devious role. Pease too insisted that the Newcastle Pro-gramme was the result of Fabian efforts. In fact the Fabian influence was not so great as they euphorically suggested. Though Webb and half a dozen other Fabians went to Newcastle in October, they did not speak; and the policy adopted there was devised and carried by the more influ-ential Radical wing of the party.

What Webb really wanted was an agreement by the Liberals to

withdraw up to fifty official candidates in working-class constituencies and allow labour men to run in their place—in effect a Liberal-labour alliance which would put a significant group of workingmen into Parliament. Such a deal would have strengthened the Radical elements in the Liberal Party in Parliament. It would have more than met the case of the "opposition" Fabians and other socialists who felt the time had come to secure direct representation of labour in the House of Commons. And it would have achieved both objectives without rousing the antagonism of the Liberals or running the risk of humiliating failure involved in running labour or socialist candidates against them.

The Liberal managers avoided the issue. They pointed out that their candidates were chosen by autonomous associations in each seat and that some of these local caucuses might adopt workingmen, as had happened in the past. Since most caucuses were controlled by the middle classes and depended on wealthy supporters for their funds, it was actually unlikely that many would choose labour men. It was a lost opportunity for the Liberals. Webb's plan would have given them a chance, at a time when their political future plainly depended upon their ability to attract the growing artisan vote, to attach the movement for labour representation to their party. Their reluctance put Webb and other Fabians who supported permeation in a difficult position. There was bound to be a general election in 1892—Parliament was by then six years old—and the Fabians had to decide where they stood. While Webb and Wallas could argue that the Newcastle Programme was as good for the nation as the London Programme had been for the metropolis, a substantial part of the Society's membership wanted to run its own candidates or to support labour men who were running independently and against Liberal nominees.

This demand was strongly voiced at the meeting in London on 6 and 7 February 1892, when, for the first time, the Fabians held an annual conference. Only half the thirty local societies sent delegates, but there were enough to join forces with the London members who opposed Webb's policy of permeation. On the first evening the delegates were treated to Shaw's brilliant but perverse account of the Society's origins and the reasons why it was superior to the SDF—a virtuoso performance in hyperbole which made discussion impossible. There was no reason why the Society should not run candidates, he said, or support labour men when they had a chance of winning—as John Burns had done

in Battersea. But, he added, "the moment you go to the poll, all concealment is at an end."[43] While a socialist party must eventually emerge, premature electoral adventures would only reduce the bargaining power
of collectivists. Shaw, after temporizing with the Bland faction for more
than two years, had decided that Webb was right and that what he
called "the permeation racket" must be given a chance.

Though Webb thought that an independent labour party in the
Commons would end with the degrading practice of selling its votes like
the Irish, and that Fabians should consider the welfare of the whole
community, he had to make concessions at the conference. He found it
necessary to second a motion, passed unanimously, which declared that
"the best way forward for the labour cause" was "by the workers acting
independently of both political parties" and wishing hearty success to
the movement for "an independent labour party." At the same time
there was substantial backing for an "absolutist" resolution calling for the
expulsion of any Fabian who held an official position in the conventional
parties.

From this hotchpotch of views the Fabians had to extract an election
policy, and Shaw was given the job of drafting a manifesto. He managed
to ridicule both the Liberals and the Tories, pointing out that there was
no reason why the working class should not have its own party if it
cared as much about politics as it did about horse racing. "Whilst our
backers at the polls are counted by tens, we must continue to drawl and
drudge and lecture as best we can," Shaw had told the Fabian conference. "When they are counted by hundreds we can permeate and trim
and compromise. When they rise to tens of thousands we shall take the
field as an independent party." He managed to put a braver face on
things with the clever prose of the manifesto, but it came to much the
same conclusion: for the present, vote for the better man against the
worse, since a small step forward was better than nothing. Webb was
equally anxious about propagandist contests which only demonstrated
the weakness of the socialist vote. "I have no intention of becoming a
candidate *anywhere* for the General Election this time," he wrote on 6
May to W. S. De Mattos, who was looking after Fabian lectures in the
provinces. "For heaven's sake don't let us have a crop of Labour candidates springing up, who, like the S.D.F. men, cannot possibly go to the
poll for lack of funds."[44] The gibe at the SDF was apposite: its plans to
run a dozen candidates had just collapsed because Hyndman had lost a
good deal of money in the Baring bank failure.

If the Fabians were divided in their political policy and election tactics, the Liberals were in graver difficulties. They were on the eve of a general election which would probably return them to office. Gladstone was by now over eighty but still in control of a party which was changing as the nation was changing. Not only was he revolted by collectivism and socialism; fundamentally he still believed in the *laissez-faire* view that social problems were not really the concern of government. Power in the party was moving into the hands of young Radicals who lacked self-confidence and were uncertain in their policies. Parnell died in June 1891, leaving his Irish group divided and leaderless. Gladstone was desperately trying to hold these disparate groups together and at the same time making a bid for the growing artisan and lower-middle-class electorate which wanted reform. No wonder Beatrice felt that, with Chamberlain on one side and socialists on the other, the official Liberals were between the devil and the deep blue sea. Queen Victoria was angry, appalled at the ludicrous "idea of a deluded excited man of 82 trying to govern England and her vast Empire with the miserable democrats under him . . . It is like a bad joke!"[45]

It was, nevertheless, a joke in earnest, for the tide was turning towards the Liberals. Parliament was dissolved on 29 June, and the Fabians threw themselves into the campaign. Sidney thought that the best the Fabians could do was to take advantage of the swing against the Tories. He told Beatrice:

> We are sending out from the Fabian Society our Manifesto & "Questions" all over the place and stirring up our members to *educate* as much as possible during the campaign, saying that we are not so much concerned with the actual result   Everywhere they are heckling candidates, selling tracts, flooding the meetings with leaflets & generally running an "unauthorised programme" with excellent educational effect . . . it is evidently our proper policy—to educate the constituencies without upsetting the coach by running Labour candidates.[46]

There was, however, some independent political action. A number of "labour" men ran at the election, and seven of them were members of the Society. One of these, and the only Fabian to be elected, was Keir Hardie, who was running in the dreary wastes of West Ham, backed by the gasworkers whom Will Thorne had organized in the Beckton strikes. He, like John Burns, who had come to an arrangement with the Liberals in Battersea and won the seat, had been given a straight fight against the

Tory. Hardie, however, did not get a formal endorsement from the Fabians. "My estimate of K.H.," Shaw wrote to Webb on 12 August, "is that he is a Scotchman with alternate intervals of second sight (during which he does not see anything, but is suffused with afflatus) and common incapacity." In West Bradford, however, Ben Tillett was helped with Fabian money and speakers, including Shaw and Webb, this action "serving nicely," Sidney said, "to emphasise our independence from the Liberals."[47] A recent strike in Bradford had led to the creation of a powerful labour union with hundreds of members; this helped Ben Tillett to do well against both a Liberal and a Conservative. The situation was further confused by the appearance of five Scottish labour candidates and the return of Champion—still suspected of taking Tory money—from a long visit to Australia. Running himself in Aberdeen, Champion also put up a hundred pounds apiece for Hardie, Burns and two other labour men in London. There was no sort of national policy. Even among themselves the Fabians made no pretence at consistency. Webb and Shaw actually backed the Liberal John Morley in Newcastle against a labour candidate because they thought the latter likely to split the vote and let the Tory in at the expense of the "progressive" Morley.

The muddle about tactics which had bothered the Society all the previous year had simply spilled over into a chaotic and indecisive intervention which damaged the Society's reputation among socialists. While the Fabians wavered and debated, the initiative was rapidly passing to the "provincials" whom Webb disparaged and the agitators whom Shaw distrusted. The elitism of the London Fabians was putting them out of touch with the emerging realities of labour politics. The election of 1892, in which three labour men were returned and others polled well, showed that they might be left on one side by the new movement.

This did not greatly worry Webb, who was much more interested in the Liberals and the prospect of influencing the holders of power. The Liberals came back with 273 seats, making them dependent on the 81 Irish members to maintain a majority over the 269 Conservatives and Chamberlain's group of 46 Liberal Unionists. Sidney told Beatrice that this narrow majority would "deliver them into our hands."[48] Pease, who had been out of things with illness for much of the year, was equally satisfied, regarding this result "as a justification for the Fabian policy of social advance."[49] It was now quite clear that at least one section of the Fabian leadership—Webb, Pease, Wallas and Shaw—thought more of influencing the new Liberal government than of helping to bring a new party of labour into being.

The election excitement over, Sidney turned his attention to his private concerns. He and Beatrice were married on the morning of Saturday 23 July in the vestry hall at St. Pancras. It was, Kate Courtney noted, "a prosaic, almost sordid ceremony—our civil marriages are not conducted with much dignity & seem rather to suggest a certain shadiness in the contracting parties. But Bee looked good—serious & handsome, the breakfast given by the Holts at the Euston Railway Hotel went off very well."[50]

"The only thing I regret," Beatrice told Sidney, "is parting with my name. I do resent that." She emphasized the point in her diary on her wedding day: "Exit Beatrice Potter. Enter Beatrice Webb, or rather (Mrs) Sidney Webb for I lose, alas, both names."[51]

11

THE QUINTESSENCE OF SHAW

"My novels are Magnificent, but they are not business," Shaw wrote at the end of 1887 to Swan Sonnenschein, the publisher of *The Unsocial Socialist*.[1] A year later when Fisher Unwin asked Shaw to do a novel for him he got a flat rejection: "I have no longer either time or inclination for tomfooling over novels. Five failures are enough to satisfy my appetite for enterprise in fiction." Sonnenschein, who thought Shaw's book "as clever a novel as we have brought out," could see from the dialogue that Shaw had promise and suggested that he should "go in for plays (which are even more suited to you in my opinion)." Shaw saw plays as a last resort. When Jim Joynes once asked him why he did not turn his talent for talk to the stage, he replied: "I may sink as low as that one day."[2]

He had first tried his hand at playwriting in 1886 when his friend William Archer, the dramatic critic, proposed a partnership—Archer to provide the plot, Shaw the dialogue. Archer produced, Shaw said, "the scheme of a twaddling cup-and-saucer comedy" in which the hero was to propose to the daughter of a slum landlord in the belief that she was the poor niece and end by "throwing the tainted treasure of his father-in-law, metaphysically, into the Rhine." He gave the piece the appropriate title *Rhinegold*. Archer assumed that this act of renunciation would be the climax of the play, expressing, in accord with current theatrical convention, the triumph of virtue over corruption. When Shaw read Archer the first two acts, he noted in his diary, "a long argument ensued, Archer having received it with contempt." He told Archer on 4 October 1887: "I think the story would bear four acts but I have no idea of how it is to proceed. . . . Will you proceed either to chuck in the remaining acts, or provide me with a skeleton for them?"[3] This, said Archer, was "like asking a sculptor to add a few more arms and legs to a statue which was already provided with its full complement." Their difference was more than a mere matter of quantity: Shaw had reversed the point of the play. The hero turns from an idealist into a cynic, taking the bride and the money. "You will perceive that my genius has brought the romantic notion which possessed you into vivid contact with real life," he explained to Archer. That was too much for Archer, who believed that a play "which opens the slightest intellectual, moral, or political question is bound to fail." The public, he argued, "will accept open vice, but it will have nothing to do with a moral problem."[4]

Archer was right about the current standards of the London theatre. Materially it was flourishing: there were sixty-one theatres and thirty-nine music halls in the capital; with the arrival of electric lighting and new stage techniques a modern London theatre was capable of handling sophisticated and sometimes astonishingly spectacular productions. Intellectually, however, the London stage was stuffy and sterile, dominated by a clique of managers, actors and writers who wanted neither realism nor satire. Their taste ran to boulevard comedies, contrived romances and melodrama; and behind them stood the minatory figure of the Licencer of Plays to ensure that the proprieties were observed in the plot and in the language. The best that could be done for an advanced play was a private reading or a single production at a matinée. There was certainly no money to be made by breaking the rules. In 1886 the playwright Henry Arthur Jones stated plainly: "there is no drama that even pretends to picture modern English life; I might also say that pretends to picture human life at all."

Shaw's partnership with Archer clearly was not going to work. When Ibsen and Strindberg could not reach the public in London with plays that were already well known in European theatres it was unlikely that the unknown Shaw would find an opening. There was not a manager in London who would encourage him in his plan to lay "violent hands" on Archer's romantic plot and to convert it into a "grotesquely realistic exposure of slum-landlordism, municipal jobbery, and the pecuniary and matrimonial ties between it and the pleasant people of 'independent' incomes who imagine that such sordid matters do not touch their lives."[5]

Shaw was now in his middle thirties and settled into a routine of living that seemed unlikely to change. "My hours that make my days, my days that make my years," he wrote, "follow one another pell mell into the maw of Socialism."[6] On 7 June 1889, however, there was a dramatic event which marked a turning point both in Shaw's own life and in the evolution of the British theatre. Ibsen's play *A Doll's House* was put on at the Novelty Theatre, with Janet Achurch playing Nora and her husband Charles Charrington as Dr. Rank. It was an immediate success. Shaw was already familiar with the play. He had taken the part of Krogstad in the private reading organized by Eleanor Marx, and on his first trip to the Continent, in April 1889, he had seen it produced in Amsterdam. William Archer was also an Ibsen enthusiast and he had translated the version produced at the Novelty. Feeling that, as the translator, he should not review the play himself for the *Manchester Guardian*, Archer asked Shaw to write the notice. Shaw was so impressed by the play that he went back twice to see it.

The play's impact was memorable, especially on the women who belonged to advanced movements. Thirty years later Edith Lees, who had met and married Havelock Ellis in the Fellowship of the New Life, recalled the first night when "a few of us collected outside the theatre breathless with excitement. Olive Schreiner was there and Dolly Radford, the poetess, . . . Emma Brooke . . . and Eleanor Marx. We were restive and almost savage in our arguments. What did it mean? . . . Was it life or death for women? . . . Was it joy or sorrow for men? That a woman should demand her own emancipation and leave her husband and children in order to get it, savoured less of sacrifice than sorcery."[7]

On Sunday 16 June there was a celebration dinner at the theatre for the cast and friends, and Shaw sat next to Janet Achurch. He immediately struck one of his flirtatious postures and, with his usual knack of instructing others in their craft, proceeded to tell her how to act. He was, he wrote to her next day, "suddenly magnetised, irradiated, transported, fired, rejuvenated, bewitched by a wild and glorious young woman." Shaw was attracted both by Janet Achurch herself and by the role she played. Nora was a rebel against a parasitic domestic life, subverting the conventions and proving that life could be fundamentally changed by an act of will. For Shaw this situation had special personal meaning: he had identified with a mother who had also repudiated her duty to her husband and children in order to emancipate herself.

It had taken nearly twenty years for Ibsen to break through the prejudices of Victorian England. As early as 1871 Edmund Gosse had noticed *Peer Gynt* in *The Spectator*, but no play of Ibsen had a commercial production until 1884. Even then it was a bowdlerized version of *A Doll's House* to which Henry Arthur Jones had given a happy ending and the sentimental title *Breaking a Butterfly*. It was William Archer who did most to promote Ibsen. He had relatives in Norway and read Ibsen's works when they appeared. In 1880 his translation of *The Pillars of Society* was given one matinee performance at the Gaiety Theatre. Even with the success of *A Doll's House* in 1889 most of the critics maintained their suspicion and hostility. Shaw was not deterred by their antagonism. Seeing Ibsen as a kindred spirit, he could identify with him and gain confidence in his own ambitions. The success of *A Doll's House* now stimulated him afresh to write a play himself, and he tried again to make something of the play he had cast aside. "Sometimes in spare moments I write dialogues," he wrote on 31 August 1889, "and these are all working up to a certain end (a sermon, of course) my imagination playing the usual tricks meanwhile of creating imaginary persons &c. When I have a few hundred of these dialogues worked up and interlocked, then a drama will be the result—a moral, instructive, suggestive comedy of modern society, guaranteed in philosophic & economic detail and unactably independent of theatrical consideration." In November he was still at it: "Wrote dialogue in the train," he noted in his diary, and again: "Writing under a lamp-post."

Shaw later liked to disclaim Ibsen's influence at this crucial period of his life. Such of his ideas as were attributed to Ibsen, he insisted, were actually "hammered out by British Socialists long before the London Press began to chatter about them," and their "novelty and blasphemy" had been "a platitude among live thinkers for the past thirty years."[8] In 1890, however, he was as eager as anyone to promote Ibsen. He could let his own ideas ride on the wave of Ibsen's popularity. When the Fabian Society was casting about for a series of summer lectures, the executive

planned a series on "Socialism and Contemporary Literature." There was
a paper from Olivier on Zola, another from Morris on Gothic architecture, one from Stepniak on the modern Russians, and an amusing disquisition on socialist novels by Hubert Bland. The contribution from
Shaw, afterwards worked up into a Fabian tract as *The Quintessence
of Ibsenism*, was given on 18 July 1890 at the St. James's Restaurant,
with Annie Besant in the chair. The lecture, it was reported, was
"couched in provocative terms," and it produced a lively debate. Bland
was critical of Shaw's apparent justification of license, and Sidney Webb
was bothered by it. "It is very clever," he wrote to Beatrice after the
talk, "and not so bad as I feared—his glorification of the Individual Will
distresses me."[9]

The talk also produced an unexpected response from Ibsen himself.
Shaw had presented him as though he were an honorary member of the
Fabian Society. A journalist who reported the lecture to Ibsen secured
a rebuttal of Shaw's attempt to nobble him as a reformer which was
published in the *Daily Chronicle* on 13 August. Two weeks later the
newspaper quoted a more cautious letter from him. "I am surprised," Ibsen wrote, "that I, who had made it my chief life task to depict human
characters and human destinies, should, without conscious or direct intention, have arrived in several matters at the same conclusions the social
democratic moral philosophers had arrived at by scientific processes."
That was good enough for Shaw to feel vindicated, although Archer
went on defending Ibsen against the "grave injustice" of those English
admirers of Ibsen, like Shaw, who set Ibsen up as a social prophet; Archer insisted that Ibsen had "no gospel whatever, in the sense of a systematic body of doctrine."[10] That was not the reaction of the radical
bohemians who packed the theatre for *A Doll's House* and responded to
Shaw's lecture. For them Ibsen's attack on dogmatism and the bourgeois
conventions showed how society could be undermined from a relativist
standpoint. The liberating impact of that demonstration against established values was far more significant than the fact that Ibsen did not
positively advocate any body of reform.

Once Shaw had taken to the world of the stage in which to perform his
favourite part of character lead or eccentric, his philandering aspirations
turned towards leading ladies. Brought up in a context of opera and

drama, and with a natural instinct to produce situations in real life on theatrical models, he already treated his comrades in the socialist movement as the stock parts of theatrical convention.

The impulsive attachment to Janet Achurch was thwarted by her departure for Australia, where she and Charrington now took *A Doll's House*. By early October 1890, however, Shaw had found a new Ibsen heroine, a thirty-year-old aspirant actress named Florence Farr. He met her through May Morris, who was teaching her embroidery; after encounters at the Arts-and-Crafts private view at Merton Abbey, where Morris had his workshops, and at a soirée of the Hammersmith Socialist Society, Shaw soon carried her off to a Crystal Palace concert. W. B. Yeats described her as a woman with "three great gifts, a tranquil beauty, an incomparable sense of rhythm and a beautiful voice." Her intellectual style resembled that of Shaw. "She spoke of actual things with a cold wit or under the strain of paradox," Yeats wrote. "Wit and paradox alike sought to pull down whatever had tradition or passion." Shaw was at once attracted, and he met her often that autumn; the meetings were a new source of jealousy for Jenny Patterson. Shaw once told Janet Achurch that he could coach her into success, but he was even more ambitious for Florence: if she would let him be her mentor, he believed, he could breathe greatness into her.

Florence, who was content to let Shaw flatter her, did not take such blandishments seriously. They were, to her, simply an agreeable variation of the down-to-earth methods of courtship she employed with her would-be suitors. Her marriage to Edward Emery in 1891 was taken lightly. Men fell in love with her very easily, Shaw amusingly recalled; "she would seize the stammering suitor firmly by the wrists, bring him into her arms by a smart pull, and saying 'let's get it over' allow the startled gentleman to have his kiss and then proceed to converse with him at her ease on subjects of more general interest."[11] Forwardness of this kind certainly appealed to Shaw, who still found it very difficult to move from extremes of verbal flirtation even to modest forms of physical contact. He was soon a regular caller at her lodgings at Brook Green near Bedford Park, a garden suburb in West London much favoured by devotees of the arts-and-crafts movement. In the early months of 1891, while Jenny Patterson was away on a vacation in the Near East, the relationship flourished. On 30 March 1891 Shaw wrote to Charrington: "I am in love with Miss Farr."

He had already found a role for her. *Rosmersholm* has a tragic heroine, Rebecca West, one of the most difficult parts that Ibsen ever wrote for an actress. Shaw encouraged Florence to play it. "We were playing, singing," he noted in his diary on 11 February, "trying on *Rosmersholm* dresses, going over the part." The play came off for two performances at the Vaudeville Theatre on 23 February. At the same time Aveling gave a paper on *Ghosts* at the Playgoers' Club, and the discussion on Ibsen's ideas at this "assemblage of barloafing front-row-of-the-pit-on-a-first-night dilettanti" was extended. "I attended two nights," Shaw informed Charrington, "and Mrs Aveling and I, being of course seasoned socialist mob orators, were much in the position of a pair of terriers dropped into a pit of rats."[12]

The Ibsen campaign, so tardily begun, was now in full spate. Archer wrote an article in the *Fortnightly Review* asking for private funds to endow a national theatre. This idea caught the imagination of a young Dutch journalist, Jacob Thomas Grein, who published an art magazine in London, worked as a tea merchant in Mincing Lane and acted as the consul of the Congo. His intention was to run a season of new English plays in which "real human emotion should be roused by the presentment of real human life."[13] When no such playwrights came forward, Grein decided to launch his Independent Theatre with *Ghosts*, which was put on for an invited audience at the Royalty Theatre on 13 March. It was, in Shaw's words, "a most terrible success." Clement Scott attacked it bitterly in the *Daily Telegraph* as "an open drain; a loathsome sore unbandaged; a dirty act done in public; a lazar-house with its doors and windows open."

Shaw was delighted that Ibsen served so well to stir up strong feelings. There was nothing he liked better than to shock as a prelude to the presentation of a novel idea. His Easter holiday in 1891 was therefore devoted to the revision of his Fabian lecture for publication. When *The Quintessence of Ibsenism* appeared in October 1891 it was clear that Shaw was using the current interest in Ibsen to elaborate his own philosophy, the similarity being sufficiently close to carry off the substitution without anyone except Archer being really aware of what he had done.

In *The Quintessence of Ibsenism* Shaw insisted that those who accept conventional morality, especially when it conflicts with their own desires and beliefs, are hypocrites. Those who seek to impose it on others, because they think it to be their duty, are immoral. Idealism thus leads to hypocrisy, and duty to tyranny, and both lead to the destruction of human happiness. The only means of escape from these traps is to assert truth against them, however unpleasant and uncomfortable that may be. That assertion was what Shaw meant by an act of will—the way in which a man might free himself from sentiment and social obligation. This, for Shaw, was the essence of heroism. To stand against the crowd for truth as one saw it was a far more moral act than conformity to principle or obedience to duty. Nora, for instance, could not be dismissed as a selfish and undutiful wife. Her repudiation of her husband, children and social responsibilities, at whatever cost, was the unavoidable price of her emancipation.

Plays based on such notions were bound to seem paradoxical and subversive. The conflict in such dramas, Shaw remarked, "is not between right and wrong: the villain is as conscientious as the hero, if not more so: in fact, the question which makes the play interesting . . . is which is the villain and which the hero. Or, to put it another way, there are no villains and no heroes." Once Shaw had seized this point, it was easy for him to conjure with paradoxes of a kind hitherto unacceptable on the London stage. Public benefactors could be shown to be thieves, and thieves—if they were honest in Shaw's sense—could turn into public benefactors. Tainted money could be used to do good, cowards could save the day, and preachers turn into braggarts and self-seekers. Such lessons, however, could not be taught in the supposedly "moral" theatre, or even by the novel idea of portraying "real life" on the other side of the footlights. For drama, said Shaw, "is no mere setting up of the camera to nature: it is a presentation in parable of the conflict between Man's will and his environment."[14] The theatre had to be made, in Archer's phrase, into "a house of correction." Shaw recognized that if this was to be achieved it was useless to harangue an audience with new ideas on the same model as the plays which exemplified the current morality. The audience had to feel the force of the parable for itself, to identify with the spiritual crisis of characters who were opposing their wills to the conventions. Nothing could be done by merely substituting one kind of villain or hero for another—making, for example, the capitalist an evil figure and the rebel a saint. For once an audience was convinced that a character was cast in the role of villain, it could relieve its discomfort by making him a scapegoat: it could relax in the knowledge that good of some kind would triumph over evil. What Shaw wanted was to question

all assumptions about good and evil. By making an audience cringe before the failings of an obvious hero and arousing its sympathies for an
apparent scoundrel he proposed to make it aware of the ambivalence of
morals and go home feeling discomforted.

Ever since Shaw arrived in London he had felt his way towards this
position. It lay behind the wit he deployed at Fabian meetings and in his
stump speeches; it had even been present in the first manifesto he drafted
on joining the Fabian Society. It had been developed in so many public
and private arguments and in his novels; it was Ibsen who made him realize its dramatic possibilities. For it was essentially a rationalization of his
own struggle. The effort to develop a distinctive personality as George
Bernard Shaw, in a family which lacked confident give-and-take, demanded the continuous assertion of will. He *had* to declare that wilfulness was freedom.

Ibsenism aroused a discussion that went on through 1891 and 1892, and
Shaw gained as much from it as anyone. *The Quintessence of Ibsenism*
had created a stir and he had completed the draft of his first play to
which he gave the new title *Widowers' Houses*. Shaw's opportunity
came when Grein found that he could not find any English plays for the
Independent Theatre. Shaw offered him his play and Grein accepted it
before he had read it—a tribute to Shaw's personality and growing reputation as a controversialist.

The first of the play's two performances was at the Royalty Theatre on 9 December 1892; the volunteer cast included Florence Farr as
Blanche. Shaw's first night, with an audience filled with friends and sympathizers as well as critics, was a lively affair. When the curtain fell he
came out front "amid transcendent hooting & retired amid cheers"; unable to resist such an opportunity to speak, he delivered a witty oration
which drew the political moral of the play. One newspaper, in fact,
reported that he had given a lecture on socialism at the Royalty Theatre
and added that it "was preceded by a play called *Widower's Houses*."
The jest was not far from the point. As Shaw wrote to Charrington a
few days afterwards, "I have proved myself a man to be reckoned with"
because "I have got the blue book across the footlights."[15]

Lowes Dickinson remembered that there was a great deal of noise
and hissing. He thought the play was effective as a socialist tract but "as

a play miserably dreary and unconvincing, all the personages unintelligible and repulsive caricatures, and even the dialogue not very clever."[16] William Archer, still convinced that Shaw had "no special ability and some constitutional disabilities" as a dramatist, claimed that the play was "a curious example of what can be done in art by sheer brain-power, apart from natural aptitude."[17] There was an outrageous puff in *The Star*, probably written by Shaw himself, but other press notices were not very favourable. Shaw did not greatly mind. What mattered to him at that point was the fact that the play had been noticed at all.

Rhinegold had been greatly changed. The parable about the guilt of riches had been developed into a dramatic exposition of the facts about slum landlordism revealed in the 1885 report of the Royal Commission on the Housing of the Working Classes. Harry Trench, a young man of liberal opinions, is genuinely shocked to learn that Sartorius, his future father-in-law, has made his money from the rents of the squalid rookeries of the poor. He then discovers that his own apparently respectable income comes from the same source. All money is tainted in a capitalist society. His sentimental illusions destroyed, Trench becomes a cynic, pockets his conscience, comes to terms with Sartorius, and takes both his money and his daughter.

The reversal of Trench's values was logically necessary to make Shaw's point that the moral pretensions of a capitalist society based on robbing the poor were simply hypocrisy. With such logic Shaw could not treat his characters as persons following their natural bent; nor could he let his plot follow a normal and credible course. The characters and the situation had to be controlled to achieve his didactic ends. *Widowers' Houses*, Shaw claimed, was "deliberately intended to induce people to vote on the Progressive side at the next County Council elections in London." The joke was serious. Shaw intended "to bring a conviction of sin—to make the Pharisee . . . recognise that Sartorius is his own photograph."[18] That was Shaw's truth as an evangelist, and it led him to devise a new kind of morality play which transferred his sermons from the stump to the stage. "I had not achieved a success," he later observed, "but I had provoked an uproar and the sensation was so agreeable that I resolved to try again."[19]

~~ PART THREE ~~

PROPHETS
AND
PERMEATORS

12

ENTHUSIASTS

"Mr Shaw's position is one of pure, unadulterated individualism," wrote one of his fellow Fabians in *Seed-Time*, the magazine which the still-surviving Fellowship of the New Life began to issue in July 1889.[1] Arguing that Shaw's exposition of Ibsen showed him to be "a mere rebel against all existing authorities," the article ridiculed his claim to be a socialist in anything but an economic sense. His attitude to moral issues, it insisted, was too selfish. This critic, harking back to the relation between morals and politics on which the Fellowship and the Fabians amiably agreed to differ in 1884, reminded the Society of that implicit division. As long as it "confines itself to politics and economics it is doing admirable work," the article added. "When it trenches on ultimate questions of ethics and philosophy, it is not only acting *ultra vires* (according to its own rules), but it is precipitating problems in which there are vital differences between its members."

The Fabian Society had managed to avoid awkward problems which tantalized more doctrinally inclined socialists by refusing to take a position on matters of marriage, religion, art and literature. This policy protected the Society from internal differences which had nothing to do with its political business. It also helped the Fellowship to continue to play its own special role. Most of its members were still Fabians. Yet its

emphasis was different. It met a psychic need to change society by withdrawing from it, encapsulating utopian idealism rather than reforming
zeal. If society was to be changed, that change must begin with individuals rather than with institutions. J. F. Oakeshott, a leader of the Fellowship and a member of the Fabian executive, expressed the Fellowship's
view "that the existing social conditions were only what might be expected from the low moral ideas which governed the lives of the mass
of the people."[2] With such beliefs, which eventually led some members
of the Fellowship into Tolstoyan communities and away from a direct
involvement in politics, it was bound to remain small.

The doctrine of the Simple Life which was preached by the Fellowship was directed at the conspicuous and corrupting waste of middle-
class life in Victorian England. "The simplification which we preach,"
Thomas Davidson wrote in *Seed-Time*, "does not involve of necessity
the abandonment of any product of civilisation which is worth the keeping; it necessitates only the abandonment of that superfluous luxury, that
multitudinous collection of needless trifles, that congestion of meaningless literature, of wearisome ornaments, . . . [of] useless servants, of
toilsome calls, condolences, congratulations, Xmas cards, and crinkum-
crankum in general, which feed neither the body nor the soul."[3]

William Morris was making a similar attack on commercial bric-a-
brac. Members of the Fellowship also shared Morris' conviction that
manual labour had a redeeming power, but, under the influence of Edward Carpenter and Henry Salt, they went much further than Morris
in their attempt to return to a more "natural" way of life. They organized "rustic gatherings"; they were vegetarians, dress reformers, amateur
craftsmen, and naturalists. It was such enthusiasm which attracted Shaw
to Salt and his circle, despite his scepticism about their philosophic pretensions. Civilization, Carpenter continually insisted, was akin to a disease, which meant a loss of wholeness.[4]

Members of the Fellowship were, for the most part, educated
lower-middle-class people earning a humdrum living as clerks, teachers
and journalists. A few had small businesses or some private means. Ethical aspirations, coloured by touches of esoteric religions, compensated
for their professional dissatisfactions and insecurity. The Fellowship was
a place where they could find a niche for themselves and at the same
time express their protest at the values of bourgeois society. Most of
them had a distaste for politics, preferring to seek the rewards of
"spiritual love," a much used phrase in the Fellowship which often

served to describe the inhibited relations between individuals with sexual repressions or homosexual inclinations. Havelock Ellis and Carpenter both wrote extensively on the theme of sexual liberation, and round the fringe of the ethical socialists there was always an element of sexual eccentricity.

Chubb had argued in 1883 that spiritual or fraternal love could best flourish in an environment where men and women lived in harmony rather than competition, and the idea of a separate community had long been discussed. One of the difficulties, as a New Lifer pointed out, was that despite their intellectual enthusiasm for manual labour the comrades were not well equipped to support themselves. The men were bad enough, but the women did not "care to use their hands for something more tangible than guitar strings or Fabian pamphlets."[5] Yet the notion of a self-governing, self-supporting commune persisted, and the Fellowship decided to take over a house at 29 Doughty Street in Bloomsbury as an experiment. Among those who tried to put their ideals into practice were Edith Lees, Emma Brooke, Havelock Ellis and James Ramsay MacDonald. It was not a success. "Fellowship is Hell," Edith Lees later sourly concluded.[6] If brotherhood was not so easily achieved, aspirations to self-sufficiency remained. Writing in *Seed-Time*, Henry Binns insisted that New Lifers should learn spinning and weaving, woodwork and smithing, leatherwork, bricklaying, pottery and basketmaking. "How great," he exclaimed at this vision of a future such as Morris had described in *News from Nowhere*, "to be able to do all one needed with one's own hands!"[7]

In 1891 Edith Lees resigned as secretary of the Fellowship when she married Havelock Ellis, and her place was taken by James Ramsay MacDonald.[8] He was twenty-five years old at that time and although he had been in London for five years he was still trying to find the right place for himself. He had had an unpromising start as the illegitimate son of a housekeeper and a ploughman and had been brought up by his grandmother at Lossiemouth in northeast Scotland. He was a spoilt and jealous child, and a combination of intelligence and a sense of superiority made him ambitious and restless. He was a keen student, reading Dickens, Robert Burns and Shakespeare; when he read George's *Progress and Poverty* his political interest was aroused.

The little town of Lossiemouth did not offer much scope for Mac-

Donald's ambitions and before he was twenty he went to Bristol to become secretary to a Young Man's Guild. He soon made contact with
the local SDF group, to whom Edward Carpenter had given five pounds
to set up a library. MacDonald became the librarian, organizing the sale
of *Justice* and other socialist publications. The little group of Bristol
socialists met in a workmen's café, and MacDonald remembered the
mood of its meetings. "We had all the enthusiasm of the early Christians in those days," he wrote. "We were few and the gospel was new.
The second coming was at hand."[9]

MacDonald did not stay long in Bristol—his employer disapproved
of his opinions—and he soon drifted to London, where he lived in cheap
lodgings in Kentish Town. Forced into a series of dead-end jobs, he
attended evening classes at the Birkbeck Institute and the City of London College in the hope of winning a scholarship to train as a teacher
at the Normal School in South Kensington. When his health broke down
from poverty and overwork he lost the chance of bettering himself
through formal education. He next found an appointment as secretary to
Thomas Lough, a rising Liberal politician, who paid him seventy-five
pounds a year. He was personable, well read, and gave an impression of
moral aspiration which encouraged people to patronize him, and he soon
had many acquaintances in Radical circles. He was a natural secretary
and before he took on the Fellowship of the New Life he served a turn
with the Scottish Home Rule Association. He also undertook literary
work for the new *Dictionary of National Biography* and was writing
for Liberal papers as well as placing articles in the socialist press.

As MacDonald came to the end of his political apprenticeship he
was potentially in a strong position. He was obviously able, a competent
journalist and a speaker with a fine voice, an excellent presence and a
resonant turn of phrase. He was also willing to work hard at the detail
which kept impoverished societies running. He was seen everywhere in
left-wing politics, making much of his Fabian membership—he joined
the Society in 1886—but taking care to maintain his links with the ethical
societies through the Fellowship. At the same time he avoided anything
which might make him unacceptable to the Radical wing of the Liberals.
By the early Nineties he was sure that he wanted to make a career in
politics. Though he considered himself a socialist, he cultivated his Liberal contacts and attempted to become a Liberal candidate in Southampton. The Fabians offered a convenient base for such activities, for Mac-

Donald strongly supported Webb's policy of permeation and he was regarded by Sidney as one of the Society's coming young men.

MacDonald soon found that the Fellowship's brand of ethical socialism was too crankish for a man with political ambitions. The Fellowship suited faddists such as Henry Salt, a dreamer like Carpenter or an eccentric moralist like Havelock Ellis; it was not much use to a man who wanted to get into Parliament. He discovered that there was a wider audience for socialist speakers who could conjure up a hazy but inspiring vision of a New Jerusalem cleansed of the moral and physical blight of capitalism. MacDonald knew what such people wanted because he was one of them. His particular form of oratory, in which ethical uplift was peppered with evolutionary catch phrases, made a considerable appeal to the self-educated men and women who were beginning to come into the socialist movement, especially in the North and in Scotland. They were idealists, but they were also interested in practical politics; unlike the Fabians, they were uninhibited enthusiasts for labour representation. Morris and Keir Hardie meant more to them than Webb and Wallas. What attracted them to *Fabian Essays* was the moral fervour of the essayists rather than their Jevonian economics.

This new mood among the provincials was a sign that socialism was beginning to break out of its original base in a cluster of small sects into something which was much more like the religious revivals which swept through Britain at intervals in the nineteenth century. It was too late for this latest awakening to take a strictly religious form. Yet the emotional patterns of Victorian faith, even the techniques of propaganda and organization employed in previous attempts at the conversion of England, continued to mould the ways in which the new missionaries worked.

This had been true of the first Fabians, but they had almost all been lapsed Anglicans from Evangelical homes. There was a Christian fringe to the London socialism of the Eighties, but this too was Anglican. The Christian Socialists came together in Stewart Headlam's Guild of St. Matthew and the Land Reform Union; and the more respectable Christian Social Union, formed in 1889—seeking in Fabian style to permeate the Anglican Church—soon attracted more than two thousand clerical members. Dissenting clergymen too began to find a place in the Fabian

Society and the London Progressives, while Unitarian churches and centres like Stanton Coit's Ethical Church provided a meeting place for believers and idealist agnostics. Yet these essentially middle-class organizations, stronger in London than in the provinces, did not appeal to the new recruits in the provinces. The newcomers were predominantly Nonconformists—Congregationalists, Methodists and Baptists. The objection common to all groups, however, was not so much to Christianity as to a social system which—as Keir Hardie continually insisted—preached Christian brotherhood but did not practice it. Socialism was, for all of them, the new Evangelism.

There were, moreover, important differences of class and education between the Fabians and the new provincial leaders. The first Fabians had been educated at good schools and at university; even such exceptions as Bland, Pease and Shaw came from literate, middle-class homes. They belonged to the middle class or identified with it, and as such they emphasized duty and social obligation; their message was essentially directed at their own class, guilty with a sense that they were not fulfilling their responsibilities to the unfortunate. Now in the early Nineties the socialist movement was attracting the self-educated—lay preachers from the dissenting chapels, voracious but undisciplined readers, articulate but rhetorical speakers. Socialism served them as a school as well as a cause; it was as much part of a process of self-improvement as mechanics' institutes and workingmen's clubs. These leaders belonged to the working class or identified with it; their emphasis was not on duty but on rights, not social obligation but social justice. They too spoke to their own class, preaching in a distinctive revivalist vernacular compounded of Biblical phraseology, inspirational poetry and texts from Henry George, Carpenter, Emerson, Whitman and Morris. They were out of sympathy with the political manoeuvres of the London Fabians and the high-minded aesthetics of the Simple Lifers. Working-class men and women concerned about securing a square meal and a good coat were not interested in giving up meat or wearing sandals. The heady rhetoric of these itinerant preachers was a powerful force, creating a sense of fellowship in a quasi-religious cause. It found an immediate response among audiences reared on revivalist preachers.

The life of these peripatetic propagandists was hard, exhausting and financially meagre. If poor men were to take politics seriously they had to get a living of some kind from the movement. John Burns raised a wages fund from his constituents in Battersea; Will Thorne, Ben Tillett and Tom Mann kept themselves going on the low wages they were paid by the trade unions they organized. Keir Hardie and Joe Burgess ran small propagandist papers. Most itinerant speakers maintained themselves with fees out of collections and with free lodgings they were given as they went their rounds.

By 1892 the missionaries had a constituency; it was one they had created for themselves, seeding new organizations as they travelled. Inevitably this group of propagandists came to dominate the movement outside London.

Sidney Webb was well aware of these developments. He was not only antipathetic to the political aspirations of the provincial Fabians but also genuinely worried by their utopian state of mind: enthusiasm could, he realized, easily degenerate into hysteria. In May 1892 he wrote to Katherine St. John Conway, who was becoming one of the most effective speakers in the movement.[10] The daughter of a Congregational minister and a graduate in classics from Newnham College, Kate Conway was the kind of New Woman who was becoming familiar in socialist circles, fusing religion, social justice and female emancipation into an emotional euphoria of the kind that Webb distrusted. He urged her to temper her enthusiasm and be more understanding of the difficulties of "our *well-meaning* opponents." He was, he told her, "persuaded of the need of thorough personal study by all Socialists, of the *facts* of modern industry rather than the aspirations of Socialists. . . . Once we have got our faith we should, I think, do better to spend our nights and days over books like Charles Booth's than over William Morris—who is for the unconverted, not for those who have already found 'salvation.' "

The revivalist temper in the provinces which caused Webb such misgivings continued to gain ground. It found expression in a successful weekly newspaper, the *Clarion*, which had been started by Robert Blatchford. "If Socialism is to live and conquer, it must be a religion," he wrote. "If Socialists are to prove themselves equal to the task assigned to them they must have faith, a real faith, a new faith."[11] He set out to arouse this faith in the industrial districts of the North, taking his texts from the Bible and William Morris and using the popular press as his pulpit to reach the emotions of the poor.

Blatchford combined the inspiration of John Wesley with the blunt style of William Cobbett.[12] Born into a bohemian family of travelling players, he had run away at the age of sixteen and enlisted in the Army. He turned to journalism in the early Eighties, working on the *Manchester Sporting Chronicle* and then the *Sunday Chronicle*.

His first reaction to socialism was hostile. After one of the Trafalgar Square demonstrations he wrote of its "hateful and insane theories" which would lead through blood and fire "to a new Utopia where there shall be neither law, nor Government, nor religion," a "godless, graceless, hopeless Commonwealth, with Hyndman for Protector, Bradlaugh for Bishop, and Kropotkin for the Messiah."[13] But he had a compassionate nature. When he undertook a series of articles on the Manchester slums—which Morris called "the vestibule to Hell"—and began to read Morris, he was converted and joined the Fabian Society.

The *Sunday Chronicle* was politically radical, and for a couple of years Blatchford used it as effectively for socialist propaganda as the London Fabians used *The Star*. His populist style, however, was very different from the solid prose of the London intellectuals. "If I desired to rouse a people," Blatchford said, "the figures I should deal in mostly would be figures of speech. Economics are for the very few; God's love is for the many."[14] And in 1891, after a series of articles by Shaw, Bland, Bradlaugh, Wallas and Hyndman, Blatchford's own contribution clearly revealed the contrast:

> Polly dead of the fever, the old mother counterpaned under the snow, the baby face white in death, the doctor sucking death and diphtheria from the patient's throat, the soldier weltering in his blood, the navvy fuddling his brains with beer, the harlot dying of disease and the frost in the streets of the City of Palaces. What does it all mean? . . . I wonder, and I wonder, Messrs Bradlaugh, Shaw and Wallas, I wonder who is right—and do our efforts matter much—I wonder![15]

Blatchford swung the *Sunday Chronicle* behind the workers in the great strike at the Manningham Mills in Bradford from which came the Bradford Labour Union, and he was asked to run as an independent labour candidate in the town. This was too much for his employer, Edward Hulton, and Blatchford was dismissed. By the end of 1891 he had launched the weekly *Clarion* from Manchester. It was an extraordinary paper, full of moral energy, attacking puritan killjoys as fervently as sweaters, romantic, patriotic, jokey, and without pomposity. Soon it was selling thirty thousand copies. Blatchford had discovered how to write for the people; his paper dealt in "Literature, Politics, Fiction, Philosophy, Theatricals, Pastimes, Criticism, and everything else" without condescension. When Hyndman and Shaw prepared a manifesto during the lockout of coal miners in 1893, Blatchford commented that the colliers would not read it and would not understand it if they did. Socialists, he insisted, must learn to write "horse-sense in tinker's English."[16]

To prove his point Blatchford wrote his own utopia, *Merrie England*, a forceful, simple and enormously effective translation of Morris into everyday speech and imagery. England, for Blatchford, was corrupted by industrialism; it could no longer feed itself, enjoy itself and provide a decent life for its citizens, who lived in squalor and drowned their misery in drink. When he put *Merrie England* out as a shilling booklet, the sales ran away even more surprisingly than had those of *Fabian Essays*. Reprinted at a penny, it sold three quarters of a million copies in a year, and before long over two million had gone out from Manchester. Its readers, the socialist preacher John Trevor said, had been introduced not to a new economic theory but "to a new life. Their eyes shine with the gladness of a new birth."[17]

The millenarian dream of making a new heaven on earth—Blake's vision of Jerusalem among the dark satanic mills—was the bridge between religion and politics for those who listened to Kate Conway or read Blatchford. The new idealism had no orthodoxy. It was, as John Bruce Glasier put it in *The Religion of Socialism*, "an all-sufficing religion of itself" which painted a "picture of a grand and gracious social order, of beautiful streets and gardens—the redemption of life from the multifarious blights of commercialism, moral, mental and physical." Bruce Glasier, like his future wife, Kate Conway, came to socialism through a crisis of faith. He had aspired to be a Presbyterian minister but lost his sense of vocation after reading Darwin and Huxley. By 1892 he had become one of the movement's itinerant missionaries.

This kind of rootlessness was a marked feature of new evangelists like MacDonald, Keir Hardie, Kate Conway, Blatchford and Tom

Mann. The appeal of "fellowship" on which they laid so much stress was a substitute for stable personal relationships, providing a generalized sense of love and evoking kindness and comradeship from local members who entertained them on their travels. Yet there was also a need to create some institutional expression for the new faith. It had to be political, but it also had to be spiritual; and so arose the idea of a Labour Church which John Trevor launched in 1891.

Trevor was an orphan brought up by Calvinist grandparents. "The continual fear of hell," he recalled, gave him a "morbid sense of exile, loneliness and self-suspicion."[18] In 1877, when he was twenty-two, his health and his faith collapsed, and on a visit to America he discovered Emerson. With recovery he became a Unitarian and assisted Philip Wicksteed at the chapel in Upper Brooke Street.[19] Through Wicksteed, Trevor came into contact with socialist ideas, and in October 1891 he set up the first Labour Church in Chorlton Town Hall in Manchester. By the second Sunday, when Blatchford delivered the sermon, the large auditorium was packed and hundreds were turned away.

In January 1892 while Beatrice Webb was in Manchester researching on trade-union archives she met Trevor. She thought him an honest man who lacked intellectual substance. He was, she wrote to Sidney, "an enthusiast and looks it—like all pseudo-religionists there is a false note in his would-be religiosity . . . this Labour Church is love of man masquerading in the well-worn clothes of love of God . . ." She decided it was "Shoddy—& it will not wear."[20] Her reaction again exemplified the gulf between the provincials and the London Fabians. She was herself disposed to religiosity, but the unsophisticated evangelism of Trevor jarred on her intellectually. This democratic Christianity was not an attempt to create a new theology—like Comte's Religion of Humanity—but a simple assertion that socialism was the practical application of Christ's teaching and that salvation was open to anyone, regardless of denomination, who would preach that gospel. Those who had broken away from the rigours of Evangelical Anglicanism found the Nonconformist style of the northern agitators sloppy and sentimental.

It was, nevertheless, a style which spilled over from the chapels to trade unionism and politics; workingmen found it familiar and appealing. In Bradford, after the great strike, a Labour Church was opened in a disused chapel which also served as the headquarters of the local Fabians and the Bradford Labour Union. By 1893 there were twenty-five Labour Churches in the textile towns between Manchester and Bradford, and Trevor had founded his own paper, *The Labour Prophet*, to advance his conviction that "the Religion of the Labour Movement is not a class Religion, but unites members of all classes working for the abolition of commercial slavery." Despite Beatrice's criticism there was an echo of the first aims of the Fabian Society in the declaration of the Labour Church Union that "the development of Personal Character and the improvement of Social Conditions are both essential to man's emancipation from moral and social bondage."

Their assemblies attracted large audiences for Sunday meetings with songs, readings and uplifting addresses. "The Swedenborgians repeated the Lord's Prayer with the Christians," Margaret McMillan recalled about the early days in Bradford. "The Social Democrats did nothing of the kind. The old chapel goers, or some of them, enjoyed the hymns but the secularists did not enjoy them. The lecture was the thing . . . all waited for that. . . . In spite of their differences they did form one real party, united by a single hope."[21] The life of the working classes, she felt, "was no longer a secret or a thing remote or a creation of the imagination." The cause had taken on "a close and thrilling reality."

Just as Margaret McMillan found that she had "friends in the Whitmanites at Bolton, in the Secularists at Leicester, and also in the various spiritualist groups," so Trevor rallied a heterogeneous coterie in Manchester. After a huge May Day demonstration in the city in 1892, he called a meeting attended by seven hundred people to found the Manchester and Salford Independent Labour Party. The president was Blatchford. On the committee, apart from Trevor, there were a former cowboy and itinerant agitator, teetotallers, vegetarians, republicans, Whitmanites and Irish Home Rulers, all dressed in "the rags and tatters of dogma" from Marx, Morris, Darwin, Ruskin, Carlyle and Mill, to say nothing of the New Testament. What held this motley band together was the idea of founding a separate labour party. The constitution of the Salford ILP ran through the usual list of aims, starting with the "nationalisation of land and other instruments of production," but its fourth clause was the most significant. It stated firmly: "All members of this party pledge themselves to abstain from voting for any candidate for election to any representative body who is in any way a nominee of the Liberal, Liberal-Unionist, or Conservative Parties."

This was upsetting to the London Fabians, especially as Blatchford

was president of the local Fabian Society in Manchester. Shaw and
Olivier both wrote to him in protest for giving his influential name to
the new venture. "I live in a country parish where the rights of the cot-
tagers and the privileges of the public in the commons are continually
threatened by the powers of the Lord of the Manor," Olivier wrote. "If
one parliamentary candidate will help and the other hinder . . . that is
another reason why I should work to put the former in and keep the
latter out."[22]

The difference between the London Fabians and the provincials
could not have been put more simply. Blatchford struck back at Shaw
and Olivier, with a sharpness of tone which sprang in part from his dislike of Shaw's "cleverness." It was true, he conceded, that "Socialists, by
sitting under the Liberal table, may pick up crumbs," but he insisted that
they would never become a "strong or formidable party whilst they remain as an appendage of Liberalism." Forming a new party would force
a necessary breach with the Liberals, who were "the enemy of Labour
whilst pretending to be its friend." Faced by a choice between permeation and principle, the enthusiasts had little difficulty in making up their
minds. If the Londoners would not go with them they would go their
independent way.

13

POSTULATE, PERMEATE, PERORATE

"After the Election we must take a clean sweep ahead and go at Socialism," Shaw wrote to Graham Wallas on 21 June 1892. All the leading Fabians had been busy in the campaign, but they were uncertain about the best way to "go at Socialism." For Beatrice and Sidney Webb it meant pressing on with their first joint venture, the history of trade unionism. Their honeymoon was a working holiday. They started in Dublin, where they investigated "ramshackle trade societies . . . combinations of Catholic artisans, claiming descent from the exclusively Protestant guilds established in the seventeenth century . . . for the express purpose of preventing Papists gaining an honest livelihood." In Belfast they interviewed "hard-fisted employers and groups of closely-organized skilled craftsmen . . . contemptuous and indifferent to the Catholic labourers and women."

It was a dispiriting experience, and Beatrice mournfully noted the "depressing climate" and "unsuccessful investigation into that ramshackle race and its affairs."[1] Two days of relaxation in the Wicklow Hills offset some of the gloom. "The people are charming, but we detest them, as we should the Hottentots—for their very virtues," Sidney wrote to Wallas on 29 July. Beatrice added a scribbled comment: "Home Rule is an absolute necessity in order to depopulate the country of this detestable race." The only bright note was her assurance that she and Sidney were "very happy—far too happy to be reasonable."[2]

The honeymoon was rounded off by a visit to Scotland, taking in the Trades Union Congress in Glasgow in early September. Beatrice thought little of the TUC: the labour movement, she wrote, "has its seamy, I would almost say its disgusting side—quarrels between sections, intrigues among individuals, and it is this side that is uppermost at a Trade Union Congress."[3]

When the Webbs returned to London at the end of September they settled into "a cosy little flat" on the top floor at 10 Netherhall Gardens in Hampstead. Their day was well organized. They started work at nine-thirty. At ten they were joined by their secretary, Galton, and all three kept at it until they lunched. Four afternoons a week, Sidney was attending London County Council meetings. At seven-thirty they had "a simple meat supper, cigarettes and then an evening of peaceful happiness." "What is needed here," Shaw wrote to Sidney on 12 August, "is a salon for the social cultivation of the Socialist party in Parliament. Will Madame Potter-Webb undertake it?" The jest was premature, for the Webbs had a simple life with few visitors. Wallas was usually there for Sunday dinner and a walk on the Heath. Shaw came less often. He was busy with the preparations for *Widowers' Houses*, and because the drains were being repaired at Fitzroy Square he temporarily moved out to Hammersmith Terrace to stay with May Morris and Henry Sparling.

This was a curious domestic situation *à trois*. Shaw afterwards described it as "probably the happiest passage in our three lives"—the continuation, he claimed, of their "mystic betrothal." Before long Shaw came to the conclusion that he "had to consummate it or vanish." In fairness to Sparling he had to go. "To be welcomed in his house and then steal his wife was revolting to my sense of honour and socially inexcusable," Shaw recalled, "though I was as extreme a freethinker on sexual and religious questions as any sane human being could be. . . . I knew that a scandal would damage both of us and damage the Cause as well."[4] This was more than vanity on Shaw's part. Sparling later told Holbrook Jackson that "after completely captivating his wife Shaw suddenly disappeared, leaving behind him a desolated female who might have been an iceberg so far as her future relations with her husband went." Sparling soon afterwards left to become a journalist in Paris and allowed May to divorce him.[5]

Sidney was not only chairman of London's Technical Education Board; he sat on the Parliamentary, the Local Government, and the Tax, Education, Housing and Water Committees of the County Council. Both he and Beatrice were also trying to push the Royal Commission on Labour in favour of legislation for the eight-hour day, working through Tom Mann, who was a member of the Commission. Sidney was so involved in the mechanics of government and in London politics that he seemed to be emerging as a natural candidate for Parliament. "Hardly a month passes but some constituency or other throws out a fly for him," Beatrice noted, but Sidney rejected these overtures. Politically he was uncommitted, and temperamentally he preferred to work behind the scenes. Beatrice supported his refusals. Her motives were mixed. In part it was self-interest: she did not want their partnership to be broken into by "that enemy of domesticity," a parliamentary career.[6] She liked the limited commitment to the County Council, which meant that Sidney was home each evening when MP's were just settling down for the night's work. In part, too, she was realistic. "I do not think that the finest part of his mind and character would be called out by the manipulation and intrigues of the lobby," she reflected.[7] Sidney was equally anxious to protect Beatrice from the hurly-burly. When Pease asked her to speak to a Fabian meeting, she replied: "The hidden masculinity of Sidney's views of women are incurable in his decided objection to my figuring among the speakers. See how skin-deep are these professions of advanced opinion, with regard to women, among your leaders of the forward party!"[8] She saw her future life as that of "a recluse, with Sidney as an open window into the world."[9]

Outside Parliament there was a great deal of argument about the best way to get socialists into it. Inside the House of Commons, after the 1892 election, the issue was what they should do once they were elected; and it was dramatized by the difference between John Burns and Keir Hardie. Burns, with a strong personal machine behind him in Battersea, had neither connections nor sympathy with the movement that was developing in the North. He declined, despite Hardie's requests, to put himself at the head of the independent labour campaign; when he and Hardie found themselves in the House they could neither get along personally nor agree on a common course of action. Hardie, a stocky, bearded, plainly dressed man, was a natural symbol of renascent labour. His refusal to play the Liberal game embarrassed Burns, but his combative tactics appealed to the rank and file.

Yet it was not Hardie but the socialist editor of the *Workman's Times*, Joe Burgess, who took the initiative in forming a new party. On 30 April 1892 he issued an appeal in his paper to those who wished to create an Independent Labour Party so that sympathizers could be put in touch with each other and form branches. He received over two thousand letters, and the work of organization began. Before the election the first groups had already formed in Bradford and the Colne Valley; Blatchford and Trevor had got things off to a good start in Manchester; and Champion established a local Labour Party in Newcastle. By June there were branches in Stafford, Bolton, Plymouth, Liverpool, Birmingham and other centres, many of them emerging from local Fabian societies or from combinations of assorted socialist bodies.

An effort to create a national leadership based on London was rebuffed by W. H. Drew of the Bradford Labour Union, who insisted: "No executive will suit the provincials that they have had no hand in forming. . . . you cockneys ought to unbend and come, say, to Bradford . . . where you will find plenty of food for reflection."[10] All Burgess could do was to set up a London ILP group. Though this had Hardie's backing it did not gain much ground in face of the refusal of the SDF, still the largest socialist group in the capital, to join in.[11] The next opportunity came when the socialists met in an informal caucus at the Trades Union Congress in Glasgow in early September. Beatrice and Sidney were both at the Congress, but they took no part in the meeting chaired by Hardie and attended by Burgess, Drew, some of the younger trade-union organizers, and Kate Conway. John Burns refused to take part; he wanted to avoid difficulties with his Liberal allies in Battersea. Nevertheless, the group sent out an invitation for a national conference. Shaw, writing to Graham Wallas on 20 September, dismissed it as "nothing but a new SDF with Champion instead of Hyndman." He expanded the point in a letter to the *Workman's Times* on 8 October: "The only vital difference between the Fabian Society and the S.D.F. is that the Fabian wants to grow the plums first, and make the pies afterwards, whilst the Federation wants to make the pies first and find the plums afterwards. This is also the idea of the Independent Labour Party . . ."

The Fabian leaders were actually in a difficulty that could not be concealed by Shaw's sarcasm. Bland had long favoured such a separate socialist party; a good many of the London members and a large part of the provincial membership were enthusiastic for it. Yet Webb, Shaw and Wallas, who all belonged to local Liberal organizations, had their gaze fixed on the new Liberal government and its Newcastle Programme that apparently promised so much. All the Fabians could agree upon was that their representatives would attend the conference called in Bradford in January 1893, on condition that there could be no question of the Society merging with the ILP or being bound by any decisions at the conference. The Fabians chose Bland and De Mattos to represent them, but Bland dropped out and Shaw took his place. Shaw made no bones about his views; two days before he left for Bradford he wrote to Pease:

> My present intention is to go uncompromisingly for Permeation, for non-centralized local organization of the Labor Party, and for the bringing up of the country to the London mark by the supplanting of Liberalism by Progressivism. I feel like forcing the fighting as extravagantly as possible; so as to make it clear to all the new men that the Fabian is the lead for them to follow. . . . If you listen attentively on Friday you will probably hear the noise of the debate in the distance.

The noise that arose in the Bradford Labour Institute, when the conference convened on 13 January under Hardie's chairmanship, was actually one of protest against Shaw, who, with De Mattos, was forced to sit in the gallery while the delegates debated his credentials—agreeing to seat him only by forty-nine votes to forty-seven. He found himself the most unpopular man in the hall.

Bradford was the obvious place for the conference. Its wool operatives had fought a notable strike and emerged from it with their own political movement, a Labour Church, a Trades Council, a Fabian Society, strong trade-union branches, and a network of twenty-three labour clubs providing education and recreation for more than three thousand members. The newly acquired Institute, formerly a Wesleyan chapel and a Salvation Army hall, now became the cradle of the new party. At the tables draped with red cotton cloths sat 120 delegates. Though there were many Fabians among them, representing other bodies as well as the dozen local Fabian societies which formally supported the conference, Shaw was the only prominent member of the parent society. "London," he wrote afterwards, "was practically out of the Conference." So too was the old guard from the Eighties.[12] Edward Aveling turned up, representing the miniscule Bloomsbury Socialist Society, but John Burns refused to attend; Champion was ill and unable to make the journey; Morris was not there, nor were the SDF leaders, and the anarchists naturally boycotted a venture intended to promote parliamentary activities. It was the new men and women, such as Hardie, Blatchford, Burgess, Trevor, Mann, Tillett and Kate Conway, who dominated the proceedings.

The attempt to prevent Shaw and De Mattos taking their seats was not personal; it was a protest against the lukewarm attitude of the London Fabians and particularly against a provocative speech Shaw made to Fabian delegates before the conference opened. He poked fun at the idea of an independent party and came out "extravagantly" for permeation. Once the conference began, however, Shaw played a useful role and worked closely with Aveling in preparing the draft programme.

There was much general agreement about the aims of the party. What was wanted was a labour party, committed to parliamentary methods and working in alliance with such parts of the trade-union movement as could be induced to support it. For that reason it was decided to exclude the word "Socialist" from its title. The conference nevertheless voted solidly for "the collective ownership of the means of production, distribution and exchange" as its fundamental objective. It then plumped for a series of reforms: the limitation of working hours, pensions for the sick, aged, widows and orphans, free education, and the provision of work for the unemployed. Apart from the overriding socialist aim there was nothing in this list which was not a commonplace among Radicals in the early Nineties.

There was no reason why the Fabians should differ with the new party on policy. They had not, as Shaw afterwards claimed, won it for Fabian principles: almost all the delegates accepted those principles already and many of them were at least nominal members of the Society or one of its local offshoots. The disagreement between the Fabians and the party's founders focused solely on two issues. The first was whether there should be a new party at all or whether the venture was premature, doomed to be abortive and likely to make it more rather than less difficult to get workingmen into Parliament. Shaw had no hope of carrying the delegates on that point; the tide of feeling in the provinces was running far too strongly against him. The second was whether the new party should leave its branches and individual members free to link up with other organizations with similar aims. The delegates were not impressed by Shaw's defence of permeation and his claim that he was "on the Executive of a Liberal Association and had taken some trouble to get the position in order to push labour interests there." On the other hand they voted down purists like Blatchford, simply to avoid embarrassing trade unionists whose organizations, like the miners' unions, had close links with the Liberal Party. There was agreement, essentially, on two points: that the creation of a labour party in Parliament was to be achieved by independent action, opposing both of the main parties and refusing to seek electoral favours from either; and that, as the decision to keep the headquarters out of London symbolized, the leadership was to be kept in the hands of the provincials.

The Fabians had been forced to show some sympathy for this policy at their conference in February 1892 and again by despatching two delegates to Bradford. Yet they disliked it, were unsympathetic to its advocates and were unaware of the strength of feeling behind it. The isolation of the Londoners from the new movement led to the uneasy reaction of the Fabians, the SDF and the Hammersmith Socialist Society, who formed a Joint Committee of Socialist Bodies. Though Socialist unity was the current slogan, nothing came out of the protracted talks held by Morris, Shaw and Hyndman but a joint May Day manifesto which, Shaw remarked, was merely "a string of the old phrases and a few ambiguities by which Hyndman meant one thing and I another."[13]

Shaw brought philandering to politics as well as to courtship. While he and the Fabian leaders continued to flirt with the idea of socialist unity, either with the Independent Labour Party or with the survivors from the Eighties, they had no enthusiasm for either venture. They preferred, as Wallas put it, to "Postulate, Permeate, Perorate."[14] In the aftermath of the 1892 elections that meant trying to extend their influence among the London County Council Progressives and working for the implementation of the Newcastle Programme by the Liberal government.

All through the first half of 1893 the provincial membership of the Fabians was slipping away; local societies survived, but some reorganized themselves as ILP branches and threw their energy into the new party. The pressure was less in London, where the Society's executive was firmly under the control of Webb, Shaw, Olivier and Wallas, and where the movement lacked the revivalist temper of the industrial districts. But by the summer it was clear that the Society could disregard neither the success of the ILP nor the growing feeling of disappointment with Gladstone's government. Something had to be done to bring the Fabians back into the picture.

Sidney Webb was slow to respond, for he was submerged in his work for the County Council and in the grind of the trade-union book. In August he and Beatrice went down to the Argoed to combine their writing with a holiday. Back at her family home, the scene of her painful encounters with Chamberlain, Beatrice brooded nostalgically over the past. Since her marriage she had been happy, but she felt the weakening of her links with her family and the separation from old friends.[15] To compensate she involved herself more closely with Sidney's circle.

Graham Wallas was invited down to the Argoed, and Beatrice began to concern herself with his future. His enthusiasm for the Society seemed a substitute for any definite purpose of his own. He was involved in social work at Toynbee Hall. He served a turn as secretary of the Fabian Parliamentary League. He was always willing to lecture or write an article. In 1890 he finally started on an academic career as a university extension lecturer, giving classes to self-improvement groups around the country. Yet in the summer of 1893, when he was already thirty-four, Beatrice wrote that "in spite of his moral fervour" he seemed "incapable of directing his own life. . . . To some men and women he appears simply as a kindly dull failure—an impression which is fostered by a slovenliness of dress and general worn-out look." Knowing his talent and making the most of his intelligent help, Beatrice asked him to read over the manuscript of the trade-union book; "he made me feel rather desperate about its shortcomings," she noted.[16]

They were soon joined by Shaw. He had been to the International Socialist Congress in Zurich, instructed by the Society to watch the business closely "with a view to the permeation of Continental Socialism with Fabianism." Shaw, Webb and Wallas now formed a private clique in the Society.

At the Argoed Beatrice had a chance to see this "Junta" at work together. Sidney, she decided, was the practical organizer, Wallas gave it a tone of morality, Shaw provided the sparkle. Each, she felt, appealed to a different element in the Society. Sidney attracted those who wanted ideas and programmes and good organization. Educated people liked the moral refinement and disinterestedness of Wallas. Shaw led the "men of straw . . . would-be revolutionists, who are attracted by his wit, his daring onslaughts and amusing parodies." Their combined influence on the Fabians was such that Emma Brooke was soon protesting that the Fabian executive was dominated by a despotism carried on from the Argoed and that the Junta was keeping all the work of the Society in the hands of its favourites.

This summer holiday also gave Beatrice a chance to know Shaw, and she found him a delightful companion. She appreciated his respect for Sidney and enjoyed his clever talk, though she decided that he had a "slight personality"—little more than "an incongruous group of qualities."[17] He was an agreeable member of the house party and he too worked his passage by revising the drafts of the trade-union book: the Fabian authors fell easily into the habit of revising each other's work.

GBS was busy himself with his third play, *Mrs. Warren's Profession*. The plot of his first play had been provided by Archer; the second, already finished in May and put aside when Shaw realized that the Independent Theatre lacked the resources to produce it, was *The Philanderer*, which plainly dramatized his flirtations with Jenny Patterson and Florence Farr (to whom he referred in his diary as "F.E.") Jenny's jealousy, intensified by Shaw's attentions to Florence, had been breaking out at intervals over the past two years. The climax came on 4 February 1893, in an episode which Shaw wrote into his play virtually unchanged.

> In the evening I went to F.E.; and J.P. burst in on us very late in the evening. There was a most shocking scene; J.P. being violent & using atrocious language. At last I sent F.E. out of the room, having to restrain J.P. by force from attacking her. I was two hours getting her out of the house & I did not get her home to Brompton Sq. until near 1, nor could I get away myself until 3. I was horribly tired, shocked & upset; but I kept my patience & did not behave badly nor ungently.[18]

The Philanderer, Shaw told Archer, was "quite as promising a failure" as *Widower's Houses*. It was a protest against the possessiveness of women in love which threatened the kind of independence that Shaw prized. The hero, Charteris, sees through the conventions, refuses to conform and is free to indulge his desires without falling into the marital trap. Since he regards marriage as a form of captivity, he is forced to lead the life of a Don Juan: the only happy marriage is one which is predicated on a mutually agreed economic bargain and not on the destructive illusion of love.

The stimulus for the third play came from Beatrice, who was bound to think well of a playwright who set out to put blue books on the stage. She proposed that Shaw write next about "a real modern lady of the governing class—not the sort of thing that theatrical and critical authorities imagine such a lady to be." Fusing this proposal with a Maupassant story told him by Janet Achurch, Shaw evolved *Mrs. Warren's Profession*. Like *Widowers' Houses*, this hinged on tainted money; brothels took the place of slum property, giving Shaw the chance "to draw attention to the truth that prostitution is caused, not by female depravity and male licentiousness, but simply by underpaying, undervaluing and overworking women so shamefully that the poorest of them are forced to resort to prostitution to keep body and soul together."[19] Unlike Trench, in *Widowers' Houses*, who would rather be a scoundrel than a hypocrite, Vivie Warren rejects her inheritance because she prefers her principles to her mother and to her mother's immoral earnings. She believes herself to be unconventional in her businesslike approach to the world, but when her mother tries to bribe her back she behaves as conventionally and priggishly as any high-minded puritan. Although Shaw's treatment of the "immoral" situation of this play could not have been more high-principled, it was not received with enthusiasm. Shaw thought it would be just the thing for the Independent Theatre, but Grein rejected it as too provocative even for a private showing—a view which was confirmed when the Lord Chamberlain refused to give it a licence.

At the end of September the Webbs and Shaw left for London. Beatrice and Sidney needed a house convenient to Spring Gardens, just off Trafalgar Square, where the London County Council held its meetings. They therefore rented, for £110 a year, a ten-room terraced house at 41 Grosvenor Road on the Embankment. It was an austere house, but Beatrice shopped for pleasant secondhand furniture and bought the wallpapers from the Morris shop.[20] When her sisters teased her, saying that they saw little socialism in such sybaritic tastes, Beatrice consoled herself with the thought that "as Sidney says we must work in order to deserve it."[21]

During the agreeable weeks at the Argoed the party had talked a lot of politics. The Liberals were losing ground, and the Fabian leadership—who had pinned their hopes on the influence of Haldane, Asquith, Grey, Buxton and Acland in the government—was embarrassed by their failure. On the day that the Independent Labour Party was founded in Bradford, Gladstone introduced his new Home Rule proposal into the Commons—partly because he was emotionally committed to this above all other measures, and partly because he thought it might serve as a distraction from the new wave of class conflict which was sweeping the country. That autumn the Lords threw out the bill, knocking down with it a set of other reforms. Outside Parliament, the long cotton strike was followed in the autumn of 1893 by a bitter lockout in the coal industry. In September, a combination of industrial militancy and socialist propaganda led the Trades Union Congress to go on record for the first time in favour of public ownership of the means of production.

Shaw was by now sufficiently worried to realize that a Fabian initiative was necessary if he and Webb were not to be discredited as mere hangers-on of the Liberals. On 8 September he wrote to Wallas from the Argoed: "We must . . . satisfy the legitimate aspirations of the ardent spirits by getting out a furious attack on the Government, rallying labor to put third candidates in the field." When Webb got back to London on 19 September he told Wallas: "Shaw and I propose that we should issue at once a political manifesto, tartly criticising the shortcomings of the Government and urging the running of third candidates whenever these can make a decent show and no advanced Radical is in the field." Wallas came to the conclusion that Shaw and Webb were "rushed" into the change of front "by fear of being thought complacent and apathetic" by the ILP.[22] Though Beatrice conceded there was some truth in that view, wondering whether it was wise "to do anything simply from fear of being left behind," she noted that for months Webb and Shaw had "been feeling the need of some strong outspoken words on the lack of faith and will to go forward" of the Cabinet.[23]

There was another reason for haste. At the Trades Union Congress in September 1893 it was decided for the first time to establish an election fund for supporting independent labour and socialist candidates. The Fabians had called for this in their election manifesto in the previous year, and such a fund appealed to them more than the concept of a separate party. Webb favoured the idea of workingmen sitting in Parliament, as a small group of them did on the London County Council. What he wanted was a means of getting them there which did not force contests against sympathetic Liberals or create such barriers to permeation as Blatchford's demand that socialists cut all ties with the conventional parties. Sidney, moreover, had learnt a great deal about the trade-union movement as he and Beatrice worked on their book and came to know both local and national union leaders. His assessment of their potential role in politics was now very different from the casual disregard of trade unionism in *Fabian Essays*.

On 1 November 1893 the *Fortnightly Review* carried a long article, nominally credited to the Fabian Society but actually written by Shaw and Webb, entitled "To Your Tents, O Israel!" Combining Shaw's sarcastic wit with Webb's precision on detail, it was a sustained invective against the Liberals. The "red spectre" of the Newcastle Programme had vanished, having served its turn; nothing more had been heard of its promises of municipal reform, new factory legislation, payment of MP's, restraints on the House of Lords, and other Radical measures. Some excuse could be made for Gladstone's failure to put through controversial bills: he had a small majority, his dependence on the Irish Party meant that Home Rule had to be given priority, and his own government was split between Whigs and Radicals on social policy. But the same could not be said of administrative matters, where individual ministers had the power to redeem some of their pledges to the unions. For several point-scoring pages the manifesto itemized what Liberals might have done by a "few strokes of the pen": Arnold Morley, running the Post Office, could have "modified the contracts under which the mail-cart drivers work fourteen hours a day." Campbell-Bannerman, instead of making speeches about the eight-hour day, could "at once have established it in all the War Department arsenals, factories, and stores" and withdrawn government orders for uniforms from the "sweaters" in the clothing industry. Lord Spencer, at the Admiralty, could have ended the "scandal of starvation wages" at the Deptford victualling yard and paid the dock-yard craftsmen the standard union rates; he had instead paid the Admiralty labourers a shilling a week less than Charles Booth's "poverty line." Sir William Harcourt, at the Treasury, could have helped the unemployed, insisted that all civil-service departments pay union wages, and used his Budget to make some progress towards social justice. The indictment ran on. All these omissions, Webb and Shaw claimed, were due simply to a lack of will. "Had the will existed, there would have been no difficulty about the way."

This blast against the Liberals was more sharply phrased than anything that had yet come from the Fabian leaders. All that currently remained of the permeation argument was the suggestion that labour might extract concessions from either party if there was a narrow majority in Parliament and if the unions kept up their pressure. Then some surprising words were inserted: "Pending the formation of a Labour Party, the working classes need not greatly care which party divides the loaves and fishes." As a step towards such a new party, the Liberal members should be converted to collectivism. Now that a beginning had been made by the Trades Union Congress, "the trade unions must do the rest" by raising "a parliamentary fund of at least £30,000, and the running of fifty independent Labour candidates at the next general election."

Webb and Shaw had waited almost a year before they came out strongly for the policy which the Fabians had opposed at Bradford. Their conversion came more from their reassessment of the potential of the trade-union movement than from any newfound enthusiasm for the provincial socialists. It failed to mollify the opponents of permeation, who claimed that the manifesto proved that they had been right all along in backing the Independent Labour Party. At the same time, it profoundly upset those Fabians who saw the Radical wing of the Liberals as the instrument for pushing collectivism. The philosopher D. G. Ritchie protested that the manifesto (reissued as *A Plan of Campaign for Labour*) was "fatuous and indecent"; the Liberals would do far more for social progress "than a whole wilderness of excitable Ben Tilletts and fanatical Keir Hardies."[24] H. J. Massingham of *The Star*, who had done much to back the Fabians in London and to assist their permeation of the County Council Progressives, resigned from the Society. He accused Webb of being "mischievous . . . mixing the most trivial complaints with the gravest political indictments." An equally angry letter went to Shaw, expressing Massingham's horror at "the foolish idea that the way out is to fill parliament with trade union delegates." Haldane, closest of all the Liberal collectivists to the Fabians, wrote sorrowfully: "Now the public and others too will not look closely enough to understand that you have not declared war on us all."[25]

There was something impulsive about the way in which Shaw and

Webb rushed out a manifesto which so wounded their Liberal friends without winning them any compensating support among the advocates of a labour party. They may have been telling "the world exactly what they had been saying in private," as Beatrice afterwards claimed,[26] but— whatever the merits of their analysis of the situation—their political judgment was poor. They had neither thought through the implications of so dramatically abandoning permeation nor considered what the Society should do if such a change of policy was accepted. Logically their argument led towards an alliance with the ILP, but they clearly had no such intention. What they had done was to preserve their virtue at the price of withholding their practical involvement with both Liberal and labour groups.

This was a matter of personality as well as politics. Shaw teased, flirted, and shied away from commitments that restricted his independence. Sidney Webb, trained as a civil servant, was much better at writing briefs for policy-makers and at devising administrative means for applying them than he was at making political decisions himself. He could advise, but not act, manipulate but not organize, and he had little understanding of the motives which governed either his Liberal allies in Parliament or the men who were trying to build the new party in the country. He thought that men of intelligence and goodwill should be able to implement policies which were self-evidently sensible and with which, to his knowledge, they agreed. Their failure to do so once they were in office seemed to him a betrayal, and this feeling accounted for the bitterness of the charges laid against them in the manifesto. His inability to appreciate the ambitions of the ILP leaders led to a similar misjudgment. He could not comprehend that unless they clung to the notion of independent action they had no stock in trade and they might as well shut up shop. Local labour leaders might make deals with the Liberals; nationally, without a party of their own, labour men had no hope of influence or careers. The Fabian leaders could afford to be intellectually superior, even if they were tactically unwise, because they were trafficking in ideas rather than votes and had no responsibility for translating their opinions into action.

"This 'behind the scenes' intellectual leadership is, I believe, Sidney's especial talent," Beatrice remarked early in 1894.[27] Part of Sidney's new enthusiasm for the political potential of the trade unions arose from the willingness of some of the leaders to use his abilities and be influenced by his advice. In the first months of the new year he was drafting the minority report of the Royal Commission on Labour which was to appear over the signature of the trade-union members. Sidney and Beatrice regarded their use of the three labour commissioners as stalking horses as "a practical joke over which we chuckle with considerable satisfaction." What amused them was the fact that the Commission, as Beatrice put it, "having carefully excluded any competent Socialists from its membership, having scouted the idea of appointing me as a humble assistant commissioner, will now find a detailed collectivist programme blazoned about as the minority report of its Labour members!"[28]

This kind of manoeuvre, at which the Webbs were quickly becoming adept, was far more congenial to them than open politics. Their aim, Beatrice remarked, was to make "our little house the intellectual headquarters of the Labour movement."[29] They felt that more progress was made by such a report, which came out for an eight-hour day enforced by law, amendment of the Factory Acts, relief measures for the unemployed, and the improvement of the conditions of casual labour, than by the creation of a political machine. Their task, as they saw it, was to define what needed doing, to demonstrate the facts about a social problem and the means by which it might be alleviated. How, politically, the reform was to be accomplished was another question.

In this respect, permeation boiled down to wirepulling—the technique of feeding facts to anyone who could be persuaded to use them. This worked well enough in the London County Council committees, but in national politics it was becoming increasingly difficult as the Liberals declined in the country and divided in government. Lord Rosebery, who led the Progressives on the County Council as well as serving under Gladstone, told a friend that the Cabinet was conducted "on prizefighting principles." Gladstone, ageing and isolated from his colleagues, wanted to go to the polls when Home Rule was rejected by the Lords vote of 419 to 41; none of the others would take the risk. There was a majority in the Cabinet for increased naval armaments; Gladstone would not agree. It was now clear that he could not last long; and on 1 March 1894 he held the last meeting of his "blubbering Cabinet."

The Cabinet had been kept going by uncertainty about the succession. The obvious choice was Sir William Harcourt, who sat in the Commons, had much experience and enjoyed the support of the "Little England," free-trade and Nonconformist elements in the Liberal Party. The enigmatic and attractive Rosebery, then only forty-seven, was known as an intelligent man, a hard worker and a committed social reformer who was backed by the more Radical members of the Cabinet and by much of the Liberal press. The Queen settled the matter by sending for Rosebery without consulting Gladstone or taking soundings among his colleagues. Rosebery had all the assets needed in a prime minister—including great wealth and the opportunity to pull his party together—save one: he had neither the taste nor the capacity for leadership. He was an aloof figure who disliked granting or asking the favours which oil the wheels of politics, and he was hypersensitive about being slighted. "He would not stoop, he did not conquer," Winston Churchill said.

With Rosebery as prime minister there was a chance that the Radicals would have more influence in government. Webb, who admired Rosebery's work on the County Council, undoubtedly hoped for better things and for the promotion of such friends as Asquith and Haldane. Yet Rosebery had scarcely been in office a week when Haldane, left out of the Cabinet, was complaining that things were as bad as ever and discussing with Webb how he could make his criticisms effective. "It was a quaint episode, when one remembered his grave remonstrance last autumn," Beatrice commented wryly in the middle of March.[30] It was also a sign that Sidney Webb, at least, was still as much concerned with the way in which the Liberals might be brought round as with the new labour campaign he had called for only four months earlier.

During the winter, Keir Hardie had given a talk to the Fabian Society suggesting that its leaders carry their enthusiasm for independent labour to the point of breaking with the Liberals. These "superior persons," he said, "were rapidly bringing upon themselves the position of being generals without followers."[31] There was truth in the charge, but it did not bother those Fabians who had neither the desire nor the intention of leading a mass movement. By the spring of 1894, Webb had moved back to his previous position. If collectivism could now be furthered by working through the Rosebery government, well and good; if not, then the tactics must be to strengthen the opposition within the Liberal Party against the day when it would split or, falling out of power, be captured by its progressive wing. Permeation, perhaps, still offered more than did Hardie's passion for propaganda.

❧ 14 ❧
PROFESSIONALS

In 1894 the Fabian Society was ten years old. It was at last beginning to make its mark, and so were its leading members. All of them were now in their late thirties and, after long apprenticeships, starting their careers in earnest. As Britain broke out of the frame of Victorian conventions those who had something fresh to say could quickly make a reputation.

The Fabians had always taken themselves seriously, even when they were no more than a small club of high-minded idealists. Members were expected to turn up regularly at meetings, go out lecturing, sell pamphlets and generally keep the Fabian name before the public. The executive made sure that this sober tone was maintained. In March 1890, for instance, it ruled that the social gathering following the annual meeting "must *not* conclude with a dance"; and in 1895 it formally decided "to have no Conference, Soirée, Conversazione, Party, or other Frivolity." From time to time there were attempts to stop smoking at meetings, one note recording that "cigarettes only" were permitted after 6 P.M. With this effort to present a solemn face to the world went a degree of self-importance, a tendency to claim too much for a society still so small in size and influence. Once again it was Shaw who set the tone. "Have you noticed that one result of the Fabians constantly telling the world how clever they are is that the world is beginning to believe them, and, of course, to pretend that it found out the cleverness for itself?" GBS wrote to William P. Johnson in 1893.[1] Such self-advertisement, he insisted, paid dividends. "Study us, my boy, and learn how to bounce," he added, "for it is only by bouncing that our little stage army can conquer the country."

Personally as well as politically, Shaw believed that people were likely to be taken at their own valuation, and he never missed an opportunity to promote himself. By 1894 he had managed to create an impression that he was a coming man in the theatre although he had not yet written a successful play. There were signs, however, that things were changing in the theatre and that his opportunity might soon come. In 1893 Arthur Pinero made a sensation with *The Second Mrs. Tanqueray*, and Oscar Wilde quickly followed with *An Ideal Husband* and *The Importance of Being Earnest*. So far Shaw had failed to find a way of appealing to the new public which Pinero and Wilde managed to reach—the veneer of entertainment over his sardonic homilies had been too thin—but he was determined to try again. The question was whether he could write a play which would force an audience to laugh even if it felt shocked and uncomfortable.

The test came in the spring of 1894. Annie Horniman, who had inherited a fortune from the tea trade and wished to support new cultural ventures, put up the money for Florence Farr to run a season of new plays at the Avenue Theatre. Shaw was asked for a play, but the one he was writing was not yet ready for production. The season opened on 29 March with a double bill. The Yeats play *The Land of Heart's Desire* was coupled with John Todhunter's *A Comedy of Sighs*, which had so bad a reception that it had to be withdrawn. Florence Farr sent Shaw a telegram asking him to go to the theatre. "Went down and found F.E. and Helmsley with *Widowers' Houses* open before them, contemplating its production in despair," Shaw wrote in his diary. "I dissuaded them from that and after some discussion took my new play out onto the Embankment Gardens and there and then put the last touches to it before leaving it to be typewritten."

The new play was *Arms and the Man*, which went into production ten days later and opened on 21 April 1894. GBS asked Helmsley to provide seats for his friends. "Sidney Webb . . . might possibly bring a cabinet minister if he has a box," he declared breezily.[2] Yeats described the impact of the play: "On the first night the whole pit and gallery, except certain members of the Fabian Society, started to laugh at the author, and then, discovering that they themselves were being laughed at, sat there not converted—their hatred was too bitter for that—but dumbfounded, while the rest of the house cheered and laughed."[3] When Shaw took his curtain call one man booed loudly. Shaw, well skilled in dealing with hecklers, replied, "I assure the gentleman in the gallery that he and I are of exactly the same opinion, but what can we do against a whole house who are of the contrary opinion?" Though the play was not a commercial success, Shaw now knew that he had hit the mark. After running with the Yeats curtain-raiser for eleven weeks it grossed £ 1,777, half of the investment, and brought Shaw £ 100 in royalties. The curtain was scarcely down on the first performance before he was involved in negotiations for the American rights; he agreed that Richard Mansfield should launch *Arms and the Man* at the Herald Square Theatre in New York. This brilliant production, as Shaw wrote to his American agent, brought in enough money to permit him "to live and preach Socialism for six months."[4]

In this first of what Shaw called his "pleasant" plays, which dealt "less with the crimes of society and more with its romantic follies," he revealed the maturing of his personality. He felt, as he told William Archer two days after the play opened, that he had "got clean through the categories of good & evil." Archer was wrong, Shaw said, in suggesting that he merely mocked at conventional ideals in the style of W. S. Gilbert. He conceded that the amateur soldier Sergius, filled with ridiculous dreams of glory, exemplified the Gilbertian view that "life is a farce . . . nothing comes of it but cynicism, pessimism & irony," but he insisted that the down-to-earth professional soldier Bluntschli was a man without illusions, "unaffectedly ready to face what risks must be faced, considerate but not chivalrous, patient and practical." Naturally he ends by carrying off Raina, the betrothed of Sergius, for such a hero is uncontaminated by false ideals.[5]

Shaw for the first time had attempted what he called "a perfectly genuine play about real people with a happy ending and hope & life in it." The flippancy which Archer disliked in his earlier plays had gone; so had the compulsion to make plays out of the raw material of Fabian tracts. Shaw was now concerned with serious motives and convincing characterization and was able to use paradox lightly to make a genuine point—that war was not glamorous and gay but boring and barbarous.

He claimed gleefully that it was a "notable artistic success" and told Archer that it shattered "your theory that I cannot write for the stage." For GBS, as he now signed himself, wanted to be taken seriously as a dramatist, not looked at merely as a propagandist who could deck out his message with clever dialogue. The contradiction between Sergius and Bluntschli reflected his own conflict between the dilettante and the professional, between vanity and self-confidence.

Arms and the Man did more than enable Shaw to preach socialism for six months. It showed him that he could achieve success at the box office without abandoning his moral purpose and that he could educate more effectively with humour than with sermons. He still believed that it would take time for the public to accept the plays he wanted to write, but he could now see how they should be written. "I shall continue writing just as I do now for the next ten years," he insisted. "After that we can wallow in the gold poured at our feet by a dramatically regenerated public."[6] Such a long haul, however, would be impossible without real commitment to the calling that he now knew was his profession.

To mark the change GBS proposed to wind up his business in Grub Street. The first move was to give up his column as a music critic. The death of his friend Edmund Yates, who edited *The World*—where he had moved from *The Star* in 1890—gave him a decent chance to drop out in August 1894. As *Arms and the Man* ended its run of fifty performances GBS told M. E. McNulty: "I have taken the very serious step of cutting off my income. . . . if I cannot make something out of the theatre, I am a ruined man; for I have not £20 saved. . . . I am about to begin the world at last."[7]

The situation was not so desperate as Shaw suggested, for the play was bringing in several hundred pounds and he celebrated his new circumstances by opening his first bank account. He turned to writing and politics with renewed vitality. In the autumn months he toiled at *Candida*, threw himself into the elections for the London School Board—at which Stewart Headlam and Graham Wallas were returned—and the local vestries, kept his end up with Fabian business, delivered two dozen lectures in London and the provinces, and managed to keep up a flow of articles and criticism in the press.

The next play did not strike the same lively note as *Arms and the*

Man. Candida was coldly received. When GBS offered it to Charles Wyndham for the Criterion Theatre, Wyndham told him that it would be twenty years before the London stage was ready for it. Mansfield, to whom Shaw also proposed it with the suggestion that Janet Achurch play the lead, was equally unresponsive. "The stage is not for sermons," he replied to Shaw; "the world is tired of theories and arguments and philosophy and morbid sentiment." In any case he thought it would fail. "If you think a bustling-striving-hustling-pushing-stirring American audience will sit out calmly two hours of deliberate talk you are mistaken—and I'm not to be sacrificed to their just vengeance."[8] It was two years before the Independent Theatre put the play on for a single performance in Aberdeen.

Its theme was close to the domestic situation which always attracted Shaw, in which two men contend for the same woman yet complement each other in the three-cornered relationship. There was more than a hint in it of the triangle at Hammersmith Terrace of Sparling, May Morris and Shaw. There was also an echo of visits to Kate Salt when Shaw and Edward Carpenter competed in playing "Sunday husbands" to her. But the "secret" of *Candida* did not lie in the obvious manner in which Shaw drew upon his friends as models for his characters: traces of Fabians and Simple Lifers could be found in all the earlier plays. It was another expression of the contrary elements of Shaw's personality. Morell, the husband of Candida, is a Christian Socialist preacher; Marchbanks, the shy poetic youth of eighteen, is anarchic, intense, wilful, and an obvious adventurer who merely wishes to deprive Morell of his wife, not to marry her himself; and Candida is a sexless coquette who uses the flirtation to increase her power over her husband. For a play with such a plot, indeed, it was astonishingly sexless, as if all the tensions were transmuted into intellectual debates. Shaw had certainly turned the tables on *A Doll's House*, as he afterwards claimed, by showing that a New Woman could win her marital battles by remaining on the domestic hearth instead of fleeing from it. It is Morell who is the household pet, and his wife who makes it clear that things are to be run on her terms. By preferring the preacher to the poet she remains spiritually inviolate. Neither man has the power to conquer a woman who remains as aloof as the Virgin Mother.

The rejection of *Candida* meant a setback for Shaw's hope of cutting loose from journalism, but he was able to turn his growing knowledge of the theatre to good account. Frank Harris, who had just become the editor of the *Saturday Review*, persuaded GBS to become his dramatic critic at six pounds a week. "It is questionable," Shaw wrote to Archer on 28 December 1894, "whether it is quite decent for a dramatic author to be also a dramatic critic." But he had to live and he could not let himself become dependent on the acceptance of his plays by managers. After a Christmas holiday with Wallas at Folkestone, he went to work for Frank Harris. His first assignment was to review the production of Oscar Wilde's *An Ideal Husband* on 3 January 1895.

Shaw was almost forty before he found his vocation. So were the Webbs, who had discovered that with marriage they had formed an ideal partnership for research. It took them two years of hard work to produce their *History of Trade Unionism*, which appeared appropriately on May Day 1894. Frederic Harrison was one who wrote to congratulate Beatrice, assuring her that the book conformed in all respects to his experience of the trade unions in the Seventies. It was, he added, "the most important book that Labour has ever called forth."[9]

F. W. Galton, who had helped Sidney and Beatrice to cull the minute books of trade unions and to interview survivors from the years in which the unions had struggled to establish themselves, described the way they worked.[10] Beatrice, he said, "was largely responsible for the plans and, so to speak, the architecture, while all the actual construction was done by Sidney . . . in the large flowing handwriting which he wrote with great speed." Sidney had the "great executive power and driving force" which Beatrice lacked, thus complementing her ingenuity and imaginative range.

They had set out to break new ground, starting without any preconceptions and not much prior knowledge of the trade unions. They decided that their task was "the precise observation of actual facts," and they assumed that from this, as they described the life history of social institutions, a scientific sociology would gradually emerge. Narrative came before analysis, and the narrative was constructed like a jigsaw puzzle, piece by piece, from the file cards which contained the facts.

This piecemeal approach was similar in its assumptions to the Webbs' belief that reforms could be separated into discrete packages each of which was intrinsically sound. Beatrice was convinced that by recording each fact on its own card and then shuffling the cards in different categories and sequences (a crude anticipation of modern factor analysis and data processing) they could arrive at "by far the most fertile stage of our investigations"—that is, at the principles of organization underlying the facts.[11] This conclusion was reached by trial and error when they were writing the trade-union history. When the book was completed, she said, "we found to our surprise that we had no systematic and definite theory or vision of how Trade Unionism operated, or what it effected." They therefore planned another book in an effort to extract "a clear, comprehensive and verifiable theory" from the mass of material they had assembled.

Before they started work on it in the summer of 1894 they took a three-week holiday in Venice and the Italian lakes: "a true honeymoon of love and common enjoyment." Back in London, the plan to work out a new theory of industrial democracy proved to be hard going. In July the summer habit of going to the country for two or three months took them to Milford, in the Surrey hills near Godalming, where they rented Borough Farm, an isolated and attractive period house. There they could walk for miles through the bracken and heather, and they were near enough to London for Sidney to go up on County Council business. The weather was depressing, misty and cold, and Beatrice had plenty of time for reflection. She fretted about the book, and for the first time she expressed regret that there were no children in her life. "Deliberately forgoing motherhood seems to me to thwart all the purposes of their nature" in women, she commented, adding: "I myself—or rather we chose this course on our marriage—but then I had passed the age when it is easy and natural for a woman to become a child bearer . . . as it is I sometimes wonder whether I had better not have risked it and taken my chance."[12]

There were a few visitors, including Wallas and Shaw. When Alice Green stayed she was astonished at the way the Junta argued fiercely at night and rose to work next day on the most amiable terms. No one took hard words to heart, whether in debate or in comment on the working drafts they submitted to each other for revision. Wallas was finishing his biography of the radical tailor Francis Place, in whose political career in the early years of the century he plainly discerned the antecedents of Fabian attitudes. He was, however, in a gloomy mood. In December 1893 he had joined the committee organizing the Progressive election cam-

paign for the London School Board, and in February 1894 he had decided that he would like to be one of its candidates. His initiation into
practical politics was beginning to estrange him from the Fabian style of
lobbying. Beatrice found his company depressing. "Like many men who
live alone and work hard," she observed, "he is a joyless being who has
to some extent lost his manners and capacity for agreeable intercourse in
the daily grind of devoted work for others."[13]

The difficulties of that 1894 summer at Borough Farm were offset by a
new challenge. In the first week of August there began what Beatrice
called "an odd adventure." Sidney received a letter from a solicitor in
Derby informing him that Henry Hutchinson, the cantankerous solicitor
who put up modest sums to support Fabian activities, had committed suicide to put an end to a long illness and had left more than half of his estate for Fabian purposes.[14] He had chosen Sidney to be chairman of the
trustees of the fund, together with his own daughter Constance, De Mattos, Clarke and Pease.

It was an odd will which could easily have been contested on the
grounds that Hutchinson was not of sound mind and that he had given
the Fabians ten thousand pounds while leaving his wife nothing more
than an annuity of one hundred. It was also vague, instructing the trustees to use the money within ten years for "the propaganda and other
purposes" of the Fabian Society, "advancing its objects in any way they
deem advisable." Wallas and Shaw were astonished when at breakfast
the day after receiving the letter the Webbs announced that they had
risen early, discussed the matter and decided to use part of the money
for founding a school of economics in London.

Sidney had long considered that Britain needed an institution devoted to the social sciences. On his American tour he had been impressed
by the work at the Massachusetts Institute of Technology; he had envied
the Ecole Libre des Sciences Politiques in Paris; and his work on the
Technical Education Board had made him see both the need and the possibility of doing something similar in London. "His vision was to found
a London School of Economics and Political Science," Beatrice noted in
September. "Last evening we sat by the fire and jotted down a whole list
of subjects which want elucidating—issues of fact which need clearing
up." Her comment clearly revealed the Webb approach to social science.

"Above all, we want the ordinary citizen to feel that reforming society is no light matter and must be undertaken by experts specially trained for the purpose." For Beatrice and Sidney both believed that reform would "not be brought about by shouting. What is needed is *hard thinking*."[15]

Before this vision could be realized, however, Sidney had to do some hard bargaining. His first decision was to double the annuity to Mrs. Hutchinson: Sidney considered that it was "common humanity" as well as "prudent administration" to protect the bequest against any challenge from her. He felt he had to carry the Fabian executive with him and the matter was discussed at the meeting on 28 September, with Shaw acting as Sidney's spokesman. Sidney's difficulty was that he wanted to keep the money under the control of the trustees so that he could divert a large part of it to his academic project, without antagonizing Fabians who might understandably assume that the legacy was intended to promote the Society's work directly.

It was not easy for Sidney to establish his larger plans. Bland argued that Webb could not both demand the executive's approval to protect himself and refuse to allow it any say in the matter. Olivier objected even more strongly, saying that only the Fabian executive could decide what were the purposes of the Society. Shaw managed to settle the matter for the moment by pointing out that a dispute might jeopardize the legacy, and by arguing that it would not be desirable to give members the impression that the Society was in funds to the extent that they could relax their own efforts. He saw the risks ahead and suggested that Bland be kept fully informed of what was intended, "to give him a proprietary interest in our projects and to keep up the camaraderie of the Old Gang." Shaw also insisted that Webb must at least tell the members through *Fabian News* how much money was involved. "You cannot treat them as children," he urged, "and now that several thousand pounds are at stake, the slightest attempt at evasion or concealment would destroy our influence at a blow."[16] Sidney therefore asked R. B. Haldane to give him a counsel's opinion whether the wording of the trust could be broadly construed to cover "the promotion of the study of Socialism, Economics or any other branch or branches of Social Science," lectures and the publication of pamphlets. Haldane replied that as long as the money was not used to finance candidates the trustees were free to do anything implied in the Basis and rules of the Society.[17]

Webb believed that the disinterested search for knowledge was likely to lead to socialist conclusions, but he knew that other influential members of the Society by no means shared this opinion. Bland and Olivier wished to use the windfall for Fabian propaganda; Shaw was inclined to agree with them, and opinion in the Society was strongly for an increase in activity if money could be found. Apart from Hutchinson's gifts it had depended heavily on the profits from *Fabian Essays*, and in the last two years its funds had been at a low ebb. While Sidney knew that his plans for a London School of Economics would succeed only if he could persuade sceptical academics, London County Council politicians, and businessmen that it would be politically neutral, he had to find a way of persuading the Fabians that the Society would benefit from at least part of the bequest. In November he wrote to all the executive members and other selected Fabians inviting suggestions for projects which would "exercise a solid and lasting influence in aid of collectivist progress." One wanted a Fabian newspaper, another a correspondence school; none of the proposals was compelling. Sidney felt that he had at least gone through the motions of consultation and that he could go ahead with the plan he had already formulated.

At a meeting of the trustees on 8 February 1895 Sidney outlined what could be done, distinguishing between social research and educational lecturing. During the winter he had worked out a scheme for starting the London School of Economics with an initial subsidy of £500 and the prospect of grants from the Technical Education Board. To keep the Fabians happy a few hundred pounds a year of Hutchinson money were to be made available to the Society. Some of the money was for general overhead: Pease had his salary raised from £50 to £150. The remainder was to be used to underwrite the costs of "Hutchinson Lecturers" who would go out to the provinces and give serious talks.

Webb originally intended to put Graham Wallas in charge of the School. Wallas was personally and politically acceptable to the Fabians, yet sufficiently moderate in his views to avoid antagonizing potential patrons of the School. But he could not be persuaded to take on the job. Eventually the position went to W. A. S. Hewins, a young economic historian at Pembroke College, Oxford, whom the Webbs had met when they were working on their book and who, although he was no socialist, impressed them by his ability and his scepticism about orthodox economics. Hewins was given a guarantee of £2,000 to underwrite the

School for three years, and a personal salary of £300 a year to cover the directorship, his own lectures and the editing of a series of monographs. The rest of the money, supplemented by other grants Sidney could scrape together, would just cover the costs of a secretary, a porter and the services of part-time lecturers. As a temporary home, three rooms were to be rented from the Society of Arts at 9 John Street, Adelphi.

The choice of Hewins and the backing of the City for the commercial courses caused more trouble among the Fabians. On 1 July Shaw wrote to Beatrice expressing anxiety about Sidney's various manipulations and the "temporary (let us hope) suspension of Webb's wits." The impression Sidney made, Shaw complained, was that "the Hutchinson trustees are prepared to bribe the Fabians by subsidies for country lectures and the like to allow them to commit an atrocious malversation of the rest of the bequest." Though GBS was ready to support the plan for the school, he thought Sidney should keep faith with his own side. "This won't do," he insisted. "Any pretence about having no bias at all, about 'pure' or 'abstract' research, or the like evasions and unrealities must be kept for the enemy . . . the Collectivist flag must be waved, and the Marseillaise played if necessary to attract fresh bequests." He begged the Webbs to avoid shocking Independent Labour Party and Fabian critics: Hutchinson's money, after all, "was expressly left to endow Socialism."

Sidney Webb's decision to divert the bulk of the Hutchinson money to teaching and research and not to "endow Socialism" marked a turning point in Fabian policy. It followed logically from his commitment to permeation, and from his belief that Fabians should be educators rather than agitators. The struggle to persuade the Fabian executive to accept his decision was the crucial test of his ability to impose that strategy upon the Society. By the end of 1894 he had already come to the conclusion that Fabians must settle for the long haul of investment, not for a propagandist spending spree.

Matters of temperament and intellectual inclination apart, there were two reasons for this cautious approach. The first was that the Liberal government was obviously doomed and nothing could be gained for the present from trying to use it as an instrument of reform. The failure of Rosebery was a disappointment. As prime minister he achieved little and annoyed everyone. He upset the Radicals by his failure to press reforms, the pacifists and free-traders by his imperialist posture, the Nonconformists by his patrician style of life and his addiction to horse racing. He could not even hold his Cabinet together. "The rot has set in," Haldane disconsolately told Beatrice. "There is nc hope now but to be beaten and then to reconstruct a new party."

The Webbs shared that view. The second reason why Sidney wanted to play a waiting game was that other Fabians saw the impending collapse of the Liberals as an opportunity to push the new Independent Labour Party. Ramsay MacDonald, active in both the Society and the ILP, made himself their spokesman. Up to the middle of 1894 he had taken the same line as Webb, hoping that some understanding could be reached with the more radical Liberals and opposing Keir Hardie's efforts to start an independent party. After a bye-election at Attercliffe in 1894, when the local Liberal caucus refused to adopt a strong working-man candidate, MacDonald changed his mind. When Webb recoiled from practical politics, the ambitious MacDonald decided that the time had come to gamble on the new movement. "I have stuck to the Liberals up to now, hoping that they might do something to justify the trust that we had put in them," he wrote to Hardie on 15 July 1894 in a letter formally applying for membership in the ILP. Now, he felt, "the time for conciliation has gone by and those of us who are in earnest in our professions must definitely declare ourselves."[18]

At the beginning of 1895, with a general election likely in the course of the summer, MacDonald proposed a trial collaboration between the Fabians and the ILP in the London County Council campaign in March. At his request Sidney Webb gave a dinner to discuss the suggestion, inviting MacDonald, Keir Hardie, and Tom Mann—about to become secretary of the ILP—with Shaw and Pease from the Fabians. The evening was a failure; the clash of personalities and policies was too sharp.[19] Hardie was caustic about the Fabian taste for "academic education and discussion on abstract principles" and said that the mass of the people could never be reached by such means. Beatrice thought that Tom Mann had reverted to the worst habits of the SDF, "stumping the country . . . raving emotions," and trying to make the ILP a new kind of church—"a body of men all professing the same creed and all working in exact uniformity to exactly the same end." She and Sidney concluded that it was best for the Fabians to continue their policy of "inoculation" which gave "to each class, to each person, coming under our influence, the exact dose of collectivism they were prepared to assimilate." She conceded that there was some truth in Keir Hardie's remark that "we were the worst enemies of the social revolution."

The immediate prospects for the ILP, let alone the social revolution, were not promising in 1895. It had enrolled about ten thousand members, but its organization was poor, it was not experienced at fighting elections and it was still very much a regional party. Of the three hundred branches formed by 1895 over a third were in Yorkshire, another quarter in Lancashire and Cheshire; the remainder were scattered in the Midlands, the North and Scotland. It was essentially a party based on the textile and engineering centres, leaving London, the South and the mining areas virtually untouched by its missionary zeal. Hardie's main assets were that zeal and the backing of Blatchford's *Clarion*, which helped to raise the four thousand pounds needed to put twenty-eight ILP candidates into the field—all but four of them running against both Liberal and Tory opponents.

In the early months of 1895 it was clear that the tide was running towards the Tories. In the March elections for the London County Council the Progressives just scraped back in, and though Sidney held his seat in Deptford he was gloomy about this setback. In May, Beatrice concluded that the Liberals were about to go "unabashed to their grave—if anything rather inclined to repent their good deeds, not to regret their lost opportunities."[20] The elections came in July, after the Rosebery government had been defeated on a snap vote and Lord Salisbury had formed a coalition of Tories and Liberal Unionists.

The Fabians could not make up their minds what line to take; they were, in Beatrice's phrase, "sitting with their hands in their laps" because "no result can be satisfactory. . . . We wish the Liberals to be beaten but we do not wish the Tories to win." And nothing was to be expected from the ILP, "splashing about in a futile ineffectual fashion."[21] The results conformed to Beatrice's gloomy prediction. The Liberals were routed—Salisbury coming back with a majority of more than 150 seats—and the socialist candidates polled only 44,000 votes, Hardie himself losing his seat.[22]

Those Fabians who, like MacDonald, were committed to the ILP were bitterly disappointed. MacDonald, receiving 867 votes at Southampton, blamed Hardie's "incapacity" for the débacle and told the young Liberal politician Herbert Samuel: "the party of progressive ideas is so badly led that it is almost suicide to join it."[23] Other Fabians, who had expected less of the ILP, thought that Rosebery's defeat might lead to a realignment of party politics. William Clarke, claiming that the Liberal Party was "a mangled corpse," hoped that it might be replaced by a new "democratic" alliance of Radicals, socialists and trade unionists.[24] The Webbs took much the same line. The result was not displeasing, Beatrice wrote. "It leaves us free, indeed, to begin afresh on the old lines—of building up a new party on the basis of collectivism."[25]

After a little reflection Beatrice decided that it was "a comfortable thought that we have a government of strong resolute men" led by Salisbury: the Fabian tactics of permeation might well be tried on the Tories and the Liberal Unionists for a change. For what she meant by a party of collectivists was very different from what the ILP had in mind. It was "a distinct school of thought," she wrote, "taking up each question separately and reviewing it in the light of our principles."[26] The decision to start the London School of Economics as a centre for research and teaching, and not to spend the Hutchinson money on propaganda, was a logical end to this argument.

The chance had come just at the right moment for the Webbs, providing a distraction from the confusion of national politics. They had also found a new recreation. With a party of friends, including Shaw, Wallas and Herbert Samuel, they spent the Easter weekend of 1895 at the Beachy Head Hotel, near Eastbourne. "In the intervals between unending talks about things in general," Samuel recalled, "we seized the opportunity to learn, on the short stretch of level road along the top of the cliff, how to ride the 'safety bicycle' that was just then coming into vogue."[27] Shaw, telling Janet Achurch that he would "not be beaten by that hellish machine," complained that his repeated falls made the coast guards laugh more than anyone ever laughed at his plays.[28] He and the Webbs kept up their practice all through the summer of 1895. Amy Strachey, the wife of St. Loe Strachey, who edited the *Spectator*, noted their rapid improvement: "I have a little picture in my mind of Mrs. Webb, who rode extremely well, scudding on before me down one of the back streets of Pimlico . . . with both hands behind her back, steering by her pedals. She was a graceful and intrepid rider."[29]

The Beachy Head party included another guest, Bertha New-

combe, an artist and a keen Fabian who in 1893 had painted Shaw as
"The Platform Spellbinder" and who had been invited because Beatrice
believed that she would make a suitable wife for GBS. It was Beatrice's
second attempt to bring them together, and she chose her moment well,
for Shaw was tiring of Florence Farr.

Shaw's vanity was easily tickled by women who openly admired
him, and Bertha Newcombe was now numbered among them. Yet, despite the fact that her deep feeling was "most injudiciously displayed,"
he did not respond in his usual way. He seemed to use the relationship to
clarify his own feelings about marriage. His conduct, Bertha Newcombe
said, was honourable in the letter, though he transgressed in the spirit.
"Frequent talking, talking, talking, of the pros & cons of marriage, even
to my prospects of money or the want of it, his dislike of the sexual relation & so on," she recalled, created "an atmosphere of love-making
without any need for caresses or endearments."[30] By the summer of 1895
he decided that he was behaving irresponsibly. When the Webbs invited
him and Wallas to spend part of the holidays at the Argoed, GBS specifically asked Beatrice not to include Bertha in the invitation. "Everybody seems bent on recommending me to marry Bertha," he wrote to
Janet Achurch from the Argoed. "She is only wasting her affections on
me. I give her nothing; and I do not even take everything—in fact I don't
take anything, which makes her most miserable."[31]

Now thirty-nine, GBS was not immune to pressure on him to
marry. His age, however, was not the only reason. He was also ex-
periencing for the first time a close association with a couple who were
happily married. "The Webbs pet one another as if they were honey-
mooning (as usual)," he noted at the Argoed.[32] There was still something in the situation of the triangular pattern, in which he commonly
played the part of the flirtatious intruder, but there was an important
difference: Beatrice did not flirt with him in that way; Sidney was his
closest and most respected friend; and both of them took him seriously.

This new kind of relationship puzzled GBS and it made him look
inward for a more sensitive understanding. On 31 August he wrote to
Janet Achurch, who served as his current confidante, that he was trying
to comprehend his attitude to Beatrice. "I—I, George Bernard Shaw—
have actually suffered from something which in anyone else I should
call unhappiness. I would give anything for a moment of really sacred
solitude, and perhaps twice as much for a moment of really sacred in-

timacy." His difficulty, he explained, was the "frightful sensation of being always on guard with another man's wife, which I escape in your
case by openly and recklessly adoring you." Since he was thrown constantly in the company of Beatrice, that feeling "seems to me to develop
itself here to a perfectly devilish intensity. . . . As an Irishman, an irregular artistic person, an anarchist in conduct, and above all, a creator
of an atmosphere subtly disintegrative of households, I am antipathetic
to her . . . we embarrass each other frightfully when we are alone together without some subject of keen and immediate interest to discuss."

This strain was not the only blight on the holiday. When Wallas
went down for a fortnight he was still in the state of moody dissatisfaction that had troubled Beatrice the previous summer. He was going
through a severe crisis which expressed itself in a political context. The
more he was drawn into the work of the London School Board the more
he found Fabianism an ideological encumbrance. Shaw noted that Wallas was "getting very uneasy in the bonds of socialism, and we all had
fearful and prolonged arguments & pleadings which had to be steered
carefully clear of ending in strained bonds & possibly broken ones."[33]
Wallas wanted to leave the Fabian Society altogether, but the persua-
sions of the group, particularly pressure from Sidney, decided him to
stay. He did, however, resign from the executive.

In September the party was joined by Bertrand Russell, the brilliant
young mathematician from Trinity College, Cambridge, who had recently married Alys Pearsall Smith, the daughter of the Webbs' neighbours in Grosvenor Road. Russell was one of the bright young people
who collected at the Pearsall Smiths' country home at Fridays Hill in the
summer of 1890. Alys, the youngest daughter of the eccentric Quaker
family, was captivated by the paradoxes and perceptions of this lively
logician with his rigorous belief in the scientific method. Her naïve enthusiasm made her a good listener, and her sympathetic intelligence led
her to idealize those she admired. For some time she was devoted to Graham Wallas and she soon extended these feelings to Beatrice.

The bicycles had gone down to the Argoed with the Webbs, and
the party found relief from the strains by recklessly swooping through
the wooded hills of the Wye Valley. When they set off one day to visit
Tintern Abbey, eight miles away, Shaw had an accident. "I was flying
down a steep hill, going at a speed which took the machine miles beyond
my control. . . . Seeing the road clear before us, I gave myself up to

the enjoyment of a headlong tearing toboggan down the hill. Imagine my feelings when I saw Russell jump off and turn his machine right across my path to read a signpost!" Russell was unhurt—though "his knickerbockers were demolished"—but GBS "flew through the air for several yards, and then smote the earth like a thunderbolt."[34] Riding back to London with the Webbs in exquisite weather, by way of Stonehenge, Shaw reflected on the stressful summer. He was not convinced that it had been a holiday at all, he wistfully told Janet Achurch.

He had actually finished a new play at the Argoed—the one-acter on Napoleon called *The Man of Destiny*. There was a current demand for curtain-raisers, and Shaw had decided to produce "a bravura piece to display the virtuosity of the two principal performers."[35] He had never been modest in his theatrical ambitions; as early as his first draft for *Widowers' Houses* he had drawn up a proposed cast list in the hope that it might be performed at the St. James Theatre, envisaging Ellen Terry as Blanche and Henry Irving as Cokane. Now he wrote *Man of Destiny* with the specific intention of attracting a top-ranking actor such as Forbes Robertson or perhaps Henry Irving, then at the peak of his fame.

To this end he revived his contact with Ellen Terry, with whom he had had a brief correspondence when he was music critic for *The World* in the summer of 1892. She responded to his engaging letters, and soon he had set up a literary relationship *à trois* with her and Irving. In November 1895 he sent her a copy of the play. It caught her interest. In a casual note for him on the margin of a copy of the *Chicago Tribune* she observed: "H.I. quite loves it and will do it finely." Writing back to her in America, where she was touring, Shaw pressed for a decision in his familiar style:

> Having no idea that His Immensity had any sort of interest in the play—having sent it to you, I swear, out of pure vanity, to steal another priceless millionth of an inch of your regard by shewing you what a clever fellow I am—I might at any moment have parted with it to Mansfield or another . . . Will you therefore befriend me to the extent of letting me know seriously whether H.I. wishes me to hold the play for him, as its production by him would of course be quite the best thing that could happen to it.[36]

Nothing came of the proposal, but the correspondence continued. GBS had found yet another leading lady as his confidante, and he unburdened his feelings—his "blarneying audacities"—to Ellen Terry in an intimate manner which would have been too threatening for him in a real relationship. This detached liaison also suited Ellen Terry. She was beautiful and clever, quick and restless, and she easily got on familiar terms with the shyest of strangers. Like GBS, however, she never sacrificed her inner self, finding it easier to pity and help people than to love them. The game she played with Shaw gave them both pleasure, and the words flowed freely because they carried no hint of action. For a man so prone to flirtation, and so distressed when his teases were taken too seriously, it was understandable that he should think that "the ideal love affair is one conducted by post."

1. *Thomas Davidson*

2. *Percival Chubb*

3. *Frank Podmore*

4. *Edward Pease*

5. *Marjorie Pease*

6. *William Clarke*

7. *Sydney Olivier*

8. *Graham Wallas*

9. *William Morris*

10. *Edith Nesbit*

11. *Hubert Bland*

12. *Joseph Chamberlain*

13. *Beatrice Potter*

14. *Sidney Webb*

15. *George Bernard Shaw and Charlotte Payne-Townshend*
16. *Beatrice and Sidney Webb*

17. *Annie Besant*

18. *Jenny Patterson*

19. *Florence Farr*

20. *The invalid Shaw at Hindhead*

21. *Ramsay MacDonald*

22. *H. H. Champion, Tom Mann, Keir Hardie and Ben Tillett in Australia in 1908*

23. *Fabian summer school at Harlech*

24. *Keir Hardie (left) with Charlotte and Bernard Shaw at Merthyr Tydvil, 1910 election*

25. *R. B. Haldane*

26. *G. D. H. Cole*

27 A & B. *Beatrice and Sidney Webb at the time of the Poor Law Campaign*

28. *41 Grosvenor Road*

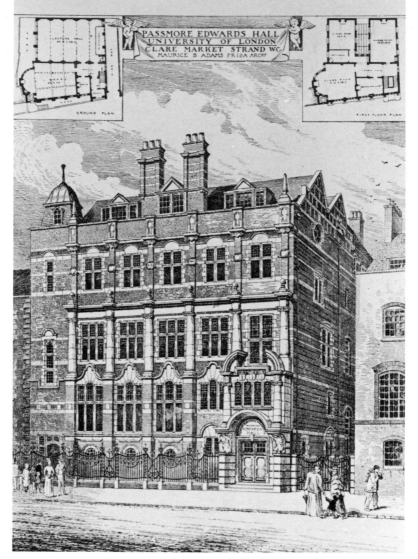

29. *The first building of the London School of Economics*

15

NEW ALLIANCES

In the first years of her marriage Beatrice dropped away from her family and her old social connections. She began to pick up these relationships again in 1895, as if a more conciliatory attitude to upper-class society were the counterpart to a decision to make political overtures to the new ruling group. At Christmas she and Sidney went down to Somerset to stay with her sister Maggie and her husband Henry Hobhouse; they moved on for the New Year to Parmoor, visiting Beatrice's brother-in law Alfred Cripps—his wife, Theresa, had died two years before—who was beginning to make his mark as a Tory politician after a brilliant career at the bar. Beatrice was pleased to find that Sidney was losing his gaucherie and could hold his own in such company; "my boy is recognised as a distinguished man!" she noted happily after the visits.[1]

Such satisfaction offset the wistful feelings aroused by the success of Joseph Chamberlain. "I shall never quite free myself from the shadow of past events," she reflected when Chamberlain emerged as the dominant figure in the 1895 election and in Salisbury's government. His opposition to Home Rule had developed into a sense of national destiny; as colonial secretary he epitomized the imperialist fervour which swept through Britain in the last years of the century.

South Africa had become Chamberlain's obsession and his opportunity. The Transvaal, reserved to the Boer farmers after an earlier clash with the British, was being swamped by emigrants attracted to the Johannesburg goldfields. The refusal of the Boer President, Paul Kruger, to allow his little republic's autonomy to be whittled away by giving political rights to the newcomers was already leading to a crisis when Chamberlain took office. Cecil Rhodes, prime minister of the Cape Colony, was bent on annexing the Transvaal. He felt confident enough, on the basis of private understandings with Chamberlain, to send his assistant, Dr. Starr Jameson, across the border on 29 December 1895 with a force of five hundred men. The invasion was misjudged and Jameson was forced to surrender three days later. In the uproar that followed, Jameson was disowned, tried and convicted by a British court; Rhodes was forced to resign; and Chamberlain repudiated the affair, sending mollifying messages to Kruger.

Despite its embarrassing failure the Jameson Raid caught the jingoist mood of Britain: "The whole mind of the country is at present absorbed in foreign affairs," Beatrice remarked; "Joe Chamberlain is today the national hero." He had "given the nation confidence not only in his administration of the Colonies but in the Conservative Govt."[2]

Beatrice's admiration for Chamberlain had warped her judgment. Before long she came to see the commercial intrigues behind his South African policy and to feel uneasy about its consequences. But neither she nor Sidney had much knowledge of foreign affairs. Their vision was much more narrowly focused on the County Council and on Parliament, and in particular upon reforms in the educational system. For Sidney had come to believe that Britain could not be effectively governed—and thereby meet the twin challenges of social progress at home and competition abroad—without modernizing its schools and training a new generation of experts. Twenty years after the introduction of universal elementary education the country was beginning to produce a moderately literate work force, but his work on the Technical Education Board had taught Sidney that, by comparison with Germany, Britain was woefully behind in vocational training. His own experience in the civil service, moreover, had made him realize the need for economists, political scientists and administrators. Without a flow of skilled people who could actually carry out new policies, reforms would not be worth the paper on which they were drafted.

The London School of Economics played a vital part in his plans, and he fussed over every detail of its development. He became chairman of its Administrative Committee, composed of the original Hutchinson trustees and some new members including Beatrice, Hubert Bland, Sydney Olivier and Bertrand Russell. He found the school larger premises, supervised the academic programme, persuaded talented lecturers to give classes, and worried about the cost of shelving for books and the quality of the linoleum on the floors. "Nothing that I can write will give you any adequate idea of the worry and anxiety I have had during the last few weeks," he wrote to William Clarke on 5 May 1896, when he was searching for a suitable house into which the expanding school could move.[3] And when the accommodation problem was settled, money was a perpetual concern. Though the running costs of the school were initially only £2,500 a year, Sidney was determined to make the Hutchinson money go as far as possible; once the institution was launched he found enough money from private gifts and County Council grants to meet the greater part of its expenses. He was, moreover, determined to make the school a centre of research as well as teaching, and from the outset he planned to create a new and specialized library.[4] Early in 1896 an appeal for funds stated the case for a library which would concentrate on political science, collecting material which other libraries neglected—reports from national and local government, both in Britain and overseas, from businesses, trade unions, cooperative societies and political parties. The library was launched as a venture separate from the school; with more than two thousand pounds coming in from contributors as diverse as the rising Tory leader Arthur Balfour, Sir Charles Dilke, Liberal financiers, bishops, and wealthy Fabians, Sidney could begin, like a jackdaw, avidly to collect books, reports and papers to stock it. Town councils and government agencies as far apart as Calcutta and Elmira, New York, were surprised to receive letters asking them to deposit their publications at the library. Within three years, with very modest resources, the library acquired over twenty-five thousand items.

Sidney also had his eye on university status for the school. Its students could enter for the external examinations of the University of London, but there was no way in which the London School of Economics and other colleges in London could combine together. There had been an abortive plan by the Liberal government in 1894 for a reorganization of higher education in London which would have created a teaching university, but the tedious negotiations had not advanced far before

Rosebery resigned. This scheme, however, had led Haldane and Webb to work together to draft a parliamentary bill establishing a new university. Despite the fall of the Liberals they went on with the idea. Haldane, indeed, had high hopes of persuading the Tories to support it, for Arthur Balfour, with whom he had good personal relations and who shared with him an interest in German idealist philosophy and educational reform, was willing to collaborate. Webb, Haldane and Balfour were all capable of putting measures before party, and on current educational issues both Webb and Haldane found themselves closer to the Conservatives than to the Liberals, whose educational policies were dominated by the Nonconformist lobby.

The decision to work through the Tories for educational reform seemed to Webb a logical application of the Fabian notion of permeation, but it made trouble for him inside the Society and particularly with Graham Wallas. In 1896 the Conservatives produced a draft Education Bill which proposed to put education under the control of county councils rather than the existing local school boards, and which also paid off some political debts from the 1895 election by offering state aid to Church schools. Webb favoured the administrative changes and he was prepared to accept the concessions to the Anglican interest as the price of progress. After a long talk with Sir John Gorst, the minister in charge of the bill, Sidney decided not to oppose it. He told the recalcitrant Wallas on 8 April that the bill was going forward in any case and that they might be able to improve it by careful lobbying.

Wallas, a fervent agnostic, was outraged by the idea of subsidizing religious teaching and found allies among the Progressives and Nonconformists, who, as equally fervent dissenters, objected to public funds being used to promote the Anglican religion in the classroom. Both Wallas and his Liberal associates wanted to preserve and even extend the scope of the London School Board, making it responsible for all types of education in the capital. Even though he was eventually won round to municipal control of the schools, he was not appeased on the matter of religious education. His irritation was intensified by Shaw's decision to support the bill and his attack on its opponents—who ultimately forced the government to withdraw it—as anti-Church fanatics. It was this issue which led Wallas to resign from the Fabian executive. Personal friendship survived, but he was no longer in political sympathy with the Webbs and Shaw.

The Webbs, in fact, were keeping different company as permeation became a life style as well as a policy. Their new interests, Beatrice remarked, combined "to force us into political society on both sides."[5] One night they dined at the House with Asquith and Haldane, the next with some Conservative ministers. They began to associate with "the superior rank of civil servants," one of these being Alfred Milner, whom Chamberlain was about to send out as high commissioner for South Africa. In all these connections Haldane played a crucial part. He was a bachelor who liked to entertain, and he often invited the Webbs. After one dinner party, which included the Asquiths, John Morley, and Lord and Lady Tweedmouth, Beatrice commented that it was "a typical Haldane dinner . . . typical of Haldane's weakness—his dilettante desire to be in every set; and his strength—his diffusive friendship which enabled him to bring about non-party measures."[6] Shaw too was drawn into the social swim, though he was less amenable to the proprieties. Asked by Haldane to dine with Asquith and Balfour, he accepted with the characteristic proviso: "Do not kill anything for me, because I simply shan't eat it."[7]

Beatrice went on picking up the threads of her old life. At Easter 1896 she and Sidney went to stay with her sister Lallie and her husband in Liverpool, going on to the Lake District to visit Rusland, another of the Potter houses where Beatrice had spent family holidays. Sidney told Wallas it was "very healthy and invigorating" and that they cycled "unhesitatingly" on "terrific hills."[8] Fabian affairs received little attention from them on this holiday—until they received a rude reminder that while they were mending their fences in high places their critics were on the rampage in the Society. A furious letter arrived from Ramsay MacDonald, accusing Sidney of abusing the Hutchinson Trust, and threatening to divide the Fabians against him.

Though MacDonald was a member of the Fabian executive, his dissatisfaction with the way the Society was run was increasing. The overt issue was a difference with Webb about the distinction between socialist propaganda and education, for MacDonald inclined to the Independent Labour Party view that the immediate task was "to make socialists" and, as Beatrice Webb caustically put it, "to organise unthinking persons into Socialist societies."[9] The Webbs, in contrast, thought the immediate need was "to make the thinking persons socialistic." MacDonald, moreover, had lately been exposed to the·enthusiasm of the provincials and he was emotionally attached to the Bristol Fabian Enid Stacey, who had followed Kate Conway into socialist evangelism. MacDonald and Enid Stacey had been appointed as the first touring lecturers to be supported by the small part of the Hutchinson funds which Webb had allocated to Fabian purposes. "How chaste one feels in starting a Fabian tour," he wrote to her; ". . . how you go forth with your express train as your steed, a black bag as your equerry, a Fabian tract as your armour of offence and defence!"[10]

MacDonald had an ambivalent personality, alternating between romantic ambition and sudden loss of nerve, and he was tetchily suspicious of other people. When Sidney Webb decided to found the London School of Economics, MacDonald apparently hoped that as an experienced lecturer he would be given some part in the scheme. Beatrice thought that he was not "good enough for that work": he had "never had the time to do any sound original work, or even learn the old stuff well."[11] Sidney had even insisted that his Fabian lectures should be "more educational" and less propagandist. MacDonald retaliated by suggesting that the Webbs were dragging the Society away from its socialist objectives. In March 1896 he told Pease that he was doubtful about running again for the executive, partly because the Webbs and Shaw were being trickily evasive about a proposed tract on women's rights; if elected, he wrote, he would "serve more for the purpose of watching developments than from any hope that the Society is going to do any useful work."

He next began to complain that the Hutchinson money had been misused. On 8 April he wrote to Pease: "If you mean that the Hutchinson Trustees have practically mortgaged the Trust for a £150 a year for the Fabian (£50 going to the office) & the rest to the School of Economics, I shall certainly oppose them and carry through the opposition to an appeal to the Society if need be."[12] Pease tried to put him off, but MacDonald kept up his campaign. The next day he declared that he was "simply amazed at the way the money seems destined to be spent. . . . The School is perfectly certain to pass out of all your hands." On Good Friday, the day he wrote to the Webbs in Cumberland, MacDonald told Pease that he would be satisfied with nothing less than a detailed accounting. He added: "You are altogether out of touch with anything but London Socialism." His ILP associations had clearly induced him to throw in his lot with the provincials, where "educational work is being handled with rare ability and success."

MacDonald was still reluctant to lose the position he had built up among the Fabians, though Webb refused to show him either the articles of the Hutchinson Trust or Haldane's legal opinion on it. In May, after being elected again to the executive, he once more threatened to resign, insisting that there was "too much of this private consultation going on & rearranging of executive decisions." He made a last attempt to divert some of the Hutchinson money back to Fabian purposes by putting forward a plan for expanding the activities of the Society at a cost of five hundred pounds a year, but he could do no more than get it accepted "in general." At this time he was also going through a crisis in his career and in his personal life. His lecture fees and journalism kept him afloat, but at the age of thirty he had no steady income and his attachment to Enid Stacey came to nothing when she married a Fabian clergyman.

His situation improved when he met Margaret Gladstone, the daughter of a distinguished scientist, brought up in a devout home and given to social work. In the summer of 1896 MacDonald proposed to her on the steps of the British Museum, where they often met. Their marriage in November not only gave MacDonald an attractive wife; it also gave him financial security, for, like Beatrice Webb, she had a private income.

With such prospects MacDonald could afford, in the summer of 1896, to carry on his feud with Webb, though he now shifted his attack from the Hutchinson funds to a direct political challenge. The Fabian Society was preparing a description of its work for a forthcoming International Socialist Congress in London. Shaw, who was asked to draft it, seized the chance to write a defence of permeation which even the moderate Pease considered to be "extreme." The more radical Fabians were so outraged that they joined MacDonald in demanding a special meeting at which they hoped to reject the document. At a crowded and lively session in July, Keir Hardie, Tom Mann, Emily Pankhurst, Kate Conway (now married to the ILP leader J. Bruce Glasier) and Emma Brooke all supported MacDonald's case against Webb and Shaw, but they were voted down by 108 votes to 33.

Shaw's policy statement, afterwards published as Tract 70, remained the formal basis of Fabian policy for the next ten years. It bore no sign of the temporary concessions to the ILP which Webb and Shaw had made in "To Your Tents, O Israel!" when they were disillusioned with the Liberals, or of Webb's scheme of financing labour candidates with trade-union money. The document declared flatly that the Society cared "nothing by what name any party calls itself, or what principles, Socialist or other, it professes." It simply stated that the Society would bring "all the pressure and persuasion in its power to bear on existing forces" and that it was not necessary for "the practical steps towards Social-Democracy" to be carried out by the Fabians "or any other specially organised society or party"; Shaw had gone right back to Webb's confident assumption in his Fabian Essay that the *Zeitgeist* would do the work.

Shaw had been deliberately provocative. Whenever there was a crisis in the Society's affairs GBS diverted the issue by insisting on the Society's freedom to decide issues on their merits and attacking those who sought to commit the Fabians to a doctrine or a party. In this case, moreover, he was determined to quash MacDonald's challenge to Webb, partly for reasons of personal loyalty and partly because he felt that the Fabians would have no useful future as an appendage of the ILP.

Shaw and Webb, moreover, were already looking in a different direction, and a close involvement with the ILP would have been an embarrassment to their plans to attempt a new round of permeation directed at the collectivists in both the Liberal and Tory parties. What they meant by "independence" was the liberty to pick and choose allies as occasion arose—allies, that is, who either had political power or had the early prospect of getting it. For the Fabian leaders, who did not want the responsibility of building and running their own movement, were dependent upon others who were professional politicians. Setting themselves up as covert manipulators and advisers—almost as a lobby of freelance civil servants—they hawked their services to those who might have the means to translate their policies into practice. Fabian purposes were to be achieved through other instruments, not by Fabians themselves.

The confusion of the Liberal Party confused every reformer. It was too decentralized to be captured, too fragmented for a decisive split, too conflicted to offer any hope of unity in the foreseeable future. Yet it was still strong enough to survive as the only practicable alternative to the Tories. It sprawled across British politics, unable to get on or get out of the way. In January 1897 Sidney Webb told Herbert Samuel bluntly that he could not support a Liberal candidate at a forthcoming bye-election, because he did not know what the party's position would be on any issue that mattered.[13] The situation had been further complicated for the Webbs, after the Liberal defeat in 1895, by the fact that their closest associates in the Liberal Party were supporters of Rosebery and the Liberal Imperialist, or "Limps," faction. Such men as Haldane, Asquith and Grey were in open opposition to the dominant trend of Gladstonian Liberalism and Nonconformity.

The Liberal failure, however, did not help the Independent Labour Party. On the contrary, the ILP suffered from the general decline in Liberal support. Though Hardie and the other ILP leaders were pressing for independent labour candidates, there was no doubt that for years to come there was little chance of building up labour representation in Parliament except by some sort of understanding with the Liberals; a new party was bound to wilt unless it could operate in the protecting shade of the Liberal organization. The ILP, moreover, was finding it difficult to maintain its own sketchy organization and the enthusiasm of its members. In London, support dwindled to the point where its organizer was told to call on Pease to patch up an agreement with the Fabians.

There was a similar reaction in the trade-union movement, where John Burns, now looking for a political career with the Liberals, had thrown his influence against the socialists in the Trades Union Congress. He had pushed through new standing orders which excluded delegates who did not work at a trade or hold office in a union—which meant that Keir Hardie was now kept out. At the same time the TUC adopted a system of card votes which strengthened the traditional unions—for the most part led by "Lib-Lab" men opposed to independent labour politics —against the struggling new unions of the unskilled.

It was a dispiriting time, coming after the five years of exciting progress which had followed the publication of *Fabian Essays*, the London dock strike, and the birth of the New Unionism. There was something symbolic about the death of William Morris in October 1896; and when Sergius Stepniak was killed in a railway accident the turnout of the socialist old guard for his funeral had a depressing impact. None of the speeches had the fire of the early Nineties. Hardie was talking of "a backlash of apathy," and from all over the country there came reports of members dropping out of the socialist groups or generally backsliding in the work. Harry Snell, a Fabian itinerant speaker, concluded that the movement had suffered "a moral disaster." It had relied too much on transient emotion, he said, and too little on intellectual and moral strength. Agitators who worked too hard and were paid too little had nothing to offer but "aimless enthusiasm."[14]

There were casualties, too, among the Fabians. In June 1897 William Clarke's depression—intensified by the death of his mother, the loss of his savings in a promoter's swindle, and the failure of the *Progressive Review*, a "New Liberal" publication which he had edited—led him to resign from the Society. He pathetically enclosed a ten-shilling postal order with his letter of resignation. Not long afterwards he sadly confessed to Webb: "I made a great mistake in giving so many of the best years of my life to barren questions."[15] Harry Snell also drew the conclusion that his energies were better spent in the ethical movement than in socialist politics, while John Trevor, who had played such a part in launching the ILP, decided that it was "attempting the salvation of the world in appalling cheap fashion, . . . attempting to bottle up all the elements of man's personal and social life in one resounding formula."[16] Resignations, nervous breakdowns, even suicide, were typical symptoms of the collapse of morale.

As the tide turned against all the socialist groups in 1896 they were forced again to face the question which seemed far simpler for the rank-and-file than for their leaders: Why should there not be a single socialist body which offered a clear alternative to the two bourgeois parties? The initiative came from the ILP. When it approached the Fabians after its conference in 1896, Webb and Shaw were in the middle of their tussle with MacDonald and in no mood to make concessions. Webb feared that any move towards closer relations with the ILP would destroy the distinctive character of the London Fabian Society as quickly as the ILP had swallowed up the provincial groups. There were, however, sufficient sympathizers with the ILP on the Fabian executive to secure a declaration that the Society was "in favour of the principle of some form of United Socialist Party." The best Webb could do was to insert the caveat that "at present the difficulties in the way are formidable." The Fabians were persuaded to wait and see whether there was any chance of bridging the gap between Hardie and Hyndman.

It was a year before informal talks between the ILP and the SDF led to the proposal that the two parties should merge. When this was put to both memberships, five thousand voted for fusion and one thousand against. But Hardie, Bruce Glasier and other ILP leaders remained sceptical, Hardie being afraid that the move would further antagonize the trade unions and Bruce Glasier bluntly objecting to the SDF's doctrinaire, "aggressively sectarian" character and its "strange disregard of the religious, moral and aesthetic sentiments of the people." It was an old and familiar complaint, which persisted even when the SDF had abandoned its early revolutionary heroics. Coming to the conclusion that merger with the SDF would drive the trade unions back to the Liberals, Hardie and his colleagues played for time and then buried the issue in long discussions that eventually petered out.

The idea of unity had turned out to be an illusion. The only result of the negotiations had been to draw the line between the SDF on the one hand and the Fabians and the ILP on the other; the complex problem of the relations between the Fabians and the ILP was still unresolved. The result was a curious ambivalence between the policies pursued by the Society's London leadership and Fabian activity in the provinces, where there were close working links with the ILP. The Hutchinson scheme still flourished outside the capital: nearly two hundred lectures had been given in more than fifty towns, the majority organized by ILP branches or by ILP members of trade-union branches and local cooperative societies. ILP branches were also the main subscribers to the Fabian book-box service and took up large quantities of Fabian tracts. Without this ILP clientele Fabian propaganda would have languished into insignificance.

Once the ILP had set its face against merger with the SDF, it needed the Fabians as a source of ideas, facts and detailed policy. The ILP leaders were skilled propagandists, and in the constituencies they were supported by local agitators who took their cue from Blatchford's *Clarion*. While the Fabians worried about the decline of lecture audiences and experimented to see if magic-lantern slides would increase their appeal, Blatchford decided to cash in on the cycling craze and the appetite for popular culture. By 1896 there were over a hundred Clarion Clubs, whose members wheeled out at weekends to take the message of socialism to street corners and village greens; there were Clarion vans, Clarion choirs, bands, jamborees and holiday homes. Yet, as MacDonald realized,

socialist rhetoric was not enough: the Fabian tracts and the Fabian lecturers were badly needed to provide more solid fare. In the autumn of
1896, for instance, Webb gave six lectures on "The Machinery of Government." Such serious material was all the more needed because the ILP
was beginning to win local elections; its members, entering town halls
and parish councils for the first time, had to rely on Fabian expertise in
municipal matters.

Webb and the other Fabian leaders were content with this informal
cooperation. Like their Positivist forebears, they were more comfortable
as cuckoos in someone else's nest. Yet, just as this compromise seemed
to be working well, a new and unexpected source of tension threatened
to disrupt it. The Society had to face the problem of foreign policy,
which Tract 70 had firmly declared was not its business at all.

16
THE IRISH LADY

At a luncheon party which the Webbs attended in the early autumn of 1895 they met as a fellow guest an attractive Irish lady named Charlotte Payne-Townshend. Beatrice afterwards noted that she was a "large graceful woman with masses of chocolate brown hair, pleasant grey eyes (*later*: they are green), matte complexion which sometimes looks muddy, at other times forms picturesquely pale background to her brilliant hair and bright eyes. She dresses well—in her flowing white evening robes she approaches beauty." Beatrice found Charlotte a receptive listener and talked to her about the Fabian Society and the London School of Economics.

It was a timely meeting for all three of them. Charlotte was rich, with an income of four thousand pounds a year, and Beatrice was fascinated at finding so much money in the hands of a woman so "genuinely anxious to increase the world's enjoyment and diminish the world's pain." Although Beatrice took to her personally, she later confessed that she first made friends with Charlotte "for the good of the cause."[1] The particular cause just then was money to set up the British Library of Political and Economic Science and premises for the infant School of Economics. Charlotte soon gave practical proof of her interest in the new school by a cheque of a thousand pounds for the library.

For Charlotte the meeting with the Webbs came when she was casting around for a long-term interest. Though she found the Webbs intimidating, she was drawn to them by their enthusiasm and sense of purpose. Already turned thirty-eight, she had so far found nothing to which she could devote her energies or substantial resources. She was by nature a rebel, Beatrice commented, "feeling any regulation or rule intolerable—a tendency which has been exaggerated by her irresponsible wealth." She was born near Cork, the elder of the two daughters of an Irish landowner. Like Beatrice Webb, Charlotte found her father the sympathetic parent, idealizing him as the innocent victim of her mother's weaknesses. She described him as "gentle & affectionate, well-educated & well-read, very *very* good, honourable & straight." Despite her affection for her father "it was a terrible home," she recalled, blaming her mother for "a perfectly hellish childhood and youth." Her mother behaved like a spoilt fidget, dominating Charlotte by her overbearing personality and her continual resort to emotional blackmail. Freedom, almost wilfulness, became an obsession; Charlotte came to fear any kind of emotional dependence, making a firm resolve "never to be the mother of a child who might suffer as I had suffered." At the same time her mother's ceaseless reproach made her feel guilty and left her with "a fearful streak of conscience, & sense of duty, complicated by a sensitiveness that is nothing less than a disease."[2]

When her father died in 1885 Charlotte was forced to be the companion of a mother for whom she had neither liking nor sympathy. She could not escape into marriage when suitors offered, for fear of losing her cherished freedom, yet as a leisured gentlewoman she had no training which would have given her an occupation. When her mother died she was thirty-four, resentful of her uselessness and driven to continue an unsatisfying round of social engagements because she knew no other way of passing the time.

In 1894, when she was in Rome, she met Dr. Axel Munthe, a Swede with a fashionable and successful practice in the city. He was a romantic figure, already well known for his courage in a cholera epidemic in Naples, and his social conscience led him to keep a surgery in a poor district of Rome. Although he was a man of pathological vanity and heartless charm he fascinated women, and Charlotte soon fell under his spell. She was flattered by his attentions and he was stimulated by her infatuation and admiration. They saw a lot of each other. His good works gave a fresh stimulus to her own desire to become a doctor and to share in his work among the poor.

Charlotte was still emotionally attached to Munthe when she met the Webbs, but on her frequent visits to them at Grosvenor Road she came across other equally stimulating people from the Webb circle. In her notes on 1896 she entered: "Met GBS first time at Webbs 29 Jan.," but Shaw apparently took no special interest in his wealthy fellow countrywoman. On 20 March he noted: "Miss Payne-Townshend 'At Home' to London School of Economics. Did not go." Charlotte felt that at last she could be useful. On 18 February Beatrice nominated her for membership in the Fabians, enclosing a donation from Charlotte of five pounds and telling Pease: "She is a good socialist and I think will prove an acquisition to the Society—the amount of her cheque showing the degree of her convictions."[3]

At the end of March Charlotte went back to Rome, where the triviality of the fashionable life palled on her more than ever. She returned to London to find Sidney bothered about his inability to find premises for the School of Economics and its library. Then Hewins found that 10 Adelphi Terrace was vacant, with a seven-year lease available at a rent of £360 a year. It was admirably situated, next door to the Statistical Society and overlooking the river near Charing Cross, but the rent seemed very high to Sidney, who could count on just over £3,600 in all to cover expenses in the first full year. Charlotte decided to take the two upper floors, paying £300 a year, so that the School could occupy the remainder almost without cost; teaching began at Adelphi Terrace in October.

Charlotte was soon recognized as part of "the Bo family," as Beatrice now began to call her entourage of relations and close friends. She was invited to join the Webbs for a six-week vacation at Stratford St. Andrew in Suffolk, where the Webbs had rented a spartan rectory with attractive grounds. Charlotte fitted easily enough into the Webbs' routine of work, walks, cycle rides and political talk. For part of the time, Shaw was the only other house guest. Since Beatrice felt ill with "rheumatic cold combined with general collapse," Charlotte and GBS were left very much to entertain each other.[4]

Shaw was as exuberant as ever despite another of his cycling mishaps in July, when he collided with a horse and cart in the Haymarket. His cycle was smashed, but he was scarcely hurt and he went off to Bayreuth to cover the Wagner Festival. He was back in time for the International Socialist Congress in London, where the German delegates regarded him "as an incarnation of Satan because he could not resist the pleasure of fanning the flames whenever there was a dispute."[5] Earlier that summer he had finished a new play, *You Never Can Tell,* and down in Suffolk he was working it up for production.

He was now trying to comply with "the requirements of managers in search of fashionable comedies for West End theatres" without sacrificing his own principles. Though *You Never Can Tell* was a farce, Shaw claimed more for it, later telling William Archer that it was a "poem and a document, a sermon and a festival all in one."[6] For its plot he drew on a familiar situation: Mrs. Clandon is a woman of forceful personality who has left her husband to live and bring up her children according to her own ideas. She accidentally meets again her stuffy middle-class husband, but neither can find the humility to make reconciliation possible. The question Shaw poses is whether her daughter Gloria, an attractive girl "raging with the impatience of a mettlesome dominative character" acquired from her mother, can conquer her pride and permit herself to fall in love with the young dentist Valentine. Gloria and Valentine at first dismiss the romantic notion of love as mere "chemistry" or as the work of the instincts—the stirrings which Shaw came to call the Life Force. Yet the young couple eventually cut through the clever talk and recognize their fate as lovers. This happy ending was not simply a concession to the box office. Shaw was being forced to find a place for love in the scheme of things.

Life at the rectory, Shaw said, was four hours writing in the morning and four hours bicycling in the afternoon every day. Beatrice was soon observing that Shaw and Charlotte had become constant companions, scouring the country together and sitting up late at night. To Ellen Terry GBS wrote on 28 August with his customary flippancy: "We have been joined by an Irish millionairess who has had cleverness and character enough to decline the station of life—'great catch for somebody'—to which it pleased God to call her, and whom we have incorporated into our Fabian family with great success. I am going to refresh my heart by falling in love with her—I love falling in love—but, mind, only with her, not with the million; so someone else must marry her if she can stand him after me." Charlotte was captivated by the same qualities of wit, charm and social concern in GBS which had attracted her to Axel Munthe. "She is in love with the brilliant Philanderer," Beatrice concluded as she watched them together, "and he is taken in his cold sort of way with her." The situation made her "somewhat uneasy," for "I doubt whether Bernard Shaw could be induced to marry: I doubt whether she will be happy without it."[7]

By 21 September all four of them were back in London, Charlotte staying with the Webbs until Adelphi Terrace was ready. In October she went to visit friends in Ireland. A letter card soon came from Shaw, begging her: "Keep me deep in your heart, write me two lines whenever you love me; and be happy and blessed and out of pain for my sake."[8] Although GBS wrote casually about Charlotte to Ellen Terry on 12 October—"there is my Irish lady with the light green eyes and the million of money, whom I have got to like so much that it would be superfluous to fall in love with her"—the tone of his letters to Charlotte was encouraging her to take him seriously. "How much longer do you intend to stay away? It is about three weeks since I heard anything of you," he wrote on 1 November. Next day, scribbling in the train on the way up to speak for Keir Hardie at a Bradford bye-election, he asked: "Why do you choose this time of all others to desert me—just now when you are most wanted?" He was pleased to have a happy letter from her. "*Be happy*," he replied; "if they love you at Mitchelstown, so do I also here in this deplorable rain. A thousand blessings grow up about you and rain down on you." Her absence was clearly affecting him. Two days later he wrote: "I wish I were with you among those hills: there are two laps in which I could rest this fagged head of mine now—Nature's and yours. . . . Imagine! past forty and still going on like this."[9] On that same day he asked Ellen Terry: "Shall I marry my Irish millionairess? . . . I am really fond of her and she of me."[10]

Charlotte naturally responded to such encouragement and wrote to tell Shaw that she was missing him. He shied off in alarm and wrote to insist:

No: you don't love me one little bit. All that is nature, instinct, sex: it proves nothing beyond itself. Don't fall in love: be your own, not mine or anyone else's. From the moment you can't do without me you are lost, like Bertha. Never fear: if we want one another we shall find it out. All I know is that you made the autumn very happy, and

that I shall always be fond of you for that. About the future I do
not concern myself: let us do what lies in our hands & wait for
events.[11]

Everyone was confused by Shaw's behaviour. When friends began
to gossip about him and Charlotte he did nothing to discourage them.
Janet Achurch told Bertha Newcombe that GBS was engaged to Charlotte, whereupon Bertha wrote to ask if this was true. GBS sent her a
farrago of nonsense about the wedding date, settlements and his future
home, which provoked the jealous Bertha into an outburst against him
for stooping to marry money; then he gleefully reported the whole episode in detail to Charlotte, as if to imply that their relationship was only
another of his larks.[12]

The bizarre nature of this courtship was highlighted by the frank
extravagance with which Shaw was simultaneously writing to Ellen
Terry, but to her—a woman whom he as yet knew only in correspondence
—he was able to reveal more of the truth. "She doesn't really *love* me," he
insisted to Ellen Terry early in November, explaining that Charlotte had
read *The Quintessence of Ibsenism*, been captivated by it, and on meeting GBS had found him "a bearable companion on bicycle rides, especially in a country house where there is nobody else to pair with. She
got fond of me . . . I got fond of her, because she was a comfort to me
down there. . . . What does your loving wisdom say to that?"[13] Ellen
replied that he was a "great silly." "If she does not dote on the quintessence of *you* she'd better marry your book. . . . How very silly you
clever people are. Fancy not knowing! Fancy not being sure! Do *you*
know you love her? 'cos if so that would be safe enough to marry on.
. . . *But a man should know*."[14]

Sidney Webb thought Shaw would hurt Charlotte with his apparently heartless trifling and gave him a "tremendous lecture."[15] GBS could
feel himself being trapped into matrimony. "My one hope," he told
Charlotte on 9 November "is that you are as treacherous as I am." He
was anxious to see her, but her return to London on 10 November would
coincide with a planned trip to Paris to see *Peer Gynt*. All the same, he
told her, "I will contrive to see you somehow, at all hazards: I *must*; and
that 'must,' which 'rather alarms' you, *terrifies* me. If it were possible to
run away—if it would do any good—I'd do it; so mortally afraid am I that
my trifling & lying and ingrained treachery and levity with women are
going to make you miserable."

In that same letter he told her that the kind of relationship he wanted was that which they had enjoyed that summer. "Stratford was so happy; better a million times leave it as it is than spoil it," he wrote. They could not continue to see much of each other unless Charlotte accepted his terms, unless, he told her, "you have the nerve to use me for your own development without losing yourself." After they had talked on the evening of 10 November he was relieved, feeling that she had taken the hint. Telling her, "I really was happy," he added significantly, "I wish there was nothing to look forward to, nothing to covet, nothing to gain."[16]

With this apparent reassurance that things could go on as they were, GBS returned to his lighthearted teasing. Charlotte learned to read his shorthand and to type. He dictated to her and she copied his notes while he alternately flattered and bullied her. "I don't find that I have made you feel anything, except nervously," he wrote. "You don't love me the least bit in the world. But I am all the more grateful."[17] He saw much of her when he was working on *The Devil's Disciple*, but while he exploited her attachment for company he continued his heartless pretence that he was her unrequited lover. To Ellen Terry, however, he could safely and frivolously write the words he denied Charlotte: "I love you," he wrote on 8 December. "You are at liberty to make what use you please of this communication."

On 17 January Beatrice wrote to Graham Wallas that Shaw and Charlotte were seeing much of each other. "Some day," she added, "they will find that it will add to the amenity of their life to spend a few minutes at the Strand Registrar's."[18] Shaw was now taking Charlotte with him when he went down to dockland to give his Sunday-morning speeches "in all sorts of holes and corners," but he reported to Ellen Terry that "these experiences make her very unhappy. At first I thought she was bored and tired and incommoded simply; but now it appears that my demagogic denunciations of the idle rich—my demands for taxation of unearned incomes—lacerate her conscience; for she has great possessions. What am I to do . . . was there ever such a situation?"[19]

Shaw found it easier to talk about his predicament than to come to terms with it. Though he had effectively dropped Bertha Newcombe after meeting Charlotte, he had procrastinated with her, leaving it until the spring of 1897 before he wrote to break things off formally. When Bertha received his letter she wrote to Beatrice, whom she suspected of some responsibility for Shaw's change of heart. Beatrice went to see her, and "with the dignity of devoted feeling" Bertha retailed the story of Shaw's ambiguous trifling. "You are well out of it," Beatrice told her gently. "You know my opinion of him. As a friend and a colleague, as a critic and literary worker, there are few men for whom I have so warm a liking, but in his relations with women he is vulgar, if not worse—it is a vulgarity that includes cruelty and springs from vanity." As Beatrice went away from this distressing interview she thought of Charlotte, "with her loving easy-going nature and anarchic luxurious ways." Would Charlotte, she wondered, "succeed in taming the Philanderer?"[20]

In April the Webbs took a pretty house with a garden on the North Downs near Dorking. Charlotte insisted on sharing the house and expenses in the hope of seeing more of Shaw. He went down to stay as often as he could, but he was hard pressed. At the beginning of May he became a member of the St. Pancras vestry. He had made a previous attempt to be elected and had been defeated in 1894, but in 1897 he was returned unopposed. He was a punctilious vestryman and enjoyed the work. "I love the reality of the Vestry," he told Ellen Terry on 28 May, "and its dustcarts and H'less orators after the silly visionary fashion-ridden theaters." He was in fact having trouble with the theatre. *You Never Can Tell* had been accepted by Cyril Maude at the Haymarket Theatre as soon as it was offered, but it had been in rehearsal for only two weeks when Shaw withdrew it. Several of the actors threw up their parts as impossible. They wanted him to "deshawise" it, but he refused to rewrite the love scenes to suit them. "They have said very nicely and sympathetically that . . . I shall lose my great chance of that splendid opportunity for a young and brilliant man," he reported to Ellen Terry on 29 April, "a first rate production at a first rate theatre in the Jubilee season that will never come again in all our lifetimes."

At the same time he picked a quarrel with Henry Irving. Disappointed that Irving had hung on to the script of *Man of Destiny*, and suspecting that he was playing the common trick of holding a play by a theatre critic as a hostage for good notices, GBS flaunted his integrity by an aggressive review of *Richard III* to which Irving took exception. Shaw, the great actor felt, had implied that he stumbled about the stage because he was the worse for drink. A note soon came from Irving's man of business to say that he was returning *The Man of Destiny*. "I am in ecstasies," Shaw pugnaciously told Ellen Terry on 17 April; "I have been spoiling for a row. . . . Watch the fun & chuckle." The bravado was all very well, but Shaw really minded enough to try a mollifying letter on Irving. He failed to move him, and, despite his breezy manner, he was put out when his current hopes for a commercial production were dashed in a matter of weeks.

When Shaw's pride was touched he became obstinate and combative, and things did not go well at Dorking. He turned for compensation to his dreamlike involvement with Ellen Terry. They were both aware that it was a pure abstraction and he threw himself into his part with abandon, knowing that she would play up to him with all the skills of a leading lady who never confused her stage roles with real life. There was no danger that she would respond to his passionate demands to come out from behind the footlights and enter his life.

> I go back to Dorking tomorrow [he wrote to her on 28 May]. If only I could bring you down with me. There's nobody there but Mrs Webb, Miss P.T., Beatrice Creighton (Bishop of London's daughter), Webb & myself. Alas! *four* too many. I wonder what you would think of our life—our eternal political shop; our mornings of dogged writing, all in separate rooms; our ravenous plain meals; our bicycling; the Webbs' incorrigible spooning over their industrial & political science; Miss P.T., Irish, shrewd and green-eyed, finding everything "very interesting"; myself always tired and careworn, and always supposed to be "writing to Ellen." You'd die of it all in three hours, I'm afraid. Oh, I wish, I wish.

Beatrice took a gloomy view. "I see no sign on his side of the growth of any genuine and steadfast affection," she concluded. Noting the way he treated Charlotte, she felt that there were "ominous signs" that he was "tired of watching the effect of little words of gallantry and personal interest with which he plied her in the first months of the friendship."[21] That was on 1 May. A week later she was even more critical. "Silly these philanderings of Shaw's," she wrote caustically. "His sensuality has all drifted into sexual vanity—delight in being the candle to the moths . . . the dancing light has gone out of Charlotte's eyes—there is at times a blank, haggard look."[22] Even when she saw Shaw's virtues she thought them shallow and lacking in genuine feeling; she thought him "an intellectual cricket on the hearth," but she recognized that he had "a sort of affectionateness, too, underneath his vanity—will she touch that?"

As Beatrice watched the progress of this ambivalent courtship she was reminded of her own unhappiness with Chamberlain. She sympathized with Charlotte and criticized GBS, but she could understand why GBS could not bring himself to a decision. He had the same kind of pride as herself—pride that had made it impossible for her to accept Chamberlain and driven her to torment Sidney when he pressed his attentions. It was, in fact, a trait which was common among the Fabian set. It was not simple arrogance or vanity; it was, rather, a sense that one's identity might be lost by submission.

The dominant personalities in the Society had been forced to assert themselves against powerful parents, discovering a distinct place for themselves in the world by sheer willpower. Their individuality, in fact, had been achieved by shedding the social and religious assumptions of childhood. Though they had filled the gap by adopting the more intellectually acceptable creed of socialism, they had been emotionally impaired by the struggle to liberate themselves. It left them feeling lonely, with a sense of difference, expressed at the personal level in pride, in politics by a posture of superiority which made it difficult for them to commit themselves or to work with others as equals. The perennial fear that the Fabian Society would lose its special identity or even be destroyed if it collaborated too closely with the Liberals, the ILP or the SDF was the political counterpart of an anxiety which the Fabian leaders felt in their own lives.

It was a brilliant summer in 1897 for the old Queen's Diamond Jubilee. In the long hot days there was something of a holiday atmosphere at Dorking to distract from the tensions created by Charlotte and GBS. Bertrand and Alys Russell went down; so did Charles Trevelyan, Herbert Samuel, Wallas, and William Pember Reeves and his wife, Maud, recently arrived from New Zealand. "Lion" Phillimore and her husband, Robert, were new members of the circle. They both sat on the vestry with Shaw, and Robert, the eldest son of a Liberal peer, was helping the Webbs with their research: he was a protégé of whom Sidney thought so well that he arranged for him to run as his fellow candidate in Deptford for the London County Council. Haldane was another visitor, running down to concert the plans for the bill to reorganize London University. Both the Webbs felt comfortable among earnest intellectual friends—always preferring those, like Haldane, who put principles before party—and they spent their time "constantly discussing hotly." The clever talk and the entertainment did not disrupt their regular work. The draft of *Industrial Democracy* was going well, and Shaw and Wallas were as usual enlisted to revise it. "Our daily life is an earthly paradise," Beatrice concluded.[23]

Back in London at the end of June, Beatrice found everyone "drunk with sight-seeing and hysterical loyalty."[24] The Jubilee celebrations provided a colourful outlet for the mood of self-righteous imperialism which was sweeping the country. Bonfires blazed from the hilltops; at Spithead the Home Fleet assembled for a demonstration of the naval power which held one seventh of the world in Britain's empire. Shaw airily told Ellen Terry, "The Jubilee business makes me sick—ugh!"[25] But he found that his first responsibility after joining the St. Pancras vestry was to sit on a committee to supervise a celebration dinner for the poor—"a ghastly wicked wasteful folly."[26] Beatrice was one of the hundred distinguished women who gave a banquet for a hundred distinguished men.[27] But generally the Fabians tried to treat the whole thing in low key. They decided not to sing the national anthem at their annual dinner, but they did subscribe one guinea towards the cost of the decorations in the Strand. *Fabian News* justified this contribution on the grounds that the Jubilee was "a national festival *from which we, as Socialists, should not dissociate ourselves.*" This was too much for Henry Salt, who wrote an indignant protest to Pease on 4 June. "The Jubilee is only 'national,'" he complained, "in the same sense as landlordism or Jingoism or gambling or drink or any other demoralising practice is 'national.'"[28]

The Webbs did not stay long in London. At the end of July they went off to the Argoed with GBS and Charlotte. Just before they left, Wallas surprised them by announcing his engagement to Audrey (Ada) Radford, the sister of the poet and barrister Ernest Radford who had been a friend of Marx, Engels and the Avelings. Ada, thirty-eight, a short-story writer of some originality, was a determined bohemian with rigid Secularist principles, whose dress and manner expressed her progressive convictions. Beatrice was generously pleased, writing to say that she and Sidney would be delighted to welcome Miss Radford into "the Bo family if she will consent to join such a humble crew." Graham and Ada were married in December. A month later Beatrice confessed her doubt whether she and Ada would become friends. "She is a woman who carries rigid principles into the smallest concerns of life," she wrote; "my distaste is really to her clothes. I could forgive them if they were not worn *on principle*."[29] Personally as well as politically the Webbs were losing touch with Wallas.

At the Argoed Shaw was clearly worn out with the struggles and disappointments of the past few months. Charlotte brought down some hammocks, but Shaw told Ellen Terry that he lacked the energy to set them up. "I can only rest myself by thinking that *you* are in a hammock, and writing to you," he wrote on 5 August, and he recounted the state of affairs with Charlotte with a heartless humour: "She is getting used to me now, I think. Down at Dorking there was a sort of earthquake, because she had been cherishing a charming project of at last making me a very generous & romantic proposal. . . . When I received that golden moment with shuddering horror & wildly asked the fare to Australia, she was inexpressibly taken aback, and her pride, which is considerable, was much startled." Charlotte could not bring herself to stand up to GBS, nor could she free herself altogether from his spell. She merely played up to his chosen role as the heartless philanderer by such remarks as "What a curious person you are" or "What an utter brute you are."[30]

Although Shaw continued to behave unkindly, he was well aware that his heartless personality bore the scars of his childhood. It was a singular fate, he told Janet Achurch in the previous year, "which has led me to play with all the serious things of life & to deal seriously with the plays."[31] He had learned to trick himself out of love. Yet he had a conscience. It was this that made the situation so tantalizing to Charlotte. She did not know which way to turn. She also had to withstand criticism from her sister and brother-in-law, who thought her Fabian friends dangerous radicals, particularly disliking Shaw. When she went off to Paris to stay with friends, seeking relief from conflicting pressures, she was no sooner gone than GBS was appealing to her again. "It is most inconvenient having Adelphi Terrace shut up," he wrote on 15 October; "I have nowhere to go, nobody to talk to."

In Charlotte's absence Shaw's luck changed. All through 1896 he had worked hard at *The Devil's Disciple*. William Terriss had made the Adelphi Theatre a success by putting on melodrama, so popular in the Nineties, and it was with him in mind that GBS set out to write what he described as "the most monstrous piece of farcical absurdity that ever made an audience shriek with laughter."[32] In *The Devil's Disciple* Shaw inverted all the conventions of melodrama into paradoxes. Setting his story in the last stages of the American Revolution, he made his hero a romantic ne'er-do-well who is so dedicated to his ideals that, despite his cowardice, he is prepared to die for them. It is the worthless devil's disciple who exemplifies the Puritan virtues and the upright revolutionary preacher who takes to his heels. Fulfilment, Shaw suggested in the spirit of his essay on Ibsen, comes only to those who are true to their own natures. He had at last made good theatre of this doctrine: as soon as the play was completed he offered it to Terriss in England and to Richard Mansfield in New York. Mansfield bought it at once and after a tryout in Albany opened with it at the Fifth Avenue Theatre on 4 October. The play "swept the board" in New York, and on 4 November GBS conceded to Charlotte that its impact was "sensational." As a result, after the first week's royalties arrived, "I am richer than ever I was in my life before—actually £314 in the bank to my credit." The play ran for sixty-four performances in New York, giving Shaw another £700 at once and twice that amount when Mansfield took it on tour in the Middle West. Its London production was set back when Terriss was murdered by a lunatic outside his theatre in December 1897. When the play did get on the London stage nearly two years afterwards it only had a brief run. But that delay was not critical. With Mansfield's production Shaw had at last established himself as a commercially viable playwright.

The Webbs too were beginning to see some reward for their investment. At the end of 1897 they finished *Industrial Democracy*. Sidney reckoned up what the book had cost them, including the money already spent on the *History of Trade Unionism*. They had, he told Pease, "sunk some £2,000 capital in this work, in actual cash outlay (quite apart from our own living expenses or any payment for our work)."[33]

Ever since *Fabian Essays* Sidney had been formulating a theory of society which could provide a context for his practical ideas about social reform. Though both he and Beatrice professed to be sceptical of biological analogies, the underlying structure of their thought—as with so many of their contemporaries—had been strongly shaped by the evolutionary ideas of Herbert Spencer, Charles Darwin and T. H. Huxley. They did not, however, believe that social evolution should proceed blindly, with competition and conflict taking the place of natural selection; that was the essential reason why they rejected *laissez-faire* economics. It had to be guided to positive ends by moral purpose. Individualism was anarchic and wasteful; collectivism could create a superior and more efficient society.

From this fusion of Spencer and Darwin with the Positivist Religion of Humanity which had so strongly affected both of them in their youth the Webbs concluded that superior societies could be built only by superior people. They had come increasingly to look for an élite which would play this role in Britain; by the end of the century they were sure that this task would be undertaken by the new class of salaried experts—scientists, social scientists, professional people of all kinds—whose skills could be devoted disinterestedly to the service of the community. They saw themselves in this light and they assumed that other specialists would work as loyally for public as for private enterprise. The civil servant was their modern counterpart to Plato's guardians and Comte's enlightened managers.

In this respect Fabianism was the ideology of the emerging salariat, and of the writers and journalists who spoke for it, providing a rationale for all those who felt that there was a "right" way of running society and that it was their mission to discover it. All through the Nineties the Fabian leaders were feeling their way towards a conception of society which could not be accommodated to the traditional theory of democracy, in which the higgling of parties was the political counterpart of the higgling of the market. If social research into "facts" would lead to a scientifically valid policy, it was wrong to assume that political problems could be settled by the catch-as-catch-can of elections, and wrong, too, to permit such issues as hours of work, factory conditions and even rates of pay to be settled by class conflict between employers and trade unions. Doubt could exist only on such matters where there was ignorance or insufficient evidence. Supply those deficiencies by education, research and training, and science could then regulate society.

Industrial Democracy was the first attempt by the Webbs to weave these ideas into a consistent pattern. It was not surprising that Beatrice claimed that she and Sidney were "developing a new view of Democracy."[34] They were writing the book at a time when the engineering industry was racked by a long and bitter strike, and when other unions were feeling the effects of adverse legal decisions. Yet they were almost as impatient with the "hopelessly incompetent" union leaders as with the obdurate employers.[35] They wanted an industrial democracy which would supersede such archaic struggles; under expert guidance, they believed, both labour and capital could move forward to what Sidney called "a scientific socialism" in which cooperation in the interests of the whole community would replace selfish sectionalism.

It was this conception of "national efficiency" which caught the mood of the moment and ensured, in Beatrice's words, that the book had "a brilliant reception." *The Times* devoted two columns to it on publication day, and the press generally was generous. Beatrice felt that they had made their mark. "It is a big plant on the public," she declared, "a new method and a new theory."[36]

The Webbs had reason to feel pleased with themselves, for the tide seemed to be running towards the scheme of things that they had sketched in their book. At the elections early in 1898 "our party," the Progressives, recovered a decent majority on the County Council. The School of Economics was "growing silently though surely into a centre of collectivist-tempered research," and their own books were "the only elaborate and original work in economic fact and theory" available to students.[37] Things were going well enough to permit the Webbs to take a sabbatical. They decided to go off on a long visit to America and the Antipodes, "seeing Anglo-Saxon Democracy."[38] Beatrice even felt sufficiently relaxed to have a "good 'go' at clothes" for the trip, though she found some of it an expression of "concrete crude vanity . . . rather comical in a woman of forty—what an age: almost elderly! I don't feel a bit old."[39]

The only worry was Charlotte, who was unhappy, restless and suffering from neuralgia. Just before Christmas 1897, not knowing what to do with herself, she went off with Lion Phillimore to Dieppe. When she asked Shaw to go with them she got a dusty answer: "I am to embark in a piercing wind, with lifeboats capsizing and ships foundering in all directions; to go to a watering place in the depth of winter with nothing to do and nowhere to go . . . No, thank you. I am comfortable as I am."[40] Charlotte was so hurt by this blunt rejection that she went away without telling Shaw. This only provoked more bullying. "What do you mean by this inconceivable conduct?" GBS asked on 8 December. "Are there no stamps? has the post been abolished? have all the Channel steamers foundered?"

When Charlotte returned to London for Christmas she was at a loss. She had stopped attending medical lectures and abandoned the idea of training as a doctor. Her miserable condition worried her friends and she was told plainly that it might be better for herself and for GBS if she stopped chasing him. The Webbs suggested that she accompany them on their trip, but this proposal came to nothing. "If she goes," Shaw coolly told Ellen Terry, "she will be away for about a year, just time enough for a new love affair. . . . You can't think what delightful agony it is to be in love with me: my genius for hurting women is extraordinary; and I always do it with the best intentions."[41] Charlotte could no longer refrain from taxing GBS with his cruelty, but he remained insensitive. "My nerves are shattered by the scenes of which I have been made the innocent victim," he wrote to her on 4 March. "I have allied myself to a fountain of tears."

A week later Charlotte packed up and left for the Continent, taking Lion Phillimore with her for a stay in Rome. On Wednesday 22 March the Webbs set off for America. "We start our journey with a light heart," Beatrice noted.[42] "Our journey will be a complete break in our life . . . Even our cats are leaving us for new homes!" Shaw was left alone in London.

PART FOUR

THE CIVILIZING MISSION

❧ 17 ❧
FRESH STARTS

"What taste! Just what one would expect from them," a Tory acquaintance remarked when he heard that the Webbs were off to tour America and the Antipodes.[1] Yet in planning their busman's holiday Sidney and Beatrice had, as usual, a purpose in mind. Neither of them had any taste for aimless sightseeing. The power of what Beatrice called "the old craving" for investigation was too strong: "tracking down facts is like any other sport to which one has devoted the best portion of one's life, one is restless unless one is indulging in it." They intended on their return to launch a massive enquiry into English local government, and their itinerary was designed to take in "sittings of about 40 different representative assemblies" as a run-up to their new project.[2]

Pease, Shaw, Wallas, Beatrice's sister Kate and other friends saw them off from Euston in March 1898. As the train pulled out Wallas turned to Shaw and said, "Webb's gone away perfectly confident that nothing will happen until he comes back." "Neither will it," Shaw replied; "nothing ever does happen unless he does it."[3] It was the first time that the Fabian Junta had been so decisively separated since they had come together more than twelve years before. Sydney Olivier also left with the Webbs, on his way to Washington for negotiations about the sugar trade. His papers and reports, Beatrice said, "lent a certain official gravity" to their party, although he spent much of the voyage working on a play.[4] They travelled in style on the *Teutonic*. Beatrice's sister Lallie was married to the shipowner Robert Holt, "whose influence at Liverpool got us a magnificent upper deck cabin," Webb wrote to Shaw.[5] "Now," he remarked, "you see what it is to have capitalist connections."[6]

On 30 March they disembarked at New York, where they found plenty of friends and lived for three days in a whirl of excitement. The United States was on the brink of war. "An unfortunate time," Beatrice noted when they arrived in Washington, "seeing that all the politicians to whom we have introductions are completely absorbed in Cuba."[7] They hung about Capitol Hill sending in cards to senators who were too distracted for academic chat about the machinery of government; they popped in and out of Congress in the hope of witnessing the declaration of war. It was all very tiring, Webb wrote to Wallas in a mood of frustration; "we intend to take some days off for bicycling."[8] They managed to meet Theodore Roosevelt, whom Beatrice found "most remarkable," with a "ready wit, splendid fighting courage and a thorough knowledge of the world he lives in," though she tartly added that she could discover in him "no particular political views except jingoism . . . civil service reforms and 'good government' generally—with a strong bias towards individualism."[9] In an extraordinary interview with Speaker Thomas ("Czar") Reed, Sidney explained to him how the committee system of the London County Council was modelled on the Congress; Reed, whom Beatrice dismissed as a man "with no ideas and no capacity for them—an ideal philistine,"[10] told them how he actually bossed the House of Representatives. Both the Webbs soon developed a distaste for the House, a body with "abominable procedure [and] no self-respect, with little intellectual leadership, with a predominantly loose moral character."[11] The Senate looked better, but, Beatrice tartly observed, "we have not been impressed by any attribute of the Senate other than its appearance and manners."[12]

By the time they left Washington they concluded that there was "no responsible government" in America, only "a hidden and irresponsible authority."[13] This impression was confirmed when they travelled back through Baltimore and Philadelphia to New York. "This people," Sidney wrote to GBS, "in all that concerns the *machinery* of government, is infantile. I suspect the St Pancras Vestry is a finished product—a masterpiece—by comparison. All good people bemoan the evil state of their government machinery, but we have found hardly any glimmering of an idea as to how to get it any better." If, Sidney added, "the American nation would sell all it has, and buy with the price the Fabian Executive, it would make a good bargain!" He and Beatrice found that their sympathies "really are tempted to go with Tammany & the other machines, which are at any rate efficient in what they set out to do."[14] Their low opinion of American politics was slightly offset by the mayor of Boston, Jo Quincy, a New England patrician who had made himself boss of the city and who reminded them of Arthur Balfour: he was, they consoled themselves, working for "Fabian Collectivism" and had given Boston government by a "public spirited . . . aristocracy working through a corrupt democracy." The City Council, Sidney decided, was a "farcical parody on popular representative government."[15] Both Beatrice and Sidney were finding it hard to comprehend the American system. They enjoyed visiting universities, such as Columbia, Harvard, and Princeton—where they thought Woodrow Wilson an "attractive-minded man . . . with a peculiarly un-American insight into the actual working of institutions as distinguished from their nominal constitution,"[16] but they were generally disappointed and puzzled. They reached Chicago on 1 June completely exhausted. Sidney was ill with a sore throat and fever, and Beatrice was sickening as well. A visit to Hull House gave them a chance to meet the pioneer social worker Jane Addams. It was she, Beatrice felt, "who has created whatever spirit of reform exists in Chicago"[17]—a city Webb described to Shaw as "an 'unspeakable' city, viler than tongue can tell." Unwell and fagged out by the heat, Sidney told Shaw that they proposed "to 'chuck' the rest of the overgrown, ugly cities, each more corrupt and misgoverned than the last, and to make a bee-line for Colorado," where they could relax for a week in the Rockies.[18]

The break made Beatrice more cheerful. She enjoyed, too, her return after twenty-five years to Salt Lake City, "the first really *self-respecting* abode of a municipal authority we have come across in the United States." The Mormons were sensible and businesslike, with a sense of public duty that the Webbs admired. Beatrice even regretted "that the experiment of polygamy was not continued by a sect exceptionally well-fitted to give it a fair and full trial and to develop the experiment into other forms of 'scientific breeding.' "[19]

The journey across the United States wearied the Webbs physically and discomforted them emotionally. When they reached San Francisco and were swept off to take part in the Fourth of July procession, Beatrice complained that "noise, confusion, rattle and bustle" were the curse of American life. It was only after they sailed for Honolulu on the *Coptic* that Beatrice was able to put down her reflections on the America of the Gilded Age. Americans, she decided, had excellent manners; they were kind, hospitable and had clean habits. "It is difficult," she added, "to be as enthusiastic over any other American characteristic." There was no time for creative thinking; the vast country had a cultural uniformity which contrasted strangely with the diversity of its population, its scenery and its climate; and the people were articulate slaves to the "tyranny of the stale platitude." No one appeared to realize that "good government rests not merely on democratic institutions but on the growth of a new motive, that of social service combined with the selection of men for the work of government according to their capacity for that work."[20] Americans were clearly not ready for Fabianism.

The *Coptic* steamed into Honolulu carrying the news that the US had annexed Hawaii. Manifest destiny had stretched across the Pacific to an island which Sidney said looked like "Skye, with Kew Gardens let loose on its beach and the temperature of a hot-house." Yet the Webbs were beginning to wilt: while the "uproar of excitement" about annexation went on around them they surf-bathed in company with Princess Kaiulani, the niece of the former Queen, and listened to gossip about miscegenation. It would, Beatrice mused, be pleasant to spend a year in such an ethnically mixed community studying "the relative rent producing faculty of various races, and what relation this rent producing faculty has to the standard of life."[21]

When the Webbs docked at Auckland on 3 August Beatrice felt a sense of relief. It was so "delightfully British," down to the mackintoshes, the umbrellas, and the "general dowdiness" of the women. As soon as they began to travel round New Zealand, however, they made the same complaint that they had raised all across the United States—the "apathy among the well-to-do about local government, and an indisposition to take part in national politics."[22] A poor and thinly populated country, where public services struggled with inadequate human and financial resources, New Zealand was behind the times, but at least it was not corrupt and the people were agreeable if uncultured. The country had an easygoing egalitarianism which the Webbs found attractive though somewhat vulgar. Its citizens seemed lethargically well-disposed to social reform, and the political system was so unsophisticated that it offered great opportunities for "a thoroughly equipped statesman" to pursue Fabian tactics. "So long as he sympathises with the general drift of democratic ideas," Beatrice noted in a revealing aside, "he could pretty well mould legislation according to his personal convictions."[23]

Another bad crossing on the *Monowai*, dirty and full of "noisy Australian commercial travellers and squalling colonial babies," left Beatrice in a tetchy state. After five months away from home she and Sidney were lacking energy to tackle Australia. Wherever they went the good words came grudgingly. When they visited the struggling Women's College at Sydney University, Beatrice complained about Australian cooking and the flashy clothes of Australian women, concluding that "the women of Australia are not her finest product." Their meeting with a group of socialists in Melbourne was a fiasco. Beatrice did not conceal her disgust at finding herself in company more suited to the SDF than to Fabians. They met their "poor relations," the believers in "socialist shibboleths," in a dirty out-of-the-way hall—"a nondescript body of no particular class, and with a strong infusion of foreigners," who showered them with "well-meaning cant." Sidney's "wily address" on permeation was clearly too subtle. When the chairman wound up the meeting he commended "Mr Webb's suggestion of taking the capitalist down a back street and then knocking him on the head!"[24]

Beatrice reacted against the desolate monotony of the Australian scenery, the vulgarity and gross materialism of the Australians. She told Kate Courtney: "Australia is the most *un*democratic as it is the most *un*aristocratic nation in the world . . . unadulterated bourgeois!"[25] Sidney, who usually left generalizations to Beatrice, was equally ruffled by the roughness of Australian life—it was the England of 1850, he told Pease[26] —but his public comments were more generous. Australia, he remarked in a newspaper interview, "must be taken seriously . . . as an adult Anglo-Saxon Democracy, full of interest and instruction to the political world."[27]

Throughout their journey Beatrice's talent for vivid observation was cramped by her negative reactions; she judged everything by her own set of ideas. Sidney's observations were also drearily limited. He had an obsession with the machinery of government—the essential Fabian belief that reforms could be treated intrinsically and transplanted from one situation to another almost regardless of social circumstances. When he found himself in a situation where he knew little of the historical background and the social problems with which his contacts were grappling, he fell back on the technicalities of politics—electoral systems, the working of committees, tax policies and the structure of government agencies. Those whom the Webbs met often found them aloof and unsympathetic, as if they were travelling inspectors who had come across the world to see if the colonials were coming up to scratch.

As soon as the Webbs and Charlotte were out of the way Shaw lapsed back into his old ways. His initial reaction to Charlotte's absence was cocky bravado. Kate Salt, who had taken his dictation on and off for over four years, came back to do his secretarial work and to play piano duets again. He soon wrote unfeelingly to Charlotte that he felt he had never dictated to anyone else. On 18 March Charlotte was told bluntly: "There is clearly no future for you as a secretary. You must get your own work, your own, own, own work. Do you hear?" GBS soon felt that "it was magnificent to be alone, with the ivy stripped off." In his letter to Charlotte on 30 March he spelt out plainly the ambiguities of his attitude to her:

> You count that I have lost only one Charlotte; but I have lost two; and one of the losses is a prodigious relief. I may miss "die schöne grünen Augen" occasionally, though the very privation throws me back, brutally great, to my natural dreamland; but then think of the other Charlotte, the terrible Charlotte, the lier-in-wait, the soul hypochondriac, always watching and dragging me into bondage, always planning nice sensible, comfortable, selfish destruction for me, wincing at every accent of freedom in my voice, so that at last I get the trick of hiding myself from her, hating me & longing for me with the absorbing passion of the spider for the fly. Now that she is gone, I realize for the first time the infernal tyranny of the past year, which left me the license of the rebel, not the freedom of the man who stands alone, I will have no more of it. . . .

While Charlotte was away GBS heard that Eleanor Marx had poisoned herself on 31 March.[28] In June 1897 Aveling had secretly and under a false name married a girl named Eva Frye. He returned to Eleanor in September and asked her to sell more of her father's papers—having already run through her legacy from Engels. He still concealed the marriage but blackmailed Eleanor by threatening to marry if she did not bail him out. A letter from Eleanor to her half brother Freddy, the illegitimate child of Marx and his housekeeper, suggested that Aveling was ready to reveal this scandalous secret, for Eleanor said that she was faced by "utter ruin—everything, *to the last penny*, or utter, open disgrace." When she received an anonymous letter telling her of Aveling's marriage she could bear no more. The maid found Eleanor dying with a final note to Aveling to say: "My last word to you is the same that I have said during all these long, sad years—love."

Shaw later used a charitable gloss on this tragic relationship as the centrepiece of *The Doctor's Dilemma*. At the time, however, the news brought on an attack of neuralgia. The most he could bring himself to write to Charlotte on the day Eleanor was cremated was a tight little note. The disastrous relationship between the Avelings had been like a nightmarish version of all that Shaw feared about passion.

Shaw's relief when Charlotte left for Rome soon changed to feeling "detestably deserted." "Oh Charlotte, Charlotte," he wrote on 7 April, "is this a time to be gadding about in Rome!" Visits to the dentist touched off his hypochondria and he complained that he was "too much done up" to face the Easter holiday; "I live the life of a dog," he wrote to Sidney.[29] There was no one to talk to in London. He had brought his troubles on himself, he admitted to Webb. "I so brutally exulted in my loneliness & freedom, not to mention my taking on Mrs Salt as amanuensis . . . that Charlotte has given up writing to me."[30] Nevertheless he wrote to her almost every day. When Lion Phillimore came back, leaving Charlotte in Rome, she invited Shaw down to the Phillimores' cottage in Hertfordshire; there, Shaw reported to Charlotte, they "bully me for hours about you & my character and my age & my foolishness & selfishness & devil knows what. . . . I have a headache now."[31] The next day, however, he cheered up, because "the vindictive Irishwoman has written at last. Ha! ha! If only I had her here in these arms: all her ribs would crack." But Charlotte said nothing about returning to England.

On 19 April Shaw was cheered by the publication of his first plays in the volume *Plays Pleasant and Unpleasant*, and that evening he cycled out to Ealing to visit his old friend Pakenham Beatty. His left foot hurt, and when he took his shoe off on arriving home he found it "the size of a leg of mutton." GBS always dramatized his aches and pains and there was nothing to suggest that the condition of his foot was anything but trivial—though he told Charlotte two days later that it was "now as large as the Albert Hall" and that he suspected gout. It got worse and he felt "a fearful wreck," hopping about his business "to the amazement of the populace."[32] Driven reluctantly to seek medical advice, he called in Dr. Salisbury Sharpe, the husband of his old girl friend Alice Lockett. Sharpe decided he was suffering from an inflamed toe joint and thought that rest and hot water would cure it in a few days. Shaw was glad of an excuse to stay at home, for he was at work on his new play, *Caesar and Cleopatra*.

When Charlotte wrote to say that she was suffering severely from neuralgia he replied on 25 April: "Come back, then. I know what your nerves need." She decided to do so, and on 1 May he hobbled to Adelphi Terrace to meet her, but she was delayed and he was disappointed. Next day she wrote a note with apologies: "Well, here I am anyway now! Yes: I *might* have telegraphed: it was horrid of me. I am a wreck, mental and physical. Such a journey as it was!"[33]

While Charlotte had been in Rome she had spent some time, Webb style, collecting material on its municipal government, and she planned to write up her researches into a book for use by students at the School of Economics. Hewins, working downstairs in the School premises and seeing Charlotte on her way in and out of her flat, sent Webb a dry comment on 30 May. He thought it a "quaint and humorous proceeding to try to smother one's love under municipal reports."[34] Charlotte was trying to find a profession for herself—she had just been elected to the Fabian executive—but her mind was still on Shaw.

On 5 May, when they went to the theatre to see Ellen Terry act, Charlotte had to collect him in a cab. The next day she went again to Fitzroy Square and carried him off to Adelphi Terrace for a long talk. She had been appalled by his home circumstances. GBS was personally fastidious to the point of being obsessional about his diet and his clothing, wearing woollen underwear, refusing to use cotton sheets, and cultivating a public reputation as a health reformer; yet he lived in squalor and disorder. In his room, Hesketh Pearson recalled, "heaps of letters, pages of manuscripts, books, envelopes, writing paper, pens, . . . butter, sugar, apples, knives, forks, spoons, sometimes a cup of cocoa or a half-finished plate of porridge, a saucepan, and a dozen other things were mixed up indiscriminately, and all undusted as his papers must not be touched."[35] His own neglect was matched by his mother's indifference. They went their own ways, and even when he was ill she made no attempt to look after him. By the time Charlotte turned up he was in a bad way. On 9 May he had an operation on his foot which did little good: he had, it turned out, a tubercular necrosis. The surgeon said it was due to undernourishment caused by his vegetarian habits; Shaw insisted that he was run down through overwork. Whatever the cause, he was seriously ill; for the first time he faced the prospect of dying. There was no chance of recovering without fresh air, rest and nursing.

Someone had to care for him and, as GBS jocularly told Beatrice Webb, "Charlotte was the inevitable and predestined agent, appointed by Destiny."[36] She proposed to find a country house where, with servants and nurses, Shaw could be restored to health. At first GBS refused to budge. He claimed that a move would interfere with his writing and his theatre criticism. Under pressure from Charlotte his resistance finally broke down. He had already told friends in April, "I shall probably marry the lady," and the matter was settled when they talked at Adelphi Terrace. The situation, Shaw confessed honestly to Beatrice, "was changed by a change in my own consciousness . . . my objection to my own marriage had ceased with my objection to my own death."[37] It was a viable bargain, because Charlotte made no sexual demands, having given up "all such illusions as love interest, happiness interest, and all the rest of the vulgarities of marriage." He protested afterwards that he agreed to marry Charlotte to avoid involving "our whole circle and its interests in a scandal" when she insisted on carrying him off to the country. To the last he presented himself, like his heroes, as the helpless victim of feminine wiles.

The odd circumstances of their marriage enabled Shaw to keep up this joke to the end. Because GBS was disabled, Charlotte made all the arrangements. She went to the registry office in Henrietta Street, where she had to explain to a boy that she wanted to get married, Shaw told Wallas. "The boy sent the news up a tube through which shrieks of merriment were exchanged, culminating in an order to show the lady up. Upstairs she found a man who became greatly excited when he learned the names of the parties, and offered to do the job any time after today for £2/17/11. She felt that it was extremely conscientious of him not to ask £2/18 and forked out." With the wedding license secured, Charlotte then "had to suffer the final humiliation of buying a ring . . . the symbol of slavery."[38] Wallas and Henry Salt were asked along as witnesses to the ceremony on 1 June. As GBS turned up on crutches and wearing an old jacket, the registrar at first took the more respectable Wallas for the bridegroom. Before they went down to Haslemere, where Charlotte had rented a house, GBS wrote his own comic version of the wedding as an unsigned gossip report in *The Star*, pretending that he and Charlotte had been forced to take refuge from the rain in the registry office, where, "in the confusion of the moment," the registrar had married "the brilliant couple."[39]

Shaw was in good spirits once the decision was made and immediately began to work hard on *The Perfect Wagnerite*. He was, he wrote to Beatrice, unwise "to tempt the gods." Coming out of his bedroom on his crutches, he lost his balance, broke through the bannisters and "was precipitated fifty fathom or thereabout into the hall," breaking his left wrist.[40] He was now a helpless invalid, condemned to a wheelchair. He made his condition worse when, thinking one night that he heard a burglar, he got up and, "walking recklessly on the bad foot, . . . did myself as much harm as possible." In July he had a second operation to remove diseased bone and he told Henry Salt that he was "unspeakably tickled" to find that four doctors had been so obsessed with his foot that they forgot to deal with his arm.[41]

Shaw was not an easy patient, and Charlotte's long honeymoon was spent worrying about him. "It is a trying thing to be married to a Sprite," GBS remarked to Sidney, "but a Sprite with necrosis is the devil."[42] He knew that he had driven himself too hard: "I have been overdrawing my account for a long time." Yet within three weeks of his operation he had finished *The Perfect Wagnerite*, a characteristic essay which "captured" Wagner as an iconoclastic revolutionary in much the same way as GBS had used Ibsen. The *Ring*, Shaw announced to Beatrice, was "jam full of Socialism in the manner of Ruskin."[43]

He was anxious to be about again. Hewins, Pease, Olivier and Massingham all went down to Haslemere. So did Wallas, full of excitement at becoming a father. Charlotte wrote to tell Beatrice that Wallas was "getting extremely fat and prosperous-looking. He described Audrey with her large gold spectacles, kneeling in awe before the baby, hardly daring to touch it for fear of injuring it."[44] But Shaw's recovery was slow. Trying to mount a new bicycle, he hurt his foot again. By November, realizing that they would have to spend some months more away from London, the Shaws took a larger house. During this period of enforced domesticity Shaw had to content himself with local interests in politics. He and Charlotte joined in a scheme to buy a public house, the Fox and Pelican, and convert it into a decent club for workingmen. They helped to elect a progressive parish council and took part in informal concerts and readings from Shakespeare. The Shaws thus settled at the beginning of their marriage into a rural pattern very different from the hectic life GBS had previously been leading—a pattern which persisted even when he recovered.

During these months at Haslemere he was anxious to start a new play for Ellen Terry, but he had first to finish *Caesar and Cleopatra*, which was not going well. "I can only spin out the same silly stuff," he told Charles Charrington on 23 October. "There is no drama in it." GBS now had no worries about money and was living in unaccustomed comfort, but his income from writing was still important to him, though in the first year of his marriage he earned only £473. So long as he could make a contribution to their joint expenses, he had no qualms about Charlotte's wealth. All the same he was sensitive to suggestions that he might have married her for money. When Charrington tried to borrow from him Shaw explained that he himself had nothing to spare and that he would not help Charrington out at Charlotte's expense. He did not, of course, object when Charlotte sent the Fabians a donation of a hundred pounds, though her current opinion of the Fabians was on a par with Shaw's dubiety about Charrington's solvency. Her experience on the executive, she wrote to Beatrice on 6 November, had put her "perfectly out of patience with the Fabians (strictly between ourselves): from my point of view it now consists of a parcel of boys and old women thinking they are making history, and really making themselves ridiculous."[45]

When the Webbs arrived back after Christmas they saw a change in both their friends. "Shaw has become a chronic invalid," Beatrice noted, "Charlotte a devoted nurse. . . . He still writes, but his work seems to be getting unreal: he leads a hot-house life, he cannot walk or get about among his equals. He is as witty and as cheery as of old, but now and again a flash of fatigue or a sign of brain irritation passes over him."[46] The Webbs had not yet given the Shaws a wedding gift, and on January 1 Sidney asked Pease to find all Shaw's early novels and books as "we want to get them artistically bound in a set" as a belated present to Charlotte.[47] At the same time Sidney took his chance to ask Charlotte to give another thousand pounds to the London School of Economics. She was, she replied, no longer "so light-hearted about giving money away." GBS, she reported, felt that Sidney would do better to spend the money on a production of *Candida*, "but such is his affection for you that he urges me to enclose a cheque sooner than disappoint you."[48]

The Webbs were soon back at work. For Sidney this meant buckling down to County Council business, the impending reform of education in London and the precarious prospects of the School of Economics. The main burden of launching the elaborate research on the evolution of local government fell on Beatrice. Reviewing the prospects for their partnership as they entered middle age, she took an optimistic view:

> Our finances are sound, our health good, and there is no reason for anxiety. We must spend, if need be, our capital on our work, and we must not be disheartened by its magnitude. We are fast becoming elderly, we have not so many years left, we must make the best use of our talents and leave the future to take care of itself. And it is useless to be downhearted because of the indifference and stupidity of the world, even as regards its own true interests. And it is childish to yearn after some sanction to the worth-whileness of human effort . . . we can but follow the still small voice of moral instinct which insists that we shall seek truth and love one another.[49]

⤳ 18 ⤶
JOE'S WAR

In January 1899 Shaw was one of the speakers at a disarmament meeting in Hindhead called to protest against the risks of a world war touched off by the scramble for Africa. He was as unorthodox as ever. Writing to Conan Doyle, who was to share the platform, GBS made it clear that he did not accept "Queensberry rules for war." The only way to ensure peace, he insisted, was "a combination of the leading powers to police the world and put down international war just as private war is put down."[1]

Shaw disliked pacifist humbug as much as he detested the moral claptrap of "Bismarck worship, Stanley worship, Dr. Jim worship." During his slow recovery, he told Ellen Terry, this scorn for the "wild-beast man" explorer H. M. Stanley and the filibustering adventurer Dr. Starr Jameson had gone into the play *Captain Brassbound's Conversion*, in which he hoped she would play the lead. "Chamberlains and Balfours and German Emperors" could not be beaten at their own game of appealing to the passions. Using the "commonsense and goodwill" of the woman traveller Mary Kingsley as his model, Shaw argued that such "slaves of false ideas and imaginary fears" could be managed only by "simple moral superiority."[2]

This was not a new idea for Shaw. It had run through all his plays since *Arms and the Man*, but by the time he wrote *Captain Brassbound's Conversion* he had come to feel sure that he could teach such lessons better by art than by agitation. In August he dismissed the work of the Fabians as "perpetuating a system that ought to be abolished." If, he told Wallas, "the practical result of our demonstration of the world's wrongness is to be a reconciliation with the world," then "there will be an end to us." So far as he was concerned, there would be no such reconciliation: "My contempt for the status quo grows from year to year; and I do not despair of expressing it yet in a mind-changing manner."[3]

Shaw's sense that the traditional mould of British politics was about to be shattered reflected an apocalyptic mood that was common as the century came to an end. The system was plainly being stretched to breaking point by internal dissensions about Ireland, by labour troubles and by a growing revolt against the Victorian conventions; and imperialist hysteria was only one of the symptoms of Britain's changing role in the world at large. The long Victorian peace was over.

Shaw was at sea when the crisis broke, as the Boer armies suddenly struck into South Africa on 11 October. He and Charlotte had gone cruising in the Mediterranean on the *Lusitania*. When he heard the news his first reaction was to write to Pease, as they sailed home, to say that it would be "too silly" to "split the society by declaring ourselves on a non-socialist point of policy."[4]

The Fabians were ill-prepared for what the new Liberal leader, Henry Campell-Bannerman, called "Joe's War." Although they had arranged a lecture series on "The Empire" during 1899, there had never been a distinctive Fabian view on imperial affairs. Many Fabians had been brought up on the moral categories of Gladstonian foreign policy and were deeply suspicious of jingoism and militarism; as socialists, moreover, they felt that the capitalist search for profits was driving the nation into foreign adventures. Among the senior members of the Society Ramsay MacDonald and Olivier took this view with fervour; and for many years William Clarke—the only one of the original essayists to touch on overseas policy—had been a passionate critic of imperialism.

Other Fabians, however, had followed Webb and Shaw in their growing hostility towards the old-style Liberalism and their distaste for the coalition of free-traders, pacifists and temperance men who were

collectively known as the "Little Englanders." Bland, who had begun as
a Tory and never had much sympathy for Radicals and Nonconformists,
was one of the few who had committed himself openly to an assertive
policy, saying that if England "did not make use of her opportunities in
this direction other countries would oust her" and that "England was the
only country fit to pioneer the blessings of civilisation."[5]

The war brought such latent differences into the open, dividing the
Society as sharply as it split the country as a whole. Its opponents saw it
as a moral outrage, an attempt to crush a nation of small farmers and to
bring their land—and the gold mines of the Rand—into a British South
Africa; they believed that Chamberlain had throughout connived with
Rhodes to this end and that Alfred Milner, Chamberlain's plenipotentiary
in the long negotiations with the Boers, had manipulated Kruger into a
hopeless fight. Its supporters were more mixed in their motives. Apart
from out-and-out imperialists, many Liberals (and a significant section
of the Fabian Society) could not tolerate the Boers, whom they saw as
reactionary religious fundamentalists standing in the way of progress.
They were attracted by the ruthless, autocratic Milner, who had a mystical belief in Britain's imperial destiny and in the civilizing power of a
superior British race. Asquith and Grey, who had been Milner's friends
at Balliol, were joined by Haldane in trying to swing Liberal opinion
behind him.

With the Little Englanders fervent against the war, and with a
mood of military hysteria gripping the country, Britain pitched into the
new century more bitterly divided than at any time in Victoria's long
reign. At dinner parties there was, as one wit remarked, "war to the
knife and fork." Old friendships were broken and families driven to savage quarrels. Beatrice Webb observed that among her eight brothers-in-
law opinion ranged from outright jingoism to the emotional pacifism of
Leonard Courtney. The split also cut deep into the socialist movement.
Robert Blatchford, an old soldier himself, had campaigned against imperialism and colonial expansion, but in October 1899 he wrote in the
Clarion: "I cannot go with those Socialists whose sympathies are with
the enemy. My whole heart is with the British troops. . . . Until the
war is over I am for the Government."[6] John Burns, now a figure of
some note in the Liberal Party, took the opposite view. One night he
was forced to defend his house with a cricket bat against a frenzied
crowd bent on looting it.

For Beatrice the war was a regrettable "underbred business." She objected to the "unsavoury" train of events, from the Jameson Raid to the "vulgarly provocative talk of Chamberlain" which had led to "war with the Transvaal Republic, that remnant of seventeenth-century puritanism."[7] Sidney felt much the same. He thought that "better management" might have avoided a conflict, but, feeling that recrimination was useless, he accepted the takeover of the two Boer republics as inevitable. Beatrice later confessed that it was astonishing that not one outstanding politician on either side "ever mentioned the claim of the native population, whose conditions of life were at stake, even to be considered in the matter."[8] The question was reduced to the crude alternative: pro-Boer or pro-British.

Immediately after the Boer commandos struck, the Fabian executive met and considered whether the next members' meeting should discuss the crisis. By seven votes to five it decided to oppose an emergency motion expressing "deep indignation at the success of the monstrous conspiracy . . . which has resulted in the present wanton and unjustifiable war."[9] On 13 October, by twenty-six votes to nineteen, the members supported the executive.

The narrow majority was an omen of trouble to come. Though Sydney Olivier held a senior position in the Colonial Office, he had no compunction about attacking his Minister's war. He had seen it coming. One day that summer he burst into the Garnetts' house at Limpsfield, quoting with rage from a confidential telegram which he thought revealed Chamberlain's true intentions. Feelings were running high. Olivier's daughters burned Chamberlain's effigy on Guy Fawkes Night that autumn. He demanded that the Fabians issue a leaflet attacking the war and claimed that if they were silent they would become nothing more than an "annexe" of the Hutchinson Trust. This time the majority for silence on the executive was only one vote.

"Olivier," Bland wrote to Pease, "has always been the 'terrible infant' of the Society, subject to sudden and feverish outbursts." What Bland feared was a quarrel, "fraught with mischief," between the senior Fabians. "It looks as though you and I and the remnant of the Old Gang . . . would have to make one more big fight to secure the Society's usefulness in the future, a usefulness which will be entirely crippled if we throw ourselves dead athwart the Imperialist, or any other, strong stream or tendency. As we cannot break up those streams, but only be broken up by them, we should try . . . to direct them. We may possibly be able to do for 'sane' imperialism what we have already done for 'sane' socialism. . . ."[10]

There was a curious antithesis between Olivier and Bland. Both had a strong streak of bohemianism. But where Olivier enjoyed a conventional family life and allowed his rebelliousness free play among the Fabians, Bland was a stickler for respectability in the Society, and his irregularities broke out in his domestic affairs. The Blands were prospering at last. Hubert was doing well in journalism and Edith had just published her successful children's story, *The Treasure Seekers*. They had recently moved to Well Hall—"a queer & ramshackle old house," Sidney reported to Beatrice, "somewhat baronial in 18th century style, right out in the country, with a moat, swans, wild ducks & rabbits."[11] But though Hubert was insisting publicly on "sanity," at home Alice Hoatson had just borne his illegitimate son while Edith had suffered the distress of a stillborn child. Both he and Olivier were emotionally on edge and Bland sensed that they were coming to a parting of the ways.

For Olivier felt just as strongly as Bland that the future of the Society was at stake. Bland, he believed, stood for the "corned-beef" rather than the "roast-beef" brand of imperialism. Writing to Pease on 20 October, Olivier insisted: "You can't get ahead of a real elementary force except by going better in elementary force yourself . . . that is what Socialism came to the front with and formed, *inter alia*, the Fabian Society." If the Society now refused to oppose the war, it would suffer from dry rot and then really there would be "no further reason for its separate existence."[12] Sam Hobson, taking the same line as MacDonald and the other anti-imperialists, wrote to Olivier on 24 October to complain that the Society was becoming weak-kneed. "We are losing all our strenuousness—our *diablerie*," he argued; "we have ceased to be feared & are only respected as amiable & harmless students of certain restricted phenomena."[13]

The first chance for Fabians to debate the war came on 24 November, when Frederick Whelen, a member of the executive, gave a lecture to a crowded meeting in which he argued that the war and the annexation of the Transvaal were inevitable. Shaw, now back in circulation, turned up to argue that the Society should abstain from taking sides over South

Africa as it had refused to take a position either way over Home Rule. But the anti-imperialists could not be subdued, and the executive was forced to arrange a special debate on 8 December, at which Sam Hobson moved a long resolution insisting that the war had "distracted the attention of the nation from domestic progress" and urging the Society to dissociate itself "from the Imperialism of Capitalism and vainglorious Nationalism." As usual in a crisis, the burden of defending the Old Gang's position fell upon Shaw, whose amendment avoided the direct issue. What the Society could reasonably demand, Shaw suggested, was that after the war was won the government should nationalize the mines of the Rand and ensure good working conditions for the miners. Otherwise the government would be charged with "having spent the nation's blood and treasure, and outraged humanity by a cruel war, to serve the most sordid interests under the cloak of a lofty and public-spirited Imperialism."[14]

Shaw's critics did not think that such a charge should be postponed until after the war. They were already making it and they resented Shaw's attempt to buy time. His speech, which included gibes at the Boers, infuriated the anti-imperialists. Shaw could not carry the meeting: though Bland and other executive members backed him, he was beaten by fifty-eight votes to twenty-seven. To avoid threatened resignations if Hobson's motion were passed the discussion was adjourned by a majority of only nine votes.

The executive could not leave matters in this state, and it reluctantly agreed to a proposal from MacDonald that the members be consulted in a postal ballot whether the Society should make an official pronouncement on the war. Four members of the executive signed the circular calling for a statement; eight, including Webb, Shaw and Bland, put the Old Gang's case that the subject was "outside the special province of the Society" and claimed that while any declaration would have no effect on the war it was bound to damage the Society.

Webb's idea was simply to play the issue down. He loathed the war and the policy that had led up to it, but he also felt that once started it had to be seen through. "Sidney does not take either side," Beatrice noted in December, "and is, therefore, suspected by both." His heart was against it, but his reason led him to agree with Haldane and Asquith. He was so uncertain of his opinions that he tried to avoid discussion about the conflict and even avoided reading about it.

Shaw had no such inhibitions. Though he was as anxious as Webb and Bland to preserve the Society from a split, he was stimulated by the fight and took pleasure in teasing the anti-imperialists. "The Socialist," he wrote to one Fabian, "has only to consider which dog to back; that is, which dog will do most for Socialism if it wins." In any case, he objected to "stray little states lying about in the way of great powers." He thought that a takeover of the Boer republics could be like a trust annexing a small shopkeeper: "a capitalistic transaction, no doubt, but one making, like all advanced capitalism, for Socialism."[15] The line of logic had led Shaw straight from *Fabian Essays* to imperialism. This was clear from a provocative speech he made to a packed meeting on 23 February 1900, the day before the postal vote was completed. The Fabians had always believed that larger units were more efficient than smaller units. The time had come, Shaw argued, to take the same line in foreign as in domestic policy.

Over eight hundred Fabians were eligible to vote, and more than half did so, with a close result. Shaw, Webb and Bland won by 259 votes to 217. Eighteen members then resigned, including Ramsay MacDonald, Henry Salt, Walter Crane, Emmeline Pankhurst and others who belonged to the ILP as well as to the Fabians.

The situation was eased a little by Olivier's departure for Jamaica, for he would have been a more formidable leader of the opposition than Sam Hobson or MacDonald. Olivier had been working in the West Indian department of the Colonial Office for some time, but in the autumn of 1899 he was appointed colonial secretary to Jamaica. He had acquired a reputation for upsetting the decorous routine of Downing Street with his intemperate expression of antigovernment views, and it was said by one of his colleagues that he was posted to the West Indies "for peace and quiet." There was a farewell dinner for him on 6 January, and on 21 January his play *Mrs. Maxwell's Marriage* was put on at the Stage Society. This was a new venture for private performances which had been launched by Frederick Whelen with the backing of the Shaws, William Archer, Crane, Charles Charrington, Janet Achurch, H. W. Massingham and other theatre enthusiasts; their intention was to give at least six Sunday performances of serious plays not tolerated by the commercial theatre.

There was little animosity in the elections for the Fabian executive in the spring of 1900. When Charrington, who was antiwar, thought of resigning from the executive, Shaw wrote him a good-humoured letter. It would, he said, "be a job to pull the Fabian through this excitement," but "it seems to me, on the whole, that keeping together is good business."[16] For once some active campaigning was necessary. Webb, Bland and Shaw each wrote to individual members begging them to avoid "plumping" for the eight antiwar candidates for the executive. Such tactics, they feared, might knock off the executive three or four valuable members who belonged to neither faction; the Old Gang, moreover, did not wish to oppose some of the antiwar candidates, "of whose claims we cannot speak too highly, though they have compelled us to resist them on this question of Fabian neutrality in the war."[17] The voting closely followed the pattern of the postal ballot. Pease, who topped the poll, secured 402 votes; Charles Charrington, with 336, headed the four anti-imperialists who were elected. The remainder of those elected were on the side of Pease, Webb, Shaw, and Bland.

Once passions began to subside, the Fabians were finding a way to pull through. The elections over, they turned their attention again to such familiar topics as municipal trading, the virtues of garden cities, the English drama, adult education and the reform of the railway system.

While the Society was preoccupied with foreign affairs Pease and Shaw were playing a minor part during the winter months in the preparations for yet another conference on labour politics. Hardie had kept up the ILP pressure within the trade unions, and in the autumn of 1899, when the Trades Union Congress met at Plymouth, the railwaymen's union proposed a resolution drafted for them by Hardie and Ramsay MacDonald. It called on the unions, the cooperatives and socialist groups to meet "to devise ways and means for securing the return of an increased number of labour members to Parliament." The majority was narrow, 546,000 to 434,000, with the powerful unions of miners and cotton operatives in opposition. The question was whether this would be yet another short-lived attempt to create a new party with the backing of the unions.

The conference was organized by a committee of ten, which included Shaw and Pease, Hardie and MacDonald, two members of the SDF, and four trade unionists. Though the committee was weighted heavily with socialists, its proposals were limited and cautious. It simply proposed an electoral alliance whereby a joint committee formed by the conference should endorse candidates put forward and financed by any of the constituent groups, so long as they had "no connections with either Liberal or Tory parties." Once elected, such candidates should form a "distinct labour group in Parliament who should have their own whips and agree upon their own policy."[18]

When the conference, called under TUC auspices, met at the Memorial Hall in London on 27 February, the outlook did not seem very promising. The gathering attracted much less attention than the founding conference of the ILP, years before. There were only nine people in the gallery to watch the 129 delegates launch the new venture, and the press virtually disregarded the meeting. The socialist groups were all there, but Pease alone turned up on behalf of the Fabians. Only four of the larger unions attended—the railwaymen, the gasworkers, the engineers, and the boot and shoe trades—and though about a third of the total trade-union membership of nearly one million was represented, the powerful and pro-Liberal miners and cotton operatives refused to have anything to do with a plan they had strenuously opposed.[19]

What Hardie wanted was a commitment in principle which would bind the unions and the socialists together. When the SDF tried to make the conference accept recognition of the class war and belief in nationalization as the test for endorsing candidates, Hardie knew he could not carry the unions so far. John Burns, representing the engineers, broke out against the "class prejudice" which was obsessed with "working-class boots, working-class trains, working-class houses and working-class margarine." He was even against the idea of a distinct labour group in the House of Commons, regarding himself and other "Lib-Lab" members as labour's legitimate representatives.

The best Hardie could do was to find common ground. His amendment called for "a distinct Labour Group in Parliament, who shall have their own whips and agree upon their policy, which must embrace a readiness to co-operate with any party which for the time being may be engaged in promoting legislation in the direct interests of labour, and be equally ready to associate themselves with any party in opposing measures having an opposite tendency . . ." This was accepted, partly because it seemed so vague; and the new Labour Representation Committee, consisting of seven union men, two each from the ILP and the SDF and one Fabian, had no powers beyond the right to endorse candidates put forward by any organization that affiliated. It also had very little money—its income in the first year was only £237—and an unpaid secretary. When the first two men approached turned down the job, it was offered to Ramsay MacDonald. Seeing its possibilities, at a moment when he was breaking with the Fabians, and being able to support himself from journalism and his wife's private income, MacDonald seized the chance. He ran the Labour Representation Committee from a room in his flat in Lincoln's Inn Fields.

Though Pease held a watching brief for the Fabians, the Society showed no real interest. The SDF almost immediately fell away, its leaders considering that Hardie had been guilty of "treachery" in opposing a commitment to socialism. And the unions were slow to rally round. In the first year only forty of more than a thousand unions bothered to affiliate, and the nominal backing remained well below half the strength of union membership in the country.

The situation seemed even gloomier in the autumn of 1900, when the Tory government believed that the war was nearly won and called the snap "khaki" election, seeking to profit from the mood of patriotic hysteria which had swept the country as the outnumbered Boers were slowly and clumsily defeated. All through the summer, the executive of the LRC had been havering about its tactics. When the election came, the LRC was ill-prepared and lacking funds. The most it could agree upon was to allow its sponsored candidates a relatively free hand. In the circumstances the LRC men did reasonably well, averaging over a third of the poll in the fifteen seats they contested. But, with the Tories picking up seats all over the country, this was not good enough. Richard Bell of the railway union, almost indistinguishable from a regular "Lib-Lab," won Derby; and Keir Hardie was unexpectedly returned for the Welsh mining seat of Merthyr Tydfil.

When the new Parliament met, therefore, Hardie was the only real labour independent in the House, Bell aligning himself for the most part with the eight "Lib-Lab" members who had survived the election. It seemed that, despite the fresh start, things had not greatly changed since Hardie had found himself in the same lonely position almost ten years before. Shaw and the Webbs were considering a quite different kind of political alliance.

In May 1900 the new Fabian executive decided that GBS should draft a tract on imperialism. With MacDonald and his strongest supporters out of the way there was a chance that Shaw's ingenuity would produce a document that was generally acceptable. He had to address himself to two questions. What was the Fabian attitude to colonial policy? What was the relationship between imperialism abroad and social reform at home? For the first time the Society conceded that the two issues were related; they had become the fundamental questions in British politics as the new century began.

Fabianism and the Empire, Shaw told H. T. Muggeridge, was a "masterpiece." Intended as a penny tract, it grew into a Fabian manifesto for the general election. There was no intention to foist it on the Society. Proofs were sent out to all members, with an invitation to amend it, and 134 of them took the trouble to send in suggestions. Almost as many turned up at a meeting at which Shaw took them through the final version. Graham Wallas thought the draft a triumph for Shaw's rhetorical talent but complained to Pease that "the points taken were not so new as to justify the apocalyptic way in which they were put." There was a sustained attack on old-fashioned Radicalism—what Beatrice called "Gladstonian sentimental Christianity"—and a long argument for a national minimum wage, for which Webb particularly had lately become enthusiastic. The heart of the booklet, however, was Shaw's case for what Olivier had called "corned-beef" imperialism.

Shaw took it for granted that the world was now to be carved up among the great powers. Small states were likely to cause "fierce patriotic, heroic, melodramatic wars"; only great powers were "big enough to have a mortal dread of war and a great deal to lose by it."[20] Would Britain play her part in this inevitable process or become nothing more than a pair of insignificant islands in the North Sea, as anachronistic as the Boer republics? For Shaw there could be only one answer. Britain and the other European states were representatives of "international civilization," and their mission was to ensure that the world was governed "in the interests of civilisation as a whole." Shaw cleverly diverted attention from the ethics of imperialism by inviting Fabians to concentrate their energies instead on schemes whereby, in Webb's phrase, the colonies might be "better managed." Once they had slipped into this assumption, all the familiar Fabian concepts could be deployed.

When the Society accepted *Fabianism and the Empire* it completed the long process of disentangling itself from the Radical cause in which so many of its members had served their apprenticeship. The Fabians were now committed, in the name of national efficiency, to the doctrine that social reform was the counterpart of Britain's imperial destiny. They had begun with the idea of a civilizing mission in darkest England; it had now been extended to darkest Africa. But it was the same doctrine of an élite offering salvation to the poor.

↝ 19 ↜
MEN AND
SUPERMEN

"All will have to be new and strange and perhaps difficult when we return," Beatrice had written in her diary before the Webbs went on their trip abroad in 1898.[1] They did, indeed, find it hard to adjust to the changes that had taken place during their absence. All through 1900 they were trying to get their bearings and to decide what direction to take in the new century. "The social enthusiasm that inspired the intellectual proletariat of ten years ago has died down," she noted, "and given place to a wave of scepticism about the desirability or possibility, of any substantial change in society as we know it."[2] There seemed to be no one on whom they could rely. They were increasingly contemptuous of the Liberals, dismissing the party's new leader, Henry Campbell-Bannerman, as both vain and stupid. Beatrice did not recognize the talents of this unruffled party tactician, seeing him merely as being "well suited to a position of a wealthy squire or a sleeping partner in an inherited business."[3]

To overcome her sense of disorientation Beatrice tried to get her life into focus. "We realize every day more strongly," she observed in October 1900, "that we can never hope to get hold of the 'man in the street': we are 'too damned intellectual,' as a shrewd journalist remarked. All we can hope to do is to find out for ourselves the actual facts and embody them in a more or less scientific form, and to trust to other people to get this knowledge translated into popular proposals."[4] Beatrice aimed at living a scholarly life, regarding social engagements as distractions that took "one's thoughts from profitable brooding over local government."[5] Her researches took her up and down the country to towns such as Plymouth, Torquay, and Leicester, and she was often away without Sidney. He found the continual round of interviewing distasteful and disliked living in uncongenial lodgings and provincial hotels. In any case he had to attend to his business in London. At Easter 1899, however, they went north together. Sidney had to take the chair at a "Conference of Elected Persons" which had been arranged to coincide with the ILP annual conference in Leeds. Over two hundred and fifty ILP members now sat as local councillors, and this was the first of a series of such meetings where Fabians dealt with municipal policy. Beatrice, who had no interest in the ILP, travelled up to start their research in Leeds and stayed on when Sidney returned to London.

Beatrice found the research work hard going even with the help of paid assistants. They had started it without much planning, intending to write a historical review of municipal enterprise from 1834, but they gradually extended its scope and found themselves driven further back historically to changes which followed the Revolution of 1688. The result was that they were acquiring a vast and almost unmanageable knowledge of the intricacies of English local government. She began to think they had made a massive miscalculation; it was six years, in fact, before they could complete the first volume.

Sidney was overwhelmed by his own problems. "I can give no kind of thought to our book these days," he told her. "What with the L.C.C., the T.E.B. [Technical Education Board] & the London School & my lectures, I feel quite absorbed." Four days later he admitted: "I got nervous (being without my Bee) last night about the London School & the University, & all the complications, thinking that it would all collapse like a pack of cards."[6] The School of Economics had got off to a good start, but it needed more money, a permanent home and academic recognition. All three tasks fell mainly on his shoulders. The Hutchinson Trust and Charlotte's substantial donations covered only part of the growing expenses; the remainder came from the London County Council through the Technical Education Board. Sidney was hoping to get that grant increased, and he had been upset to hear from Hewins while he was in Australia that there had actually been an attempt to reduce it. New premises required capital, and though Sidney had induced the Council to provide a site in Clare Market made available by the construction of the new Aldwych road scheme, it took him several months to persuade Passmore Edwards, a philanthropist interested in libraries, to put up the ten thousand pounds needed to start the first building. The question of academic status was even more complex, for it was dependent upon the planned reorganization of London University. Sidney and Haldane were closely involved in the matter; since legislation was needed they had to win the support of Arthur Balfour, who had succeeded his uncle Lord Salisbury as the Tory premier.

Sidney was not satisfied with the compromise scheme that emerged, but it did meet the two essential requirements. First, it created a federal structure for the university which could accommodate individual colleges such as the School of Economics while leaving them a considerable degree of autonomy. Second, its academic pattern made room for his view that economics was a science: the school could now teach for the degree of B.Sc (Econ.). "This divorce of economics from metaphysics and shoddy history is a great gain," Beatrice noted with satisfaction on 20 February 1900.

There was one more battle to win before the school was safe. The County Council had to be persuaded to provide more cash, and Ramsay MacDonald, now openly hostile to the Fabians and sitting on the Council as an ILP member, took the chance to make things difficult for Webb. When Sidney was first trying to persuade his fellow Fabians that by using the Hutchinson money for disinterested social research he would be advancing the cause of socialism, MacDonald had declared that this was nonsense. Now he took the opposite line to attack Sidney. The School of Economics, he declared, was so much under Fabian control that it could not be considered truly independent. The ensuing row forced Sidney to write to the vice-chancellor of the university denying that the school was being used "to promote some particular creed." Conceding his own "Radical and socialist" beliefs, Sidney nevertheless insisted that he was "also a profound believer in knowledge and science and truth," and he set out clearly and in detail the assumptions on which he had founded the school: "I thought that we were suffering much from lack of research in social matters. . . . I believed that research and new discoveries would prove some, at any rate, of my views of policy to be right, but that, if they proved the contrary, I should count it all the more gain to have prevented error, and should cheerfully abandon my own policy."[7] Only in scientific study, he told Charlotte, lay the hope of remedying social evils: "I am furious when I read of bequests to the Poor Box, or the Lifeboat Society, or the Hospitals—it is worth more to discover one tiny improvement that will *permanently* change conditions . . . than to assuage momentarily the woes of thousands."

"This last year," Beatrice wrote on New Year's Day 1901, "we have seemed to drift upward in the strata of society."[8] It was their effort to raise the status of the School of Economics which drew the Webbs into the social round of lunches, dinner parties and afternoon calls. They were also caught up in a stimulating political world. In March 1901, in what she described as a week of dissipation, she met Lord Rosebery at a dinner given by Haldane in "an attempt to piece together an anti–Little England combination out of the most miscellaneous morsels of political influence." She thanked Haldane for seating her next to Rosebery, but could not refrain from telling him that if she were "four-and-twenty hours in the same house with that man" she would be rude to him.

Beatrice was genuinely ambivalent about their new style of life. She recognized that their excursions into society furthered the interests of the School and gave Sidney valuable contacts. She also teased herself with the prospect of influence through dinner-table politics. It flattered her vanity but touched her adolescent anxieties about self-indulgence and neglect of duty. She felt an uneasy sense of "skating on rotten ice which might suddenly give way under me," confirming that she feared "weakness in my own nature & incapacity to keep my intellect and heart set on our own work, undistracted by personal vanity or love of admiration."[9]

These feelings were given an added stimulus when, in July 1900, she met Chamberlain again for the first time in thirteen years. They met by chance on the terrace of the House of Commons when she and Sidney were attending a dinner given by Haldane. She introduced Sidney as "a former civil servant." Chamberlain opened the conversation gracefully: "I think you were once in my office, Mr. Webb." Sidney pedantically replied, "That is hardly quite correct. When I was there, you were not."[10] The contrast between Sidney's gaucherie and the glamour of Chamberlain touched off her old emotions. She raked over old diary entries and letters and was troubled by the memories aroused. She felt there was some inexplicable link between such uncontrolled "romancing" and the undisciplined social life she and Sidney were leading in "the inner circle of the political and scientific world."[11]

She also felt that in this new milieu they were drifting away from old friends such as Shaw. "Charlotte Shaw does not specially like me," Beatrice noticed, "and while meaning to be most friendly, arranges her existence so as to exclude most of Shaw's old friends." The Webbs spent more and more of their time with friendly acquaintances rather than intimates; in fact, "a sort of universal benevolence to all comers seems to take the place of special affection for chosen friends."[12] There were growing links with a younger generation. Their friendship with Bertrand and Alys Russell prospered, and the Webbs stayed several weeks at the Russells' house at Fridays Hill in the summer of 1901 and 1902. Russell thought the Webbs were "the most completely married couple" that he had ever known.[13] He admired Sidney's industry but was aware that he was somewhat earnest, not liking jokes about sacred subjects like political theory. He admired Beatrice, respecting her integrity and ability, and both the Russells found her a warm and kind friend. Beatrice, on her side, responded to Russell's intellectual stimulation but was troubled by this lack of sympathy and intolerance of other people's emotions; she remarked that he was "almost cruel in his desire to see cruelty revenged."[14] This ruthless aspect of his personality and his puritan ideas of perfection gradually affected his marriage. Beatrice was so concerned about Alys Russell's mental health that she took her off for three weeks' holiday in Switzerland in July 1902.

The Webbs had also come to know H. G. Wells, and they found it refreshing to talk to this "explorer of a new world."[15] Wells's public reputation as a writer of science-fiction stories and novels of lower-middle-class life was already established when he came into the Webb circle, and he was branching out into speculations about a new social order which naturally interested the Webbs. Wells found Beatrice rather formidable but was flattered by the attention of such an influential couple.[16]

Work was Beatrice's answer to the allurements of society. She felt greatly relieved when, in April, they were able to get away to spend three months in a thatched cottage near the sea at Lulworth and "London life, with its constant clash of personalities, its attractions and repulsions, its manipulations and wire-pulling could be set aside."[17] Sidney was more relaxed, having comfortably retained his County Council seat in an election that had strengthened the Progressives. He was "perpetually working," with his influence ramifying "through many organisations and persons, the outcome of multitudinous anonymous activities."[18]

But the holiday calm did not last. Beatrice was confused and restless. She felt that this "emotional and imaginative phase, whilst it gives me a certain magnetic effect on others, knocks me to pieces myself."[19] Rosebery wrote to her on 25 July 1901, trying to dispel her anxieties: "You must not talk of personal failure. You are rich in good gifts and high pure ambition and cannot fail to succeed in the long run."[20]

Beatrice had been further upset in January by the death of her old friend Mandell Creighton, the Bishop of London, who had shared the Webbs' interest in education and research and backed their work for the School of Economics. He seemed to her the ideal churchman, spiritually tolerant and with a vision of the Church as an instrument of what Beatrice called "mental hygiene"—a means of giving the state "its consciously religious side" and preventing its citizens from becoming "purely rationalistic and selfish."[21] She was feeling a renewed craving for the spiritual comfort which as a girl had led her to sample esoteric religions. Though she was agnostic, she was beginning to search for a spiritual home which would meet her inner need for moral order and social discipline. "Our object," she wrote, "is to enable the Church to grow out of its present superstitious doctrine and obsolete form."[22] She had always found a comfort in prayer. It allowed room for a sense of mystery, an indeterminate emotion, which Beatrice needed to express but could not satisfy in the ordinary occasions of life. In these years her religious need and interest grew; she sometimes went to St. Paul's for evensong, and she took to reading religious texts.

She deliberately offset the self-indulgence of her political and social life by a new regimen of personal self-abnegation. In September 1901, after an unsatisfying holiday in Yorkshire during which she felt unwell and full of morbid thoughts, she and Sidney met a diet faddist who believed that one cause of disease was eating too much at too frequent intervals. Beatrice was at once won over to his ideas and from that moment set herself on a strict diet aiming at reducing her food consumption to less than one pound each day. To outsiders like Bertrand Russell it appeared that she had become addicted to fasting in the belief that starvation made her more spiritual. He noticed that she took no breakfast and a meagre dinner, with lunch as the only solid meal. She weighed herself each week at Charing Cross station, and before long she had reduced her weight to well below eight stone. She maintained this strict regimen for the rest of her life, gradually cutting out meat, tea and coffee, and restricting her addiction to cigarettes. She felt that she had now set herself on a healthy course to counteract the "chatterings of personal vanity."[23]

One of the things which were exciting Beatrice was the intrigue, in which their friend Haldane was playing a key role, to resurrect Rosebery as a national leader. After the Liberal defeat in the 1900 election, Liberal Imperialists such as Haldane, Asquith and Sir Edward Grey found their party in Parliament under the control of Campbell-Bannerman and David Lloyd George, a young Welsh solicitor who entered the House in 1890, apparently bent on the revival of Gladstonian Liberalism. They had four choices: to acquiesce, sticking to their own opinions but doing nothing to jeopardize their prospects of office if the Liberals won the next election; to make a bid for control of the party by making Rosebery its leader; to break away, as Chamberlain's Liberal Unionists had done earlier; or to try to form a new centre party by wooing the Liberal Unionists away from the Tories. The number of possibilities made it difficult for them to settle on any one of them. They were too indolent politically, since all of them were enjoying the life of London society and making their own professional careers, to face the grind of a new venture seriously. And the situation was complicated by Rosebery's own ambivalence. He flirted with the idea of power, and he waited to be called to office. At one point he actually discussed with King Edward VII the possibility of forming some kind of coalition government on Salisbury's retirement, but he would never go beyond arcane indications that he was available if the moment should come. The Liberal Imperialists were thus in the frustrating position of campaigning for a leader who had given no clear sign that he was willing to lead. "He is a Puck in politics," Haldane said with exasperation in July 1901.[24] Without any warning Rosebery suddenly told the City Liberal Club, "I must plough my furrow alone"—yet again implying that he might rally the dissident Liberals behind him.[25] Unlike his distressed lieutenants, Beatrice felt that Rosebery had at least made it clear that he had broken with an "obsolete Liberalism."[26]

It was Shaw, however, who decided that it was time to promote

Rosebery, and that Sidney Webb should take the initiative. On 24 July 1901 he wrote to Beatrice: "*Our* policy is clearly to back him for all we are worth: I think Webb might do worse than write a magazine article about it. . . . I would do it myself if my reputation were of a nature to help R. But it isn't; and Webb's is."[27] As GBS insisted to Sidney two days later in briefing him on what he ought to say, Rosebery could achieve nothing unless he matched his imperialism with social reform. If the country merely wanted a secondhand Bismarck, this role was already filled by Chamberlain. The party system could be reconstructed only by a leader who would make himself a spokesman for collectivism.

Shaw recognized that he was setting Sidney a difficult task in casting Rosebery in that role. As he wrote to Beatrice at the end of July, it would be fatally easy for Sidney to give the impression that he had abandoned the Fabian cause. "Nothing is more unpopular in England than hauling down a flag," GBS said; "we are committed for life to Socialism; & any appearance of backing out of it would leave us less influence than Hyndman or Keir Hardie."[28] What Webb had to do was to show that neither socialism nor imperialism was in itself the basis of a new party— the supporters of both doctrines were riddled with dissensions and quite unable to agree how to translate their shibboleths into measures. If, Shaw concluded, "Lord Rosebery wishes to become a political entity he must become a personified program." It was Sidney's business as a Fabian to provide him with one.

"We have succumbed to his flattery," Beatrice said of GBS.[29] With suggestions from her and with Shaw's help in polishing his prose, Sidney composed for the September issue of the *Nineteenth Century* an article called "Lord Rosebery's Escape from Houndsditch." The leaders of the Liberal Party, Sidney suggested, were a set of tailors (Houndsditch being a centre of that trade) who were "piecing together the Gladstonian rags and remnants" to make "patched-up suits." Lord Rosebery was the only person who had "turned his back on Houndsditch and called for a complete new outfit." In place of outmoded individualism, Rosebery could offer a programme aimed at regenerating England and bringing efficiency into every aspect of national life—"the rearing of an imperial race." That programme would have to deal with the sweated trades and the scandalous inadequacy of the Poor Law, use municipal enterprise to provide decent housing, create a comprehensive educational system, reform the "silly procedure" of Parliament, modernize the Army and the Navy, and give the country a competitive economic system.

The article made a stir. Rosebery himself unbent sufficiently to write to Beatrice on 3 September to hope that she would "keep Webb out of London, or have him protected by the police, for his life can hardly be safe since the publication of his article . . . the most brilliant article I have read for many a day."[30] Haldane too wrote to thank Sidney. A few days later he told Beatrice that the time was at hand when Sidney ought to go into Parliament: he could provide "an expert element . . . which would give life to the whole business."[31] When Beatrice demurred, Haldane pressed his point. If the Liberal Imperialists did get into power, he insisted, Sidney was the man they would need to turn the watchword of efficiency into practical politics. By the end of the year, Beatrice had concluded that they had best press on and finish their book so that if Sidney were to be drawn into national politics he would be regarded as the great authority on local government as well as on labour questions. The idea of Sidney as home secretary in a Rosebery administration, promoted so assiduously by Haldane, had begun to appeal to her.

On 16 December 1901 Rosebery spoke at Chesterfield in Derbyshire. While making a conciliatory gesture towards the pro-Boer majority in the party, he called for "a clean slate" in domestic policy and for a new programme of efficiency. He attacked the basic concepts of party government, suggesting that it brought forward not those most fitted to govern but those most eligible from a party point of view. Campbell-Bannerman, who stood for all that Rosebery attacked, thought the speech was mischievous and silly—"a mere réchauffé of Mr. Sidney Webb who is evidently the chief instructor of the faction." Haldane, indeed, told Beatrice that the Houndsditch article had done its work. It was certainly a paper victory for Webb, but its effect was negative: Rosebery's tactics were so confused that his prospects of becoming premier actually receded from this point. He came out against Home Rule for Ireland, but his antagonism to Chamberlain made it almost impossible to consider an alliance with the Liberal Unionists which might have brought him back to office. His purpose was to discomfort those in office rather than to seek it himself. It was typical of Rosebery that when the Liberal League was formed, early in 1902, with himself as president and Asquith and Grey as vice-presidents, he was at pains to insist that it was not the nucleus of a new party: he claimed that it was merely a means of preventing the Liberal leadership from driving him and other imperialists into the wilderness.

Haldane and Webb, however, thought the League could develop into a party of national efficiency, and for some months in 1902 Sidney was an active member of it. Yet the more the Webbs saw of the "Limps," the more doubtful they became.[32] Reviewing this ill-assorted and ineffective team, Beatrice asked: "Why are we in this galley?" The only answer she could find was that they had "drifted" into it, partly because Haldane and Rosebery had been helpful over the School of Economics and the reorganization of London University, partly because they flattered the Webbs by listening to them, by being socially pleasant, and by taking much the same line on "the Empire as a powerful and self-conscious force." There was, moreover, no other group of politicians with which the Webbs felt any sympathy. "The leaders of the other school of Liberalism are extremely distasteful to us," Beatrice admitted; "we disagree with them on almost every point of home and foreign policy." Rosebery's idea of the clean slate offered some chance to "get the new ideas and new frame of mind accepted."[33] Beatrice did not shirk the logic of their position: "If Sidney is inside the *clique*," she decided in spite of her uneasiness, "he will have a better chance of permeating its activities than by standing aloof as a superior person and scolding them. So I am inclined to advise him to throw in his lot with them in their days of adversity and trial."

The Webbs had calculated and miscalculated: the consequences of their decision were profoundly damaging to their influence. Their naïve commitment to the Rosebery intrigue ensured that they would be distrusted by the main body of the Liberals. They had already cut themselves off from the Independent Labour Party. They had antagonized the left-wing Fabians by their attitude towards the war. Sidney had fallen out with the Nonconformists in the Progressive Party over education policy. Now, writing off Campbell-Bannerman as a fuddleheaded nonentity and annoying the other Liberal leaders with the gibes that Shaw had inserted into Sidney's article, they were needlessly making enemies of the only men with any prospect of leading a reformist government. Permeation had degenerated into a dinner-party cabal. Beatrice consoled herself with the thought that politics was "a mere by-product of our life" and that "we should have to choose our comrades more carefully" if "we came to throw our main stream of energy into political life."[34]

Their disappointment was all the more bitter because they had suspected all along that they were philandering politically with men less serious-minded than themselves and yet had been unable to resist their

blandishments. By the middle of March 1902 Beatrice was ready to write
them off: Asquith was "deplorably slack," Grey "a mere dilettante,"
Haldane "plays at political intrigue and has no democratic principle";
Rosebery was a bad colleague and "suffers from lack of nerve and persistent purpose."[35] Shaw too was backing out of a manoeuvre which he
had instigated a few months before, writing dolefully to Sidney on 24
March 1902 about the utter emptiness of the Rosebery campaign and
suggesting that they might after all have to try and "collar the I.L.P." If
he were seriously bent on politics, Shaw added, he "would not waste another five minutes on permeation."

The political outlook seemed bleak indeed. The Webbs could see
that labour was gaining ground politically and that Campbell-Bannerman
was weaving together an alliance of "all the antis—anti-war, anti-United
Kingdom, anti-Church, anti-capitalist, anti-Empire." All possible combinations seemed to Beatrice "equally temporary and equally lacking in
healthy and vigorous root principles."[36]

The Webbs spent much of the summer of 1902 away from London,
"camping out" in a girls' school at Crowborough in April to work at a
solid chapter on the Commissioner of Sewers. They stayed for a time
with the Russells, and after Beatrice returned from Switzerland with Alys
Russell they went off to Chipping Camden in the Cotswolds for another
stint of writing. They were currently obsessed with the idea of efficiency: it was the touchstone they used in their assessment of municipal
enterprises as they worked at their history, and they rigorously applied
the same standard in their own lives. In her letters Beatrice often referred
to their domestic and professional activities in terms which revealed her
preoccupation with time, effort, money and the results to be expected
from a given expenditure. This calculating attitude, which even spilled
over into their pleasures, struck many of their friends as tiresome; it
gave an ungenerous, almost mean impression which was intensified by
their lack of a relaxed sense of humour. In the summer of 1903, for instance, when they spent a week touring Normandy with the Russells,
Bertrand described their style of sightseeing to Gilbert Murray: "They
have a competent way of sizing up a cathedral, and pronouncing on it
with an air of authority and an evident feeling that the L.C.C. would
have done it better. They take all the colour out of life and make everything one cares for turn to dust and ashes."[37]

While the Webbs were out of London in the summer of 1902 they had mulled over the notion of a new dining club which they proposed to call the Co-Efficients. It was Beatrice who chose the name, and the scheme followed up the suggestion that Sidney had made in his article a year before for a brains trust for national revival. He had then called for "a group of men of diverse temperaments and varied talents, imbued with a common faith and a common purpose, and eager to work out, and severally to expound, how each department of national life can be raised to its highest possible efficiency."[38]

Although the political tide had begun to run away from the notion of "imperialist" coalitions, they managed to get together an apparently impressive set of people. Each of its twelve members was selected as an expert in a given field. Haldane, at whose home the first dinner was held, on 8 December, represented the law; Sir Edward Grey represented foreign policy; W. A. S. Hewins was there to speak for economics, Bertrand Russell for science, W. Pember Reeves for the colonies, and Sidney for municipal affairs. There were, besides, Halford J. Mackinder, an academic geographer from Oxford whose "geopolitical" concepts provided a rationale for Liberal Imperialism; the financier and Morgan partner Sir Clinton Dawkins; a retired naval officer and journalist named Carlyon Bellairs; and, as a military specialist, Leopold Amery. A Fabian at Oxford, then political secretary to Beatrice's brother-in-law Leonard Courtney, Amery had made a reputation as the *Times* correspondent who had used his Boer War experience to point out the need for army reform. There was a xenophobic journalist called Leo Maxse, whose energies were mainly devoted to arousing the country to the threat from Germany. The last of the Twelve Wise Men was H. G. Wells. His best-selling book on the scientific potential of the new century, called *Anticipations*, had greatly impressed the Webbs, who liked his idea of "New Republicans"—an élite which could regenerate the nation. In a letter to Wells which Sidney wrote from Chipping Campden on 12 September 1902 he set out the details of the scheme: "It is proposed to . . . arrange for about 8 dinners a year, mostly at a restaurant at the members' own expense; that the subject of all discussion should be 'the aims, policy and methods of imperial efficiency at home & abroad'; that the club is to be carefully kept unconnected with any person's name or party allegiance . . ."[39]

The Co-Efficients were significant as one minor expression of a change in the national mood which cut across the parties and social classes, a mood rather different from the jingoism of the Boer War. For the first time in a century there was a sense of national danger, of a need for forthright leadership which could stiffen the country's moral fibre and strengthen its ability to fend off foreign threats and competition. Ideas about racial improvement by selecting out the efficient were widely discussed, and Shaw was working these "eugenic" notions into his new play *Man and Superman;* Beatrice Webb called it "the most important of all questions, this breeding of the right sort of man."[40] Beatrice summed up such feelings in a letter to R. C. K. Ensor in May 1904: "At present the whole official Liberal Party . . . is wholly blind to the ghastly tragedies of the mental & physical decrease of the mass of our race," she wrote, adding that there must be "a compulsory raising of the standard of health & conduct."[41]

The Webbs were naturally attracted by the current talk of a new party of national efficiency. Such a notion fitted precisely into their conception of collectivism, designed to serve the whole nation rather than merely to improve the lot of the working classes, which Sidney had so assiduously defended against successive attempts to pull the Fabians into independent labour politics. In the congenial company of the Co-Efficients Sidney was associating with men who believed, as he did, in the cult of the specialist, who wanted strong leadership, who favoured large efficient units, whether these were great powers, big commercial enterprises or agencies of public administration. Above all, they were avowed élitists, intolerant of the cumbersome and apparently wasteful processes of democracy, who wanted to see England ruled by a superior caste which matched an enlightened sense of duty with a competence to govern effectively. All of them, moreover, shared Sidney's belief—which had led him to spend so much effort on London education and on the School of Economics—that social improvement depended upon the training of the superior manpower needed to carry out schemes of reform. Shaw was suggesting in his latest play that universal suffrage was a disaster, putting power into the hands of the "riff-raff" and setting the country on the road to "national suicide." Webb, who could not wait until a new race of supermen had been bred up to establish the millennium, felt that improved education and intelligent politics would at least start the necessary process of national regeneration. The Co-Efficients—deliberately called together as a kind of shadow Cabinet for the new party that the

Webbs hoped would emerge—were beginning to seem a much more attractive instrument for their purpose than the argumentative and divided Fabians.

"I am getting old and demoralized," GBS told Janet Achurch on 8 May 1903. "The more I try professional art, the greater becomes my horror and weariness of it." He was forty-six and still had not made a name for himself in the theatre. He had a reputation only on its fringes, and even there his impact had been more as a critic than as an author.

There had been some changes since his marriage. His London home was now Charlotte's comfortable maisonette in Adelphi Terrace and they had a rented cottage in Surrey. Charlotte was content and she devoted herself to caring for Shaw and doing all she could to further his career. She settled a considerable part of her income on him and they lived easily but simply on three thousand pounds a year. She too became a vegetarian in 1903. Shaw continued his work on the St. Pancras vestry and remained an active member of the Fabian Society, but he was seeing less of his old friends, for Charlotte was jealous of her position and discouraged these ties. Although the Webbs came regularly for dinner on Thursdays, when Beatrice gave a lecture at the School, the old intimacy had gone. There were no more duets with Kate Salt, no casual visits from Janet Achurch, no holidays with Wallas. The style of Shaw's life was gradually changing.

While he achieved no big theatrical success, his plays were not quite forgotten. They had been given scattered performances by the Stage Society run by his Fabian friends. It put on *You Never Can Tell* at the Royalty Theatre in November 1899 and again at the Strand Theatre in May 1900. *Candida* was also performed by the Society in that year. *The Devil's Disciple* was given thirteen nights at Kennington in September 1899, and Forbes Robertson took it to Leeds a year later. In an effort to make his mark Shaw started to put his work out in published form. *Plays Pleasant and Unpleasant* appeared in 1898, and in January 1901 *Three Plays for Puritans* followed it.

Such frustrations no longer mattered to him financially and they did not abate his combative cockiness. While he was convalescing in 1898 he had written *Caesar and Cleopatra*, and there was no modesty in his assertion to Archer "I am by a very great deal the best English language playwright since Shakespeare."[42] Once again, in his play, Shaw was using the theatre as a "battering ram" to make a point about contemporary life. His Caesar was a Victorian empire-builder, a wily man given to bluff and bombast. But the topical analogy was wasted, for it was seven years before anyone would risk a production of a play which required elaborate sets, several scene changes and many extras.

Captain Brassbound's Conversion, written specially for Ellen Terry, fared no better. When she told GBS, "I couldn't do this one," damning it further by saying, "I believe it would never do for the stage," Shaw retorted, "Oh Ellen . . . this is the end of everything."[43] Still, he persevered. In December 1900 the play was put on by the Stage Society with Janet Achurch and Charrington in the leads. It was then that Shaw met Ellen Terry for the first time.

In 1901 not one of his plays was produced, though *The Admirable Bashville*—a dramatization of his early novel *Cashel Byron's Profession* in banal blank verse—was put on to preserve the dramatic copyright. Undismayed, Shaw was hard at work by midsummer on *Man and Superman*, with an idea that he had been turning over in his mind for some time. If the playgoing public was not fit for plays intended to entertain them, he decided, he would abandon his efforts in that direction: he would use a dramatic form simply as a vehicle in which to present his metaphysical beliefs, publishing the play as a book if it could not be performed. He was now as taken by Nietzsche and Schopenhauer as he had been by Ibsen ten years earlier. "My next play will be a horror—and a masterpiece," he told Richard Mansfield's wife in January 1900; from time to time he issued similar reports on its progress. "The new play . . . is stupendous," he wrote to Frederick Evans;[44] later that summer he told Henry Salt that it was "one of the most colossal efforts of the human mind."[45]

He had conceived a work which was Wagnerian in scale and style. Its theme was the same as *Parsifal*—the dialogue between the sensual and spiritual lives. Jack Tanner's struggle against love was the same that Shaw had fought. How can a man be truly free, preserve his individual will, yet accept the demands of society and his species? Shaw had rehearsed that question many times. Now he had found his answer. Man cannot defeat the pursuing Woman on her own terms. She is the Life Force, embodying the instinctual drive to preserve society and the race, and love is her conquering instrument. He must submit, sacrificed into the martyrdom of marriage. Yet in surrendering his body he can save his soul: as he becomes the passive victim of sensuality his spirit soars up into immortal spheres, where reason is superior to instinct.

For Shaw this notion had already become more than a metaphor. He had begun to believe that the human race must transcend its animal origins and seek salvation in the eternal life of the mind. "Man, as he is, never will nor can add a cubit to his stature by any of the quackeries, political, scientific, educational or artistic," Jack Tanner declares. "Our only hope, then, is in evolution. We must replace the man by the superman." For Shaw, already rejecting Darwinism, ordinary evolution was not enough. Some years before, T. H. Huxley had suggested that the one hope of humanity might lie in using what he called "the ethical process" to combat the "cosmic process" which made man the doomed slave of Nature. Now Shaw, like his contemporaries Samuel Butler and Henri Bergson, was pushing that idea towards the doctrine of "Creative Evolution" in which the mind can triumph over matter and shape it in a desired direction. The vision of the superman, using will to bend destiny, to "eliminate the yahoo" and create a new and superior race, was one that had been implicit in Shaw's life and work. He now made it explicit, and henceforward it remained his formula for survival.

His Fabian friends liked the play. In January 1903 the Webbs were staying on Lady Battersea's estate at Overstrand on the Norfolk coast and they invited Wallas and Shaw down for a week "with their wives as chorus." It was a long-awaited reunion, and Shaw gave them three "delightful evenings" reading *Man and Superman*.[46] Beatrice was enthusiastic. "To me it seems a great work," she wrote; "quite the biggest thing he has done. He has found his *form:* a play which is not a play; but only a combination of essay, treatise, interlude, lyric."

William Archer was more critical, reading GBS a severe lesson about his career: "In no way are you making the mark, either upon literature or upon life, that you have it in you to make." It seemed to Archer that Shaw was always adopting "somebody else's war-cry, with only the addition of your own Irish accent." To Shaw's claim that his men were Wagner, Ibsen, Tolstoy, Schopenhauer and Nietzsche, Archer pointedly retorted: "I should reverse it & say that you are *their* man. . . . The moment someone comes along with a nostrum, you seize upon it as the last word in human wisdom."[47]

In November 1900 a young Austrian playwright named Siegfried

Trebitsch had visited Archer, whose theatre criticism and translations of Ibsen he much admired. Archer then told him about Shaw and the growing list of unperformed plays. Trebitsch read them and decided that it was worth translating Shaw into German. Archer sent him to see Shaw, but the diffident young man was somewhat overawed by the "amiably mirthful giant," who at first declined to cooperate. Then, on reflection, Shaw gave him permission to translate three plays, on condition that if he failed to find a producer within a year the rights reverted to GBS.

Things went well from the beginning. GBS admired Trebitsch's industry and skill, and Trebitsch did not challenge Shaw's fervent refusal to alter anything he had written. The moment managers "begin to sing that old song about alterations & modifications," Shaw told Trebitsch on 26 June 1902, they should be brusquely informed "that I know my business and theirs as well." Shaw was all the more prepared to be adamant because he approved of the translations that Trebitsch produced; "I prefer them in many respects to the originals," he told Archer on 12 January 1903. Trebitsch also succeeded in making arrangements for productions in Austria and Germany. *The Devil's Disciple* was presented in Vienna on 23 February 1903 and *Candida* a year later. When Shaw saw that he was being taken up in Europe, he became even more disillusioned about his neglect at home—for which he blamed the "illiterateness of the managers." "As to the public," he told Trebitsch in March, "we cannot even guess whether I shall ever hit their fancy."

In this letter, however, Shaw made a prescient remark. With patience, he said, "things will gradually change. The older men will die out; the contemporaries will surrender."[48] GBS had been a rebel, trying to urge new ideas and styles upon managers—and audiences—who were conservative in taste. With the new reign, things were different. Edwardian England was much more likely to listen to Shaw. As the taboos broke down, and a new generation emerged, the rebel could be transformed into a prophet.

WIREPULLERS

"Politics are very topsy-turvy just now," Beatrice wrote in December 1903 to her sister Georgie Meinertzhagen; "one never knows who is to be one's bedfellow."[1] The Webbs had drifted into the role of lobbyists, pushing their plans for coaching civil servants, devising schemes for politicians and ghosting reports to feed into the political machine. There was, Beatrice confessed, an element of sport in watching their ideas "wending their ways through all sorts of places," and a certain thrill in exercising anonymous influence.[2] Despite her doubts about the morality of "intrigue," she was fascinated by the gossip, intellectual stimulation and flattery of the *haut-monde*. She was good at salon politics, and Sidney sometimes had to appeal to her common sense against her vanity. In the summer of 1904, when they were invited to three fashionable parties in one week, he told her the cautionary tale of the ambitious Sir Gilbert Parker, of whom it was said that in the dead of night he could be heard "climbing, climbing, climbing." It was undesirable, Sidney said, "to be seen in the houses of great people." Curbing "my lower desires," Beatrice tore up the invitation cards and put away her new party dress. "Know them privately if you like," Sidney added; so Beatrice resolved to restrict herself to small dinners.[3] On such occasions she could talk shop all evening and feel that good was being done unostentatiously.

The Webbs had fallen into the practice of covert manipulation.

They saw themselves as independent experts rather than professional politicians: they were interested in ideas and issues and promoted both by pulling whatever wires seemed appropriate. Their interests, moreover, cut across party lines and enabled them to work with sympathetic people who had access to the levers of power. This suited Sidney's temperament and his training as a civil servant. He had no inhibition about collaborating with Tories such as Arthur Balfour, Liberal Imperialists such as Haldane and Asquith, or with the Progressives on the London County Council. In choosing allies, indeed, he and Beatrice were always more attracted to individuals who were currently in a position to make practical decisions than to those who, out of office, could do little but raise a clamour about principles.

The complex problems of educational reform in London were a case in point. For some years Sidney Webb had been at odds with such influential Fabians as Wallas and Stewart Headlam on this issue. Both of them served on the London School Board and had been antagonized by Sidney's support for a Conservative plan in 1889 to abolish the Board and put the schools directly under the control of the County Council. When the Society considered the draft of a new tract, *The Education Muddle and the Way Out*, Webb argued at a Fabian meeting in May 1899 that all education should be run by municipal bodies and not by the cumbersome procedure of electing special boards. Wallas and Headlam attacked him so hard that the tract had to be held up for two years while the discussion continued; when it did appear it contained significant concessions.

The strong feelings aroused by this apparently technical problem reflected a fundamental difference of approach. Webb's sympathies increasingly lay with experts such as Robert Morant who were trying to engineer a more efficient educational system managed by specialists. The supporters of the old School Board believed that democracy demanded the direct involvement of its members in the running of the schools. This division of opinion was accentuated by political factors. The Tory reforms envisaged subsidies to denominational schools, a move which Webb favoured on the grounds that it was the only way of bringing Church schools up to a minimum standard. The School Board, however, was dominated by Liberal Nonconformists led by Dr. John Clifford, who bitterly opposed the idea that the ratepayers should be forced to underwrite Anglican education.

This situation had not been resolved by the end of 1902. By this time Sidney was more than ever convinced that the Tories were right in trying to modernize the system, nationally as well as in London, and he had privately become closely involved in shaping the proposed legislation. He was in a difficult situation, because he was publicly the foremost spokesman on education for the Progressives who controlled the County Council, and the Progressives both objected to the proposed changes on grounds of policy and believed that by beating the sectarian drum they could win back votes from the Nonconformist middle class which had swung to the Tories.

On the one hand, therefore, Sidney was trying to stiffen the resolve of a vacillating Tory administration to make a thorough job of educational reform; on the other hand he had somehow to win the Progressives round to accepting the change. "I want to use the present revolution to make a new start," he told Graham Wallas in January 1904, "however, I am overruled and boycotted by the Progressives."[4] He was engaged in a complicated and risky manoeuvre in which his main assets were his position as an acknowledged expert on education and his extraordinary capacity for hard work.

It was a supreme test of his ability to get results by wirepulling. All through 1903 and the early months of 1904 he was trying to inch the conflicting interests towards a compromise. He had, first, to persuade the Tories to hand over education to the County Council—a course about which they had become increasingly doubtful; they were more inclined to create a new ad hoc body to run the whole school system or else to pass the work over to the local borough councils in London. Second, he had covertly to stir up the Anglican and Catholic lobbies to offset the Nonconformist pressures on the Progressives. Third, he had to persuade the suspicious and recalcitrant Progressives to jettison their favoured School Board and to agree to County Council control of a school system which included the disagreeable concessions to the churches. He had, fourthly, to work with Robert Morant and the other civil servants drafting the legislation. Finally, through Haldane—who was willing to work against his Liberal colleagues on this issue—he had the ear of the Tory Prime Minister, Arthur Balfour.

In this situation the support of the Fabian Society was vital to Webb: he needed it as a base. In all the other groups with which he was working he had no firm position; even in the Progressive Party, to which he had given fifteen years of hard work, he was jeopardizing all the in-

fluence he had built up by loyal service. "I don't feel sure what is going
to be the end result," he told Pease as early as March 1903; "I don't intend to budge, and I hope the F.S. will hold on and keep the faith."[5] It
was, however, difficult to convince some of the Fabians that the Webbs
themselves were keeping faith. There was gossip that they were hobnobbing with Balfour in the hope that Sidney would be given a government
post as a reward for his efforts. At times the outlook seemed black. There
was, Beatrice wrote, a "slump in Webbs" on the political market. Mac-
Donald was stirring things up against Sidney on the County Council
and spreading a rumour that Sidney himself was drawing a salary from
the money he induced the Council to grant to the School of Economics.
The government, losing two bye elections and sensing a swing of opinion
to the Liberals, was on the point of capitulating. And the Progressives
were declaring that they would not implement the Education bill even if it
was passed. All over the country the Nonconformists were running a
campaign of "passive resistance," refusing to pay rates to support church
schools.

The Webbs and Haldane were spurred to throw in every scrap of
influence they possessed. Sidney drafted amendments and scurried round
to whip up support for them. Some were first passed through a Fabian
meeting as a means of keeping the Society in line. It was not until the
middle of June that the bill struggled through its committee stage in
Parliament. Webb's formula had won the day. Against all the apparent
odds, the London County Council was to have control of education, and
the Progressives were persuaded to accept the new system.

The political confusion over educational reform was only one example
of a general state of muddle and uncertainty. For all Rosebery's havering, up to May 1903 it still seemed possible that some new political
grouping might be formed by a combination of the Liberal Unionists
and the Liberal Imperialists. On 15 May, however, Chamberlain delivered a speech in Birmingham which wrecked forever the chances of such
a coalition. He came out flatly for tariff reform as the means of national
salvation. To meet the challenge of foreign rivals, he insisted, British
industry needed protective tariffs. To hold the Empire together there
must be a system of imperial preference—a kind of customs union. And
to ensure the support of the people there must be social reforms, such as

old-age pensions, financed out of import duties. The logic of Chamberlain's imperialism had led him to this Bismarckian formula, jettisoning the traditional policy of free trade on which Britain's industrial supremacy had rested. The Liberal Imperialists, otherwise sympathetic to his position, could not accept his tariff policies. Where Chamberlain spoke for the industrialists who saw the Empire as a protected market, Rosebery and the other "Limps" were closer to the financial and commercial interest of the City of London, whose prosperity rested upon their role in world trade. They were therefore driven, on this one issue, back towards orthodox Liberalism.

Chamberlain's policy was bound to create a serious split among those who had dreamed of a new party of national efficiency. Sidney wrote to Pease that he expected an early election on the issue and he revealed the difficulty in which he and his friends had been placed: "I am disposed to stand & say nothing myself. But I am dead against taxes on food; & also against protective tariffs—& I think the artisan in the North & the rural labourer will be also. All the same I think Chamberlain (as with Old Age Pensions) has hit on a fundamentally right *idea*, which he ignorantly & rashly spoils by plunging on an impracticable *device*."[6]

Sidney realized that the Co-Efficients were being torn apart. Hewins, Mackinder and Amery came out openly for Chamberlain. And there were signs that the Fabians too might divide again as sharply as they had disagreed over the war and education. Even the Webbs themselves did not see eye to eye on the matter. Beatrice thought that Chamberlain's import duties might be one way of providing a national minimum through social services, while Sidney felt that tariff reform was a distraction from the struggle for a social policy which, he told a Fabian meeting in June, was needed to make Britain more efficient, mentally and physically. His intention, Beatrice noted, was to get the Fabians "to prepare the ground for some intermediate plan combining imperialism with sound national economy."[7]

By the time the Webbs came back from their retreat in the Cotswolds, it was evident that the Fabians could not avoid the issue. Shaw, for one, had come out as "a Protectionist right down to my boots," as he told John Burns in September.[8] Bland was also afraid that the Fabians would cling to free trade, telling Pease on 22 September that he was worried that the Society was "going to anchor itself up a financial backwater. . . . I suppose every 'advanced' society gets left high & dry at last."[9] Webb was always susceptible to pressure from Shaw. He had been carried along when Shaw decided to back Rosebery and when *Fabianism and the Empire* was being drafted. Now GBS was at work on a new tract, *Fabianism and the Fiscal Question*, and Sidney was afraid that Shaw would sweep him into the Protectionist camp. He had reason to be anxious. On 6 October GBS wrote to Beatrice asking her help "to anaes- thetise Sidney" while he extracted the last fragments of classical Liber- alism from him. He recognized that Sidney was slow to change his opin- ions, whereas "I switch off the old current & switch on the new with treacherous & disconcerting suddenness."[10] A month later he was still trying to induce Sidney to abandon free trade, suggesting half seriously that Sidney would find himself in the Cabinet if Chamberlain could form a government.

Sidney, however, was unwilling to align himself with Chamberlain. He was especially concerned lest the controversy damage the London School of Economics, since from the early summer Hewins had been a strong Chamberlain supporter. "We must at all costs get the 19th cen- tury well buried," Hewins wrote to Beatrice at the end of May, ex- plaining why he was a Chamberlain man, and he sent Sidney several letters arguing that so long as he behaved impartially as director of the School he was free to help Chamberlain privately.[11] This did not reassure Sidney. The more Hewins pressed him, the more he felt that he had to protect the impartiality of the School by making it clear that he was not a tariff reformer. At the same time he had no desire to see the control of the School fall into the hands of Gladstonian free-traders. When Hewins was offered a salaried post as secretary to the Tariff Commission set up by Chamberlain and resigned from the School of Economics, he was replaced by Halford Mackinder, equally strong for tariff reform but less publicly partisan.

The tariff issue thus intensified the political difficulties that the Webbs had run into as a result of their alliance with the Liberal Imperial- ists. An attempt to hitch their programme of social reform to Chamber- lain's protectionist campaign would have led to an open break with the Fabians and an alliance with the Tories at a moment when their chances of winning the next election were beginning to look very slim. Con- versely, if the Webbs followed the "Limps" back into the Liberal fold they would be forced into the uncongenial company of unreconstructed Gladstonians, Nonconformists and anti-imperialists. Appreciating their dilemma, Hewins told them as he left the School of Economics that they had best press on quickly with any educational changes they wanted, "because some of the instruments on which you reckon at present may turn out worse than useless, and you yourselves may be isolated."[12] The best that they could do was to temporize and to focus opinion instead on their schemes for social reconstruction without taking sides on the conflict between protectionists and free-traders.

That was Shaw's brief for the Fabian tract. To make it palatable he resorted to the same device that he had employed in *Fabianism and the Empire*, cleverly shifting the ground from the facts to a discussion of a policy that might be viable if only the facts were different. His ability as a debater helped him to put over his muddling of the "is" and the "ought." But it was more than just a trick to get out of a tight corner. It was characteristic of the Fabian avoidance of unpleasant political realities by harping on some ideal—though unrealizable—state of affairs. Thus, for Shaw, it was not protection itself that was wrong; it was unacceptable because it was a tool of "our present class governments and their lobbies." If, however, it could lead to "the deliberate interference of the State with trade," then socialists should welcome it as a means to "the subordination of commercial enterprise to national ends." This was good enough for the majority. It was too much for Graham Wallas, who wrote to Pease on the eve of the meeting to complain that despite the verbal concessions to free-traders the draft was "thoroughly bad." It was "virtually a plea for a Chamberlainite Ministry," and "insincere and mischievous as a whole."[13] On 22 January, when his free-trade amendment was defeated, Wallas resigned from the Society. The breach with Wallas had been a long time in the making; it had come finally on an issue on which few Fabians were willing to follow him.

The intense social life of the Webbs between 1902 and 1905 was set in a milieu very different from that of most middle-class Fabians and even further from the impoverished idealists who were trying to build up a socialist movement in the constituencies. They were no longer in touch with the labour leaders, and on the London County Council MacDonald had lined up the handful of workingmen against Sidney. When, at the instance of Haldane, Sidney was appointed by the Tory Premier Arthur Balfour to a new royal commission on trade-union law, Beatrice

naïvely assumed that this would "have the incidental advantage of bringing us again into communication with the trade union world."[14] When
the unions decided to boycott the commission Sidney's membership only
served to intensify suspicions that the Webbs were sitting "behind the
scenes, touching buttons, pulling wires, making the figures on the stage
dance to their rhythms," as their journalist friend A. G. Gardiner described them.[15] To their modest table, he added, came "the great and the
powerful to learn their lessons."

One frequent visitor was Arthur Balfour. The Webbs had met him
first at a party arranged by Haldane in November 1902, when the Prime
Minister—as Haldane told Beatrice—wished to show that he was grateful
for what they had done in supporting his education policies.[16] In the
summer of 1903, even more in Sidney's debt, he went to "a brilliant little
dinner" at Grosvenor Road. Beatrice took the trouble on occasions like
this to have her sister Mary send up flowers from Gloucestershire and to
provide particular recipes to serve the occasion. She responded at once
to Balfour's urbanity, finding him a man "of extraordinary grace of mind
and body—delighting in all that is beautiful and distinguished—music,
literature, philosophy, religious feeling and moral disinterestedness—
aloof from all the greed and grime of common human nature."[17] The
attraction was reciprocal. Over the next two years they met frequently,
finding that they had similar interests and much the same high-minded
outlook on life. Balfour was almost the ideal foil for Beatrice. "But what
a strange being to be at the head of the nation's affairs," she wrote to
Mary Playne after one dinner party; "regarding all questions as unsettled problems to be debated academic-wise, & cordially detesting social
& economic issues as ugly and irrelevant to the life of a Distinguished
Soul."[18]

Balfour was one of "the Souls"—the set of smart, clever people who
had made literature, art and ideas fashionable in society, who processed
through country houses such as Stanway, Wilton and Taplow, and
through London salons such as Lady Desborough's, taking up talented
writers and rising public figures whom they found amusing. When the
Webbs spent holidays in Gloucestershire they were made welcome by
Lady Elcho, Balfour's particular friend, at Stanway. Beatrice was critical
of "the Souls," but she found company of this kind more stimulating
than the "coarse-grained" politicians with whom Sidney rubbed shoulders in the County Council. Even the best of them, Beatrice complained,

were "a good deal below the standard of our intimate associates—such as Hewins, Mackinder, Haldane, Russell, etc.—and the ordinary Progressive member is either a bounder, a narrow-minded fanatic, or a mere piece of putty upon which any strong mind can make an impression."[19]

By the end of 1903, in fact, Beatrice and Sidney were wondering whether Sidney could much longer hold his ground in a party so marked by "class, sectarian and professional jealousy." With the County Council elections looming in the spring of 1904, they were thinking how they might engineer a result which would "tame" the Progressives by leaving them only a small majority or perhaps bringing in the Moderates. In January 1904, when Sidney published his *London Education*, he was lobbying newspaper editors to take a strong line against the Nonconformists. With the political tide running strongly against the Tories, the manoeuvre was hopeless; the Webbs' "underground attack on the size of the Progressive majority," Beatrice confessed as the Progressives romped home easily in March, was a complete failure.[20] The Webb tactic of striking temporary alliances was beginning to undermine their standing. "It is unpleasant," Beatrice admitted, "this perpetual transit from camp to camp, however hostile these camps feel to one another. It is perilously near becoming both a spy and a traitor—or rather, being considered such by the camp to which we officially belong."[21]

The reputation for political perversity which was proving a handicap to the Webbs was even more justified with Shaw. Despite his delight in teasing paradoxes, he had worked conscientiously in St. Pancras as a vestryman and then—after the system was reformed—as a borough councillor. But in 1904 he ran for one of the two London County Council seats. It was the first time he had fought an important election, and he found it difficult to play the traditional game. Charlotte, who had asked Webb to find a seat for GBS, hoped to see him in respectable politics. Sidney, out of friendship and also anxious to ensure that his ally was not discredited, tried to get the Fabians to rally round. Yet Shaw insisted on showing what Beatrice called "his bad side . . . vanity and lack of reverence for knowledge or respect for other people's prejudices."[22] He told churchmen that he was an atheist, cancelling out the support Sidney had tried to drum up for him among Anglicans; he laughed at the stuffiness of the Nonconformist conscience; he ridiculed the Catholics, upset

the publicans and the temperance interest equally. It was a romp, characteristic of his wilful individualism, which put an end to Shaw's chances of
ever again being considered as a serious candidate. "I have been defeated
—wiped out—annihilated at the polls," he wrote to Trebitsch a week afterwards, "mostly through the stupidity of my own side. Consequently I
am furious. It is no use sending congratulatory telegrams about that silly
old *Candida*."[23]

Yet the production of *Candida* by Max Reinhardt in Berlin on 4
March was more than a consolation for electoral disappointment. It coincided with a real and long-awaited breakthrough on the London stage,
where six matinées of the same play were scheduled for the following
month. In Germany Shaw had Trebitsch to thank; in London it was a
young actor named Harley Granville Barker, who had played the part of
the poet Eugene Marchbanks in the Stage Society production of *Candida*
in July 1900. Barker, GBS told Archer on that occasion, "was the success
of the piece. It was an astonishing piece of luck to hit on him. He is a
very clever fellow."[24] Later in the year, when Barker played opposite
Ellen Terry in *Captain Brassbound's Conversion*, Shaw's approval was
confirmed. "Barker was *very* good. We must stick to Barker," he told
Janet Achurch that Christmas.[25]

Granville Barker was then only twenty-three. He was attractive
and his reddish hair, dark eyes, thin frame and irrepressible vitality gave
him an air of nervous intensity. In temperament he was self-willed and
industrious, as interested in producing and writing plays as in acting.
The fact that Barker was an intellectual actor enabled him to respond
exactly to what Shaw wanted; his readiness to serve as Shaw's apostle
enabled GBS to play a paternal role. For most of his life he had been accustomed to bullying his elders and chiding his contemporaries; now that
he felt himself to be one of the old generation he was able to be generous
to the young. Charlotte too liked this self-neglected young man who was
willing to let her mother him.

Barker soon showed that he had a taste for politics as well as a talent
for the stage. He joined the Fabians and eventually became a member of
the executive. He was also attracted by Archer's dream of a national
theatre and sat on a fund-raising committee for that campaign. Though
nothing came of it for over fifty years, the idea of a centre of theatrical
excellence and innovation became a ruling passion of Barker's life. It lay
behind the proposal he made to Archer on 21 April 1903 "to take the Court

Theatre for six months or a year and to run there a stock season of the uncommercial drama."[26] The plan, in effect, was to extend the work of the Stage Society from a Sunday subscription theatre to afternoon productions that would get at least a fortnight's run. Later in 1903, the lease of the Court was bought by J. H. Leigh, a businessman and amateur actor who proposed to mount a Shakespeare series. After two flops, Archer advised Leigh to bring in Barker. As part of the arrangement Barker agreed with Leigh's manager, the astute and meticulous J. E. Vedrenne, to put on *Candida* for six performances in the afternoons. The Stage Society production had not pleased Shaw, and he told Barker that his plan was "hideous folly." But, unknown to GBS, Charlotte had privately underwritten the venture financially. Barker excelled in the part of Marchbanks when the play opened on 26 April. Shaw had always been ambitious for the best actors to play his leads—Irving, Ellen Terry or Forbes-Robertson. Now he had found his man, and the man had found a way to put his patron before the public.

In May 1904 Charlotte took GBS off on a long visit to Italy. Then they spent much of the summer in Scotland, part of the time at Rosemarkie on the Cromarty Firth within cycling distance of the Webbs, who had retired there for three months. "O, these holidays, these accursed holidays," GBS wrote to Barker.[27] Shaw was anxious to finish the new play he was writing for Yeats, who, with Lady Gregory, was setting up the Irish National Theatre in Dublin. *John Bull's Other Island* was finished in September, and Yeats approved of it. "You have said things in this play which are entirely true about Ireland," he wrote to Shaw, "things which nobody has ever said before."[28] His company was less enthusiastic about a play which mocked Irish illusions almost as much as it derided English follies. When Yeats decided to drop the play, Barker opened with it at the Court on 1 November.

Shaw declared that the play was "a sort of political farce, of no use to anybody but cranks."[29] In fact it was Shaw's first attempt to express his own complex féelings about the country he had fled more than thirty years before. If the play was muddled, its moral unclear, so was GBS. Part of him sympathized with the impatient property developer, Broadbent, almost a Fabian and recognizably as full of modernizing zeal as a member of the Co-Efficients, who wants to convert a bankrupt estate

into a resort; Broadbent may be insensitive and clumsy, but he is as much
the agent of the civilizing process as Chamberlain's imperialists. Part of
Shaw, too, speaks through Broadbent's assistant, the expatriate Irish
cynic Larry Doyle, who has seen through the mist of Irish fantasy,
knows that the villagers will succumb to Broadbent and yet is unable to
prevent their inevitable ruin. "An Irishman's imagination never lets him
alone," says Doyle; "it makes him that he can't face reality . . . he can
only sneer at them that do." Doyle, the displaced person, stands between
the light of progress and the Celtic twilight. And Father Keegan is the
prophet of a different Ireland: he is the man of visions, who can talk elo-
quently about salvation but is actually powerless to stop Broadbent ruin-
ing his people in the name of his efficiency and their prosperity.

The Irish question had haunted British politics for a generation, but
Shaw dramatized its paradoxes so successfully, with dour comedy, that
the play caught the public imagination. Beatrice Webb took Balfour to
see it, and he was so enthusiastic that he went five times—taking Campbell-Bannerman to one performance and Asquith to another. Any play
which could induce a Tory Premier to take the two leaders of the Liberal opposition to the theatre had clearly touched a popular nerve, and it
was revived twice in the following year. Edward VII requested a special performance, and this sign of royal approval not only opened London society to Shaw but also stimulated American interest. Vedrenne
and Barker now signed a new agreement, to run for three years, which
meant that it would be possible to put on evening productions employing
actors at full commercial rates. The Court had met the box-office test.

Shaw was a tireless worker right up to the moment the curtain rose
on a play. He demanded much from his actors, but he had also schooled
himself so well in his trade that the demands were seldom resented and
he was able to create an unusual degree of collaboration between himself
and the actors. "There was inspiration, originality and discipline in the
Court productions," Lillah McCarthy recalled. "We were members of a
theatrical House of Lords: all equal and all lords." She, like other young
actors such as Lewis Casson and Edmund Gwenn, made her reputation
as part of this talented team in partnership with Shaw. He was a wild
man, "with his pocket full of plays," she felt when she came into the
cast of *John Bull's Other Island*, yet he was "serious, painstaking, concentrated, relentless in the pursuit of perfection." Years later she recalled
the magic of his presence at rehearsals: "With complete unselfconscious-

ness he would show us how to draw the full value out of a line. He would assume any role, any physical attitude, and make any inflection of his voice, whether the part was that of an old man or a young man, a budding girl or an ancient lady. With his amazing hands he would illustrate the mood of a line. We used to watch his hands in wonder."[30]

In the first season at the Court under the new arrangement twelve plays were produced, four of them by Shaw—including *Man and Superman* in May 1905. The management even made a little money. Shaw's theatre had emerged at last.

The wave of new attitudes was beginning to lift Shaw's fortunes. His next piece, *How He Lied to Her Husband*, came on at the Court in February 1905—a trivial curtain-raiser to serve as an alternative to *Man of Destiny*. He was suddenly in demand, "quite maddened by the business . . . that my recent boom has brought me," he told Florence Farr. "If I would consent, the whole 13 plays would be produced simultaneously about the middle of April."[31] Under such pressure he was working relentlessly, taking up a new play as soon as the last was done. Charlotte had long wanted to show GBS her childhood home, and *Major Barbara* was completed during the three months they spent in the summer of 1905 at Castle Townshend on the south coast of Ireland.

It was a difficult play to finish. Before it came on at a Court matinée on 28 November Shaw had slaved away at rehearsals, and, displeased with the last act, he had quickly written a new one to replace it. His reputation was now good enough to fill the house, though few of the critics liked the play. Shaw told the actress Eleanor Robson that the audiences were "pained, puzzled, bored in the last act to madness; but they sit there to the bitter end and come again & again."[32] Beatrice Webb took Balfour, in the dying moments of his government, to see what she called "a dance of devils . . . hell tossed on the stage—with no hope of heaven."[33] Set in the East End slums, the play was curiously appropriate to the occasion. Five days before, Balfour had appointed Beatrice to the new Royal Commission on the Poor Law.

The Fabians had begun by asking: Why Are the Many Poor? The question was still relevant twenty years later. Though middle-class standards were rising, a recent setback in trade was a grim reminder that millions lived on the verge of destitution; and the setting up of the Commission was an admission that the government had not yet found an effective way of coping with the masses of paupers who thronged the workhouses and lived on the verge of starvation. In middle life GBS and Beatrice had both come back to the theme which first brought the Fabians together.

Beatrice's negative reaction to the play, however, revealed the difference between her and GBS. She, like his Major Barbara, was a rich man's daughter who had gone among the poor with a sense of compassion and duty, believing that they could be helped to help themselves. She was repelled by Shaw's insistence that self-sacrifice was self-deception. Barbara Undershaft, the daughter of the munitions millionaire, lives on money produced by the very evils she seeks to alleviate. When her father diabolically destroys her faith by making her confront this fact, she accepts his dictum that true revolutionaries must change the conditions under which men live before evangelists can make them virtuous. The poor, Undershaft declares, would rather doff their hats to the landlord than burn his slums, sooner embrace Christ for a cup of tea in a Salvation Army mission than listen to a socialist preacher. Only men of destiny who control the money and the gunpowder can impose the new order. They have no illusions, but they have a will to action; they may use any means to achieve their ends because all other crimes are less than the crime of poverty. This dogmatic rejection of the saving role of conscience made Beatrice feel that the play ended in "the triumph of the unmoral purpose."[34] She was still in the position of Barbara at the end of the first act arguing with Undershaft; she was appalled by Shaw's argument that the choice is not between villainy and virtue, but between the energy which is the essence of salvation and the infamous submission to one's fate which is the hallmark of the damned, that Undershaft's guns can blow up evil while Barbara's prayers perpetuate it. For Beatrice that paradox seemed an intolerable reversal of values. Unlike Shaw she could not follow the logic of her own implicit élitism into accepting Undershaft's benevolent autocracy.

"The smart world is tumbling over one another in the worship of GBS, and even we have a sort of reflected glory as his intimate friends," Beatrice remarked as Shaw became "the adored one of the smartest and most cynical set of English society." Some people, she added drily, "might say that we too had travelled in that direction."[35]

The senior Fabians had certainly made a mark. Olivier came home from Jamaica in 1903, but when a hurricane hit the island soon afterwards he returned there to help in the work of relief and rehabilitation, staying until September 1904 in the role of acting governor. Bland was a journalist with a national reputation and his wife a successful writer of stories for children. Shaw was the dramatist of the day, Sidney an acknowledged expert on local government and Beatrice a member of an important royal commission. Yet all these successes had taken them further away from the growing labour movement. It was left to Pease, as the Society's nominee on the Labour Representation Committee, to keep them loosely in touch, and he seldom stirred himself to be more than a sleeping partner.

There were personal reasons for the indifference of the Fabian leaders, notably the antagonism between them and MacDonald and their distaste for Hardie's sentimental style of campaigning. There were also political differences. For the first five years of the century the Webbs and Shaw had been openly contemptuous of Gladstonian Liberalism, Radical Nonconformists and anti-imperialists; the Independent Labour Party and the trade unions were just as openly allied with the Radicals on most of the main issues. MacDonald was already talking of the Labour Party eventually becoming the heir of traditional Liberalism.

For the immediate future MacDonald's strategy was that which the Fabians had followed in the early Nineties and then abandoned: to collaborate with the Liberals so long as they offered a programme of reform, and to be ready to join with the Radicals in creating a new party if the Liberal Party broke into pieces. As a first step, it was essential to get a group of labour men into Parliament who would preserve their independence but generally support the Liberals. Things had been at a low ebb when MacDonald became secretary of the infant Labour Representation Committee, but the situation had now changed. In 1901 the House of Lords had decided that the railwaymen's union must pay £23,000 to the Taff Vale railway company in South Wales as damages for trade lost in a strike. This judgment, which put the finances of every union at risk, made them see that they needed spokesmen in Parliament to work for legislation to reverse it. Within a year the affiliated membership of the LRC had trebled and the powerful engineers and cotton workers had swung behind it.

MacDonald had now arrived at the position which Hardie had foreseen and for which he had worked hard for twenty years—an alliance between the socialist enthusiasts and the moderate unions. It was a viable formula on which to create a Labour Party, though it meant that henceforth MacDonald had to run a tricky course between two interests: he had to veer sufficiently towards socialist purposes to maintain the morale of the rank and file while keeping close enough to practical matters to retain the support of the unions. MacDonald also had an external problem to solve. The vital question was how far he could move towards at least a tacit understanding with the Liberals without jeopardizing the independence of the Labour Party or provoking the socialist enthusiasts on whom the constituency organizations depended. He needed a deal whereby the Liberals would let more workingmen into Parliament and reverse the Taff Vale judgment, while the Labour Party would go into the next election pledged to support a Campbell-Bannerman government. By the early months of 1903 he was involved in secret negotiations for such an electoral pact with Herbert Gladstone, the Liberal chief whip.

Gladstone himself had been thinking of such a move for the past two years. He believed that the Liberals would win a larger share of the working-class vote if they accepted candidates backed by the trade unions. The loose structure of the Liberal Party, however, meant that he had little control over the local party machines and no funds which he could use to support such candidates. He was convinced that the problem could be solved if some constituencies could be induced to give a labour man a clear run in exchange for labour's agreement not to split the anti-Tory vote in other seats. The fact that the LRC would meet the expenses of such candidates removed the difficulty about financing them.

An understanding of this kind was thus attractive to both Gladstone and to MacDonald. Both of them had to be discreet, for a public agreement ran the risk that it might be repudiated by both parties. MacDonald made this clear in a letter to Campbell-Bannerman on 7 August 1903, just after he and Gladstone had struck their bargain. "People are talking great nonsense about the need of an understanding and arrangement," he wrote, "but if they would only hold their tongues and allow us to work quietly, we should be all right." Next day the Liberal leader replied that "such a degree of harmony" was "very creditable."[36]

In the next two years it was difficult to make the pact work in some bye-elections. Both in Scotland and in Yorkshire the Liberal associations were recalcitrant; and socialist candidates over whom the LRC had no control cropped up in seats where labour was supposed to withdraw. Both Gladstone and MacDonald kept their heads, and a year before the Balfour government resigned a list of seats where the pact would apply had been agreed. The LRC would sponsor fifty candidates, and thirty-two of these would either have straight fights or run in a double-member seat with a Liberal. These were indeed favourable terms, especially since a number of union leaders were running as official Liberals outside the terms of the agreement. MacDonald had reason to be pleased with himself. His variant of permeation had proved successful. He was a politician making deals on the basis of parliamentary bargaining power, whereas the Webbs were idealists attempting to foist their ideas on influential friends: they had nothing to offer but their schemes.

The contrast in tactics was pointed by the character of the Cabinet which Campbell-Bannerman formed after Balfour's resignation on 4 December 1905. "Our friends the 'Limps' have romped into all the leading posts," Beatrice noted jubilantly; "the great coup is to get Haldane to take the War Office."[37] She was too quickly pleased. Asquith, Grey and Haldane had abandoned a last-minute conspiracy to block Campbell-Bannerman when Asquith was won over by the offer of the Exchequer with the implication that he would be the next leader of the party. Grey and Haldane had then been put respectively in the Foreign Office and the War Department, where both were isolated from domestic policy. The key posts, so far as the Webb interest in social reform was concerned, had gone to anti-imperialists such as Lloyd George and other Radicals over whom they had no influence. During the past five years Shaw and the Webbs had been so preoccupied with the idea of "filling the gap" with a domestic programme for a possible Rosebery government that they had never seriously considered that the real gap might appear in an administration led by Campbell-Bannerman.

In the general election in January 1906 Little England took its revenge for "Joe's War." The Tories were cut back to 157 seats in the worst defeat they had ever suffered; the Liberals, appealing to every dissatisfied minority but lacking a positive and coherent policy, were astonished to find that they were swept back with 377 seats, giving them an absolute majority of 84 and an even larger working majority when the 83 Irish members and the 53 labour men were taken into account.

Not all the labour men were official candidates backed by the Labour Representation Committee: 24 of them were "Lib-Labs," mostly from the mining and cotton unions, who did not follow Hardie and MacDonald. The election of 29 official Labour members was nevertheless a decisive breakthrough, making a Labour Party in the House of Commons a reality for the first time. It was not, of course, a socialist party, though more than half the Labour group belonged to the ILP and four of them were Fabians. Shaw sourly remarked in the *Clarion* that the victory had produced nothing more "than a nominally independent Trade Unionist and Radical group. . . . I apologise to the Universe for my connection with such a party."[38] Yet Hardie and MacDonald had won the argument which Shaw had been conducting with the ILP ever since it was founded at Bradford in 1893. The alliance between the socialists and the trade unions had worked. Almost all the gains came from the industrial areas of the North, where the socialist evangelists had at last reaped the fruits of their labours.

≈² PART FIVE ²≈

JUDGMENT DAYS

◈ 21 ◈
MODERN
UTOPIANS

Edwardian England had a glamorous veneer, but the lower depths were as miserable and soul-destroying as ever. Charles Booth's survey had described the squalor of subsistence in London's slums in the early Eighties. Twenty years later, Seebohm Rowntree followed up Booth's work in the relatively prosperous city of York and showed that "in this land of abounding wealth, during a time of perhaps unexampled prosperity, probably more than one-fourth of the population" were living in poverty. No civilization could be sound, he added, "which has at its base this mass of stunted human life."[1] Many of those with steady jobs had a struggle to clothe, feed and house their families. Large numbers of children went to school barefooted, were plainly underfed, often verminous and sickly. Yet the worst sufferers were the casualties of the system; for the chronic sick, the workless and the aged there was nothing but scraps of charity and the dreaded harshness of the Poor Law, an archaic, ramshackle and personally humiliating means of dealing with paupers that dated from 1834 and relied upon the hated workhouse as the ultimate resort of the destitute.

The Poor Law was administered by elected local boards of guardians who raised their money by rates, or property taxes. They controlled the workhouses and provided a limited amount of "outdoor relief," pay-

ing small sums under stringent conditions to registered paupers. There
was no uniform policy: some guardians were lenient, others severe; some
were philanthropic and others thought their main duty was to limit the
burden on the ratepayers. There were obvious defects in the whole system, but there was no agreement about the way it might be reformed.

The underlying principle was that of "less eligibility"—the doctrine
laid down in 1834 that the condition of the pauper supported from public
funds must always be inferior to that which could be obtained by working at the lowest-paid job available. To enforce this doctrine it was necessary to keep outdoor relief to a minimum, lest men prefer idleness to
labour, and to make the prospect of incarceration in the workhouse a
haunting terror. To these deterrents were added the "stigma" of the
pauper, who had to sell up before help was granted and who had to accept the loss of all political rights while on relief and for a period thereafter.

The dominant view all through the nineteenth century had been the
belief that the poor were poor of their own volition and that if they
failed to help themselves the responsibility of the state was merely to
provide them with a roof and to stop them actually starving. Long after
it was evident that poverty was the result of old age or bad times or bad
weather or bad health or simply low wages, both public policy and
private charity continued to argue that a systematic attempt to help
them would discourage thrift and undermine self-respect. Working-class
families, said C. S. Loch, the secretary of the influential Charity Organisation Society, should take care to save for bad times—as if this were a
feasible proposition for millions who lived on the threshold of destitution even when they had work.[2] The unemployed man, remarked James
Davy, the chief inspector of the Local Government Board, "must stand
by his accidents" and "suffer for the general good of the body politic."[3]
Such a refusal to face the social causes of poverty was compounded by
the high moral tone in which all relief work was conducted. People
talked of the poor in moral categories such as the "deserving" and the
"undeserving." A system which sought to classify the unfortunate by
personal merit rather than by need simply could not cope with the irre-
ducible mass of poverty caused by social conditions.

The Royal Commission on the Poor Law which Balfour set up in
the last days of his government had a mixed and potentially antagonistic
membership which epitomized the confusion over the sources of poverty

and the means of alleviating it. The civil servants, such as Davy, were primarily concerned to tidy up anomalies and to make the Poor Law more rigorous; as Beatrice Webb put it, they hoped "to stem the tide of philanthropic impulse that was sweeping away the old embankment of deterrent tests."[4] There were keen members of the Charity Organisation Society, such as C. S. Loch, Helen Bosanquet and the veteran philanthropist Octavia Hill, who wanted a better system but still saw the problem as one of providing individual remedies for individual cases of distress. There were representatives from boards of guardians, clergymen, economists, a couple of labour men—one of whom was George Lansbury, whose Christian Socialism had sprung from his experience of East End poverty—and two social investigators, Beatrice and her relative Charles Booth.

Every member of the Commission, as Beatrice quickly realized, had a special interest; groups of members formed factions; and no one except the officials, who had intended to use it as a means of endorsing changes they already had in mind, had any clear idea how it was to proceed or what it was to do. Beatrice herself, who had decided so early in her career to make the study of "chronic destitution" her life work, saw that the Commission would give her a chance to launch a series of enquiries which would reveal the causes as well as the character of different kinds of poverty. She proceeded at the outset to make things difficult by raising points of procedure designed to make the Commission work effectively. "It is a new experience to me to *have* to make myself disagreeable in order to reach my ends," she noted on 15 December, adding that she was "refusing altogether to be over-awed by great personages who would like to pooh pooh a woman who attempts to share in the control of affairs."[5]

On the day that she was appointed, Beatrice wrote: "Enter Royal Commission No. I for me, No. II for the firm!" She and Sidney had already decided that the partnership would give the Commission's work priority, though their normal roles were reversed. She was now the public figure, attending the Monday meetings in the Foreign Office committee room, cross-examining witnesses, going about the country to take evidence; Sidney became the offstage expert, coaching Beatrice on tactics, drafting papers, and planning their joint strategy. She was, however, far less experienced than Sidney in the ways and wiles of committees, less patient, more pushing and less discreet; before long her manner was antagonizing both the officials at the Local Government Board and many of her fellow commissioners. She was determined to ride out the hostility she evoked, to make the Commission listen even if it would not agree with her, and to take the chance it offered of bringing the Webb policy into the public eye.

For the first time since she had given up her work to ally herself with Sidney, subordinating her career to his, Beatrice found an opportunity to assert herself, and she intended to make the most of it. She felt that the chance might never come again. "We are becoming elderly," she remarked in June, "and our days of work are obviously limited."[6]

Though she was still under fifty, she had lost three of her sisters. Theresa, who had a "saintlike asceticism," had died first. Blanche, given to "wild melancholy," had committed suicide. And in May 1906 Lallie died, unhappily, after years in which her husband and children had turned against her. Reflecting on the Potter sisters, Beatrice felt that the one quality that seemed to bind them together was "impulsive generosity . . . towards individuals and towards causes. . . . They each and all *spent themselves* for others." She was resolved to keep up this family sense of mission by adding her mite "to the world's generosity of feeling, of thought, of action." With her sister Mary Playne, who shared her feelings of mystic dedication, she discussed her utopian dream of something like a religious order "embodying faith in a spiritual force, the obligation to love and thankfulness, and abstemiousness from all harmful, if not unnecessary physical indulgence or vain display." She was, she felt, "too old and worn to start it," but "some younger woman may."[7]

It was this asceticism which made Beatrice feel so uncomfortable with her own modest privileges and brought on her bouts of guilty self-denial. Harnessed to a purpose, it was also a source of strength which enabled her to press on in the face of opposition and sustain the long and exhausting grind of her work. She seemed priggish, even censorious, to a degree that made others feel uneasy in her company. Sidney's gentle modesty was a vital foil to her when she was in this prickly mood, but in the Commission she had to manage publicly without his restraining presence. Her determination to get things done seemed like an attempt to dominate her colleagues; her cleverness gave the impression that she was trying to make fools of them. In the privacy of her diary she confessed her misgivings about the effect she had on the commissioners; at the same time she frankly admitted her impatience with those who could not share her moral passion to reorder the world.

From the start the Fabians had always been bound together by a shared sense of moral earnestness. Whatever their political disagreements, and whatever their other concerns, they maintained that bond: it enabled them to tolerate differences without questioning motives, and to debate fiercely without reducing arguments to personalities. The style had been set in the early days; it had been preserved for twenty years largely because Fabianism was a state of mind rather than a doctrine.

By 1905 the members of the Old Gang were getting old in a real sense and their other interests were making increasing claims upon them. They still did their share of routine business, attending the executive, giving lectures and keeping a close eye upon the production of Fabian tracts. Yet they were beginning to wonder how much longer they could run the Society as something like a family business and whether it was time to set it on a new course. Its composition was changing. Though there was still a core of veterans, almost two thirds of those who had joined in the boom of the early Nineties had dropped away, and after MacDonald had fallen out no new potential leaders of comparable stature had emerged.

The most active newcomers were younger people. A few were children from Fabian families. The Olivier girls had come in, so, too, had Hubert Bland's daughter Rosamund. One eager recruit was Cecil Chesterton, the younger brother of Gilbert; another was Robert Ensor, a bright young journalist who had started a university group at Oxford; Clifford Sharp, another clever young man, had joined in 1901; and Leslie Haden Guest, a romantic revolutionary who combined an interest in the theatre with a medical career, was clearly bent on shaking up the Fabians. In many ways they were similar to the young middle-class idealists who had founded the Society. They were intellectuals, excited by ideas; they were distressed by the contrasts of wealth and poverty; they were gripped as much by social conscience as by political conviction; and they were impatient for change. While Fabianism attracted them temperamentally, they felt that the Society itself had fallen into a humdrum condition and that it was essential to revive it. Though they admired the Old Gang, they were in revolt against their elders and were becoming increasingly vocal in their criticisms. They wanted the Fabians to do something, though they were not certain what they hoped the Society would do, or how it might do it.

The nature of the Society made it difficult for a consistent opposition to polarize. The older leaders did not have an agreed policy which could be challenged. On most issues the executive was as divided as the Society as a whole, and it always avoided attempts to commit it to a particular policy or to impose any discipline upon its members. It was, to all effects, run by an oligarchy, yet its temper was democratic and the rights of members were respected as scrupulously as their heterodox opinions. Its publications were thoroughly and sometimes exhaustively discussed—although none was presented as binding upon all members—and its service of lectures, book boxes and information was available to anyone who chose to make use of it. Part debating society, part a focus for research and propaganda, part social club, the Society had survived precisely because it was a unique combination of interests without any of them becoming its sole purpose. Unlike other socialist groups, where factions could fight for control, the Fabians had no machine which could be captured: there were no funds to speak of, no staff beyond Pease, a typist and an office boy, no journal apart from the parochial *Fabian News*, and only a small, loosely organized membership. The Society's main asset was a prestige out of all proportion to its resources, and that was an intangible asset which no group of rebels could hope to cash merely by taking control. Such a victory would simply have destroyed the Society.

One reason for the turnover of membership was the difficulty that enthusiastic recruits had in grasping this point. People often came into the Society expecting to find it an active socialist body like the ILP or the SDF. Such hopes had accounted for the influx of members in the early Nineties which had almost swamped the Society, as well as for the subsequent dropout when they discovered their mistake and left in disappointment. It was difficult for outsiders to understand how it worked, and why the leadership seemed so reluctant to expand it. Joining, H. G. Wells said after he became a member in February 1903, took "as much fuss and trouble as one takes to make a member of a London club."[8] After twenty years, there were still fewer than seven hundred Fabians; and fewer than a hundred of these formed the active nucleus of the Society which organized and attended the meetings in Clifford's Inn, gave the lectures and wrote the tracts.

H. G. Wells was sponsored by Shaw and Wallas. He had known Shaw slightly since the days when they were both scratching a living as journalists, and he had met Wallas through Ada's sister Florence Popham, a neighbour at Sandgate, where Wells and his second wife, Catherine (always known as "Jane"), settled in 1899. Wells had been quickly taken up by other Fabians when his book *Anticipations* appeared in 1901, for his vision of a future society run on collectivist lines by a managerial elite was very close to Fabian thinking. Beatrice commented that it was "the most remarkable book of the year" and thought his work "full of luminous hypotheses and worth careful study by those who are trying to look forward."[9] On 10 January 1902 Pease, equally impressed, sent a note to ask "if you've yet met the Webbs: they are the pioneers of your New Republic. We have lived for years on Webb's new ideas of politics. We want someone else who can also think ahead."[10]

Sidney and Beatrice were soon invited down to stay at Sandgate. Wells reported to Pease that they were "wonderful people & they leave me ashamed of my indolence & mental dissipation & awfully afraid of Mrs Webb."[11] The Webbs took up Wells and invited him to select dinner parties at Grosvenor Road as well as including him in the first group of Co-Efficients. They had, it seemed, found a celebrity who was a match for Shaw—a clever publicist, an amusing talker, an impish little man who believed in making things hum.

Wells was thirty-five when he met the Webbs, and his reputation had been made in the previous five years by such books as *The Time Machine*, *The War of the Worlds* and *The Invisible Man* and by his short stories.[12] The son of a ladies' maid and a gardener turned shopkeeper, he had grown up poor and endured a miserable youth as a draper's apprentice. Struggling to educate himself, he won a scholarship to train as a science teacher, gave that up after a series of illnesses and turned to Grub Street for a living. He had shown little serious interest in politics until, as Beatrice deduced from reading *Anticipations*, he began to apply his lively imagination and his knowledge of science to social problems.

Success had changed him. His early work reflected the innate depression which had dogged his early years—a sense of impending doom derived from the Evangelical religion of his mother which led him to the notion, taken from his mentor T. H. Huxley, that evolutionary laws would result in the extinction of the human race unless it could find a means of saving itself from this gloomy fate. When both his health and his fortunes improved he began to speculate on the way in which the species might be saved and on his own contribution to that task. Even though he had abandoned the puritan faith in which he was raised, he had never broken out of the apocalyptic frame of mind which made him obsessed with the idea of salvation. Fusing the Book of Revelations with the *Origin of Species*, he developed that idea into a secular version of the Second Coming in which a new and superior breed of men would "take the world in hand" and create "a sane order." In *Anticipations*, *Mankind in the Making* and *The Food of the Gods*, he had already started to map out this doctrine; at the time he fell in with the Fabians he was filling in the outline in *A Modern Utopia*. He was taking himself so seriously as a new kind of sociologist that his first lecture to the Society was a ponderous disquisition in March 1903 on "The Question of Scientific Administrative Areas in Relation to Municipal Undertakings." The title suggested that he was anxious to be taken as a true Fabian.

Though Wells wanted to impress the Webbs as a social scientist, the bohemian streak in his personality made him gravitate towards the Blands and their eccentric entourage. It was, Wells said, "a place to which one rushed down from town to snatch one's bed before anyone else got it."[13]

The Blands lived extravagantly, mainly on the earnings from Edith's books once *The Treasure Seekers* made her name, though Hubert also prospered as a columnist on the *Daily Chronicle*. Their ménage was still eccentric, but as the years passed it had settled into a style. Wells noted that one found unattached young women and children of doubtful parentage about the place. Edith now "detested and mitigated and tolerated" Hubert's amorous intrigues and found them "extremely interesting." Wells felt that her success aggravated Hubert's promiscuity as a compensation for her "wit and freaks and fantasies."[14] She had always been a good talker, and she both impressed and helped the young people in their set. Cecil Chesterton's wife remembered "the sheer magnificence of her appearance," especially on festive occasions when she dressed in "a trailing gown of peacock blue satin with strings of beads and Indian bangles from wrist to elbow." Everyone called her "Madame"; she smoked incessantly "and her long cigarette holder became an indissoluble part of the picture she suggested—a raffish Rossetti, with a long full throat, and dark luxuriant hair, smoothly parted." Hubert, as smartly dressed as ever, looking like "a dashing company promoter at a Convocation of Rural Deans," had his own protégées, "a springtide of femininity fluttering round him."[15]

Wells got on better with Edith than with Hubert. He liked dominating women who flattered him, whether they were Fabians or the
hostesses of the Edwardian smart set who had begun to patronize him
and invite him for weekends. Soon after he became a Fabian he came to
know the Pember Reeves family, and once again it was the wife, Maud,
who attracted him rather than her priggish husband. She was a New
Woman, keen on Ibsen, who had been active in the suffrage movement
in New Zealand. By 1904, indeed, Wells had got on easy terms with the
inner circle of Fabians—the only outsider who had successfully worked
his way to something like equal status with the Old Gang.

For a year Wells did little in the Society. He was busy with *Kipps* and
A Modern Utopia. Suddenly, with characteristic impetuosity, he decided
to resign. He was very close to Wallas, and when Wallas decided to
leave in protest against the tract *Fabianism and the Fiscal Question* Wells
also proposed to quit. If he had the time to attend meetings regularly, he
told Pease on 21 January, "I would do my poor best to establish my
views . . . against the prevailing influences, in spite of my distinguished
ineptitude in debate."[16] Pease tried to mollify him, pointing out that it
was unusual to resign in a democratic organization simply because one
was in a minority on a particular issue. Shaw, who saw Wells as a potential asset for the Fabians, read him the first of many lessons on tactics.
"I don't believe you have any views on Free Trade or any other subject,"
GBS wrote. "I believe that you are so spoiled by living in a world of
your own invention, peopled by your own puppets, that you have become incapable of tolerating the activity or opinions or even the phrases
of independent individuals."[17] It was a blunt but prescient analysis. The
Webbs went down to Sandgate to appease Wells and then invited him
to dinner with the Shaws and Balfour to show that they still valued
him. "I highly disapprove of the Fabian Society," he wrote significantly
to Pease, grudgingly conceding that he would stay in the fold.[18]
    When *A Modern Utopia* appeared in 1905 it was clear why the
Fabians did not want to lose Wells. Shaw had tried to put blue books on
the stage; Wells now proved that he could translate Fabian tracts into
fiction. The Fabians had never lacked talented journalists to put their
case, but in Wells they had acquired for the first time an author who
could reach a large popular audience. He turned out articles, short

stories, novels and social predictions. In his *Utopia* he showed that he could discuss such solid Fabian topics as collective ownership, social welfare and industrial efficiency without boring his readers. His ideal state was a benevolent dictatorship run by a public-spirited caste of social engineers which, in the current vogue for things Japanese which followed Japan's unexpected victory over Russia, he called the Samurai. This quasi-religious order, another version of his "New Republicans," he teasingly told Beatrice, "will pander to all your worst instincts."[19] Sydney Olivier, coming home from Jamaica, was immediately taken by the idea. The Fabian Society, he said to Wells in a letter introducing himself and seeking his acquaintance, had been "ossified" since 1897. Now, he remarked admiringly, "I recognise your trumpeting angel of the Samurai as my desire for the League of Sane Men"—a group of talented and educated leaders who could defend society against "the increasing insanity of our compatriots."[20]

Wells was flattered by the praise, which touched the messianic streak in his personality. Ever since the success of *Anticipations* he had been vacillating between a career as a novelist and as a publicist, putting politics into his fiction and using his imaginative powers to enliven his propaganda. He now began to see himself as a political prophet. He needed an outlet for his fantasies of salvation, even if this meant neglecting his literary ambitions. He decided that the Fabian Society, in which he had been so readily accepted, could serve his purposes. Talking to Ford Madox Ford in the summer of 1905, he declared that he was "going to turn the Fabian Society inside out and throw it in the dustbin."[21]

Wells sensed that the Society was ripe for change and that the younger members were becoming restive. Shaw was also aware of the new mood. In June 1905 he scribbled a note to Pease suggesting that it was time to review the achievements of the last ten years. "I think a stock-taking would do us no harm," he wrote, believing that an enquiry might answer the perennial question "What does the Fabian Society do?" If it had done very little, GBS concluded, "the sooner we have a definite eye-opener on the subject, the better."[22]

In the early summer Wells was consorting with some of the younger members, especially Leslie Haden Guest, who wrote to him on 11 June to say, "We must get our attack on the Fabian definitely in focus."[23] Shaw's proposal showed that the leadership had no strong objections to rejuvenating the Society; he welcomed anything that jolted it out of its complacency and he encouraged the executive to start a discussion. "All I want," GBS told Pease on 4 July, "is a stir up and a stock-taking to make Fabianism interesting again." He thought that the best way to do this would be to call for two reports. "If you and Webb were to make out the best case you could for the old policy & the Old Gang," he told Pease, "and Wells, Guest & Chesterton were to do all they could to explode us, we should get something that would really give us an overhauling."[24] The idea seemed simple and sensible, if the game was still to be played by the traditional Fabian rules. The question was whether Wells, as the potential leader of the opposition, either knew the rules or was willing loyally to abide by them.

❧ 22 ❧
NEW WORLDS
FOR OLD

Wells fired the first shot in his campaign on 12 January 1906, when he gave a talk to the Fabians called "This Misery of Boots," cleverly satirizing England from the bottom up. His idea was that it should serve as a model for the kind of propaganda with which to revivify the Society. Wells was not at his best as a speaker: he had little presence, a poor delivery and a reedy voice. Yet his text was witty enough to get a response from an audience which was bubbling with the excitement of a general election. He had chosen his moment well. The landslide for the Liberals and the return of thirty Labour candidates both reflected and touched off a wave of radical feeling.

In less than a month he followed up his first attack with a stinging indictment of the Society. In "The Faults of the Fabian" he told the members that they had "an air of arrested growth" and that the Society had failed "either to organise, develop, or represent the spirit of social reconstruction that is arising all about us . . . to use the prestige it has accumulated, to fulfill the promises it once made to the world." It was too small, too poor. It so wasted good intentions, time and energy that only a "little dribble of activities" came out of the "miserable cellar" in which it had its office. He scorned the traditional habits of the Society, rejected the Basis—the Society's written constitution—and attacked the

Old Gang, deriding the Webbs as petty-minded and complaining that Shaw's levity reduced "this high business of Socialism" to "an idiotic middle-class joke." The Society, he insisted, had taken the wrong Roman general as its model. Fabius Cunctator had begun his campaign against Hannibal by being cautious and ended in impotence: it was the energetic Scipio who had taken the war to the enemy and destroyed Carthage.[1]

The tirade was Wells at his most priggish and demagogic. Yet it did not provoke the Fabians to repudiate him. On the contrary, it fitted the current mood of rebellious euphoria so well that they applauded. Many members felt that the Society had become a mere tool for the political manoeuvres of Webb and Shaw, and they saw Wells as a symbol of protest and as a potential leader. It was not merely the younger generation who thought a Wellsian thunderclap would startle the Society into useful activity. Olivier, always willing to challenge stodgy respectability and to assert socialist first principles, encouraged Wells. So did some other members of the executive. Marjorie Pease, who normally took little part in the Society's affairs, reflected the new mood. She told Jane Wells on 24 March: "The more I think of Mr Wells' Fabian Reforms the more do I welcome them & if only everyone will be sensible & broadminded I foresee a new era for Fabianism. Sixteen years ago I felt very dissatisfied with the Society. It seemed so narrow & exclusive & I always likened it to a Baptist Chapel, dominated by Deacon Webb! My Socialism then and now is much more catholic & democratic & comprehensive."[2] Pease himself thought Wells was suffering from "imaginative megalomania," but even he was willing to see what Wells would make of his bid. Most of the younger Fabians had no doubts: he was just the man to give the Society "whoosh" and an effective place on the new political scene.

The upshot was that the executive was instructed to set up a committee to consider the future structure and activities of the Society. It was easier said than done. They were at once plunged into procedural difficulties. Wells, who thought it was his committee, wanted to pick the members for himself, but executive members were reluctant to sit in judgment on themselves and their colleagues. Wells was suspicious that their refusal to join implied a plot against him. Shaw, Pease and Sam Hobson all wrote to assure him that the executive was friendly, and even Charlotte sent a sympathetic letter explaining, "The whole business is a little ticklish & difficult to *start* & wants diplomacy. If we get splits &

quarrels we shall lose a lot of useful work that we may rope in by care and patience." She warned Wells, "Mr Bland is in a very obstreperous mood, & I strongly advise his being *ménagé* just a little!"³

Bland was one of the minority who were sceptical of Wells's good intentions and, indeed, of his capacities and character. The Webbs, naturally enough, were also critical, and neither of them took his attack very seriously. Beatrice confided to her diary on 1 March, "H. G. Wells has broken out in a quite unexpectedly unpleasant manner." What upset her was the "odd mixture of underhand manoevres and insolent bluster" which he displayed towards such friends as Webb and Shaw. She suspected that he might not have "the skill and the persistence and the real desire to carry a new departure" and that it was "more for 'copy' than for reform that he has stepped out of his study."⁴ Their suspicions would have been confirmed if they had seen Wells's cynical remarks in a letter to E. V. Lucas, the essayist, on 22 February. "I have been up to my eyes lately," he wrote, "in 'straordinary intrigues to upset the Fabian Society by making buttered slices for an old lady. Most amusing."⁵

Bland and the Webbs suspected that Wells was engaged in an irresponsible game. Bland was angry and the Webbs tried to dismiss him, but Shaw took a different view. He was ambivalent. While he was critical of Wells's tactics, even perhaps suspicious of his motives, he recognized that HG was voicing genuine discontent within the Society. "Do not under-rate Wells," he told Sidney Webb later that year, "you do not appreciate the effect his writing produces on the imagination of the movement."⁶ He was afraid that an ill-considered rebuff to Wells could easily lead to a split within the Society. He wanted a genuine debate about policy.

The special committee, it was finally agreed, should include three members of the executive: Headlam, Charlotte Shaw and G. R. S. Taylor. The chairman was Sydney Olivier; Jane Wells was secretary; and there were two moderates, the Reverend Stanton Coit and W. A. Colegate, to balance Wells's supporters Maud Reeves and Haden Guest, and HG himself. The first meeting was held on 28 February. Wells was anxious to get it working before he left on a visit to the United States on 27 March. His own first contribution before he left was the draft of a new Basis for the Society. Shaw quickly punctured his arrogant enthusiasm, warning him against a reckless rampage among the Fabians. His tone was that of a headmaster rebuking a recalcitrant prize pupil. It was easy to draft a new Basis, Shaw pointed out. Anyone could have done the job, but it would not have conciliated all the factions in the Society. ". . . you amuse yourself by treating us to several pages of cheek to the effect that the imperfections of the Basis are the result of our own folly and literary clumsiness . . . you are too reckless of etiquette. . . . You must study people's corns when you go clog dancing." Shaw was trying to make Wells realize how the Fabians managed their affairs: "you must identify yourself frankly with us, and not play the critical outsider and the satirist," he wrote. "You haven't discovered the real difficulties of democratic work—and you assume that our own folly and ill-will accounts for their results."[7] Wells was not interested in such advice. "You leave my committee alone while I'm in America," he replied defiantly on 26 March. "If I'm to identify myself with 'us,' who's 'us'? I'm not going to identify myself with your damned executive, nohow!"[8]

Wells's absence gave the Fabians a breathing space; they too could give time to their own affairs. Sidney kept to his grind on the London County Council and his devilling for Beatrice's work on the Commission. She was beginning to find her fellow commissioners as narrow-minded and recalcitrant as Wells found the Fabians, and she was treating them with equal contempt. She decided to launch her own investigations, hiring her personal research staff with money provided by Charlotte Shaw. She and Sidney continued to dine out with politicians like Asquith and Balfour, but Beatrice could not allow herself to enjoy it. She was shocked by the contrast between the glamour of London life and the misery of pauperdom. When more than a third of all Londoners over sixty-five were paupers Asquith's grand style of living was unsuitable, she thought, as "the entourage of a democratic minister."[9] At the sumptuous home of Sir Julius Wernher, the millionaire from South Africa who had been persuaded by Haldane and Sidney to put up the money to launch the Imperial College of Science, she felt that wealth screamed aloud. "There might just as well have been a Goddess of Gold erected for overt worship," she wrote.[10]

In April GBS and Charlotte went to Paris: Rodin had invited GBS to sit for a bust. Lillah McCarthy and Harley Granville Barker had married on 24 March, and they stopped by on their way to a honeymoon in Germany to go with Shaw to Rodin's studio at Meudon—"a huge

room, floating like an ark upon the sea of a wonderful garden," said
Lillah. The bust was a success, and, back in England, the Shaws went
down to Mevagissey in Cornwall for two months. Granville Barker
wanted a new play for the Court, and on August 11 GBS started to write
The Doctor's Dilemma.

Meanwhile Wells was preparing for the next act in the Fabian
drama. His visit to America had stimulated his grand ideas. During July
and August he worked on the draft of the special report to have it available to the executive by September. Worried about his plans, the Webbs
went down to Sandgate in the middle of July to see how things were
going and to ease the strain, but Beatrice found HG conceited and contemptuous of "us poor drudgers." He made it clear that he thought Shaw
and Webb would have to retire if they would not go along with his
schemes. He seemed to be longing for something like the magical transformation scenes of his books as a way of achieving utopia. His report
was little more than a repetition of the arguments of "The Faults of the
Fabian." He wanted the executive replaced by a council of twenty-five
members which would appoint three triumvirates—one to control propaganda and membership, one for publications and one for general purposes and finance. There should be an energetic recruiting drive, and the
name should be changed to the "British Socialist Society." Permeation
should be abandoned and the Fabians should collaborate with like-minded
bodies to run socialist candidates for Parliament.

Copies were sent to members of the executive, but reactions were
not encouraging. Charlotte Shaw was outspokenly cross. "You must
know quite well that I can't sign this report," she wrote from Cornwall.
"You have let me in in the most abominable manner, you treacherous
man . . . The Committee has been nothing from its very first meeting
but a Committee of Public Safety to try the Executive; with the fore-
gone conclusion that we are to be condemned . . . I don't agree with
you and I won't sign your report . . . the impossible triumvirates, the
magnificent publishing business, the grand suite of offices, the bringing
of everything to the test of ordinary business success; in short, your
commercial utopia."[11] Charlotte assured Wells that she was quite
friendly still, but she got a cold reply. "No! dear lady, you have betrayed me," he insisted. "You want everything better and everything just
the same & it can't be done."[12] Sidney, writing on 3 September, was more
cordial but just as critical. "Frankly," he concluded, "I don't believe that

either the necessary capital or the necessary income can be obtained. But by all means try." He did not think the senior Fabians would give up enough time to make the triumvirates work, or the Society agree. "I am sorry," he told Wells, "as I had hoped it would gain from your new impulse."[13] Wells was also being rebuffed by Pease, who told him on 7 September that publication of "This Misery of Boots" by the Society was being held up until he agreed to delete personal gibes against Shaw and Webb.

Wells tried to drum up support outside the Society and wrote to a number of prominent socialists asking them to back his campaign, but he had little success. Keir Hardie wrote to tell him that it was "more or less a waste of time and effort and not quite fair to endeavour to convert the staid and steady-going Fabian Society into a semi-revolutionary organisation."[14] He urged Wells to join the ILP if he seriously wanted to get into socialist politics. But Wells had no intention of throwing in his lot with the working classes or taking the stump for labour candidates. He was not a politician but a romantic with ambitious dreams.

In the Days of the Comet, which was published that September, described how a Wellsian utopia was brought about by a trail of mysterious gas from a comet. The idea amused his friends but did nothing to persuade them that he was a serious political tactician. Pember Reeves, writing to congratulate him, asked point-blank whether the story was "a parable applicable to the transformation to be wrought by H. G. Wells in the Fabian Society."[15] Shaw took up the same metaphor, telling Wells: "You want to play the part of the Comet . . . You cannot go on spinning comets out of your head for ever . . . You must . . . learn your business as a propagandist and peripatetic philosopher if you are ever to be anything more than a novelist bombinating in vacuo."[16]

Throughout the autumn Shaw argued with Wells about his proposals for the reform of the Society, but it soon became clear that HG was not amenable to rational argument. He was not fighting on issues but was making an ill-considered takeover bid without any serious idea of what he proposed to do with the Society if he won control of it. Shaw confessed that the Old Gang was willing to give up if Wells meant business: "if you will steer that crazy little craft for five years to come, making the best of it no matter how ridiculously it may disappoint you," Wells could have his turn.[17] But Wells was expressing a mood rather than advancing an alternative policy. Shaw, though sympathetic to the mood,

saw the practical danger. Wells was facing the Society with a disruption
far worse than any of the earlier rows simply because he had personal-
ized the issue—something the Fabians had always avoided. Shaw had gone
to Ireland with Charlotte that autumn, but he corresponded with Sidney
about tactics when the battle was joined in the Society. He wanted to
stage-manage the drama so that everyone would have their money's
worth and the ending should be the way he wanted it.

   Wells's provocative attitude was leading him into trouble outside
the Society as well as within it. *In the Days of the Comet* had evoked
savage criticism as an immoral book. Wells had already hinted at some
kind of group marriage in *A Modern Utopia*, and now it seemed he was
advocating the Great Change as much for sexual freedom as for socialism. *The Times Literary Supplement* attacked the novel for implying
that under socialism both wives and goods would be held in common.
"Free love," it suggested, "is to be of the essence of the new social contract."[18] Before long Wells found himself denounced in press and pulpit
as an advocate of promiscuity; he seemed to confirm the charges when
he elaborated his theories in a Fabian lecture on "Socialism and the
Middle Classes" in October. Addressing the largest audience the Fabians
had ever attracted, he made another onslaught on the "unimaginative"
Webbs for promoting socialism like "district visitors" and then launched
into an indictment of bourgeois marriage as the moral counterpart of private ownership. He spelled out his ideas of endowed motherhood: the
state and not parents was really responsible for children; women would
never be liberated from control by men until they achieved economic
independence. This flaunting of the conventions was a calculated appeal
to younger Fabians as well as an attempt to turn the current interest in
female suffrage onto a broader base. The discontent of women, he urged,
was "a huge available source for socialism."

   A speech that was so shocking to the conventional naturally stirred
up the members. Younger members responded emotionally to his bold
and romantic notions; older members were confused and suspicious.
Bland, writing to Pease on 14 October, said: "I am afraid that Mr Wells'
lecture did no sort of good to the propaganda. Judging by what I heard
afterwards a lot of people were quite upset."[19] Beatrice felt that the audience as a whole was against him. To her he was "gambling with the idea
of free love—throwing it out to see what sort of reception it gets—without responsibility for its effect on the character of hearers. It is this reck-
lessness which makes Sidney dislike him."[20] Her comment revealed a

common reaction. Even those Fabians who disliked what Wells was saying were forced to notice what he said: morality was a problem they
had so far evaded. After the meeting Beatrice read *In the Days of the
Comet* and thought afresh about the "women question." While she rejected unequivocally the idea of free love, she decided that her own advantages had made her too insensitive to the problems other women
faced in marriage and work. On 2 November she wrote a letter to the
moderate suffragist Millicent Fawcett, published in *The Times* three
days later, explaining that she had now withdrawn her opposition to
votes for women. "Mrs Wells will rejoice that I have at last thrown in
my lot with Women's Suffrage," she wrote to HG. "See what you have
accomplished by your Propaganda! Far more important than converting
the whole of the Fabian Society!"[21]

Many Fabians had seen Wells as a useful missionary for their ideas,
but it was becoming plain that he saw himself as a prophet with a mission
of his own. Nobbling the Fabian Society was simply one means to that
end. Before he presented his special report to the Fabians he went off in
November for a holiday in Venice. He not only wanted to escape the
hue and cry of his critics but was also working on a new propagandist
volume, *New Worlds for Old*, elaborating his view of socialism as "a
plan for the reconstruction of human life."[22]

Shaw could see what was happening and he was worried. The problem was to find a satisfactory forward policy for the Society which
would conciliate some of the rebels like Haden Guest, G. R. S. Taylor
and Sam Hobson and win them away from Wells. GBS suggested to
Webb the idea of a Fabian parliamentary committee which might serve
as a step towards a new party, both more socialist and more middle-class
in character than the Labour Party. What Shaw wanted was a formula
which would revive the Society while preserving it as an autonomous
body able to resist attempts to convert it into a political machine or the
adjunct of any political party. To offset the Wells campaign he set off
on a round of lectures in London and the provinces.

Charlotte took advantage of Shaw's absence to move into the rectory at Ayot St. Lawrence, not far from Welwyn in Hertfordshire,
which they had now settled on as their country home. It was a gawky
late-Victorian villa with a large garden set in very plain country. Charlotte took on a couple at thirty shillings a week to do the housekeeping
and gardening.

"The storm in the Fabian teacup," as Wells later called it, was only one of Shaw's worries. He was also under pressure to finish *The Doctor's Dilemma* and prepare for its opening at the Court on 20 November. He was so overwhelmed with work, he told a French journalist, that he had "narrowly escaped a breakdown."[23] But he was optimistic about the play. He told Lillah McCarthy in September, "It will be a lucky play, a complete success for you, for me, for the Court & for the universe."[24] And so it proved. Not only was it crisp and amusing but it touched on current controversies. He poked fun at the medical profession, having long regarded doctors as incompetent and even murderous quacks. The central question of the play, however, was the relative value to the world of the irresponsible genius Dudebat and the earnest slum doctor Blenkinsop. GBS was again reflecting the dualism in his own nature, as he had done in *Candida*, between the egotist and the altruist, the bohemian and the reformer. The play also reflected the dialogue with Wells, who had argued in his lecture to the Fabians that the state had a responsibility to the individual. In his play Shaw put the converse question: Is anyone, even an artist, free from a moral responsibility to society?

With the success of his play assured, GBS put his mind to the Fabians. The Wells report, printed and circulated along with an alternative report from the executive, was to be the subject of the members' meeting in early December. To ensure that the meeting was handled dexterously and with humour and thus avoid a damaging split, he nominated himself to be the executive's spokesman. It was clear to everyone that not only was the Old Gang on trial but the future direction of the Fabian Society was at stake.

The Fabians had never before seen such a dramatic confrontation; over a third of the entire membership of the Society crowded into Essex Hall to witness it on the evening of Friday 7 December. Shaw moved the executive's proposal, which said, in effect, that the time had come to organize middle-class opinion as effectively as the ILP and the Labour Party were promoting working-class representation in Parliament. It conceded that some of the suggested reforms were admirable as aspirations if money could be found: a new Basis could be drafted; the executive could be enlarged; there could even be new branches outside London if these were not just a device to swamp the Fabians with ILP enthusiasts.

Wells then rushed in, usurping Olivier's right to present the special committee's report and trying by the procedural device of an amendment to make the meeting endorse his views and reject the old executive. It was a serious tactical error, though he was given his head and allowed an hour to repeat his gibes at the Old Gang. By the time he sat down there was little time for more than a plea for loyalty from Webb and a bid for change from Olivier. The meeting was adjourned to the following week.

Shaw was expressing the common view when he wrote to Bland afterwards to say that Wells's speech was a damp squib. It was "AWFUL-SHOCKING," he added.[25] Wells had in fact upset some of his allies by shifting the ground away from a substantive discussion of the Society's policy to what amounted to a vote of no confidence in the Old Gang. Clifford Sharp went so far as to write to Wells asking him to withdraw. "Sidney Webb may be a bit of a conservative," he wrote, "but really one cannot afford to give him up in exchange for Haden Guest."[26] Maud Reeves and some of the more ardent women in the Society were also beginning to vacillate: Shaw had privately assured them that, if they did not rock the boat at this critical time, the Basis might soon be amended to include support for female suffrage. Wells, indeed, made such a poor showing that Shaw was afraid the supporters of the executive might not bother to turn up on 14 December, in the belief that the matter was already settled. He circulated a printed postcard to the members making it clear that he and his colleagues would resign if Wells got a majority.

The stage was now set for the final scene. Despite Shaw's fears, the meeting was larger than ever and the discussion quickly got going. Maud Reeves appealed for unity. Bland drily poked fun at Olivier and Wells by remarking that the "flamboyant self-constituted championship of youth had not come from the young but the elderly and middle-aged members of the Special Committee." Sam Hobson and Clifford Sharp said they could not go along with personal attacks on the Old Gang. Headlam suggested that the revolt was really against wirepulling behind the scenes and that younger members should be given a bigger say in the Society. By nine o'clock, when Shaw rose to wind up the discussion, the tide was clearly running against Wells.

With humorous but effective malice Shaw attacked Wells for misrepresentation, for inventing grievances, for trying to throw out those who had built and sustained the Society for so many years. The Wells amendment meant, he said, "not only dismissal but dismissal with dishonour." To call for a vote, as some of the executive wished, would be unwise. "We cannot force friends like Mr. Olivier and Mrs. Reeves into the dilemma of having either to desert Mr. Wells on the amendment or vote for our ignominious expulsion." There was then nothing Wells could do but rise with the best grace he could muster and withdraw the amendment.

Wells had lost the battle, disastrously, but it was not certain that he had yet lost the war. Shaw had outdebated him and outmanoeuvred him without the real points at issue being considered. There were many who were worried by the manner of Shaw's victory. Wallas, looking on as an outsider, wrote to Wells on 16 December to say that he "loathed the mixture of gerrymandering, bluffing, browbeating, quibbling, baiting and playing to the gallery" by which Wells had been defeated.[27] Taylor wrote to Pease to say he felt like resigning because at the crucial moment, instead of defending the substance of their case, the Old Gang put up Shaw to defend their personal position; this might be fair and clever, but it was not heroic.[28] Beatrice too thought the mauling by Shaw "an altogether horrid business" even though Wells had brought it on himself. "The odd thing is," she concluded, "that if he had pushed his own fervid policy or rather enthusiasm for vague and big ideas, without making a personal attack on the Old Gang, he would have succeeded . . . But his accusations were so preposterous—his innuendoes so unsavoury and his little fibs so transparent that even his own followers refused to support him."[29]

"I am reluctantly taking up a secondary position for a time," Wells wrote to Pease early in January 1907.[30] He was harbouring, as he admitted, "a very lively resentment" at the way he had been treated. Everyone was anxious to win back his goodwill, but it was difficult to overcome his suspicions: "the worse he behaved the more he was indulged, and the more he was indulged the worse he behaved," Shaw commented afterwards.[31]

"Don't desert us," Maud Reeves wrote to Jane Wells on 6 January. "Can't *you* join the Reform Group even if Mr Wells has to keep out of it? . . . You simply must keep in touch with us . . . Tell the dear man that it is almost impossible to do anything without him."[32] Shaw too had written Wells a long and friendly letter, on 17 December, telling him, "You can easily retrieve the situation if you will study your game."

Wells grudgingly agreed to go on attending the meetings of the ginger group which had backed the special committee and to work for the election of more of its members to the executive in March—a task made easier by increasing its numbers to twenty-one to permit a more balanced representation of opinion. But his associates were finding him difficult to work with, and there were signs that he was losing the respect of some of them. After one meeting to discuss the draft of the reform manifesto, R. C. K. Ensor, a young Oxford graduate starting a career as a journalist, noted drily: "Wells absurd, the others reasonable."[33] Haden Guest, who had egged Wells on all through 1906, told him firmly that he must cooperate. "You will make it easier by endeavouring to imagine the possibility that your views and judgments may occasionally be wrong," he wrote. "My fear is that your mental peculiarities may—despite the great value of your ideas & your writings—isolate you in the socialist movement & render any attempt to realize your ideas very difficult."[34]

Despite the setback in December, the reform group still included influential Fabians and the most vocal of the younger generation. They were not insignificant in numbers. When the reform caucus met on 7 January, thirty members turned up, including Olivier, Maud Reeves, Wells, Guest, Taylor, Pethick-Lawrence, Emily Townshend, Aylmer Maude and H. T. Muggeridge. The problem that they faced was only partly due to the erratic personality and impulsive tactics of Wells. They were also unable to agree on what they wanted beyond the generality of livening up the Society—whether its future lay with the ILP or the Labour Party or in striking out boldly for a new middle-class party of socialists. The best they could decide on in the early months of 1907 was to promote their own ticket for the executive elections. In March their candidates, Wells among them, secured nine of the twenty-one seats. Though none of the crucial issues had been effectively debated, this result seemed to open the way for a realistic dialogue about the future of the Society.

Wells continued to harbour a grievance against the Webbs, believing that he had been a victim of a plot to humiliate him, but neither Sidney nor Beatrice paid him much attention. They had problems of their own. Sidney was more concerned about the elections to the County Council than he was about the poll for the Fabian executive. There was a real danger, with the tide running strongly against the Progressives in

London, that he might lose his seat in Deptford. Beatrice was too busy
to help very much, sending a secretary down to Deptford in her place.
In a desperate attempt to save the day for Sidney the Fabians rallied
round in full strength; on polling day three hundred of them were mobilized and deployed in the wards under Shaw, Pease, Reeves and other
friends. In the event Sidney scraped home by two hundred votes on a
day when the Progressives were at last swept out of office.

Beatrice was delighted with Sidney's success and full of admiration
for his calmness and strength in contrast to her own overwrought condition. She was totally absorbed in her work on the Commission but was
quite unable to come to terms with her fellow members. She told her
sister Mary that the Commission was "a regular *Scramble*—anybody's
game—each member having a different view of what its function is." In
this situation she felt free to act as "Solicitor, Barrister, Judge and Jury
all in one" to push her own case.[35] She was indiscreet to the point of dis-
loyalty to her colleagues, showing Commission papers to Haldane and
other influential friends and criticizing the commissioners in an attempt
to manipulate opinion against them. She knew that she was behaving
badly, which only made matters worse. "I lack discretion in the spoken
word—to that extent I lack manners," she noted on 18 January 1907.

Suffering from indigestion and insomnia, Beatrice went down to
Beachy Head in the middle of February to recuperate, blaming her colleagues for her collapse. "Eleven more obstinate men I never did know,"
she told Wells. "Moreover the fact that they *are* men & resent a woman
with secretaries (not to mention a husband) to help her, makes the tussles
between us assume a less pleasant tone than might otherwise be."[36] Her
desire to get her own way whatever the cost was largely the cause of her
difficulties. By April she was confessing, "I have become wholly indifferent to the Royal Commission. I merely work as hard as I know how
in my own direction without caring much what happens."[37] While she
felt "it is my business to be hostile" to the conventional attitudes to the
relief of poverty, she did have misgivings as the months went by about
her trick of "promoting every dissension among my colleagues." At the
end of the year she conceded that her colleagues might be "justified in
their dislike of me—I have played with the Commission."[38] She could
only console herself with the thought that by "persistent discourtesy"
her colleagues had absolved her "from obligations of good fellowship."

Beatrice found little relief from anxiety even in moments of relaxation. The Webbs were still "dallying with fashion,"[39] as she put it, but she could neither give it up nor enjoy it. They were particularly friendly with Balfour; Sidney got on with him as well as anyone except Shaw. There was no house in London where Arthur Balfour more enjoyed a dinner than at 41 Grosvenor Road, Beatrice was told by Balfour's sister-in-law Betty, Gerald's wife.[40] Weekends with Balfour in the country also provided a welcome break from the pressures of London. They were together at Lady Elcho's house, Stanway, in February and again in March. On both occasions Balfour came down in his automobile, so that they were able to spend delightful days motoring—"brilliant and pleasant was the talk as we whirled through the countryside." Beatrice found Balfour captivating with his "wonderful gift of intimacy."[41] She and Sidney went to stay with him at his country home, Whittinghame, on the Scottish border. After one such visit Balfour told Lady Elcho that "the talk was abundant but strenuous: Mr & Mrs W. being little moved by the more frivolous side of life! But they were extraordinarily pleasant and interesting."[42] Balfour had touched the heart of the matter. Beatrice could not accept and enjoy these friendships for their own sake. Thinking about Balfour, she wondered whether there was "any good purpose served by his friendship,"[43] justifying it to herself only if it served a political end. She decided that he might be a useful political card to keep up their sleeves, and she took care to see that both the Tory leader and his brother Gerald, who had been the minister who originally set up the Poor Law enquiry, were kept as well informed about the Webb plans as were their contacts among the Liberal leaders.

Wells too was dallying with fashion. His amour-propre, bruised among the Fabians, found gratification in society. He was an occasional guest at Stanway; he stayed with the Sassoons; he went to Taplow Court at the invitation of Lady Desborough. *New Worlds for Old* was coming off the press, he was excited by his new political melodrama *The War in the Air*, and he was already writing his major novel on the condition of England, *Tono-Bungay*. His work might be provocative, but it was successful enough to make him a focus of curiosity and admiration, lionized by influential men and women. All through the early months of 1907, nursing his wounded pride, Wells was looking for new emotional outlets. From the easy sexual mores of the Edwardian smart set to philandering among the more bohemian Fabians was a short step, and by the summer of 1907 he was increasingly surrounding himself with a bevy of attractive young women. There was a flirtatious intimacy with the young writer Violet Hunt; there were the young Fabians who had set up their own informal group in 1906 called the Fabian Nursery. His particular favourite was Hubert Bland's daughter, Rosamund. These young people saw Wells as a powerful and seductive hero who would somehow bring about a new golden world. For his part this role of prophet was more flattering and comfortable than the dreary grind of Fabian committees. He might have failed to capture the Society, but he had seized the imagination of many of its members.

"The little boom in the Fabian Society continues," Beatrice noted on 3 May. She told her sister Mary that it was "mostly the increasing reputation of GBS and H. G. Wells—perhaps even of 'Sidney & Beatrice Webb'—which is leading the young intellectuals to join us in such numbers compared to the slow growth of former years."[44] There had been nothing like it since the boom in the early Nineties. Now, in the course of 1907, the membership doubled to two thousand. Members who had lapsed rejoined, and new recruits were committing themselves with all the fervour of religious converts. Some were ILP activists, notably Philip Snowden and his wife, Ethel, and many of the younger members such as R. C. K. Ensor were influenced by ILP ideas and tactics. Most of the newcomers, however, were middle-class idealists who were temperamentally and intellectually cast in the same mould as the Society's founders. Fabianism was a congenial way of espousing socialism, especially as the labour movement was predominantly working-class and provincial.

   At Oxford and Cambridge there were small groups who turned to the Fabians as a political variant of the philanthropic settlement work which served as an outlet for uneasy consciences among young intellectuals. The Webbs, in particular, attracted fervent and brilliant young men whose first experience of politics was good works in the East End, at Toynbee Hall or some similar "settlement." It was from such people that the Webbs selected their own team of neophytes to help their research or to choose their candidates for public appointments. At Cambridge there was a lively set. Rupert Brooke, who, with Ben Keeling, Hugh Dalton, James Strachey, Clifford Allen and Amber Reeves, was involved in the Cambridge Fabians, caught the mood of his contemporaries with his critical sympathy. He was impressed by the Old Gang—

"they're really sincere, energetic, useful people, and they do a lot of good work." Yet he found them "rather hard." He wanted the Fabians to take "a more human view. . . . They confound the means with the end; and think that a compulsory Living Wage is the end, instead of a good beginning."[45] He went through a phase of soul-searching before he decided to join the Society: on 8 April 1908 he wrote to Hugh Dalton that he had made up his mind through such influences as "the wee, fantastic, Wells," Fabian tracts and "private meditation and prayer. . . . Spiritually the thing is done (not without blood and tears). . . . What steps can I take, even now? Where write? What say? . . . Tell me . . . I am eager as a neophyte always is, for action."[46]

The Fabians had always appealed to political amateurs—educated people on the fringes of the professions, such as the clergy, doctors, social workers, civil servants, teachers, writers, journalists, actors and artists. During this Edwardian boom young writers who were being carried up on the wave of new journalism, new fiction and new taste in art were prominent among the new recruits. Apart from Wells and Arnold Bennett, notable newcomers included the humourist Jerome K. Jerome, St. John Ervine, and Edgar Jepson, who was soon to write a novel, *Tangled Wedlock*, about his Fabian associates.

Holbrook Jackson, a young writer from Leeds recently arrived in London, wrote to Pease in December 1906 to say that in the last two decades the Society had "created a definite Socialist attitude in both Politics & Sociology" and to ask why it should not "do the same for ART and PHILOSOPHY."[47] With his friend Alfred Orage, Jackson had already started an Arts Group in Leeds to promote reform in art, manners and culture. Now that they had both moved to London they wanted to repeat this venture among the Fabians. The Fabian Arts Group was one of a number which grew up to cater for the enlarged and more diverse membership. There were similar clusters among members with special interests in biology, local government and education. There was an amateur dramatic society, but in 1908 the executive, with Shaw in the chair, decided that the Society could not countenance a Dramatic Group! Within a few months a Women's Group had been added to the list, and the veteran Fabian Charlotte Wilson became its active secretary. It was, however, the Arts Group which had the liveliest impact, attracting writers such as G. K. Chesterton and Hilaire Belloc to its meetings and becoming a forum for wide-ranging debates on manners and morals. The sculptor Eric Gill recalled that it was given to "vague efforts to deprive Fabianism of its webbed feet."[48] Orage was the moving spirit. He had been a schoolteacher in Leeds and had taken to Theosophy and Nietzschean philosophy. Like many of his contemporaries he believed in the force of will to change fact, the power of ideas to make a new world. He made an unhappy marriage, he found teaching a bore, and he descended on London to make a fresh start.[49]

In the spring of 1907 a small weekly review called the *New Age* came up for sale for a nominal sum. The name and the opportunity appealed to Orage and Jackson, and they decided to buy it. They went to Shaw for money and got a promise of five hundred pounds if they would "raid the City" for the remainder: half the capital came, anonymously, from a Theosophically minded banker named Lewis Wallace. Shaw also undertook to write articles for nothing and to encourage his friends to contribute. Orage was an odd, eclectic character. He said that his socialism was an anthology of the mediaeval stained glass of Morris, the sandals of Carpenter, Keir Hardie's cloth cap and red tie, and Shaw's jingling bells and cap. He was interested in vegetarianism, the Simple Life, occultism, arts and crafts. Such heterogeneous interests were valuable assets on which Orage could capitalize as an editor. Coupled with his distaste for orthodoxy of any kind, they enabled him to appeal to a wide range of progressive readers. His policy was to publish anyone who had something to say and said it well; he simply held the ring while pacifists, suffragists, sexual reformers, anarchists, syndicalists and every variety of socialist argued out their ideas.

Nominally Fabian, Orage was out of sympathy with the bureaucratic collectivism of Webb and closer to the Fabian mood of earlier days. Without overtly challenging the Old Gang, the *New Age* became in effect the champion of every kind of radical dissent from the conventions of art, literature and politics. It was time, Orage wrote to Wells in June 1907, to ask "whether the Fabian Society has not ceased to be the medium of free discussion, whether in fact, it has not become so dogmatic as to make its future as an intelligent organ of discussion and enquiry very doubtful."[50] For many Fabians it provided an attractive alternative outlet for their energies and ideas. Haden Guest was its dramatic critic, Clifford Sharp and Cecil Chesterton wrote many of its political notes, the early psychoanalyst M. D. Eder wrote about politics and medicine, Florence Farr and Beatrice Hastings were the chief women contributors, and for two years Arnold Bennett wrote a book column under a pseudonym. Wells, Belloc and G. K. Chesterton were all liable to drop into the smoking room in the A.B.C. restaurant in Chancery Lane where each Monday afternoon Orage held his informal editorial meetings and everyone read the proofs of the next issue. Such meetings became a running seminar for all those who wanted new worlds for old.

Feminism was an important ingredient in this ferment. The New Woman was good copy and by 1906 an unavoidable political topic. Socialist groups had never found it easy to cope with the question of women's rights, which raised strong and divisive feelings. Many active feminists, like Emmeline Pankhurst, had hived themselves off into separate organizations. She had begun as a Fabian, become one of the early leaders of the ILP and then, in 1903, founded her own militant Women's Social and Political Union. In all the socialist groups there was a faction which sympathized with the suffragettes, and the *New Age* offered them a platform from which to agitate. Its pages reflected the swing of opinion among the women Fabians, who, by 1907, constituted over a quarter of the total membership.

The Fabians were slowly adjusting to the new climate of opinion, but they found it difficult to translate their general excitement into an agreed course of action. The underlying issue, epitomized in the Wells affair, was the nature of the Society and its future political role. The Old Gang had no desire to stand pat; in making concessions to the reformers, however, it tried to avoid being stampeded to the point where the Society would lose its distinctive character. The reformers still could not agree on a coherent alternative and were busy arguing out their ideas in the pages of the *New Age*.

In an effort to make some progress it was decided to set up a new Political Committee for the Society and to promote "local socialist societies of the Fabian type, with the object of increasing the socialist representation in Parliament as a party co-operating as far as possible with the Labour Party, while remaining independent of that and all other parties."[51] These terms of reference, deliberately ambiguous on the disputed points in order to produce a compromise, drew an immediate protest from Wells. He was also suspicious about the composition of the new committee. Webb was to be the chairman; Olivier, who would have been more acceptable to Wells, had been fêted by the Fabians at a dinner in the Holborn Restaurant and sent on his way to become governor of Jamaica. Wells thought Webb and Shaw were packing the committee in favour of a new middle-class socialist party. "What an extraordinary & total misconception of my bias," Webb coldly told Wells, pointing out that the membership of the new committee might have been different if Wells had taken the trouble to attend the preliminary meetings. In any case it represented the main currents of opinion among the Fabians, and five of its members were known sympathizers with Wells.[52]

On 15 June Pease wrote to Wells asking him to sit on the committee himself, and Webb wrote on the same day to assure him that his suspicions were "quite baseless." The pressure of the last few months forced Sidney to spell out more clearly than ever before the assumptions upon which the Old Gang had run the Society and on which he felt it should continue to be based. He told Wells plainly what the Society was and how it worked:

> The Society never was very homogeneous because it was deliberately kept heterogeneous. But the danger now is of its becoming . . . a mere philosophical debating society. Now it has been, since 1888 at any rate, a very definitely *political* society, with essentially *political* aims, pressing *political* proposals, and exercising a good deal of political influence. Personally I am not in it for anything else. . . . I don't know whether you really differ from me in this; sometimes I think we don't use words with the same meanings. Perhaps it may not be useless to explain that by "political" I mean simply "state institutional" & not at all necessarily forming a separate party, or any party, or indeed having anything to do with elections or electioneering! . . . Personally I do not work & strive & find money to satisfy my intellectual curiosity. . . . I want to diminish the sum of human suffering. I am not concerned about this party or that, but about getting things done, no matter who does them. Elections & parties are quite subordinate—even trivial—parts of political action. More is done in England in politics whilst ignoring elections & parties than by or with them. Nevertheless, they, too, form a part of life which the Socialist cannot ignore.[53]

Wells might disagree with this point of view, but it was at least a friendly attempt to clear up the confusion. Maud Reeves, personally friendly with Wells and in sympathy with his attempts to liven up the Society, felt it necessary to urge him to take the Fabians honestly on their own terms. "Do be good," she wrote on 15 June. "The fact is we are too humdrum for you. But you would never get along with 14 other H. G. Wells. Think of it!"[54]

With summer coming on, there was no chance to move beyond a first formal meeting of the new committee. There was also "humdrum" business to be done, but there were signs of a more expansive mood. On 1 July the telephone was installed in the Society's office as "a labour-saving device," and Pease was given a raise in salary from £150 to £250 a year. The former office boy, E. J. Howell, who had served the Fabians for seventeen years, now handled all the literature sales and worked as a shorthand typist; even Webb conceded that his pay should be raised from two pounds a week to forty-five shillings. A social committee, set up to make the new members feel at home, ran a soirée at the Suffolk Street Galleries. The executive agreed that Cecil Sharp's Morris dancers might perform but on a majority vote decided that no ices were to be served. Despite its austerity, it was a successful occasion: over four hundred came, including the old antagonist Henry Hyndman and the former Fabian Annie Besant. She was now sixty and for the past ten years had been living in India, where she had been converted to Hinduism and had become the world leader of the Theosophical movement. Although she eschewed direct involvement in politics, she appeared once more before a Fabian audience in July, to give a lecture on "The Future Socialism."

The most original sign of a new spirit among the Fabians to meet the challenge of what *Fabian News* called the "all-pervading younger generation" was the introduction of a summer school. The idea had come from F. Lawson Dodd, a Fabian dentist who thought the Society might usefully fuse the idea of a cooperative holiday home with the German scheme of lecture holidays for young people. Shaw quickly responded to the proposal. It was his approval and a financial underwriting by Charlotte that made the first of a long series of summer schools possible in the summer of 1907. The Society managed to rent a large house, Pen-yr-allt, at Llanbedr on the North Wales coast near Harlech. Fabians were invited to attend for any period between 24 July and 14 September at a cost of thirty-five shillings a week. To ensure success the Shaws themselves took a house nearby for the whole summer, and GBS threw himself into the affair with gusto, giving lectures on marriage, education, foreign politics and socialism, reading from his plays and spending hours in informal talk. Over a hundred Fabians turned up at one time or another—a mixed crew of university students, lower-class professionals, a bevy of young girls from the Fabian Nursery, a handful of MP's and academics, and a number of elderly ladies who found it a lively and cheap way of taking a holiday.

The Welsh weather was bad, but it did not dampen the high spirits. "The first fixture in the morning was an hour's Swedish drill," *Fabian News* reported, the costumes worn by the participants rather startling the Methodist Welsh. There were lectures and discussions on four days of the week, all-day excursions on Wednesdays and Saturdays, and improving entertainment in the evenings. "Intellectual zest," *Fabian News* went on, "was intermingled with the long walks and climbs, the parties and games and gymnastics." Shaw was tireless, taking a lead in the expeditions and indulging his enthusiasm for swimming—on one occasion narrowly escaping drowning when he and Robert Loraine, one of his favourite actors at the Court, were swept out to sea. Sending a long account of the incident to Wells, GBS noted that the younger Loraine had "a much worse time," being "badly handicapped as a meat eater" in anything demanding physical stamina![55]

Shaw had hoped to persuade Wells to take part in the summer school: it seemed a good chance to get him back on the rails. Shaw invited HG and Jane to stay, and Charlotte backed up the invitation with a letter to Jane on 7 August,[56] but Wells would not leave Sandgate. He was busy entertaining his own guests, among them the attractive and clever Amber Reeves, then entering her last year at Newnham College. The Webbs also stayed away. The Shaws had lent them the house at Ayot St. Lawrence for the summer and they went there to get on with their work, taking three secretaries along to cope with Beatrice's Commission enquiries and to lend a hand on their next volume on local government.

Although Shaw was much occupied with the Fabian jamboree, he too had work to do. Things had not been going well at the Court. The Ellen Terry production of *Captain Brassbound's Conversion* had lost money, and the plays put on in the first months of 1907 had not been popular. GBS had insisted on a production of *The Philanderer* against the advice of Granville Barker and Lillah McCarthy; then Lillah had gone into hospital after a miscarriage at the dress rehearsal, and her understudy had not been adequate. A revival of *You Never Can Tell* had done better, and Barker proposed that the autumn production might do better if they moved to the Savoy in the West End. Shaw was sceptical but agreed to put up two thousand pounds to back the scheme. "The game is up at the Court," he wrote philosophically to Barker in April, "it has not yet begun at the Savoy. Four years is enough to give to any one move in the way of high art. . . . Debating societies which always begin on a wave of public interest in something begin to die after four years; and the Court is nothing but a debating society. The Shaw boom, in its novelty phase, cannot last longer."[57] Up at Llanbedr that summer he was at work on *Getting Married* in the hope that the new play might postpone that predicted decline.

For all the sprightliness GBS displayed among the Fabian holiday-makers, he was beginning to feel that at fifty he could rest on his laurels. "I have done my turn" became a familiar phrase. He was making a considerable income, telling his old friend Matthew McNulty that he had touched as much as thirteen thousand pounds in one year. The vigorous enthusiasm of the Court days had gone and could not be recaptured at the Savoy. When they opened there with *You Never Can Tell* on 16 September Barker failed to make the play sparkle. *The Devil's Disciple*, which followed, was undistinguished; Max Beerbohm was one critic who thought the production was "thoroughly bad." In November Forbes-Robertson, who had been touring America with *Caesar and Cleopatra*, brought it to the Savoy for a five-week run that was a financial flop. In December Shaw complained to Arnold Daly, the American actor-manager: "Business here has been disastrous . . . theatre stalls have been empty. The cheap seats have been faithful; but London rents depend on the $2½ people, not on the widow's mite."[58] In fact, Shaw told Gertrude Elliott on 4 December, "unless we can retrieve the situation with *Arms and the Man*, Vedrenne, Barker and Shaw will have to go round with a street piano." With Barker playing Serge and Lillah playing Raina, the play came on as Shaw's last card in the Savoy game.[59] It ran until March 1908, when the hapless Savoy tenancy ended. Though Vedrenne and Barker continued a desultory partnership, Shaw had been essentially right: the boom at the Court had been their heyday. Shaw's difficulties were a symptom of a change of style in the theatre. The Edwardian vogue for reforming plays was coming to an end. By 1911 the avant-garde had turned to Chekhov, Strindberg and Wedekind, to the work of Max Reinhardt, Gordon Craig and the Moscow Arts Theatre.[60]

GBS was certainly in no mood in the autumn of 1907 for more knock-about turns with Wells, and Wells himself showed no sign of fight. On 11 October, as if to demonstrate his waning interest, he resigned from the Society's Finance and General Purposes Committee and its Publication Committee. After the excitement earlier in the year Fabian affairs seemed to be slipping back to a more normal pace. "All I want to do just now," Shaw wrote to Sidney on 21 October, "is to talk and push the middle-class propaganda . . . I find that my line of telling the middle class that they are getting badly left between Labour & Plutocracy in Parliament, & that the cost of pensions & all other reforms extracted by Labor will be thrown on their rates & taxes if they don't organize, is effective. . . . What we want is a couple of years of this sort of talk rather than any immediate attempt to organize anything or formulate anything." He was, in fact, feeling "rather lazy" about reconstructing the Fabians.

Wells, meanwhile, was rollicking about, "having just as good a time . . . as I can."[61] After *New Worlds for Old* was published in March 1908 he impulsively took up the draft for a new Basis which Shaw had sent him almost a year before. He wanted to amend it to work in a scheme for children's allowances to make women independent. When he sent his proposals to Shaw and Webb on 9 March and called for an early discussion before his version was sent round to members, he got discouraging replies. Shaw thought there was no chance of persuading Fabians to accept it as it stood. It contained, he said, "a devil of a lot of Liberal Children's Bill to a very little Socialism and no Democracy—not even Women's Suffrage."[62] As he was busy trying to finish *Getting Married*, he had no time to work on it himself. Sidney was equally pressed and he told Wells that he thought his plan of campaign was wrong. "I can't imagine anything more regrettable than to turn the local Societies & Groups away from work in order to spend some months of time discussing a Basis."[63]

The Old Gang had never shared Wells's enthusiasm about a new Basis, and now that the Society was attracting new members and finding new things to do it seemed to them little more than an intellectual exercise. But Wells went on fussing; it had become the scene for another battle of wills. The Basis, Wells replied to Sidney, was "the worst enemy the Webbs have in the Fabian Society. I happen to be something of a teacher & I want to get rid of that piece of apparatus very much. Why can't you & Shaw let me think it out new. . . . You two men are the most intolerable egotists, narrow, suspicious, obstructive, I've ever met."[64]

Sidney sent a testy but conciliatory reply: "I am honestly willing to confer about the Basis. Only—just as you could not take it up some months ago, so I can't very well take it up now. . . . We can't all be disengaged when you are."[65] GBS was not so willing to let the snub to Webb pass without reproof. "You are forgetting your committee manners," he wrote to Wells on 22 March, "if a man can be said to forget what he never knew." People could give and take hard knocks in private, but the "art of public life consists fundamentally in respecting political rights. Intimate as I am with Webb, I should no more dream of treating him as you have treated him than of walking into the House of Lords & pulling the Lord Chancellor's nose."

The edge of the joking was becoming sharper. On 30 April Sidney told Beatrice that Wells was "breaking out again" and that he had raked up the old MacDonald complaint about the maladministration of the Hutchinson Trust. Shaw had earlier feared that Wells might make trouble on this issue, for it would be difficult to sustain the argument against his expansive scheme if it could be shown that the Society had hidden reserves or that Webb was guilty of abusing the trust. As the trust had now been wound up and the residual money distributed to the London School of Economics and the Society, it was easy for Pease to reply to Wells that the trust no longer existed.[66]

Maud Reeves was one of the few executive members who bothered to respond to Wells's new plans for reorganizing the executive and enlarging *Fabian News*, but she could not back them. Her reply was guarded because she was friendly with HG and grateful for his encouragement of her daughter Amber. "She adores you both," she wrote to Jane Wells after the Easter holidays, which Amber had spent at Sandgate. "She has gone up to Cambridge full of spirits & confidence . . . You are good fairies to all these young people. It must be very pleasant to realise what a lot of happiness you give them."[67]

Wells stood at the executive elections in 1908, again coming fourth, but he continued to embarrass his colleagues. Winston Churchill, who was fighting a bye-election in Manchester as a Liberal, received a letter of support from him although a socialist candidate was also running. Many Fabians regarded this as treachery, and Wells was sharply rebuked at the annual general meeting on 22 April. Webb tried to defend the right of Wells to take his own line. Sidney was himself in an embarrassing situation, since he was making private approaches to Churchill to win him over to the Webb schemes for reforming the Poor Law. He tried to soften the criticism of Wells by saying that his fault was nothing more than a failure to inform his colleagues of his views in advance. This gentle reproof was too much for Wells: he ostentatiously walked off the platform. "We all know our Wells" was Webb's only comment.

This was not, however, just another fit of petulance. After four years the comet was swinging out of the Fabian orbit. The next day Wells wrote to the *Fabian News* implying that he was ready to quit the Society. He did nothing for the next six months, but when Pease returned from his summer holiday on 16 September he found a letter of resignation from Wells. HG had thought of launching yet another vigorous campaign, he told Pease, but "when I calculate the forces against such a campaign, the inevitable opposition and irritation that must ensue, and the probable net results of what would certainly be an irksome and distressing conflict, I am forced to conclude that the effort is . . . not worth making." The chance of converting the middle classes to Fabianism had "found us divided and undecided . . . it is to other media and other methods that we must now look for the spread and elaboration of those collectivist ideas which all of us have at heart."[68] Ten days later the executive agreed that it was best to let him go his own way. Formal regret was tempered by relief.

The Fabians were at last done with Wells; but Wells was not yet done with the Fabians.

⟪ 23 ⟫

LUXURIOUS
PERVERSITY

"When will all this wicked misery cease—misery that leads to wickedness and wickedness that leads to misery? An abomination!"[1] Beatrice exclaimed after visiting workhouses and labour yards for the unemployed early in 1908. At Hollesley Bay Colony, a bleak settlement on the east coast, she saw three hundred broken-down men who were part of an experiment in rehabilitation.[2] She went on to Hadleigh Farm, where the Salvation Army had a similar scheme for released convicts, tramps and other human wreckage; and though she had doubts about the religious pressures put on hungry men she thought the Salvationist officers "a Samurai caste" with a "beautiful spirit of love and service."[3] Back from a tour in Lancashire and Yorkshire, she was soon off to Ireland with a group of the Commission, examining the local variant of the Poor Law. "The misery is genuine," she remarked. "There is heaven and there is America—and according to whether they are the children of this world or the next, they desire to escape to one or the other."[4]

Beatrice returned to London impatient with bureaucrats who stood in the way of reform. A grand design of her own was gradually taking shape, and she was coming to the view that she must submit her own plan to replace the Poor Law. She had no misgivings about this; she and Sidney, indeed, were beginning to show some anxiety at the prospect that the other commissioners might accept too many of their ideas and make it difficult for them to put forward what Sidney later described to Pease as a complete revolution of the whole system. In early December 1907, when Beatrice put an outline of her scheme before the Commission, Sidney sent it to Haldane, saying: "Its effect on the majority was like the bark of a shepherd's dog—it drove them helter-skelter into the Chairman's fold!" Rather than accept anything from Beatrice, he added, they had accepted "a blurred outline which may . . . come to the same thing." Fortunately, he said revealingly, "it just leaves her an excuse for a Minority Report in favor of the Break-up of the Poor Law which we are going to do in the grandest style."[5]

As Beatrice became more determined to push the Webb plan and to ensure that they got credit for it, her contempt for her fellow commissioners increased. She was arrogant and defiant at the meetings, which were marked by coldness and sharp words. Though she could count on the two labour men, she had no other allies and she had alienated her old associate Charles Booth, who resigned in January because he found the divided Commission too uncomfortable.

Haldane, as a friend and long-time ally, was one of the first to be shown the draft of the Webbs' proposals, but they were soon busy lobbying other political acquaintances. Their scheme was sent off "in confidence" to more than half the Cabinet, including Asquith, Lloyd George, Churchill and John Burns; to an equal number of Tory leaders; and to favoured civil servants, journalists and other public figures. Beatrice also gave a series of dinner parties, whose guests included labour men as well as Balfour, Asquith, Haldane and Churchill. These occasions, she noted on 10 February, were "speculative investments in the minds of rival politicians." It was necessary to keep up with both government and opposition: "We are inclined to plunge heavily on all parties—give freely to anyone who comes along." There was such a scramble for new ideas that politicians were "mendicants for practical proposals." She and Sidney were still pinning their hopes on the old tactic of permeation.

In April Campbell-Bannerman died and Asquith replaced him as prime minister. Beatrice was exultant at his elevation, feeling that Asquith seemed "inclined to carry out our ideas."[6] She was even more hopeful of Churchill, who had been offered the Local Government Board and turned it down as "full of hopeless and insoluble difficulties," going instead to the Board of Trade, where he would have a chance of dealing with unemployment.[7] When Beatrice first met Churchill, in July 1903, she had written him off as "bumptious, shallow-minded and reactionary . . . with a certain personal magnetism . . . not of intellect but of character."[8] She now saw him as having "the American's capacity for the quick appreciation and rapid execution of new ideas, while hardly comprehending the philosophy beneath them." He was, she thought, "beginning to realise the preposterousness of the present state of things" when he dined with them on 10 March, a favourable reaction induced in part by the discovery that he had "swallowed Sidney's scheme for boy labour and unemployment, had even dished it up in an article in *The Nation* the week before."[9]

Beatrice was euphoric. "To my schemes of reform there are, at present, no rivals," she claimed in May when the Commission adjourned for the summer.[10] It was hard, she wrote with some excitement, "to keep one's head cool and free for downright grind" when so many possibilities of influence seemed to be coming their way again.[11] The Webbs, however, wanted anonymous influence. When a newspaper cartoon in March drew attention to their manipulations, Beatrice was worried: "One great advantage we have is that we are never mentioned in the newspapers. . . . we always see our friends in little private meetings."[12] There were disadvantages too in such discreet tactics. Naïve about political realities, the Webbs were prone to overestimate their influence as experts and were puzzled when professional politicians such as Asquith were socially agreeable, willing to listen and yet unwilling to implement the schemes the Webbs devised for them. They also found it hard to understand how their backstairs methods embarrassed and alienated their associates.

Their political insensitivity did not help in their handling of their old colleague John Burns and the officials of the Local Government Board, the department responsible for applying the Poor Law. Burns was self-important, inexperienced and unsophisticated; his department was underfinanced, overburdened with work, and poorly run by old-fashioned officials. He was in fact becoming the prisoner of his officials. The Webbs had kept up good relations with him until the end of 1906, and even after that date Burns made several pompous but well-intentioned overtures to them. But, as the Commission wore on, Beatrice made a dead set at his senior officials, and both she and Sidney became contemptuous of Burns. When, in May 1908, Burns suggested that Sidney might move into the Local Government Board as his permanent secretary, Beatrice "pooh-poohed the idea as impossible."[13] They noted that Burns was losing ground in the Cabinet. Asquith himself increasingly bypassed the Board, letting Churchill at the Board of Trade deal with unemployment and allowing Lloyd George as chancellor of the exchequer to work on his own new schemes of social insurance, which owed more to Bismarck's Germany than to the Royal Commission on the Poor Law. The Webbs therefore decided to attack Burns from the rear and to intrigue for the appointment of their friend the talented Robert Morant. It was several months before the matter was settled against Morant, but in the process the Webbs annoyed Asquith as well as Burns by their attempt to insert their protégé into a key post.

The Webbs had got into the habit of patronizing and promoting the careers of young men who exemplified their notion of efficient public servants. Morant was one. Another was Llewellyn Smith, who had helped Ben Tillett in the great dock strike, worked with Charles Booth on his social enquiries and become the senior official in the Board of Trade. The young academic William Beveridge also benefited from their patronage. Like Smith and others in the Webb entourage he had served his apprenticeship in the East End settlement at Toynbee Hall. On the recommendation of the Webbs, Churchill took on Beveridge to help with his scheme of labour exchanges.

The Webbs themselves had come to serve as something like a private labour exchange for young professionals—the kind of person that the London School of Economics was intended to train. Sidney still kept a close eye on the school as chairman, and when H. J. Mackinder resigned in 1908 to work with Milner on imperial policy for the next Tory government the Webbs had to find yet another director. They finally persuaded William Pember Reeves to resign his post as the London representative of the New Zealand government and take on the job.

With the School in safe hands, Sidney and Beatrice were free to get on with the minority report. They went off to spend the summer at Luton Hoo, the Bedfordshire estate of Sir Julius Wernher, where their thoughts were haunted by the antithesis between Mammon and the misery around them. There was the great house with fifty-four gardeners, thirty house servants and ten electricians, run at a cost of thirty thousand pounds a year and used for only a few weeks in the year; half a mile away was the "drunk, sensual, disorderly" industrial town of Luton.[14] This disturbing contrast spurred them on to work at what Sidney described to Wallas as the biggest thing they had yet tackled. Beatrice feared that they might not be ready with their own report before "this mad dog of a Commission rushes at the public."[15] She no longer cared what the commissioners thought of her, even taking a perverse satisfaction in her isolation. "By the time that Commission ends I shall be a well-hated person," she wrote on 29 October 1908. When she saw the draft report of her fellow members she haughtily dismissed it as valueless save for its admission that the old Poor Law had collapsed.

At the same time Beatrice was beginning to adopt a take-it or leave-it attitude to the Liberals. Churchill was friendly. In July he wrote a cordial letter to Sidney saying: "You will always find the door of my room open whenever you care to come & I hope you will feed me generously from your store of information & ideas."[16] In October she and Sidney were invited to breakfast at 11 Downing Street, where Lloyd George tried to interest them in his new plans for social insurance, which he proposed to launch with modest noncontributory old-age pensions. They rebuffed him at once, Beatrice telling him bluntly that she was against paying out public money as a right without imposing any obligation upon the person who received it—"the state got nothing for its money." She still felt that relief "ought to be conditional on better conduct"; the aim of public policy should be to force self-improvement.[17] Haldane, who was also present, tried to find a compromise, but the division between Lloyd George and the Webbs was never bridged. They had become so obsessed with the virtues of their own proposals that they failed to seize any of several chances of collaborating with Churchill and Lloyd George in the drafting of Liberal social reforms. Beatrice told Haldane that if the Liberals would not adopt the Webbs' scheme they would give it to the Tories.[18]

Beatrice was clearly overwrought. "I have had a collapse," she wrote to Graham Wallas in July; "the pressure of getting the Report finished was terrific."[19] She fasted and prayed to sustain herself through the final strains; her dedication to her cause was turning to fanaticism. Only three commissioners joined her in signing the minority report: the labour men, George Lansbury and Francis Chandler (secretary of the Carpenters Union), and one of the clergymen, Russell Wakefield. Beatrice no longer minded. The three-hundred-page report which she and Sidney

had compiled was another child of their partnership. It was their utopia
in a blue book.

For three years Beatrice had ridiculed the commissioners, sneered at
their ideas and predicted that the Webb plan would make a big bang. In
fact it landed with a dull thud. When both documents reached the newspapers in February 1909 Beatrice had to confess, "We feel a trifle foolish," for the majority report was given an excellent press.[20] The most
she could say for their own report was that it got "a fair look in." In
their disappointment they were less than fair to the majority, which had
actually criticized the existing Poor Law as outmoded, recognized the
evils of the general mixed workhouse, suggested the abolition of the
guardians and proposed a reformed system of "public assistance" under
municipal control—a policy sufficiently in advance of its time for another twenty years to elapse before it was fully adopted.

It was true that the minority report was conceptually more coherent than the patchwork proposals of Lord George Hamilton and the majority of the Commission, but the Webbs had become so obsessed by its
virtues that they had lost their perspective on the whole matter. They
were unwilling to compromise, or even to say a good word for anything
that deviated significantly from their own far-reaching—and politically
unacceptable—proposals. This was, in part, a carry-over from Beatrice's
irrationally negative attitude towards her colleagues. It was also the result of the Webbs' attempt to shift the ground from the Commission's
original terms of reference. All through its sittings Beatrice showed little interest in any improved and more effective way of dealing with the
relief of paupers—the same kind of indifference which the Webbs displayed towards Lloyd George's plans for alleviating the symptoms of
poverty. What they wanted and what they had spent so much effort devising was a completely different pattern of welfare as a means to national efficiency. "Nothing will avail to save a nation whose workers
have decayed," they wrote in the minority report. On the meanest cal-
culation of profit and loss it was necessary "to clean up the base of
society."

To do this, they insisted, it was essential to begin by establishing a
national minimum and to provide a variety of means for dealing with
those who fell below it. They rejected the idea that there was a single

undifferentiated mass of paupers all of whose problems should be dealt with by a single agency such as the Poor Law—old or new. Such an approach, in their opinion, inevitably led to the classification of paupers by type of person rather than by type of need. Beatrice had already pointed out to the Commission that such a policy was undesirable and inconsistent. The Webbs argued that it would be logical to scrap the Poor Law completely and replace it by a series of specialist agencies, each coping with a specific aspect of poverty. There should be a public-health service which dealt with sickness, one of the great causes of poverty, whether the beneficiary was in or out of work, young or old. There should be similar services for employment, for mental illness and to provide pensions and other support for the elderly; the education service should deal with the social problems of children as well as with their schooling.

Such an elaborate system seemed like an administrative nightmare to their contemporaries, who complained that the Webb plan would force a poor family with several kinds of need to run from one office to another to secure help—for the father to seek medical attention or work, for the grandparents to get pensions, for the children to get school meals. There was an even greater objection to the idea that welfare services should be offered at public expense to anyone who was not, formally speaking, a pauper. The notion of a coordinated system of social services was too novel to be grasped in the middle of the Edwardian age, especially when the most pressing need still seemed to be the degrading poverty of the lower depths.

The Webbs were well aware that the idea of enforcing "personal responsibility" died hard—that the majority spoke for a good deal of public opinion when they argued that such provision as the Webbs envisaged would discourage thrift and might even make the pauper better off than the man who was taxed to assist him. They had to meet that case, and parts of the minority report revealed the lengths to which they were prepared to go to discourage waste and selfishness. They believed that labour exchanges were necessary to ensure that no one who declined to work should be helped. They talked about moral and physical invalids who would need training to improve their "faculties of body and mind." And they went so far as to recommend detention colonies of a most severe kind to which "industrial malingerers" would be sent if they refused to work. Like Shaw, who declared that poverty was a crime, they saw destitution as a public danger which demanded the most rigorous measures to "drain the morass." Where most of the current debate was concerned with ways of containing and managing the problem of pauperism, the Webbs used it to advance their doctrine of national regeneration.

They arranged to put out a cheap Fabian edition of their plan distinct from the official publication, which Beatrice described as the minority report "encumbered with the Majority Report."[21] Having failed with the Commission and making no headway with friends in the Cabinet, they now felt that their main purpose was to rouse public support for their scheme. In that task they turned to the Fabians as the most suitable organization to hand. Sidney told Pease: "We must have a concerted 'boom,' organizing every member of the FS so as to go full tilt at the walls of the confounded old Elizabethan Jericho, which we must destroy."[22] Their opponents guessed what they had in mind. "You have declared war," wrote one of the inspectors of the Local Government Board, "and war this will be."[23]

The Victorians were convinced that philanthropy should not merely relieve distress but also promote middle-class morality. The Webbs took this link a step further when they sought to transfer this "civilizing mission" to the state. This belief that social policy should simultaneously tackle destitution and improve character was what they meant by matching communal and individual responsibility. It had been a persistent Fabian theme from the first meetings, when the founders had agreed that their "ultimate aim shall be to help on the reconstruction of Society in accordance with the highest moral possibilities." Such a change was to be brought about by idealists through an effort of will and intellectual persuasion, not by the class struggle, the victory of the proletariat or any of the other Marxist notions which the Fabians had rejected in their early years.

It was an attitude which Shaw clearly expressed in a letter to Henry James on 17 January 1909: "I, as a Socialist, have had to preach, as much as anyone, the enormous power of the environment," he wrote. "We can change it; we must change it; there is absolutely no other sense in life than the task of changing it." Shaw was disagreeing with James on exactly the same grounds as those on which Wells broke with James two years later. Both Shaw and Wells believed that the human race was to be

saved by a superior elite with missionary zeal, which would show mankind how to break out of the cage of evolutionary laws and circumstances. GBS had already remarked that when Wells talked about his
Samurai, or New Republicans, he meant much the same thing as Nietzsche's superman. Such an elite could triumph only by making will the
master of fact—and art must be subordinated to that end and made the
instrument of change. "What is the use of writing plays, what is the use
of writing anything," Shaw asked James, "if there is not a Will which
finally moulds chaos itself into a race of gods with heaven for an environment, and if that Will is not incarnated in man?"

Shaw was writing to James to tell him what he disliked about the
dramatic version of *Owen Wingrave* which James had submitted to the
Stage Society. "People don't want works of art from you: they want
help," Shaw insisted. This attitude, for James, spelt death to the creative
spirit. Works of art, he replied to Shaw, "are capable of saying more
things to man about himself than any other 'works' whatever are capable
of doing. . . . The artist undertakes to represent the world to us." For
Shaw to set his autocratic doctrine against the free play of the imagination, James asserted, was "a luxurious perversity."[24]

The wilful Shaw, whose ability to write clever dialogue and to manipulate his characters through sheer stagecraft disguised his brittleness
as an artist, had no patience for the case that James was making. His plays
had always been a vehicle for the ideas of the preacher rather than the
insight of the playwright. He had come to the point where the message
was becoming increasingly fanciful and perverse. Although GBS told
Wells on 22 March 1908 that *Getting Married* was "a dramatic masterpiece," he came closer to the truth in a letter to John Martin Harvey on
3 January. "I am getting too old now for melodrama—even Shavian
melodrama," he admitted. "All my recent plots have been long & preachy:
the next one will probably be quite unplayable."

Getting Married opened at the Haymarket on 12 May 1908 to "a
torrent of denunciation" from the critics, who trounced it as a dull failure and not even a play in the usual sense of the word.[25] This familiar
complaint, however, no longer kept audiences away now that Shaw's
reputation was at its peak, and he considered the play's commercial success a great triumph. It was a long wrangle about the rights of men and
women which intellectualized the topical middle-class concern with the
marital conventions. One couple in the play solve their problem by

striking a contract which sets out the terms on which they will continue to cohabit; another couple are reconciled by accepting a *ménage à trois* in which the interloper's role is to relieve the husband's boredom and to be the plaything of the captive wife. Shaw knew both situations. He had opted for the first in his own marriage after playing through the second with the Salts, the Sparlings, the Charringtons and the Blands. He claimed that the play was another instalment in his struggle to force the public to reconsider its morals because he believed that contemporary morality on economic and sexual matters was disastrously wrong.

Shaw was invariably free with his advice, but paradoxically he was embarrassed when others took it literally and behaved as he had done in his philandering youth. He had for some time been pursued by Rupert Brooke's young cousin Erica Cotterill, to whom he responded with long letters counselling a more conventional view than might be inferred from his plays. When he suggested that she marry someone of her own age to distract her from plaintive hero worship, she merely intensified her declarations of love, moved near the Shaws and tried to inveigle herself into their household. GBS read her a lecture on the "iron laws of domestic honour" which contrasted starkly with the flirtatious insouciance of *Getting Married*. "Now that I have taught you some respect for business and the law," he wrote, "let me assure you that marriage is more sacred than either, and that unless you are prepared to treat my wife with absolute loyalty, you will be hurled into outer darkness for ever." Charlotte might have "to tolerate worshipping females . . . who bore her to distraction with their adoration of me; but it is my business to see that her patience is not abused."[26]

Wells was one of the younger socialists who saw the contradiction in Shaw's position. To him such sentiments seemed priggishly Victorian. Though GBS was willing "to play about with ideas like a daring garrulous maiden aunt," Wells complained, in real life he showed "the instincts of conscious gentility and the judgment of a hen."[27] Wells was angry because Shaw had reproved him for dalliance among the younger Fabians and for causing a backstairs row with the Blands that had further embittered the last stages of the Wells campaign. For Wells had become entangled with the attractive Rosamund, and Bland had come the heavy father. Fabian gossip said that Bland had hauled Rosamund off the train at a London terminus when she was about to run away with Wells and had threatened HG with public exposure. There was no open scandal, 'but Wells felt that the fuss had blighted his career among the Fabians. "Damn the Blands," he wrote to Shaw.

There had always been a streak of bohemianism among the Fabians. Behind the Society's puritanism there were instances of homosexuality and lesbianism as well as free unions and transient affairs. Bland and other Fabians set up the Anti-Puritan League as a gesture against prudes and killjoys. But Wells was one of the few Fabians with the consistency and bravado to come out openly as a prophet of sexual liberation and to risk the criticism of the watchful purity movement. He consistently tried to get the Fabians to repudiate the bourgeois family and to support his scheme for endowed motherhood. Their failure to do so had, indeed, been the nominal cause of his resignation: "to leave the mother and child economically dependent upon the father is to me not socialism at all but a miserable perversion of socialism."[28]

In fact as well as in theory Wells found domestic responsibility suffocatingly restrictive, and he longed, like the hero of the new novel he was planning, to "throw everything to the winds"[29] for passion. His ideas were essentially a rationale for his emotional needs. He and Jane—who had been one of his students and with whom he had eloped after the failure of his first marriage, to his cousin Isabel—kept up conventional moral appearances, but they had privately struck a bargain in which they were released from emotional and sexual dependence. Jane was caught up in the new ideas and saw herself as one of the New Women. In 1908 she engaged a governess for her two sons, was elected to the Fabian executive, became active in the Women's Group, and did some short-story writing; it was all part of her own move to make an independent place for herself.

Family photographs at Sandgate in this period showed Wells and Jane surrounded by female admirers. Among them was the clever and rebellious Amber Reeves. In September 1908, just after Amber graduated with a double-first from Cambridge, Beatrice noted that "a somewhat dangerous friendship" was springing up. "If Amber were my child I should be anxious,"[30] she commented. They were considering what Beatrice afterwards called "the advantages to their respective development of a polygamous relationship." Wells, she thought, was trying to "lead a double life—on the one hand to be the respectable family man and famous litterateur to the world at large, and on the other, to be the Goethe-like libertine."[31]

The struggle with Wells between 1906 and 1908 was the last set piece in which all the Fabian Old Gang played leading roles. By 1908, with the onset of middle age, they were settling to their separate concerns and styles of life. Shaw noticed this change. Writing to William Stephen Sanders, who had become Pease's assistant, he suggested that the Society, like an individual, had passed through several phases of growth. The "revolutionary stage in which the patient breaks away from all his moorings, and sets up a vague but fierce revolt against every human institution from his father to the Prime Minister," he said, was "a stage in which he is no use even as an agitator." The socialist rebel became really effective only on "resuming his place as a member of society—no better and no worse than the rest, but with certain definite measures of reform to advocate."[32] The Old Gang, he implied, had reached that stage, and it was time the younger socialists learnt the lesson.

Settling down, however, meant that though the old friendships remained, they were decreasingly channelled through the common Fabian interest. Wallas, who had become a lecturer at the London School of Economics, was devoting himself to his pioneering work *Human Nature in Politics,* and he had dropped away from his Fabian connections after his resignation. Olivier, off in Jamaica, retained an intellectual interest in Fabian affairs, but he returned to London only for leave and brief official visits. Bland, whose health was not good, was having trouble with his eyesight; his energies went mainly into his journalism. The Webbs were absorbed in their Poor Law campaign, and Shaw was preoccupied with the theatre.

GBS had now settled down at Ayot St. Lawrence. His one complaint was that Charlotte, who had spent her youth moving from one place to another, was tiresomely restless and found it dull at Ayot. She badgered GBS to take holidays, arguing that he overworked and that he needed regular breaks to avoid the migraine attacks which were brought on by strain. In the summer of 1908 she took Shaw off on a long tour of Sweden and Germany, but he found the constant movement irritating.[33] "I am fed up with vagabondage," he wrote to Granville Barker, "and with the cat and dog life I lead with poor Charlotte, who takes every unguarded expression of my loathing for travelling as a personal insult to herself. Another month and it would end in divorce."[34] They had hired a car to make their tour through Germany, however, and he liked it so much that on their return he ordered a De Dietrich car and employed a chauffeur. In the spring of 1909, after writing *The Shewing Up of Blanco Posnet*, he adventurously went off with Charlotte and her sister to motor around Algeria. Once again the trials of travel upset him; burst tyres, flies, heat and dust were recurrent nuisances. But Shaw had become such an enthusiast that in August the car again went with them on a visit to Ireland. The downstart from Dublin returned in the style of the successful Edwardian man of letters.

On 19 May 1909 the Fabians gave a testimonial dinner and soirée for Sidney and Beatrice Webb. Two hundred members turned up to celebrate both the minority report and the second volume of the Webbs' massive history of local government, which had been published late in 1908. As a gesture to old friendships Graham Wallas took the chair. It was Beatrice that evening who in effect gave the Society new marching orders, declaring in her speech that she would be "no longer an appendage of the Old Gang" and that she "wanted to make a new start."[35] In her own way she had become as militant as the feminists who were then making life difficult for Asquith and the Liberals by demonstrations, clashes with the police, and hunger strikes which led to the scandal of forced feeding. The brutal treatment of Lady Constance Lytton, the sister of Beatrice's friend Betty Balfour, became a *cause célèbre* in the women's movement. Beatrice too had decided to become a campaigner, "to start on the war-path at the head of a contingent of young men and women."[36] She was refreshed after a long holiday which she and Sidney took in Italy, and she was now determined to push the minority report "without thought of ourselves or what people think of us and our work."

Beatrice undoubtedly saw this new campaign as an outlet for the enthusiasm of the younger Fabians, just as she needed their energies to get it launched. It was an issue which fitted precisely the Fabian pattern of education, organization and conversion, and it bypassed the recurrent demand of Fabian reformers for a new socialist party free of the compromises forced upon labour in Parliament. As a concession to this demand Shaw and Pease went down to the Labour Party conference in Southsea to urge more socialist policies, upon threat of Fabian withdrawal. The Society also set up a parliamentary fund, with Bland, Pease and Webb as its trustees, to sponsor Fabian candidates on the Labour ticket in suitable constituencies. Within a few weeks over £2,500 had been collected.

Beatrice proposed to divert this militant feeling behind a National Committee for the Break-up of the Poor Law, starting with "very little money and a good deal of zeal on a crusade against destitution."[37] Most of the work would be done by young idealists, to whom she would act as "moderator and councillor" and for whom the crusade would be a cause with "real comradeship." This movement, which she described as "a great social drainage scheme" to clear up the swamp of poverty, was also to be the culmination of the Webb partnership.[38] If they could "commit the country to a policy of complete communal responsibility," Beatrice felt, it would be "the best way to spend the remainder of our two little lives."[39]

For the first time the Webbs came out into the open, setting themselves up as public figures. They had always seen themselves as missionaries. Now at last they were in command of their own revivalist movement. Beatrice felt compelled to act, yet she was ambivalent about her reactions. She was nostalgic about "the quiet life of research and pleasant friendship, which we enjoyed before the Royal Commission came in to upset our lives." She disparaged the "curiously demoralising life" of the agitator, realizing that the acclaim gave her the thrill of feeling "admiration and willing obedience to my will."[40] Yet, at the same time, she was emotionally keyed up by the sense of leadership and overstimulated by the "raging, tearing propaganda" for the conversion of England. All the same, once the decision was made, she threw herself into the work with her usual dedication and thoroughness. Writing to her sister Georgiana from the summer school at Harlech in August 1909, she reported: "I practise voice production between 6:30 am and 8 am every morning on the beach—orating to the waves! . . . It is rather funny to start on a new profession after 50."[41]

The offices of the National Committee were just off the Strand, between the Fabian Society's premises and the London School of Economics—"a sort of middle-term between avowed socialism and nonpartisan research and administrative technique," said Beatrice. "The staff of the three organisations and the active spirits of their management are all the same persons," she added, noting that they all reflected the Webb philosophy of "a rapid but almost unconscious change in the *substance* of the structure of society."[42] From these offices Beatrice directed a campaign of meetings, conferences, summer schools, study circles and propaganda leaflets which within a few months had recruited over sixteen thousand members and had set up branches across the country. Its energies came largely from young people. Rupert Brooke, pedalling around the Cambridgeshire villages with his campaign literature, collected the litany of names for his famous poem on Grantchester, and many aspiring politicians on the left served their apprenticeship in the campaign.

To promote its propaganda, the National Committee founded its own journal, *The Crusade*, edited by the young Fabian Clifford Sharp. He was well suited to run such a campaign, as he came from a deeply religious family which had supported the evangelism of Sankey and Moody. An imposing list of sponsors was collected. Apart from economists, prominent clergy, trade unionists and a scattering of Liberal, Tory and Labour MP's, it was endorsed by such literary figures as G. K. Chesterton, John Masefield and Gilbert Murray, and by Forbes-Robertson, Beerbohm Tree and Harley Granville Barker from the theatre. Beatrice, indeed, tried to find a dramatist willing to put the Poor Law onto the stage, and in May 1909 she wrote unavailingly to John Galsworthy, Masefield and Barker, inviting them to turn out plays for her campaign. Her only success was to promote a playlet called *Our Little Fancies*, which had a fleeting production at Manchester. According to *Fabian News* in July 1911, it was "not didactic" but did answer the question "Given good management, what is wrong with the General Mixed Workhouse?"

The Webbs had found it possible to do for their own purposes what they had rejected as impossibly ambitious when Wells had proposed a similar effort for the Fabians. Wells had claimed that the time was ripe for a campaign on this scale among the middle classes and that the resources could be found to support it. The Webbs had hit on an issue which could win wide support; an attack on destitution was specific, emotionally charged and nonpartisan politically. They were in fact articulating the latent middle-class and intellectual desire for a programme of social reform. The pent-up demand among Fabians for a new party was released into an agitation intended to create a new political climate.

The Webbs, however, had not thought through the implications of their decision to launch a mass movement for the conversion of England.

They had rushed into public controversy without realizing that this was a very different game from the politics of permeation and manipulation with which they were familiar. Churchill saw what had happened. "You should leave the work of converting the country to us, Mrs Webb," he told Beatrice in October 1909; "you ought to convert the Cabinet." That would be sufficient, Beatrice replied, if the Webbs merely sought a change in the Poor Law structure, "but we want to *really change* the mind of the country."[43]

There was no doubt that the Webbs were caught in a dilemma. They would have preferred to push their scheme in the old style of salon politics. "If we were quite certain that our proposals would be accepted if we withdrew ourselves," Beatrice remarked at one point, "we would retire at once for good and all." But they had become progressively estranged from their influential contacts.

They were not deterred. They took little interest in the election early in 1910, when the Liberals came back with a reduced but still substantial majority, or in the important drama of the Liberal struggle to curb the House of Lords. They soldiered on. In February 1910 Sidney left the London County Council, to which he had given so many years of devoted service, and all his energies now went into the campaign. Both he and Beatrice travelled tirelessly, "converting the country to the *philosophy* of our scheme." Since there was no chance of insinuating their plan into party politics, at least in the short run, they were shifting their ground, consoling themselves for the loss of immediate influence with the thought that they were preparing the way for a new phase of public life. Beatrice compared their campaign to the Progressive victory in London at the end of the Eighties which had heralded twenty years of municipal reform. They were establishing, she wrote, "the new principle of a National Minimum and the joint responsibility of the individual and the community for a given standard of individual life."[44] This approach, Beatrice told Betty Balfour, offered the chance of creating a new movement which would have a "strictly limited character," uniting experts and idealists in "a Common Social Faith." The trouble with "Socialism & even Fabianism" was that they were "far too vague and far too theoretical and comprehensive a basis to attract persons of sufficient intellect & character & practical experience."[45] The vision of a socialist, she explained late in 1910, could stand as a long-term aim, but in the meanwhile something had to be done "with the millions of destitute persons which constitute an infamous & wholly unnecessary accompaniment to an Individualist State."[46]

There was no loss of momentum. The revivalist spirit had taken hold of their followers. Early in 1910 the campaign had eleven paid employees, four hundred lecturers on call, and a large membership. But by May Beatrice was beginning to wonder where this evangelizing impulse would lead. "Having discovered in myself the faculty of the preacher and the teacher," she wondered, "shall I be able to withdraw to the life of research?"[47] There was a partial but disquieting answer to that question in July when the Webbs went off to Switzerland for a month's holiday and discovered that things went awry in their absence. Paternalistic rather than democratic, they could not find a way to convert the campaign into a stable, self-sufficient movement. In the middle of 1910 Beatrice was noting that the local branches were unstable and that it was largely the drive and reputation of the Webbs that was keeping the movement going. "We may never be quit of leadership again," she remarked anxiously.[48] They had become the captives of their own success.

Things would have been simpler if they could have swung their supporters behind a political party. But any attempt to give the campaign an overtly socialist bias would have driven off much of their nonpartisan support. Beatrice had already attributed Tory and Liberal hostility to "an active fear of Socialism." And though the campaign was essentially Fabian in character it drained energies and resources away from the Fabian Society. Pease was driven to complain that the Webbs had diverted the younger and more active Fabians to provide their cadre of energetic volunteers, and that the other work of the Society was suffering from the distraction of effort. The Shaws too were critical. They felt, Sidney reported to Beatrice, that the Fabian Society had been "a little left behind by the National Committee & that a new departure must be found for it."[49]

This fact was brought home to Beatrice at the Fabian summer school in 1910. The first two weeks were devoted to a meeting of the Poor Law campaign workers, which she described as an unqualified success. There followed a conference of university Fabians. One of them was Rupert Brooke, who wrote to a friend, "I was acting on my Conscience in going there. . . . And acting on one's Conscience is always rather fun."[50] For Beatrice the conference turned out to be an "absurd failure," and it upset her. She castigated the frivolity and egotism of the young university men for preferring "boisterous, larky entertainments" to the "*technical* and *specialised* discussion which will attract a better type."[51] It was just this intellectual priggishness that many people found so distasteful. Despite his enthusiasm, Rupert Brooke remarked in August 1908, "Oh, the Fabians, I would to God they'd laugh & be charitable."

When Wells had wanted to turn the Fabian Society inside out by launching a huge national campaign Shaw and Webb had protested that his plan would decisively change the Society's character, swamping its committed members with excited recruits who preferred immediate results to the long haul of education and research. By their determination to impose their own remedy for destitution the Webbs had created the situation they had feared when Wells was demanding action. Wells did, indeed, recognize his own ideas in the campaign. In February 1909 he told Beatrice that the minority report was "quite after my own heart," and he lent his name to the National Committee.[52]

By the summer of 1909 it was personal rather than political differences that divided Wells from the Fabian Old Gang, for he was now in the midst of an acute emotional crisis. Amber Reeves was pregnant and she and Wells had run away to Le Touquet. The elopement was impulsive and unsatisfactory. Wells was miserable in temporary exile, and before long he and Amber returned to England. Amber tried to resolve the situation by marrying, in July, Rivers Blanco-White, a young lawyer and a fellow member of the Fabian Nursery who had previously proposed to her and now, aware of the new circumstances, repeated his offer. But she and Wells could not so easily abandon each other. HG sold his house at Sandgate and bought a home for Jane and their two sons in Hampstead, installing Amber in a cottage at Woldingham in Surrey, where he continued to visit her while she awaited the birth of the baby at the end of the year.

This was the situation when the Webbs came to hear of it. Maud Reeves was beside herself with grief; Pember Reeves was wild with rage, exacerbated by what Beatrice called "an impudent letter" from Wells claiming that Maud had condoned his intimacy with Amber. There was soon a buzz of gossip running through the Fabians. W. A. Colegate, who was the personal secretary of the Webbs, talked indiscreetly and resurrected the earlier scandal about Rosamund Bland. Beatrice grew alarmed and took it upon herself to warn Olivier, over from Jamaica on leave, to keep his daughters away from Wells. This infuriated HG, who complained bitterly to Beatrice on 11 September that she and Sidney were defaming him: "You know best how far my name will be worth anything after you have finished this campaign against me." He threatened that unless it was called off he would provoke "a public smash to clear up this untraceable soaking nastiness about us."[53]

Beatrice was anxious to avoid public trouble. She had, she told Amber frankly on 11 September, "a quite genuine desire to see H.G.W. saved from a big smash."[54] She had already urged Colegate to hold his tongue. Shaw, still in Ireland with Charlotte, was playing his usual role of go-between. He had heard about the scandal from Maud Reeves and he had written an understanding letter to Wells. At the same time, in a long and levelheaded letter to Beatrice he suggested that the affair be treated simply as "a questionable social experiment," arguing that there was no point in striking moral attitudes or even trying to sort out the rights and wrongs of the case. The immediate need was to damp down the gossip: "The consequences of a blow-up are far too serious to be faced if we can possibly avert them." Asking Beatrice "to prevent Reeves from advertising the affair by betraying his feelings about it," he suggested that Wells would eventually back down under pressure and that Amber's bravado would collapse.[55]

Beatrice, who was genuinely fond of Amber as well as a close friend of the Reeves family, had been trying to persuade Amber to choose "between a happy marriage and continuing friendship with H. G. Wells." She promised to "shut people up as quickly and conclusively as I can,"[56] but when she visited Amber she could not persuade her to give up Wells.[57] All through the autumn Amber and Wells clung on, though the pressure on them was increasing. Pember Reeves was rampaging against "the blackguard Wells and his paramour," and the story was running around the clubs and dinner parties. The fuss was no longer private. In October 1909 *Ann Veronica* was published, and this novel provoked a fresh attack on Wells as an immoral writer, some of his critics being quite aware that it was a thinly disguised account of his personal life. The most ferocious onslaught came from St. Loe Strachey's *Spectator*, which denounced the "pernicious teaching" of this "poisonous book" and described "the muddy world of Mr Wells' imaginings" as "a community of scuffling stoats and ferrets, unenlightened by a ray of duty or abnegation."[58]

Wells was in serious trouble. People had begun to ostracize him.

He resigned from the Savile Club, which had "turned into a barroom of rant & lies about me," he wrote to his friend and lawyer E. S. P. Haynes.[59] At the moment when his popular influence was at its peak and his books were selling excellently, his attempt to practise the freedom he preached was bringing him close to ruin. By the end of 1909 he was forced to yield and give an undertaking that he would stay away from Amber and give her marriage a chance. Amber's daughter was born on New Year's Eve 1909. There was still a risk, as Beatrice noted early in 1910, that Wells and Jane would be "permanently dropped"—Jane, in fact, was asked to resign from the Fabian executive—but it was not so easy to crush the ebullient and unrepentant Wells. Two years afterwards he was claiming that the attempt of "a group of eminent and influential persons . . . to obliterate" him had failed, that his books were more popular than ever, and that he had "become a symbol against the authoritative, the dull, the presumptuously established, against all that is hateful and hostile to youth and to-morrow."[60]

Wells had, however, left a trail of wreckage behind him, and in his final parting with the Fabians there was a flick of revenge. The story of his erratic flight through Fabian politics was told again in *The New Machiavelli*, which lampooned Beatrice and Sidney as the characters Altiora and Oscar Bailey and also retailed the affair with Amber in a form so thinly concealed that Macmillan, his publisher, refused to handle the book. Beatrice thought the novel "really very clever in a malicious sort of way," though it revealed the personal tragedy of Wells—"his aptitude for 'fine thinking' and even 'good feeling,' and yet his total incapacity for decent conduct." She attributed his animus to a sense of guilt at the "baseness" of his deception of the Reeves family and his other Fabian friends, but she thought the book such "a pretty bit of work" that it would "probably enable him to struggle back into distinguished society. . . . I shall take no steps to prevent this," she added, "so long as no one expects us to meet him on terms of friendship."[61]

How had the whole sad business come about? Beatrice felt it demonstrated that "we none of us know what exactly is the sexual code we believe in—approving of many things on paper which we violently object to when they are practised by those we care about."[62] This ambivalence between the bohemian and the conventional was not merely a matter of sexual morality, though recent events had made Beatrice see it in that context. The same ambivalence made the Fabians individualist in private and collectivist in public, rebels demanding freedom from bourgeois constraints and regulators whose new order would impose restraints on others. Ellen Terry had spotted this trait in Shaw as early as 1906. "Aren't you funny," she wrote to GBS, "preaching against marriage, and marrying? Against other things, and doing 'em."[63]

GBS continued to express that dichotomy in his work and his life. In October 1910 he was again berating Erica Cotterill because she did not appreciate "what loyalty men and women owe to one another in that very delicate and difficult relation" of marriage, but in his plays he was still exploring what Beatrice called "anarchic love making." While he was in Ireland he had started to write *Misalliance*, and when it was finished at the end of November he read it to the Webbs. "It is amazingly brilliant," Beatrice decided, "but the whole 'motive' is erotic—everyone wishing to have sexual intercourse with everyone else—though the proposals are 'matrimonial' for the most part."[64] When it was put on for eleven performances at the Duke of York's Theatre in February 1910 she decided that it was "disgusting," comparing it unfavourably with Galsworthy's sobering attack on the legal system in *Justice*. Shaw maintained that his play was merely a frolic, but the critics took it seriously and hammered it. *The Times* called it "the debating society of a lunatic asylum—without a motion and without a chairman . . . it is madness." It had a wildly improbable plot, with everyone talking hysterically about love; in fact no one was capable of love, the children rejecting their parents as futile, the parents regarding their children as a punishment for their sins, and all the possible couplings being evident misalliances. It was a prime example of what Henry James had called Shaw's "luxurious perversity."

If the play was perverse, so was Edwardian society. GBS had put on the stage a domestic paradigm for a social system that was visibly breaking up as Edward's reign came to an end. The King died on 6 May 1910, with the country in a combative mood. George V succeeded in the middle of a constitutional crisis, having to face the Liberal demand for the creation of enough peers to swamp the recalcitrant diehards who proposed to fight a last-ditch for the power of the Lords. The trade unions were gripped by a mood of militancy unmatched since the struggle of the early Nineties, and great strikes were looming. The suffragette

movement, drifting towards direct action, converted the sexual repressions of the Victorian age into political rebellion. The Irish question was
lurching towards another confrontation between Unionists and Home
Rulers. Public life had become a mêlée of wills in which all values were
subordinated to conflicting ambitions and ideals.

·· 24 ··
HEARTBREAK
HOUSE

In the middle of June 1911 the Webbs left Liverpool for Quebec on a long-planned journey round the world. They had worked unsparingly to complete their commitments before leaving, and they were tired and also somewhat dispirited. "In spite of all our work," Beatrice admitted, "the National Committee does not seem to be gaining many new members and our friends are beginning to melt away."[1]

Lloyd George was winning his political battles, and the Webbs were losing theirs. Speaking at over eighty meetings in the last months of 1910, the Webbs could still arouse enthusiasm by their attacks on the Poor Law, but their supporters were really demonstrating against destitution, not for the Webb plan. It was hard for audiences to understand why the Webbs thought that Lloyd George was wrong in proposing cash payments to relieve poverty and that they were right in seeking to abolish it by a complicated exercise in "administrative science." At the end of 1910 Beatrice ruefully conceded: "Lloyd George and Winston Churchill have practically taken the *limelight*."[2] Lloyd George's attacks on wealth in his budgets, and his simple slogan "Ninepence for fourpence," which summarized the system of contributory social insurance, caught the public's imagination. It was all very well for Beatrice to insist that his schemes were "badly contrived, owing to his ignorance and hastiness," and that

he was putting them forward "as a way of one class despoiling & humiliating another class" rather than "as a fulfillment of a great national obligation";[3] the fact remained that he had the political power to implement
his reforms and that the Webbs led nothing more than an articulate pressure group. Beatrice might console herself with the thought that they
had "practically converted England to the obligation of preventing
destitution,"[4] but in terms of practical politics they had, as John Burns
gleefully remarked, been "dished" by Lloyd George. It was clear that
they were leaving Clifford Sharp and his colleagues of the National Committee to fight a forlorn rearguard action against Lloyd George as his
Insurance bill was pushed through Parliament.

The Webbs were also worried about Sidney's position at the London School of Economics, where he was under attack for preferring
"agitation to science," as *The Times* put it in accusing him and Beatrice
of letting "their political passion" run away with them. In a case known
as the Osborne Judgment the House of Lords had swept away the financial base of the Labour Party by ruling that trade unions could not use
their general funds to pay election expenses and to provide salaries for
members elected to Parliament, where MP's were still unpaid. In an address to the Amalgamated Society of Railway Servants on 17 September
1910 Sidney mildly criticized the decision. The School of Economics for
some years had received special grants from railway companies to support studies in transport economics. It was suddenly confronted by the
resignation of four governors who represented the railway interest and
a request for Sidney's resignation as chairman on pain of the School being
denounced as a centre of socialist propaganda. Since the chief critic was
Lord Claud Hamilton, the brother of the chairman of the Poor Law
Commission, and since *The Times* had linked Beatrice into its complaint,
the Webbs concluded that this was yet another sign that "the hostility
to us will grow."[5] If, Beatrice decided when the row had blown over,
"we are to continue an agitation on a great scale as at present, we shall
have to drop into the background in the School's life."[6]

The life style of the Webbs had changed with their entry into political agitation. The days of fascinating dinner parties were over, and
the Webbs had fallen away from their old social circle. The link with the
Balfour family was almost the only one of their old contacts with the
political *haut-monde* that had survived the stresses of their new life.
"Their lives are so rounded off by culture and charm, comfort and

power," Beatrice remarked of Haldane and the other Liberal leaders, "that the misery of the destitute is as far off as the savagery of Central Africa."[7] The Webbs fell back on their young lieutenants for companionship and admiration. They may have been losing their impact on politicians, but they were still extremely influential with young intellectuals from Oxford and Cambridge. To students the Webbs looked quite different from the impression they now made on their contemporaries. They listened to the problems of the young and helped them with their careers. At Christmas 1910, when Gerald and Betty Balfour lent the Webbs their house at Fisher's Hill, Woking, they took with them a group of young friends—Clifford Sharp and his wife (he was now married to Rosamund Bland), W. A. Colegate, Mostyn Lloyd, a young social worker and Fabian active in the campaign, Rivers Blanco-White and Amber, who, Beatrice noted, had settled down with her husband and apparently made up her mind to play straight.

In the aftermath of the Wells row the Fabian Society had been left to drift along without any real leadership and without much concern with the exciting issues of the day. Shaw complained to the Webbs in March 1911 that "apart from pure routine" there had been "absolutely no *raison d'être* for the Society" of late.[8] Even the scheme for running socialist candidates soon languished. In March 1910 Hubert Bland complained to Webb that one procrastination followed another, and that the members were "fed up with defeat. . . . The Fabian policy of delay is to delay the enemy but not to delay yourself."[9] The Society was going through a crisis not of dissent but of indifference.

Bland alone of the older Fabians seemed aware that the Society was losing touch with "the socialism of the Basis" and worried that it was becoming simply a tail to the Webb kite. The obsession with welfare problems, he told Shaw in October 1910, had "sidetracked" the Fabians. "If everything we have been proposing were carried out tomorrow we should be no nearer . . . to Socialism or to anything worth fighting for than we are today. . . . Consider all this ferment and unrest in the labour world just now. The Society does not think about it, much less say anything about it."[10] A year later, Bland took Pease through a similar analysis of the way in which the Fabians had progressively watered down their socialism in the quest for palliatives. The campaign for Bea-

trice's minority report had been the last straw. Such issues should be left
"to the large crowd of people whose sympathies we have enlisted," while
Fabians should start working again for socialism.[11] In what proved to be
his valedictory address to the Society, at the Memorial Hall on 5 July
1912, Bland repeated this argument, saying that the success of "Lloyd
Georgism" had set the Fabians free to pursue their "proper business,"
which was not to mitigate poverty but to secure "the extinction of private property."[12]

New blood and new policies were clearly needed. Early in 1911,
Shaw announced that the day of the Old Gang was over and that control of the Society should be handed over to younger people. Bland, in
any case, was resigning from the executive for reasons of health. Sidney
Webb was going abroad for a year. Granville Barker, Stewart Headlam
and Ensor were also ready to quit, and Shaw proposed to go with them.
To avoid "the smash-up which might be effected by the retirement of
the entire Old Gang from the management of the Society," he proposed
to create a "sort of House of Lords" whose members would have the
right to attend the executive meetings but not to vote.[13] His resort to
this cumbersome device revealed the dilemma of the old leadership,
which was able neither to get on with Fabian matters nor to get out of
them. The members were equally ambivalent, wishing to hold on to the
Society's prestigious founders and yet irritated by the way they kept the
Society in leading strings.[14] Every three or four years, it seemed, the Fabian Society had to cope with a protest movement. Clifford Sharp said of
one of the young Cambridge enthusiasts, Ben Keeling, that he tried to
combine a revolutionary spirit with evolutionary methods. That kind of
paradox was endemic among the Fabians.

The smouldering discontent in the Society broke out again in the
autumn of 1911 with the formation of a Reform Committee supported
by many of the young people who had served their apprenticeship in
the Fabian Nursery. Its angry manifesto amounted to little more than a
renewed demand to join with the ILP in making the Labour Party something other than "an expression of working-class discontent." It attacked
permeation as putting the middle-class socialist in the position vis-à-vis
the Labour Party of "lecturing it from above."[15]

The demand for Fabians to play a more significant role in the Labour Party was a sign that times had changed. Before 1910 Fabian rebels
had shown little interest in the Labour Party, to which the Society was

nominally affiliated. Now the Labour Party could no longer be ignored as a political force. It had come back stronger from the two elections in 1910, and the weakened Asquith government needed its support in the House of Commons. In exchange for Labour votes Asquith was prepared to offer concessions, such as salaries for MP's, to offset the trouble caused by the Osborne Judgment, some reforms in trade-union law, and the Lloyd George social-insurance schemes. All these proposals were attractive to the moderate trade unionists who dominated the Labour Party in Parliament, and under MacDonald's leadership the party seemed to be little more than an appendage of the Liberals. Such tactics seemed over-cautious and compromising to socialists. The ILP seethed with frustration. Its members felt that they were shackled to a parliamentary machine controlled by men whose primary loyalty was to the trade unions, not to the socialist cause.

There was, moreover, growing dissatisfaction with parliamentary methods among the trade unions themselves. Direct action fitted the current mood of confrontation, and it was stimulated by a fall in real wages which produced the great strikes of 1910 and 1911. The dockers, the railwaymen and the miners came out successively in bitterly fought disputes, and the prospect of an apocalyptic class struggle was raised by the formation of the "Triple Alliance" binding these unions to concert their future demands. There was rioting in Liverpool, with troops called out and cruisers sent to the Mersey. "It made me feel," Betty Balfour wrote anxiously to Beatrice Webb in Japan, that "the French Revolution had come upon us again."[16]

This unrest was given a new turn by the theory of syndicalism imported from France. Syndicalists believed that the unions should develop the strike as a political weapon for social change, aiming ultimately at a revolutionary general strike. They also broke with the classical socialist ideas of public ownership and bureaucratic collectivism so long advocated by the Fabians. The syndicalist society of the future was to be based upon associations of producers, who would abolish wage slavery without thereby putting the exploiting state in the place of the exploiting capitalist.

This reaction against political socialism was not confined to militant trade unionists. Cecil and G. K. Chesterton, with Hilaire Belloc, had swung away from the Fabians to a neo-mediaevalist "distributivist" theory, attacking Fabianism as the road to the servile state. Belloc, for instance, wrote an article in the *New Age* condemning the Webbs' proposals for eliminating poverty as an expression of their "inhuman interest in figures without vitality" and of their "itch to manage the affairs of others" by organizing "the poor into a flock of sheep."[17] The Chestertons and Belloc soon set up their own shop in the *New Witness*.

While Alfred Orage did not agree with the Catholic romanticism of what Shaw christened the "Chesterbelloc," he too had abandoned the Fabians; and early in 1909 Sam Hobson decided that twenty years of Fabianism was enough. Always an unruly and barely reputable member of the executive, Hobson made a last attempt in January 1909 to persuade the Society to cut its ties with the Labour Party and launch a truly socialist party. Orage supported him in the *New Age*, claiming that the Labour Party would always "remain indifferent to the squeals of the impotent Fabian" and that he was tired of an organization in which everything depended upon "the acuteness of Mr. Shaw's last headache, or the weaving of the latest political Webb." The *New Age* thereupon began to cast around for a new platform. Orage had been a close friend of the architect A. J. Penty, who had published a book in 1907 called *The Restoration of the Guild System* in which he harked back, like William Morris, to a fantasy of a mediaeval England, in which the craftsman found fulfilment in creative work and the economy was controlled by self-regulating guilds. He was therefore sympathetic when Sam Hobson began to fuse this vision with the currently fashionable syndicalism, suggesting that the unions could be made into a modern counterpart of the guilds.

Guild socialism offered a different challenge to the Fabians. For more than twenty years the Society had rested on the fundamental assumption that socialism would slowly come by the extension of state and municipal enterprise—what Sidney Webb later summarized in his famous phrase about "the inevitability of gradualness." There had never been any doctrinal orthodoxy in the Society, but this collectivist brand of socialism had been tacitly accepted, differences arising more over the means to implement it. Now this new romantic vision of a society built around productive labour caught the imagination of young socialists, focussing particularly around a group of Oxford graduates. The Cambridge group had largely veered off to interest themselves in the philosophy of G. E. Moore, who had just published one of his influential books on ethics. Lytton Strachey described the remarkable scene when he and Rupert Brooke "tried to explain Moore's ideas to Mrs Webb while she tried to convince us of the efficacy of prayer."[18]

One of the leaders of the group from Oxford was G. D. H. Cole,[19] a clever but hot-tempered young man, born in 1889, who had been converted to socialism while still a schoolboy at St. Paul's by reading William Morris's *News from Nowhere* and had joined the ILP before he went up to Balliol in 1908. By the time he graduated he was already at work on the first of his many books, *The World of Labour*, in which he eulogized the unions as the revolutionary force which would transform society. He was soon drawn into the Poor Law campaign and attracted the attention of the Webbs as a promising recruit. Beatrice thought him "the ablest newcomer since H. G. Wells."[20] Cole and friends like William Mellor moved into the Fabian Society because it was intellectually prestigious and its blend of bohemianism and spiritual earnestness was temperamentally appealing. But these Oxford men were avowed revolutionaries, impatient and out of sympathy with bureaucratic state socialism and with the Labour Party. They were openly defiant of their respectable elders, singing political doggerel and flaunting red ties. They made no secret of their intention to use the Fabians as a base for their new faith. Their aim was not an amelioration of the lot of the labouring classes but their emancipation from the "slavery" of wage labour.

The Webbs went away from England at a critical time and they were effectively out of touch for almost a year, returning home in April 1912. It was an expedition which they had carefully planned and eagerly anticipated. In the event it was something of an anticlimax. They hovered uneasily between tourism and social investigation and seemed unable either to relax or to work effectively. Once again they behaved like itinerant government inspectors, as if the habit of collecting facts and making judgments had become an end in itself. They visited factories, hospitals, prisons and nurseries; Sidney interrogated a Japanese prostitute —paying appropriately for her time—about her earnings and hours of work. They docketed, catalogued, praised and criticized, approving of the cleanliness of Japan and the idealism of its people, objecting to the squalor of China and to the Chinese "lack of capacity for the scientific method."[21] They escaped from Peking, in the throes of the 1911 revolution, with the help of an English railway guard who was a member of the ILP and who, recognizing Sidney from a picture in the *Labour Leader*, hauled them through the window of the goods van on the last train to leave for Tientsin. India upset Beatrice, who took a poor view of the British officials and a poorer one of their policies; she was both disgusted and fascinated by Hinduism and left feeling that she was "converted to the Nationalist position."[22] So much travel had worn her out, and before they reached Egypt she was in a state of chronic anxiety and fidgeting to be about her own more familiar business once more.

Before the Webbs left England they had been uncertain where to turn politically; their absence intensified their isolation. Things were not going well for the National Committee. In the autumn of 1911 there had been a falling demand for its lecturers, the branches were mostly moribund and there was not enough work for the staff. Many of the volunteers, Sharp told Beatrice, "after two years of envelope addressing are anxious for other work."[23] Pease was complaining again about the way that the Webbs had poached Fabian resources for the campaign. Sharp was wondering what to do next. It was clear that by the time the Webbs returned Lloyd George would have put his Insurance bill through Parliament; despite the opposition of Lansbury and the bulk of the ILP and the Fabians, who had joined in a last-ditch resistance, the Labour Party had decided to back it. Sharp advised, "We shall gain nothing by continuing a hostile *tone*," and asked Beatrice to consider how the fund of helpers attracted by the Poor Law campaign might be shifted to tackling such social problems as sweated labour, factory conditions, working hours and housing. "I can't believe that it would be very difficult to get most of the Labour Party to look to *you* instead of Lloyd George for their gospel," Sharp concluded.[24] But Beatrice was reluctant to become embroiled with the Labour Party. She told Sharp that MacDonald was so securely entrenched and so antagonistic to the Webbs that it might be better for them to stay out of Labour affairs altogether.

For two months after their return Beatrice struggled with "waves of depression and panic." To get abreast of things she went to the Trades Union Congress in September, but her reaction was sour: "The bulk of the delegates are the same solid stupid folk they have always been," though the "extreme left" of twenty years before, the state socialists, were "now on the defensive against the new left," the syndicalists.[25] "Syndicalism has taken the place of the old-fashioned Marxism. The angry youth, with bad complexion, frowning brow and weedy figure, is now always a Syndicalist"; so, too, were "the glib workman whose tongue runs away with him" and the "inexperienced middle-class ideal-ist" who "accepted with avidity the ideal of the Syndicalist as a new and exciting Utopia."[26] She was equally critical of the Labour Party, which she thought was "drifting into futility. . . . J. R. MacDonald has ceased to be a socialist, the trade union M.P.s never were socialist." They were all cynics except Lansbury; her old ally from the Commission had be-come "a raging revivalist preacher of general upheaval" and had quixoti-cally resigned his seat to fight a hopeless bye-election on the principle of woman suffrage.[27] He was defeated by seven hundred votes. Sending condolences, Beatrice told him of her "depression about the future of the Labour and Socialist movement." She informed Lansbury, "I have joined the ILP," and begged him not to "leave it just as I am coming in."[28]

After so many years in which the Webbs had opposed or ignored the ILP and deprecated its evangelistic rhetoric, they had come to feel that after all they had much in common with it—a feeling partly engen-dered by the conversion of the Webbs themselves to public agitation and partly by their increasing reliance on young men and women who wanted socialism rather than reform. The Webbs, in any case, had few other possible allies left. They had broken with their Liberal and Tory friends, and their antagonism to MacDonald made it hard for them to see any useful role for themselves in the Labour Party. The purism of the ILP suited their mood.

Sometime in 1912 Beatrice decided to make herself the effective head of the Fabians. During her absence she had been elected for the first time to the executive, running a few votes behind Sidney at the top of the poll. After her return she began to assert herself and to impose her style on the Society's organization and its work. On 2 September 1912 she wrote to Pease to say that she agreed with the younger mem-bers who felt that the Fabian tracts had been concerned too much with reforms under the existing capitalist system. This work, she suggested, was "practically exhausted": there was "great lack of clearness of thought [in the Society] with regard to the ultimate aims of Socialism."[29]

Her first move was to wind up the remains of the National Com-mittee. Next, she and Sidney had plans for a joint campaign with the ILP for their new policy of the "national minimum." And to underpin this work Beatrice decided that the Fabians should make a new start on research. In a circular sent out at the end of October 1912 she called for subscriptions to support two Fabian committees to draft new policies. "I cannot help feeling," she wrote, "that the present extraordinary 'unrest' in the Labour World, and the growing consciousness among the middle-class that 'all is not well' make a call upon us for redoubled activity, alike in investigation and propaganda."[30] One committee, on rural problems, was led by a wealthy Fabian, Henry Harben, who was the largest shareholder in the Prudential Insurance Company and backed both George Lansbury's rebellious *Daily Herald* and Christabel Pankhurst's militant suffragette campaign. The other, on the control of industry, took over the keen young research staff of the Poor Law movement. It soon became the Fabian Research Department, housed in the old offices of the National Committee at Norfolk Street and effectively run by G. D. H. Cole and William Mellor.

Pease, who had already objected to the way the Webbs had directed Fabian resources, was unsympathetic to Beatrice's independent posture, but he could do nothing to stop her bid for control. He had served the Society as a loyal steward through all the vicissitudes of the Fabian years; now he was played out. Beatrice regarded him as untrustworthy politically: he was friendly with MacDonald and content with the pragmatic methods of the Labour Party. From her point of view it was fortunate that at this time Pease inherited £28,000 from his uncle Joseph Fry, for it made his retirement possible. He was persuaded to relinquish the secretaryship to William Sanders, a forty-year-old protégé of Stanton Coit who had moved out of the ethical movement to become assistant to John Burns in Battersea and then gone into the Fabian office as Pease's assistant. Pease formally handed over at the end of 1913, thirty years after the Society was founded in his rooms. To mark the occasion there was a formal dinner in May 1914, when Shaw presented a set of the *Encyclopaedia Britannica* as a farewell gift.

The Webbs also decided to close down *The Crusade* and to replace it by a new political weekly, again to be edited by Clifford Sharp. They had made up their minds about this while they were away, and as soon as they were back they started to raise funds and to recruit contributors and subscribers. They turned first to Shaw, but he was cool about the idea. On 10 July 1912 he told them: "My fear in the matter is that we are too old. . . . Unless you can find a team of young lions (coaching them to some extent at a weekly lunch or dinner) and give them their heads, the job cannot be done."[31] Reluctantly prepared to put up some capital, Shaw was not keen to take any editorial share in what Beatrice admitted was "a mad adventure," but he finally gave a thousand pounds; so did three other well-to-do Fabians, Henry Harben, Ernest Simon and Edward Whitley. Another thousand was made up of smaller shares.[32]

By December 1912 Sharp was formally appointed to edit what, on Balfour's suggestion, was to be called *The Statesman*, only to be renamed *The New Statesman* on its second issue to avoid confusion with the well-known Calcutta newspaper. To get the two thousand postal subscribers essential to float the paper, circulars were sent off to all supporters of the Poor Law campaign and members of the Fabian Society. Personal letters also went out from Beatrice, Sidney and—to people in the theatrical world—from Shaw. The response was gratifying, dispelling criticism by journalists such as the former Fabian H. W. Massingham, then editing the similar *Nation*, who thought the paper would be "the Webbs flavoured with a little Shaw and padded with the contributions of a few cleverish but ignorant young men."[33]

The Webbs chose their staff well. Sharp, a priggish man with tendencies to drinking and womanizing which were to be his eventual undoing, was nonetheless an effective editor who had served his apprenticeship profitably on *The Crusade*. So had Julius West, who became the company secretary. As literary editor Sharp chose Jack Squire, from the *New Age;* Desmond McCarthy took on the dramatic criticism; and a Fabian stockbroker named Emil Davies started a City column. The main difficulty was with Bernard Shaw. The Webbs had counted on his reputation to attract readers and on his journalistic skills to hold them. He agreed to write but refused to sign his articles. For the first three years he and Sharp battled over everything from politics to punctuation, until their temperamental incompatibility ended in a row and Shaw's resignation in October 1916 as a director. GBS wanted to make the journal a spokesman for all the voices of revolt, as Orage had done so effectively for a time with the *New Age*. Sharp and the Webbs were determined to create an intellectual weekly which would exemplify the old Fabian tradition of research, education and discussion. Within two years they had shown that they could succeed, for with modest annual subsidies *The New Statesman* survived to make a serious name for itself. Once again, Sidney took over the daily chores of guiding the partnership's new offspring through its infancy.

Relations between the Webbs and the Shaws had been strained before the attempt to make Shaw an active partner in *The New Statesman*. In the spring of 1911, when the Webbs spent a day at Ayot to say goodbye before their trip, Beatrice had noted that GBS was getting both restless and depressed. He annoyed Sidney because he kept talking about the sex question, "which does not interest Sidney as GBS has nothing positive to propose." She thought it sad that such old friends should come to the point where "there does not seem much reason for meeting—and therefore we seldom meet, and when we do the conversation tends to be made up and not spontaneous."[34]

Shaw had run into a bad phase of middle life. His headaches troubled him; he was perverse and irritable with Charlotte, feeling bored when they were at home and finding her company oppressive when they travelled. He seemed to be hankering for some stimulus to reassure him that he was not as old and domesticated as he felt and that he could still do good work as a writer. As early as October 1909 he had told Vedrenne, "My bolt is shot as a playwright,"[35] and his despondency about the theatre was intensified when Barker—whose partnership with Vedrenne finally petered out in March 1911—confessed that he too could see little future for himself as actor, producer or author. Lillah McCarthy was also looking for a fresh experience. She had already been thinking of going into management on her own account and she asked Shaw for a new play. "Get a theatre and the money and the play will be there," he replied, and then he himself put up some of the cash with which she took the Little Theatre in John Street to present *Fanny's First Play* in April 1911.[36] It was a cheeky satire on the critics who had lately given him a hard time. This time they were kinder: the play had a rapturous reception. "The Court Theatre has come back to us with all the magic and laughter," one of them wrote; and Shaw was so pleased by its good reception and so in need of the reassurance of success that for the first time he let a play run itself to death in the usual commercial manner. It lasted for 624 performances.

For years Shaw had written a series of curiously ambivalent works in which the badinage of drawing-room comedy was used to carry his personal doctrine, but the preacher was always struggling with the artist. Dissatisfied with the play as a vehicle for this purpose, he increasingly felt obliged to spell out his philosophy in the long prefaces which came to serve as its canonical books. He claimed that *Androcles and the Lion*, which he wrote in 1912, was a fable for children, written as a riposte to Barrie's *Peter Pan* in the style of a Christmas pantomime. As the subsequent preface—setting out Shaw's view of Christianity—made clear, it was in fact a passion play, in which Shaw used the theme of martyrdom to exemplify again his thesis that all progress is the work of exceptional individuals who can serve the Life Force only by refusing to be bound by the constraints that regulate the common man. His Christian heroine defies the laws and conventions of Rome and is prepared to die for her defiance. The assertion of will has become the sign of grace, though Shaw adopted the puritan conception of salvation to his own religion of Creative Evolution. The elect are not saved by a faith in God the Creator; they are saved by the victory of will, which is divine. Man himself thus becomes godlike. Shaw saw himself as a prophet of this religion of the superman: the description of Jesus in the preface came embarrassingly close to a self-portrait.

Such a rationale for rebellion, with its messianic undertones, ran consistently through Shaw's writings and through his life. By 1912 it was beginning to possess him to a degree that affected his personal behaviour, for he was becoming tiresome as vanity got the worse of him. Charlotte too was unhappy. In April 1912, for the first time in fourteen years of marriage, she went off to Italy for a holiday on her own. They had been getting on each other's nerves.

In 1897 Shaw had written to Ellen Terry to say that he would like to write a play for Forbes-Robertson and Mrs. Patrick Campbell, "in which he shall be a West End gentleman and she an East End dona in an apron and three orange and red ostrich feathers."[37] That old idea was the seed which grew into the new play *Pygmalion*. On 26 June 1912 Shaw read it through to Mrs. Campbell in the hope that he could persuade her to play the flower girl Eliza Doolittle. Mrs. Pat was then at the peak of a career which had begun with her success in 1892 in Pinero's *The Second Mrs. Tanqueray*. At forty-seven she was still strikingly attractive, with thick raven-black hair and a deep resonant voice. Her personality was already a legend for unpredictability, outrageous egotism, jokey humour, and snobbery. Yet for all her preposterous vanity she was fun, overpowering but charming, and it was this vivacity that saved her from being quite impossible.

GBS had followed Stella Campbell's rise since his days as a dramatic critic and had corresponded intermittently with her since 1899. Reviewing her performance in *The Notorious Mrs. Ebbsmith* in 1895, he had revealed her fascination for him. "She creates all sorts of illusions," he wrote, "and gives one all sorts of searching sensations."[38] Though Shaw had written the part of Cleopatra with her in mind, she had played it only in a single copyright performance of *Caesar and Cleopatra* and had not appeared in any other Shaw play. Now Shaw tried again, hoping to interest her in a quite different role. Four days after reading the play to her he wrote to tell Barker: "I fell head over ears in love with her— violently and exquisitely in love. All yesterday I could think of nothing but a thousand scenes of which she was the heroine and I the hero. And I am on the verge of 56. There has never been anything so ridiculous, or so delightful, in the history of the world."[39]

Mrs. Pat responded to his flattery, and the familiar flirtation of his youth began again. When he could not see her he wrote provocative letters protesting that he was heartsick but insisting that it was all a gay lark. "I must now go and read this to Charlotte," he told Mrs. Pat as he completed a letter on 3 July. "My love affairs are her unfailing amusements: all their tenderness recoils finally on herself. I love an audience."[40]

A few weeks later Mrs. Pat was badly shaken up in a collision between two taxis, and she was confined to bed for six months. She found GBS among the more consoling of her visitors. "Himself living in dreams, he made a dream-world for me," she recalled. "Only those who can understand this can understand the friendship Bernard Shaw gave to me by my sick-bed—the foolish, ridiculous letters he wrote me, and his pretence of being in love with me."[41] She certainly did not take Shaw's lovelorn blandishments too seriously, particularly as she was also encouraging the suit of George Cornwallis-West. For Shaw, however, lapsing into a congenial triangular situation, the matter was more complicated and Charlotte knew it. She was aware that GBS had reverted to his old habit of flamboyant courtship and she was irritated by the way in which he could not stop talking about Mrs. Pat. Ill with asthma, lonely, restless as ever and patently bored, Charlotte had lost interest in Fabian politics, had come to dislike the theatrical world and cared little for most of Shaw's old friends. Her earlier interest in medicine revived in the form of a hypochondriacal belief in spiritual healing and she started going to Christian Science lectures. She took GBS off to Germany in the summer of 1912, and while she took the waters he motored to France with his chauffeur. In March 1913 they went off to Ireland, and Charlotte gradually got well again.

Charlotte, however, was still jealous and GBS continued to provoke her. In May 1913, after overhearing a telephone conversation between GBS and Mrs. Pat, she made a scene which led Shaw to tell Mrs. Pat, "I throw my desperate hands to heaven and ask why one cannot make one beloved woman happy without sacrificing another." Charlotte was undoubtedly very miserable, and in July 1913 she complained bitterly to Beatrice about the way GBS was carrying on. GBS himself recognized that he was caught up in an uncontrollable fantasy. "You are a figure from the dreams of my childhood," he told Mrs. Pat, "all romance . . . I will hurry through my dream as fast as I can; only let me have my dream out."

When Mrs. Pat realized that the dream was threatening to take over from real life she reacted sharply. In August she went down to Sandwich on the Kent coast to recuperate, having begged Shaw to let her be "alone by the sea—how are strength and steadiness to come to me otherwise. . . . It's getting difficult not to love you more than I ought to love you." Unexpectedly Shaw turned up at the hotel. Apart from her desire for some privacy, Mrs. Pat had another reason for brusquely turning him away: she was now engaged to George Cornwallis-West, who proposed to marry her as soon as he secured his divorce from Jennie, the widow of Randolph Churchill. She sent GBS a note, pleading with him to return at once to London. "If you wont go, I must—I am very very tired and I oughtn't to go on another journey. Please don't make me despise you." Shaw was not moved and stayed on in the hotel, sending her a harsh letter. "Very well, go," he wrote. "The loss of a woman is not the end of the world. . . . You have wounded my vanity: an inconceivable audacity, an unpardonable crime." Mrs. Pat was driven away to Littlestone-on-Sea, where she wrote to Shaw bluntly: "You have lost me because you never found me—I have nothing but my lamp and flame—you would blow it out with your bellows of self. You would snuff it with your egotistical snortings—you elegant charmer—you lady killer—you precious treasure of friendship. Do you think it was nothing to me to hurt my friend?"

The shattering of the fantasy hurt Shaw deeply. He still wrote to her, but the extravagance was gone from the letters. He turned to more practical matters. There was work to do: Mrs. Pat did not go back on her agreement to play Eliza, which Herbert Beerbohm Tree—the best character actor of his day—was to produce at His Majesty's Theatre with himself as Higgins. The play had been given its first production in Vienna in October 1913, and its success had persuaded Tree to take it on.

He had not bargained to take on Shaw as well, and the rehearsals were a stormy struggle of wills. GBS wanted to impose himself as he had done in the early days at the Court, but he was not dealing with malleable young actors. Mrs. Pat was a prima donna who wanted to do things in her own way; Sir Herbert Tree was accustomed to dominate his own productions. Sometimes the rehearsal stopped while Tree recovered from a Shavian comment; sometimes Mrs. Pat refused to go on until GBS had left the theatre. She sent Shaw notes of apology. "I wanted *you* to produce the play," she wrote in one of them, "and Tree not to be sufficiently insulted by you as to 'throw it up'—in this I have succeeded—though there are a few more days! For myself the last three months and more particularly the last five days have been full of anxiety." The root cause of the trouble, in her view, was that GBS did not want the actors to think for themselves because he felt that he had done all the thinking necessary for "us poor players."[42] The final crisis came five days before the opening night. On 6 April Mrs. Pat married Cornwallis-West, and they disappeared for a short honeymoon. She returned for the dress rehearsal without apology.

Yet the first night on 11 April 1914 was a triumph; no previous Shaw play had been so well received. There was, Mrs. Pat said, "such joyousness. The 'bloody' almost ruined the play: people laughed so much."[43] Charlotte missed the opening, having gone off to America with Christian Science friends. "The play last night got boomed to an amazing extent," Shaw told her; Mrs Campbell played superbly and ravished the house almost to delirium."[44] For all the applause, he was oddly pessimistic, thinking it would not run. It actually turned out to be the most successful of all his comedies, establishing him as the leading contemporary dramatist and helping to make him the richest. In the first three months it earned £13,000, coming off simply because Tree could not stand the strain of playing Higgins to Eliza. Mrs. Pat then took the play to America, and translations were soon being played round the world.

Shaw had come through his depression and his emotional vacillations with a superb comedy, satirizing the English class system with poignancy and wit and giving a modern twist to an old fairy tale by turning Cinderella into a New Woman. He had, moreover, accommodated his own eccentricity more comfortably to his medium: it was a play of characters rather than prosy declamation. But the characters were essentially Shavian. The conventional happy ending of the fairy story was impossible if Higgins was to remain true to himself, and it is he who embodies Shaw's message. The intellect must rise superior to passion, for salvation lies in single-minded dedication to one's vocation, not in a surrender to the physical urge disguised as love. Higgins may be a tyrannical egotist, but his unbending will redeems him: mind is superior to the grossness of matter. Tree objected strongly to this conclusion and took advantage of the ambiguity in the last lines of the play to suggest that Higgins has finally surrendered. His trick was to have Higgins throw a bouquet to Eliza.[45] "My ending makes money; you ought to be grateful," he told Shaw. "Your ending is damnable; you ought to be shot," was Shaw's reply. It was impossible for Shaw to accept that interpretation without betraying his own nature. Mrs. Pat understood the truth about him. "I have sometimes thought," she wrote afterwards, "that perhaps it is only his human heart he hides and fears."[46]

The success of *Pygmalion* did little to raise Shaw's spirits. Mrs. Pat had turned and left his overpowering presence, just as Eliza walked out on Higgins. While he was pursuing her he had let other friendships languish. The old connection with the Barkers had fallen away: they were tied up with their own Shakespeare repertory at the Savoy, which ran from September 1912 to the summer of 1914. Barker had long dreamed of a national theatre, but the war put an end to his effort to put the repertory on a permanent footing, and he and Lillah went off to America. Before long they were divorced and he married the rich Helen Huntingdon; she could not get along with Shaw, and the old comradeship faded. For a time, Shaw helped the unhappy Lillah, but when she too remarried that association came to an end.

"Old friends drift apart," Beatrice commented in the summer of 1913. The Webbs rarely saw Graham Wallas. Sydney Olivier had come back from Jamaica that year to run the Board of Agriculture, but they had seen him only twice in eight months. Hubert Bland, who had been blind and ailing, died on 14 April 1914; Pease, formally representing the Society, was the only one of the first Fabians to attend the funeral.

Shaw, however, still kept in touch with the Webbs. They went for a walking holiday together to Devon and Cornwall in January 1914, when Beatrice felt that he was "getting rapidly old physically" and that he was "mortified by the refusal of his generation to take him seriously as a thinker and reformer."[47] With the loss of Mrs. Pat he took more interest again in Fabian affairs. He was still willing to lecture for the Society; his debates on socialism against Chesterton and Belloc were memorable occasions, and he was planning a series of Fabian lectures for the autumn of 1914.

"It is remarkable how limited one's circle becomes when one is at once elderly and hardworking," Beatrice observed.[48] The Webbs had in fact come full circle, for their attention was now focussed on the Fabian Society.

They were also involved in trying to bring together the socialist groups which had spent the past twenty years going their separate ways. The Socialist International summoned the executives of the ILP and Hyndman's British Socialist Party for a meeting in London in an effort to impose the unity which had so long evaded them. Sidney was chosen to preside over the meeting, and Beatrice was selected to chair a standing joint committee to create a United Socialist Council. The scene of the meeting on 13 December 1913 was, ironically, Anderton's Hotel, from which the Fabians had been asked to remove themselves after the noisy shouting match with the anarchists and the SDF in 1886.

This initiative made little headway, but during the early months of 1914 Beatrice found herself again consorting with old ILP leaders such as Hardie and Bruce Glasier, and with SDF stalwarts such as Hyndman and Dan Irving. Differences of policy and temperament now seemed less relevant than the need to reassert the socialist part of the Labour alliance and reduce the influence of the moderate trade unions. The key role played by the Webbs was significant. It marked the end of their belief that the Tories or the Liberals could be manipulated into collectivism; for the first time they made a definite commitment to working-class politics. "I am afraid you & we will have to remain in harness within the socialist movement for some years longer," Beatrice wrote to GBS on 13 June 1914. "If we could safely steer the Fabians into a Unified Socialist party, & leave it provided with a philosophy & a programme, and a Research Department & an Organ issuing out of the Research Department, we could comfortably retire into our old age."[49]

The old Fabian Society had run its course and the Webbs had sketched out a new strategy. The question now was who would play the role of the Old Gang and ensure that it was implemented. Beatrice felt that the Webbs must do so, at least for a transitional period, because there was no one with "the combined conduct, brains and faith" to enable the Society to flourish without them.[50] The Society was not an institution which could easily arrange the transfer of control to new directors. Its founders were rebels, and like had attracted like, so that a rebellious posture was an essential part of the Society's life style and each generation of recruits sought to establish its identity by a conflict of wills with the Old Gang. The Society was more like a family of strong-willed people reflecting the personalities of its elders, as if the first Fabians unconsciously transferred to the Society the family pattern against which they had originally reacted.

Only the Webbs were left in this parental role by 1913. They turned to the latest group of eager rebels, led by G. D. H. Cole, who were willing to take on the grind of the Fabian Research Department on which Beatrice thought the future of Fabianism now depended. In less than two years the Cole group was creating trouble and making Beatrice feel doubtful whether her scheme for ensuring the survival of the Society was viable. At the summer school at Keswick in 1914 Cole and his comrades went on the rampage, upsetting the staid little Lake District town by singing revolutionary songs in the marketplace as an evangelical convention was assembling, turning all the discussions into disorderly demonstrations for guild socialism, heckling, and walking out in a body when they were called to order. When, a year later, Cole angrily flounced out of the Fabian meeting, throwing his resignation on the table, the Society had become little more than a holding company, and its only vital component, the Research Department, had been snatched from the hands of the Webbs by the guild socialists.

During that hot summer at Keswick the Fabians talked about socialist
theory and listened to Douglas Cole telling them how the world might
be changed by an apocalyptic general strike. But another kind of doom
was in the making. All through the July weeks, Beatrice said afterwards,
"there had been the rumblings of the coming earthquake without our
awakening to the meaning of it."[51]

Shaw caught the rumblings of that earthquake in the allegory of
Heartbreak House, which he began in 1913 and finished after two years
of war. It expressed his contempt for a society which was as doomed as a
set of first-class passengers chattering aimlessly while the sinking ship
settled in the water. Captain Shotover's strange house was the "ship that
we are all in, this soul's prison we call England." Its inhabitants were
spiritually dead: "We are useless, dangerous, and ought to be abolished,"
says Hector Hushabye. Like the rulers of England, Shotover's guests do
not heed the mysterious drumming which heralds their fate. They embrace the coming disaster with euphoric relief. "The judgment has
come," says Captain Shotover. "It's magnificent," shouts Mrs. Hushabye.

The fear that the world was doomed unless it listened to a message
of salvation had run like an undertone through the lives of the first
Fabians. It lay beneath their belief in a civilizing mission, beneath their
conviction that the enlightened expert had both the capacity and the
duty to regenerate society, beneath their enthusiasm for education and
propaganda, beneath their search for a disinterested elite which could
govern the people for their own good. It was a fear born in part of a
sense of guilt—from which sprang their concern with personal duty and
social obligation—and in part of the depression and anxiety which had
affected all of them in their youth and made them seek, in the hope of
remaking the world, a secular faith which would fill the void left by the
collapse of religious certainties. Now, in middle age, they had a sense of
failure, of profound disappointment at the inability of ordinary, sensual
men to see the light and create a new moral order. They had achieved
much, but they were still unsatisfied; and thirty years after the Society
had been founded they had a feeling that, after all, the judgment days
were upon them. "I am haunted by the fear that all my struggles may be
in vain," Beatrice wrote, "that disease and death are moving with relentless certainty."[52] As the world slid into the holocaust, she could not, like

Shaw, feel that the slate might be wiped clean and that the chance might come afterwards for the supermen who would set it to rights. Her despair was too personal, less dramatic. Yet she knew, in that tragic summer, that the Fabian vision of a Religion of Humanity was still no more than a dream.

EPILOGUE

In the summer of 1937 Beatrice Webb was nearing her eightieth birthday, and a large party of her relatives and friends assembled at Passfield Corner, the comfortable house in rolling country on the Hampshire–Surrey border where the Webbs had made their retirement home. Among them were over a hundred descendants of Richard and Laurencina Potter. Though all Beatrice's sisters save the youngest, Rosy, were dead, there were many nieces, nephews and their children, as well as Shaw and other old Fabian friends and Labour politicians. It was, in effect, a leavetaking; the Webbs were at last withdrawing from public life. Beatrice had yet to finish *Our Partnership*, the second volume of autobiography based on her diaries, but it was nearly done. Sidney was failing in health. A few months later, in January 1938, he had a stroke which left him a lingering invalid able to do little but read.

More than twenty years before, Beatrice had thought that their useful working days were over and that neither they nor the Fabian Society would last much longer.[1] Yet they had survived through the years which saw the rise of Fascism and Communism, the emergence of two Labour governments in Britain, and the reappearance of mass destitution as a result of the Great Depression. The Society too had kept alive in a modest way, seeing many of its ideas adopted as Labour policy and many of its members holding office in Labour Cabinets. At the time of the party at Passfield Corner, plans were being made to amalgamate the Society with the New Fabian Research Bureau, started in 1931 by G. D. H. Cole and his wife, Margaret, which had independently continued the Fabian style of work. In the Coles the Webbs had found the successors that they had sought before the First World War; when the merger took place a luncheon party to celebrate the reunion was held at the London School of Economics, and Beatrice was made president of the revivified Society.

Other Webb ventures had also prospered. *The New Statesman*, which had seemed such a gamble in 1913, had struggled through to solvency, taken over *The Nation* in 1931 and under the editorship of Kingsley Martin become Britain's leading intellectual weekly. The School of Economics, started on a few thousand pounds of Hutchinson money, was a flourishing and world-famous centre of teaching and research in the social sciences.

Such successes, however, had not made the Webbs complacent in their old age or deterred them from still seeking some public certainty to ease the private uncertainties which, so long ago, had led them to seek a new social order combining faith and works. Their experience in democratic politics had done nothing to reassure them about democracy, and the political events of the Twenties and Thirties had made them even more sceptical about its virtues and prospects.

Before the outbreak of the First World War the Webbs had reluctantly decided that their political future lay, after all, with the Labour Party— "the new thing," Beatrice then said, "round which all who are discontented with the old order foregather."² In 1916 Pease persuaded Webb to become the Fabian representative on the Labour Party executive. At the time it seemed unimportant, but it was a decisive step for Webb, who was soon accepted as a member of the inner group; and in Arthur Henderson, who had succeeded MacDonald as the party's secretary, Sidney found a new colleague with whom he could work as congenially and effectively as he had once done with Shaw in the Fabian Society. With Henderson and MacDonald—the old animosity now muted—he drafted *Labour's War Aims,* and he and Henderson drew up a new constitution for the Labour Party, which for the first time began to recruit individual members and to create its own organization in the constituencies. In the closing stages of the war Sidney then wrote the party's manifesto for the future, *Labour and the New Social Order*, which proclaimed that the "individualist system" had served its time and set out a comprehensive programme for public ownership, social welfare and political reform. The essential ideas of Fabianism had at last become official Labour policy.

Sidney was happy in this new role as adviser-in-chief to the Labour Party; he had become, in effect, its intellectual leader, accepted as an expert and welcomed as a colleague to a degree that had never been true of his uneasy collaboration with the Tory and Liberal politicians. His involvement in Labour politics was symbolically and practically significant. For three decades the Fabians had kept aloof from the working-class movement, arguing that they were independents who had a special role to play in promoting collectivism among the middle classes. Now they threw in their lot with the unions and the provincial enthusiasts. In 1919 the change was formalized. The Basis was amended to declare unambiguously for the first time that the Society was "a constituent of the Labour Party."

This change in Sidney's political position again altered the balance within the Webb partnership. He was busy and in demand. Beatrice had little to occupy her and she felt depressed and lonely, "beaten by events."[3] By the middle of the war she feared that she had cancer; but she soon realized that much of her bad health was due to mental distress —"partly war neurosis, partly too persistent work to keep myself from brooding over the horrors of war, partly I think from general discouragement arising out of our unpopularity with all sections of the political and official world." She often thought of death. "I now feel that I am packing up," she wrote when she made up her mind to begin her autobiography—"so that I may be ready to depart when the time comes."[4]

While Beatrice withdrew, Sidney came forward. He took up again his old idea of going into Parliament, though the backstairs role that he had played so long was so familiar that he hesitated until the eve of the 1918 election, in which he stood as a Labour candidate for one of the two London University seats. He lost, but the Labour Party polled 2.5 million votes and became the official opposition to the Lloyd George coalition government. Then, in 1919, he represented the mineworkers' union at the hearings of the royal commission on the troubled coal industry, a task he performed so impressively that he topped the poll for the Labour Party executive and was sponsored by the miners as candidate for the seat at Seaham Harbour in the Durham coalfield. He and Beatrice took this new opportunity seriously, preparing energetically for the next election. They started what Beatrice jokingly called the "University of Seaham," running local educational classes and writing a short history of the local miners' union. In November 1922, when Sidney was sixty-three, he was at last sent to the House of Commons with a stunning majority.

"I really believe he is going to enjoy Parliament," Beatrice wrote;[5] she felt that he was "like a boy going for his first term to a public school."[6] She was less cheerful about the prospect for herself, feeling that the partnership could not continue on the old terms. Though she and Sidney still had work to do on their local government volumes and on their massive history of the Poor Law, and though they had been able to collaborate on *The Decay of Capitalist Civilisation* and the *Constitution for a Socialist Commonwealth of Great Britain*, she realized that with Sidney in active politics it would be some time before she could fulfil her vision of "two old folks living in comfort, and amid some charm, writing endless works, and receiving the respectful attention of an even larger public." In the meantime, she occupied herself with the story of her youth, which she called *My Apprenticeship*, and searched for a country home to which the "old folks" could eventually retire. In 1923 they bought a cottage at Passfield Common, set in eight acres of fields and woodlands, and Beatrice happily superintended its modernization and extension.

Sidney found the House of Commons less agreeable than he had hoped. Its procedures were very different from the London County Council he knew so well, where the management of committees was the heart of the business and he had direct contact with the officials. The back-bencher in Parliament needed another kind of skill, and Sidney's deficiencies as a speaker made it difficult for him to settle to the cut-and-thrust of debate. He was, nevertheless, a conscientious member, and outside the House he was kept busy with Labour Party affairs, becoming its chairman in 1923.

In December of that year the Labour Party's chance came to form a government for the first time when it won 191 seats; supported by 148 Liberal votes, MacDonald was able to form a minority administration against a Tory opposition with 258 votes. Among the ten Fabians given office, Sidney Webb, as president of the Board of Trade, and Sydney Olivier, as secretary of state for India, held senior posts in the Cabinet. Beatrice's brother-in-law Alfred Cripps—now Lord Parmoor—had swung away from the Tories and was a nonparty member of the government; and Haldane, who had drifted to Labour when Lloyd George took the Liberals into a coalition with the Tories, became lord chancellor. At long last the first Fabians were to have a real responsibility for government. The formation of a Labour government was an exciting and bewildering surprise. After the swearing-in, the Webbs gave a party where, Beatrice said, everyone was "laughing at the joke of Labour in office."[7] Things seemed less of a joke when the new and inexperienced ministers, enjoying the rewards of office, found it difficult to fulfil its obligations. The Cabinet did not settle as a team; each minister was caught up with the problems of running his own department, and MacDonald was so concerned at proving that Labour was "fit to govern" that, precariously dependent on Liberal backing, he made little attempt to implement the Labour programme.

It was hard for trade union leaders and old ILP propagandists to adapt to the task of governing; the social problems of their sudden elevation were also troublesome. Beatrice decided that she should try to help the new members and their wives to adjust to the manners and mores of the unfamiliar milieu in which they now found themselves, and she played a leading part in setting up the Half-Circle Club near the House of Commons as a social centre for the party (a well-meant effort that was denounced by Robert Smillie, the left-wing leader of the miners, as "a school for snobbery").

The MacDonald government survived for nine months, plagued throughout its life by its inability to cope with the problems of unemployment created by the postwar slump. Labour politicians were discovering that effective measures were far more elusive than effective propaganda, and they were under pressure both from their own left-wing supporters and from the *laissez-faire* Liberals on their right. The government fell on a different issue, however—the mishandling of a sedition charge against a Communist journalist. In the ensuing election the Tories worked up a scare about the Zinoviev letter, alleged to give Moscow's instructions for revolutionary activity in Britain; by November they were back in office with a comfortable majority.

Beatrice was relieved that the trying experiment was over and hoped that she and Sidney could settle back to a quiet retirement in the country. "These three years have been nerve-wracking," she observed in December 1925.[8] "I have not exactly enjoyed my association with the Parliamentary Labour Party; I have done my level best. . . . I do not and have never liked political life." Since Sidney had decided that he would not run at the following election—both he and Beatrice disliked the separation which kept him in London through the week—it seemed that they would soon resume the kind of life they liked best. Living mostly at Passfield, Beatrice began to find new pleasures. She took an interest in birds and plants, and through the BBC she discovered a taste for music.

She enjoyed entertaining at their new home. Political associates and old friends went down for weekends and were taken on the long walks that the Webbs found both healthy and relaxing. Graham and Audrey Wallas were among those who went to stay, and the old friends resumed their habit of discussing each other's current work. Wallas too had achieved success and was no longer dispirited. He had found a respected academic niche for himself at the School of Economics, and his books had given him an international reputation. It was in his writings that his basic scepticism found expression. He had no use for the Fabian Society, the Labour Party or the trade-union movement, and his dislike of organized religion had become an obsession. As early as January 1921, after reading *Human Nature in Politics*, Sidney had commented to Beatrice on Graham's "querulous discontent with Democracy itself"; this underlying lack of confidence in democracy, indeed, was characteristic of the ageing Fabian Old Gang. It showed in Shaw's contempt for popular government and his flirtation with autocracy. When the Shaws went to Passfield in November 1925 GBS was working on his *Intelligent Woman's Guide to Socialism and Capitalism*, and Beatrice was disturbed by his praise for the Soviet practice of teaching a Communist gospel to schoolchildren.

Shaw soon gave further proof of his taste for sensational perversity. In October 1927, returning from eight weeks in a luxurious hotel at Stresa where he had been courted by Fascist officials, he announced that Mussolini's dictatorship was superior to the ramshackle arrangements of democracy. Mussolini, in fact, conformed to Shaw's old conception of the superman as hero. The Webbs were distressed by Shaw's newfound enthusiasm for Russian Communism and Italian Fascism; Beatrice called them "two sides of the worship of force and the practice of cruel intolerance," and she worried whether Britain could move towards a collectivist society without losing its democratic faith.[9] "Our great ones in the world's esteem, Haldane and GBS, H. G. Wells," she noted, "are showing unmistakable signs of scuttling from a ship manned by so disorderly and half-trained a crew."

Yet the disillusionment with the slow and apparently incompetent processes of democracy which Shaw and Wells were displaying in the Twenties had long been implicit in their attitude. Shaw in particular had always disliked the bourgeois order, derided its hypocrisies and insisted that it would eventually be swept away by a new breed of men whose will to change the world would triumph over human stupidity. His rebellion had been expressed in moral preaching, satire and drama; and his ideal revolutionaries were men of destiny, imposing the Shavian order upon mankind.

Casting himself in that prophetic role, Shaw had never softened his opinions to suit critics or circumstances. Denunciation simply strengthened his conviction that he was right and that he was suffering the fate of all prophets. He had fought all his battles on the plane of intellect; lacking imaginative sympathy, he seemed to be perversely argumentative, attacking men's minds rather than appealing to their hearts. His reaction to the outbreak of war in 1914 was characteristic. He declared that it was an act of insanity and wrote a long supplement to *The New Statesman* called "Common Sense about the War," attacking militarism, diplomacy and the popular hysteria against all things German. Though it appealed enough to pacifist sentiment among Liberals and socialists to sell 75,000 copies, it attracted a storm of protest. Wells, who had become a demagogic patriot, said that GBS was "an idiot child screaming in a hospital," and Henry Arthur Jones called him "a freakish homunculus, germinated outside lawful procreation." Shaw was hurt by such abuse and by the blacklisting of his plays, but all through the war he kept up his defiant stance, sustained by his pride, his vanity and his sense of martyrdom.

Shaw had always identified with the outcast, whose stigma he saw as the mark of redemption. During the First World War he began explicitly to formulate the religious ideas implicit in his earlier work. His

Fabian colleagues had filled the gap left by the collapse of their Evangelical faith with pseudoreligions such as Comteism, Theosophy or assertive Secularism. Shaw had found his road to salvation in Samuel Butler's creed of Creative Evolution, and from Ibsen, Nietzsche and Bergson he had drawn the idea of will as the mainspring of that process. The human race was not recovering from original sin—Shaw found the doctrine of the atonement the most repugnant aspect of Christianity—but was discovering its divine potential: an elect of supermen would be the harbingers of a future of unlimited wisdom and unlimited power. Traditional Puritans had taught that men must undergo a change of heart; Shaw ingeniously inverted that idea into the belief that men must undergo a change of mind. Describing himself as "the conscious iconographer of a religion," he set out his faith in the elaborate epic *Back to Methuselah*, which he finished in 1919.

GBS described these almost unperformable tracts as his masterpiece, a testament which used the theatre as Wagner had used opera in *The Ring*. It was, however, *Saint Joan*, which followed in 1923, which put Shaw's new evangelicalism into successful dramatic terms. Joan's martyrdom is the proof that she is one of the elect. "I am His child," she retorts to her judges, "and you are not fit that I should live among you." Embodying the emergent will, her suffering and death are trivialities beside her demonstration that mind will triumph over matter. Self-sacrifice is not an atonement for the sins of mankind but a rejection of responsibility for them: Shaw's saints do not save sinners, they liberate themselves. Writing to Beatrice Webb in August 1914, Shaw had put the point explicitly: "As you very properly say, the whole world is a fool and I alone am right. Otherwise, what am I?"[10]

As Shaw grew older his perversity and eccentricity were accepted as the oddities of a respected man of letters. As his self-esteem was satisfied his natural kindness came through, and he and Charlotte were happy together. He still liked to make striking gestures: when he was awarded the Nobel Prize in 1925 he gave the money to promote the works of Strindberg in Sweden. He enjoyed hobnobbing with the famous: his friends ranged from Gene Tunney, the boxer, to Lady Astor. He adored being painted and photographed. And although he was making a great deal of money—in 1928 his plays brought in over £40,000—he complained bitterly about the burden of taxation at the same time as he was campaigning for equal incomes under socialism.

Sidney believed that he was finished with the strains of government and, as an ironic sequel to his old feud with MacDonald, had arranged that at the next election he should retire and that MacDonald should take over his seat at Seaham Harbour. But in 1929 the Labour Party came back strongly enough to form a second minority government with Liberal support. MacDonald, short of experienced men to meet the constitutional need for ministers in the House of Lords, gave Sidney a peerage as Baron Passfield and made him secretary of state for the Colonies. His brother-in-law Lord Parmoor became lord president of the Council and leader of the House of Lords. Though there were more Fabians than ever in the government—eight in the Cabinet and ten holding junior posts—this time Olivier was not given a ministry but was sent off to investigate the sugar industry in the West Indies.

The parallel between Sidney's career and that of Joe Chamberlain was not lost on Beatrice: both started in the Board of Trade and finished with the Colonial Office. For Sidney there was the added twist that he now headed the department in which he had made his career as a civil servant. Yet this promotion brought its problems. Beatrice would have nothing to do with the "paraphernalia" of aristocracy. She was unwilling to accept a title, feeling it was against the grain of her views on the caste system and the monarchy. She was equally reluctant to refuse it lest the gesture be considered pompously self-important. She compromised by declining to use the title of Lady Passfield, thereby hoping to do something "to undermine the foundations of British snobbishness," but she agreed to attend court functions and to curtsey to the Queen should the occasion arise. Spending most of her time in the country, she was able to keep clear of public occasions she found tiresome, but she complied reluctantly with at least some of the social demands on the wife of a minister. The Webbs gave up the house in Grosvenor Road at last and kept a small flat in London simply as a *pied-à-terre*.

Sidney, now past seventy, was soon faced by the problems of an important ministry. There were demands for native rights in Kenya, the agitation of the increasingly strong nationalist movement in India, and the Zionist claims for the promised national home in Palestine, governed by Britain under a League of Nations mandate. Unaccustomed to dealing with such intractable problems, lacking the traits of personality and the political experience required of a minister, Sidney began to flounder. Beatrice quickly realized what was wrong. "When he is acting in a responsible administration," she wrote in November 1929, "he is, in fact, an excellent civil servant—his instinct is to obey the orders of his chief, and make the best of the business."[11] Now that he was a chief giving the orders he was at a loss; both his training and his belief that experts could find their way through to rational solutions led him to rely increasingly on his advisers. Instead of imposing himself on them he identified with them. He dealt with Kenya's problems by appointing a committee of enquiry. Dominion affairs were taken out of his hands in May 1930. When his Palestine policy turned out to reflect the traditional pro-Arab stance of Whitehall he was again bypassed, Henderson as foreign secretary taking over the delicate negotiations with Chaim Weizmann. "People will say," Sidney sadly confessed to Beatrice, "that your husband has not been a success as a minister."[12]

Sidney's failure as a minister derived from his personal posture and his assumptions about politics. It touched the flaw in his beliefs in the rule of the expert, which could lead only to an autocratic society and the abnegation of personal responsibility. The imagination required of democratic government was beyond his range. But his was not an isolated failure. In such a period of crisis the quality of the whole government was tested, but it lacked the experience and confidence to sustain itself. Most of its members disagreed instinctively with the conservative policies of retrenchment adopted by the former Fabian Philip Snowden, now chancellor of the exchequer, but lacked any alternative solution. The Labour Party, Beatrice noted in February 1931, had "completely lost its bearings."[13] By the summer the government was facing financial disaster. Fear took hold of the government and the people, and there was a sense of helplessness in the face of catastrophic forces. "Where as a nation are we going?" Beatrice asked. The collapse came in August 1931. MacDonald, breaking with the party to which he had given his life, bolted into a coalition with the Liberals and the Tories, leaving the majority of his colleagues to a ruinous defeat at the ensuing general election.

MacDonald's government had finally disillusioned Beatrice with democracy. The political game offered neither a faith nor efficiency. There was some compensation when the Poor Law was abolished in 1929—"the old Webbs are chuckling over their chickens!"—but that was merely a footnote to an earlier passion. Looking back, she now believed that the

Webbs had been on the wrong track in trying to win the support of Liberal and Conservative politicians for their schemes by permeation. She also had second thoughts about the Fabian dismissal of Marxism from the earliest days at the Hampstead Historic Society meetings. "Where we went hopelessly wrong was in ignoring Karl Marx's forecast of the eventual breakdown of the capitalist system."

While Sidney was struggling with the daily detail of office, Beatrice began to look for an alternative to the social system which seemed to be collapsing around her. What she had always called "the average, sensual man" had not proved to have the makings of a new society. For all her earlier doubts about the Soviet system she was coming to wonder whether Communism might be the key to salvation. She read books on the Soviet Union and a private diary kept by the old Fabian friend Henry Harben, who had made a tour of Russia. She and Sidney had become friendly with the Soviet ambassador, G. J. Sokolnikov, who gave them information about the Soviet regime and made it clear that they would be welcomed on a visit. Still sceptical—in March 1931 Beatrice was talking about the "fanatical brutality" of Soviet Russia—both the Webbs began to feel, as the crisis developed, that if the choice lay between the kind of individualist capitalism exemplified by America and Russian collectivism "without doubt we are on the side of Russia."[14] The problem which they were honest enough to appreciate was how to achieve equality without an unreasonable loss of individual freedom. They were abandoning capitalist individualism because of its failure to provide equal opportunity and a minimum wage, but could Russia succeed as an egalitarian state without sacrificing human liberty?

Shaw had no such doubts. In 1928, before MacDonald had taken office for the second time, he wrote *The Apple Cart*, a savage burlesque on a self-important blundering Labour government with the clear implication that democracy was a farce and that new men of power were waiting in the wings. In 1931 GBS went to Russia with Lady Astor and returned full of enthusiasm, declaring that the Stalin regime was nothing but applied Fabianism—the old Webb notion of a threefold state of citizens, consumers and producers united by a moral creed and efficient organization.

It was the creed which appealed most to Beatrice. In January 1932 she conceded, "It is the invention of the religious order as the determining factor in the life of a great nation that is the magnet which attracts me to Russia." She felt that at last one country was trying to implement the ideas which she and Sidney had held when they were young. "Practically that religion is Comteism—the Religion of Humanity. Auguste Comte comes to his own."[15] As Fabians the Webbs had rejected conventional creeds, but they had never lost the puritanical drive to save the world. That need now led them to look towards Soviet Communism as its modern expression. Despairing of the way the world was going, the Webbs could not resist the chance to see for themselves whether that belief was really true. Beatrice recognized its emotional significance when she wondered whether "a pilgrimage to the Mecca of the equalitarian state led by a few Fabians, all well over seventy years of age, will bring about the world's salvation."[16]

The Webbs were delighted with their visit to Russia in 1932. On their arrival in Leningrad in May they were greeted, in Sidney's phrase, like "a new type of royalty." During their three-month stay they were plied with documents, taken on prepared visits and given long interviews with senior officials. In the mood of converts, they took everything at face value, not wishing to probe the darker side of Soviet reality. Dismissing reports of famine in the countryside and of forced labour and deportations as inevitable shortcomings in a backward country, they were fascinated by the discovery that the formal structure of Soviet society corresponded so closely to their own notions of a socialist state in which the individual was subordinated to the collective, public morals were ascetically puritanical, and private profit was replaced by planning for social purposes. In what they called "the Religion of Scientific Humanism," moreover, they found the quasi-religious dedication for which Beatrice had been searching, and in the strict discipline of the Communist Party they saw the "new religious order" which Beatrice had so often insisted must assume the task of making a new civilization.

On their return they reported these revelations in their vast compendium *Soviet Communism*. It was Beatrice whose emotions provided the vitality to prepare what she described as their last will and testament. "Old people," she remarked, "often fall in love in extraordinary and ridiculous ways—with their chauffeurs, for instance: we feel it more dignified to have fallen in love with Soviet Communism." Even when the Stalinist terror began in 1934, while the book was still being drafted, they saw no reason to change their minds. Sidney, together with Beatrice's niece Barbara Drake, paid a return visit in September 1934 to have the manuscript checked in Moscow. "See, see, it works," was his response to any suggestion that things were not as they seemed or as the Webbs described them.[17] They had no more resources to face another disillusionment.

Their conversion came as a surprise to many of their friends. Yet it was not the turnabout that it superficially seemed. The Soviet system touched deep-rooted elements in both their personalities—the streak of elitism and authoritarianism, intellectual dogmatism, the need for an all-embracing faith, the desire for a planned and efficient order, the belief in the rightness of the expert, the lack of sympathetic imagination for ordinary people and distrust of the people's capacity to govern themselves. In the depressing conditions of the early Thirties, when many intellectuals had begun to flirt with totalitarian solutions, Communism had come to seem to the Webbs the only hope for a genuinely new order of things.

Sidney's intellectual and Beatrice's emotional needs were now satisfied. To the end of her life Beatrice did not waver, listening regularly to broadcasts from Moscow, taking in Communist publications and entertaining Soviet diplomats. Writing to the C.P. leader R. Palme Dutt in 1942, she described herself and Sidney as "non-party Communists." In the final years of their partnership their only political interest was in the survival of the Soviet state which they saw as the Fabian utopia.

With the Fabian Society itself the Webbs, like Shaw, retained a nominal contact, but they had played no great part in its affairs since 1914. They had, Shaw remarked sixty years after the Society was founded, ceased to be Fabians and become "celebrities with public reputations."[18] A new generation had grown up in the Society, men like Hugh Dalton, Herbert Morrison, Clement Attlee and Harold Laski, who were deeply involved in Labour politics and, after the debacle of 1931, had faced the hard grind of rebuilding the party and of fitting it to defend democracy against both Fascism and Communism. Carrying on the element of the Fabian tradition which had produced the early tracts on policy, the detailed advice to local councillors, the summer schools and the hard slog of propaganda, the Fabians became again, as in the Nineties, a brains trust for the labour movement. Joined by the Coles and their group in 1938, when war came a year later they had the nucleus of an organization which could both promote and benefit from the leftward swing in politics. Before the Second World War ended, the Fabians had more than ten thousand members, a network of local societies, an impressive range of policy documents, and a new reputation; more than half the Labour MP's who came in to form the staggering Labour majority in 1945 were Fabians, and the Society's hand could be seen in much of the reforming legislation which followed from a government which included forty-five Fabians—ten of them in the Cabinet.

The octagenarian Fabians were too old to share in the third and greatest Fabian boom. The war, making travel difficult, cut them off from public life and from one another; it did nothing to change their basic attitudes. They still felt themselves, in Shaw's phrase, to be "missionaries among the savages," superior people despairing of human frailty and folly.[19] In the First World War Beatrice had cried out that the human race had "disgraced itself" and "shown neither intelligence nor goodwill." In the Second World War she again felt that mood of Heartbreak House: somewhere beyond the miseries of the shipwreck there must be a hope of salvation, for without such a hope life was dismally meaningless.

For the ageing Webbs, hope lay in the social system of a distant country which they had briefly visited and whose language they did not speak. For Shaw it lay in the emerging immortality of the intellect. For Wells it was to be found in the dream of a world state controlled by elites of scientists and airmen—symbols of a secular Second Coming which would establish the rule of the saints on earth. The Evangelical heritage fell heavily upon them all. It was a depressing inheritance, combining anxiety and guilt, the need for moral redemption and a compulsion to regenerate the world. Nothing, in reality, could ultimately appease such powerful drives, for no achievement could ever match the dream of perfection. One by one the first Fabians had fallen away into disillusionment or sought relief in new faiths. William Clarke had despaired of humanity as well as of the Fabians before he was struck down prematurely by diabetes in 1901. Frank Podmore, who did so much to launch the Society died in 1910 in circumstances that suggested suicide. Hubert Bland, before his death in 1914, had come to the conclusion that the Fabians had failed in their true mission. Graham Wallas, for all his academic success, never shed his basic pessimism. The obstacles to the good society, he concluded, were not institutions which could be reformed but the irrational elements in human consciousness which made men unable to will the new order. He died in August 1932. Sydney Olivier, living in a long retirement in the Cotswolds and then in Sussex, also felt the frustrations of human stupidity. "It has taken eighty years for what appeared reasonable to us to appear reasonable to the nation," he wrote to Wells in 1942. And shortly before he died in February 1943 he tartly repeated what "I long ago said in the Fabian Society: 'this world is no place for a gentleman.' "[20] Annie Besant, the greatest evangelist of all of them, turned to the comforts of reincarnation. Before her death in 1933 she had moved on from leadership of the Theosophical movement to proclaim that the Second Coming was at hand in the person of the child saviour Krishnamurthi, the new Christ, whose twelve apostles were led by Annie herself.

There was little left for the survivors in their last years but the vestiges of old friendships. The Webbs, living at Passfield, were too far from the Shaws at Ayot to meet often, but they kept in touch. In 1934, believing the Webbs to be hard up because of their investment losses in the slump, Shaw sent them a gift of a thousand pounds. Sidney, thanking him, reflected on the years since they had met at the Zetetical Society. That meeting, he wrote, "led to nearly half a century of a friendship and a companionship which has been most fruitful to me. I look back on it with wonder at the advantages and, indeed, the beauty of that prolonged friendship. Apart from marriage it has certainly been the biggest thing in my life, which without it would have been poor indeed."[21] Shaw felt much the same. His last comment to Sidney, twelve years later, was, "I never met a man who combined your extraordinary ability with your unique sympathy and integrity of character."[22]

It was, as Sidney recognized, the success of his marriage which had made his life, and he never ceased to wonder at his good fortune in a partnership continually enriched by intellectual comradeship and deep affection. In her last years Beatrice was worried only by the thought of parting: it was the thought of leaving Sidney alone that kept her going after his stroke and through her own deteriorating condition. At the beginning of 1943 she wrote to Shaw's secretary, Blanche Patch: "If it were not for my beloved partner I would be glad to quit life. We have lived the life we liked and done the work we intended to do. What more can a mortal want but a peaceful and painless death?"[23] She died of a kidney disease on 20 April 1943.

Charlotte Shaw, more content in the final years of her marriage, told Beatrice in October 1940, "We feel we have lived our lives & had a very good share of the best that was going." Crippled with arthritis and suffering from troubling hallucinations, she lived six months longer than Beatrice, dying peacefully at the age of eighty-six. GBS wrote moving letters to their friends about her last hours, in which she had rallied and seemed her old self again.

Sidney, increasingly enfeebled, survived for another four years. When he was awarded the Order of Merit in 1944 he regretted that Beatrice could not have been included in the citation, since her contribution had been as great as his own. His ashes were buried with hers in the garden at Passfield Corner, as he wished. But Shaw was determined that the Webbs should be recognized together among the elect, and he wrote to *The Times* proposing their reinterment in Westminster Abbey "to commemorate an unparalleled partnership." On 12 December 1947 Clement Attlee, the second Fabian to become prime minister, gave the address at the Abbey funeral ceremony.

GBS, still active, and delighted by the fuss made of him on his ninetieth birthday, was at work on yet another play when he fell and fractured his leg. He no longer had the strength to cope with the complications, and he died at Ayot on 2 November 1950. His ashes were left, as he instructed, scattered with Charlotte's in their garden.

The last survivors were the first of all the Fabians. Edward Pease died in 1955, only two years short of his centenary, after a forty-year retirement at Limpsfield in which he still followed Fabian affairs like a gruff but benevolent uncle. Percival Chubb, who spent most of his life in the service of the Ethical Church movement in the United States, died in 1959, a year before his hundredth birthday.

All their lives the first Fabians had sought to reconstruct society on new moral principles. Looking back, however, Beatrice made a wry comment on the five partnerships of the Old Gang: the Peases, the Oliviers, the Shaws, the Wallases and the Webbs. "Have there ever been five more respectable, cultivated and mutually devoted and successful couples?", she asked. They were "the utter essence of British bourgeois morality, comfort and enlightenment."[24]

REFERENCES

The main source of material for Sidney and Beatrice Webb is the Passfield Papers, a large collection which includes letters to and from the Webbs, miscellaneous documents and the diaries of Beatrice Webb (BWD). These papers are in the British Library of Political and Economic Science (BLPES), which also holds some Shaw material and a large part of the Wallas papers. The bulk of the Shaw papers are in the British Library, and a part of the Wallas papers are at Newnham College, Cambridge. The John Burns papers are in the British Library. The papers of R. C. K. Ensor are in Corpus Christi College, Oxford. Apart from files of *Fabian News* and other Fabian publications in the offices of the Fabian Society, the surviving records of the Society are at Nuffield College, Oxford (Fabian Papers). The Haldane papers are in the National Library of Scotland. The papers of Thomas Davidson (which include letters from early Fabians) are in the Yale University Library. Percival Chubb's papers are held by his son, R. Walston Chubb, of St. Louis, Missouri. The Wells Archive is at the University of Illinois, Champaign-Urbana. The ILP archives are at Bristol. The Shaw letters quoted below, unless otherwise stated, come from the two volumes of *Collected Letters*, edited by Dan H. Laurence (London, 1965 and 1972). Pease family papers are in the keeping of Nicholas Pease; Olivier family papers are held by Dr. Benedict Richards; and the MacDonald papers are at the Public Record Office. There are Pease and Webb letters at the University of Texas. Additional material will be found in three forthcoming books: the biography of Sidney and Beatrice Webb by Royden Harrison; the biography of Ramsay MacDonald by David Marquand; and *The Letters of Sidney and Beatrice Webb*, edited by Norman MacKenzie.

1. THE NICEST SET OF PEOPLE

1. On the politics of the crisis see Burn, W. L., *The Age of Equipoise* (London, 1967); Ensor, R. C. K., *England, 1870–1914* (Oxford, 1936); James, R. R., *Lord Randolph Churchill* (London, 1959); Lynd, H. M., *England in the Eighteen-Eighties* (New York, 1945); and

Magnus, Philip, *Gladstone* (London, 1954).

2. "Faith and Verification," *Nineteenth Century*, IV (1878).

3. The main sources for Pease's life and opinions are his unpublished MSS "Recollections for My Sons," written March 1930, and "Notes on My Life," written December 1950; and "Reminiscences of E.R.P.," by Marian Pease, written October 1953. All these are in the possession of the Pease family.

4. On the SPR, see Gault, Alan, *The Founders of Psychical Research* (London, 1968).

5. Letter in possession of the Pease family.

6. On the socialist revival, see Harrison, Royden, *Before the Socialists* (London, 1965); Hyndman, H. M., *The Record of an Adventurous Life* (London, 1911); Jones, Peter D'A., *The Christian Socialist Revival, 1877–1914* (Princeton, 1968); McBriar, A.M., *Fabian Socialism and English Politics* (Cambridge, 1962), which includes an excellent bibliography on Fabianism; Pelling, Henry, *Popular Politics and Society in Late Victorian Britain* (London, 1968); Pierson, Stanley, *Marxism and the Origins of British Socialism* (Ithaca, 1973); Tsuzuki, C., *Henry M. Hyndman and British Socialism* (Oxford, 1961); and Wolfe, Willard, *From Radicalism to Socialism* (New Haven, 1975).

7. Hyndman, H. M., *op. cit.*

8. Letter of 19 July 1882, Pease family.

9. Ellis, Havelock, *My Life* (London, 1940).

10. Chubb's letters are in the Davidson collection in the Yale University Library, which also contains relevant letters by Podmore, Ellis and Clarke. On Clarke, see Burrows, H., and Hobson, J. A., *William Clarke* (London, 1908), and Weiler, P., "William Clarke: The Making and

Unmaking of a Fabian Socialist," *Journal of British Studies*, 1975.

11. Knight, William, *Memorials of Thomas Davidson* (London, 1907). See also Davidson Papers.

12. 12 June 1882, Davidson Papers.

13. 22 Jan. 1883, *ibid.*

14. 27 Dec. 1882, *ibid.*

15. 24 May 1883, *ibid.*

16. 2 May 1883, *ibid.*

17. 25 Oct. 1883, *ibid.*

18. 6 Nov. 1883, *ibid.*

19. 13 Nov. 1883, *ibid.*

20. 6 Dec. 1883, *ibid.*

21. 15 Dec. and 21 Dec. 1883, *ibid.* The full text of the draft constitution can be found in Pease, E. R., *History of the Fabian Society* (London, 1916).

22. 21 April 1884, to Davidson.

23. Letter in possession of R. Walston Chubb.

24. On the Blands, see Moore, Doris Langley, *E. Nesbit*, rev. ed. (London, 1967).

25. H. M. Hyndman, *The Record of an Adventurous Life* (London, 1911).

26. Letter of 18 March 1884, in possession of R. Walston Chubb.

2. THE DOWNSTART

1. Of the many books on Shaw, for biographical details see especially Ervine, C. St. John, *Bernard Shaw* (London, 1956); Henderson, Archibald, *George Bernard Shaw* (New York, 1956); Irvine, William, *The Universe of George Bernard Shaw* (New York, 1949); Pearson, Hesketh, *Bernard Shaw* (London, 1942).

2. Shaw, G. B., *Sixteen Self-Sketches* (London, 1949).

3. Shaw, G. B., "In the Days of My Youth," *Mainly about People*, 17 Sept. 1898.

4. See Weintraub, S. (ed.), *Shaw—An Autobiography* (London, 1970).

5. Ervine, C. St. John, (ed.), *Ellen Terry and Bernard Shaw Correspondence* (London, 1931).
6. Weintraub, S., *op. cit.*
7. "Why I Am and What I Think," *Candid Friend*, 11 May 1901.
8. Weintraub, S., *op. cit.*
9. Munro, John, *Frederick James Furnivall* (Oxford, 1911).
10. Ervine, C. St. John, *op. cit.*
11. *Collected Letters*, 19 Aug. 1884.
12. See George, Henry, Jr., *The Life of Henry George* (New York, 1930); Birnie, Arthur, *Single-Tax George* (London, 1939); Lawrence, Elwood, *Henry George in the British Isles* (East Lansing, Mich., 1957).
13. In Irvine, William, *op. cit.*
14. "The New Politics," a Fabian Lecture by Shaw on 20 Dec. 1889.
15. *Ibid.*
16. "Why I Am and What I Think," *loc. cit.*
17. See Rodenbeck, John von B., "Bernard Shaw's Revolt against Rationalism," *Victorian Studies*, June 1972; Hummert, Paul A., *Bernard Shaw's Marxist Romance* (Lincoln, Nebr., 1973).
18. Shaw, G. B., "How I Became a Public Speaker," *Sixteen Self-Sketches* (London, 1949).
19. "Mr. Bernard Shaw's Works of Fiction as Reviewed by Himself," *Tinsley's Magazine*, 1892.
20. 8 Jan. 1884, Lloyd Papers, Wisconsin State Historical Society.
21. 12 Dec. 1884, Davidson Papers.
22. Davidson Papers.
23. 5 May 1884, Shaw Papers.
24. Fabian Tract No. 2 (1884).
25. Shaw's speaker's notes 1884–88 are in the British Museum.

3. BOHEMIANS

1. See Nethercot, Arthur H., *The First Five Lives of Annie Besant* (London, 1961); West, Geoffrey, *Annie Besant* (New York, 1928); Shaw, G. B., *et al., Dr. Annie Besant: Fifty Years in Public Work* (London, 1924).
2. Smith, W. S., *The London Heretics* (London, 1967).
3. On their relationship see Nethercot, *op. cit.*
4. Hyndman, H. M., *The Record of an Adventurous Life* (London, 1911).
5. Pearson, Hesketh, *Bernard Shaw* (London, 1942).
6. Tsuzuki, C., *The Life of Eleanor Marx* (Oxford, 1967); Kapp, Yvonne, *Eleanor Marx*, Vol. I (London, 1972).
7. Tsuzuki, C., and Kapp, Yvonne, *op. cit.*
8. On the split, see Thompson, Edward, *William Morris* (London, 1955).
9. On the links between early socialists and the health, food and clothing reform movements, see Newton, S. M., *Health, Art and Reason* (London, 1974).
10. Shaw's diary in BLPES.
11. Moore, Doris Langley, *E. Nesbit* (London, 1967).
12. Shaw *et al., op. cit.*
13. Hulse, James W., *Revolutionists in London* (Oxford, 1969).

4. ACQUAINTANCES IN TROUBLE

1. Shaw, G. B., *Sixteen Self-Sketches* (London, 1949).
2. To Sydney Olivier, 17 July 1885, Passfield Papers.
3. A list of his successes, and some limited biographical materials, can be found in the Passfield Papers.
4. To Graham Wallas, 2 July 1885, Passfield Papers.
5. Olivier, Margaret, *Sydney Olivier* (London, 1948).
6. Olivier's reminiscences are in Olivier, Margaret, *op. cit.* Some

additional MS fragments are in the possession of his grandson, Dr. Benedict Richards.

7. The majority of the Graham Wallas papers are in BLPES, including some biographical materials. Biographical materials collected by his daughter, May Wallas, are with other personal papers at Newnham College, Cambridge. See also Wiener, Martin J., *Between Two Worlds* (Oxford, 1971).

8. Family papers: Dr. Benedict Richards.

9. Letter to Shaw, 11 Aug. 1883, Shaw Papers.

10. *Church Reformer*, March 1884.

11. Olivier, Margaret, *op. cit.* See also Harrison, Royden, *Before the Socialists* (London, 1964) on the political impact of Positivism; and Smith, W. S., *The London Heretics* (London, 1967).

12. Olivier, Margaret, *op. cit.*

13. 24 Oct. 1886, University of Texas.

14. "Lecture on *Progress and Poverty*" (London, 1883).

15. Webb, Sidney, *Economica*, November 1932.

16. Shaw Papers.

17. "Bluffing the Value Theory," *To-Day*, 1889.

18. Herford, C. H., *Philip Henry Wicksteed* (London, 1931).

19. Winsten, S., *Salt and His Circle* (London, 1951); Salt, H., *Company I Have Kept* (London, 1921); Forster, E. M., *Lowes Dickinson* (London, 1934).

20. Passfield Papers.

21. To Shaw, 5 Aug. 1885, Passfield Papers.

22. 26 July 1885, Passfield Papers.

23. 17 Aug. 1885, Passfield Papers.

24. To Beatrice Potter, 11 Oct. 1890, Passfield Papers.

25. Passfield Papers.

26. Pease, E. R., "Recollections for My Sons," Pease family papers.

27. The fullest account is in Moore, D. L., *E. Nesbit* (London, 1967).

28. 16 Nov. 1887, University of Texas.

29. *The Practical Socialist*, February 1886.

30. The minute books are in the Fabian Papers.

31. To G. Burne-Jones, in Henderson, Philip, *William Morris* (London, 1967).

5. ENGLAND, ARISE!

1. Magnus, Philip, *Gladstone* (London, 1954).

2. Perkin, H. J., "Land Reform and Class Conflict in Victorian Britain," in Butt, J., and Clarke, I. F., *The Victorians and Social Protest* (Newton Abbot, 1973).

3. In "Locksley Hall, Sixty Years After."

4. In Pierson, Stanley, *Marxism and the Origins of British Socialism* (Ithaca, N.Y., 1973).

5. Letter to Mrs. Pakenham Beatty, in Shaw, *Collected Letters*.

6. Fabian Tract No. 41.

7. *The Practical Socialist*, January 1886. On "Tory Gold," see Tsuzuki, C., *H. M. Hyndman* (Oxford, 1961).

8. *Weekly Dispatch*, 16 May 1886.

9. *The Practical Socialist*, October 1886.

10. The papers relating to the Trafalgar Square riots are in the Home Office archives. See also Critchley, T. A., *A History of Police in England and Wales* (London, 1967), and *The Conquest of Violence* (London, 1970).

11. Fabian Tract No. 41.

12. *Aberdeen Journal*, 18 Feb. 1886.

13. *Time*, July 1885.

14. See *The Practical Socialist* for July 1886; a manuscript report of the conference is in BLPES.

15. Letter to Pease, University of Texas.
16. Printed as an appendix in Pease, E. R., *History of the Fabian Society* (London, 1916).
17. Wallas Papers.
18. Fabian Tract No. 41.
19. Edward Pease left a manuscript note of this little-known meeting.
20. Wallas Papers.
21. Critchley, T. A., *op. cit.*, for Warren's reports.
22. Letter to William Morris, 22 Nov. 1887.

6. STUMP AND INKPOT

1. For the reactions of the socialist press, see *Justice*, 19 Nov.–24 Dec. 1887; *The National Reformer*, 20 Nov. 1887–15 Jan. 1888; *Our Corner* for December 1887 and January 1888; and *Commonweal*, 12 Nov.–24 Dec. 1887.
2. Nethercot, A., *The First Five Lives of Annie Besant* (London, 1961).
3. *Ibid.*
4. Quoted by Henderson, A., in *George Bernard Shaw* (New York, 1956).
5. Fabian Tract No. 41.
6. Webb to Marjorie Davidson, 12 Dec. 1888, Pease family papers.
7. Webb to Wallas, 17 Sept. 1888, Wallas Papers.
8. Webb to Wallas, 13 Oct. 1888, *ibid.*
9. Pease to his sister May, 4 Dec. 1888, Pease family papers.
10. Marjorie Davidson to Shaw, 2 Jan. 1888, Shaw Papers.
11. Webb to Marjorie Davidson, 12 Dec. 1888, Pease family papers.
12. Marjorie Davidson to Shaw, 27 Jan. 1889, Shaw Papers.
13. Olivier to Marjorie Davidson, 31 Jan. 1889, Pease family papers.
14. Marjorie Davidson to Shaw, 27 Jan. 1889, Shaw Papers.

15. Shaw to Janet Achurch, 17 June 1889, *Collected Letters*.
16. Weintraub, S. (ed.), *Shaw: An Autobiography* (London, 1970).
17. To E. D. Girdlestone, 10 and 18 Sept. 1890, *Collected Letters*.
18. Weintraub, S., *op. cit.*
19. Olivier, M., *Sydney Olivier: Letters and Selected Writings* (London, 1948).
20. "Communism," in *William Morris: Selected Writings*, ed. Cole, G. D. H. (London, 1934).
21. Weintraub, S., *op. cit.*
22. *Ibid.*
23. To C. Charrington, 28 Jan. 1890, *Collected Letters*.

7. ANGELS ON OUR SIDE

1. Reported in *Labour Elector*, 3 Aug. 1889. On the congresses, see Cole, G. D. H., *Socialist Thought: The Second International, 1889-1914*, Part I (London, 1956).
2. Hyndman's comment is in his foreword to Burgess, J., *John Burns* (Glasgow, 1911). On Burns see also Kent, William, *John Burns: Labour's Lost Leader* (London, 1950).
3. See Torr, Dona, *Tom Mann and His Times* (London, 1956); *Tom Mann's Memoirs* (London, 1956).
4. Thorne, W., *My Life's Battles* (London, 1925).
5. Tillett, Ben, *A Brief History of the Dockers' Union* (London, n.d.).
6. For contemporary accounts see Smith, H. L., and Nash, V., *The Story of the Dockers' Strike* (London, 1889); Champion, H. H., *The Great Dock Strike* (London, 1890).
7. Burns, John, *The Liverpool Congress* (London, 1890).
8. Quoted in Cole, G. D. H., and Postgage, R., *The Common People* (London, 1946).
9. See Pelling, H., *The Origins of the Labour Party* (London, 1954).

10. On the establishment of the LCC and the Fabian attitude towards it, see McBriar, A. M., *Fabian Socialism and English Politics, 1884–1914* (Cambridge, 1962).

11. 11 Dec. 1888, *Collected Letters*.

12. Letter to William Sanders, 28 March 1889.

13. All the following quotations from *Fabian Essays*, the edited version of these lectures, come from the edition of 1889.

14. Shaw's marginal comment on the MS of Pease, E., *The History of the Fabian Society* (London, 1913), in BLPES.

15. Shaw to Emery Walker, 12 Sept. 1889.

16. Shaw to Charles Charrington, 28 Jan. 1890.

17. Pease, E., *op. cit.*

18. Fabian Tract No. 45.

19. "Richard Cobden," *British Quarterly Review*, January 1882.

20. "The 'Spoils' System in American Politics," *Contemporary Review*, October 1881.

21. 22 Oct. 1884, Lloyd Papers, Wisconsin State Historical Society.

22. Clarke, W. (ed.), *Essays Selected from the Writings, Literary, Political and Religious, of Joseph Mazzini* (London, 1887).

23. "Toynbee Hall," *The Christian Register*, 8 Sept. 1887.

garet, *Beatrice Webb* (London, 1945), and Muggeridge, Kitty, and Adam, Ruth, *Beatrice Webb* (London, 1967). References to the diary are not given where they are clearly identifiable in the text.

2. The work on this book is described at length in *My Apprenticeship*.

3. *My Apprenticeship*.

4. *Ibid.*

5. *Ibid.*

6. See the comments of Michel Chevalier, whose visit is described in Taine, H., *Notes on England* (London, 1872).

7. *My Apprenticeship*.

8. BWD, 8 April 1884.

9. BWD, 31 March 1883.

10. *My Apprenticeship*.

11. *Ibid.*

12. *Ibid.*

13. See Fraser, Peter, *Joseph Chamberlain* (London, 1966).

14. BWD, 22 April 1884.

15. The period of work in the East End is recalled at length in *My Apprenticeship*.

16. The letter, undated, is in the Passfield Papers.

17. BWD, 15 Sept. 1885.

18. The will is copied into the diary.

19. The letter, dated 13 Feb. 1886, is inserted in the diary.

20. The letters are in the Passfield Papers.

21. Passfield Papers.

8. LITTLE BUSY BEE

1. Beatrice Webb's Diary (BWD) is in the Passfield Papers at the London School of Economics. Substantial parts of it were quoted by her in *My Apprenticeship* (London, 1926) and *Our Partnership* (London, 1948). Margaret Cole published two further volumes of extracts (London, 1952, 1956). On the life of Beatrice Webb see also Cole, Mar-

9. A YEAR OF LOVE

1. BWD, 26 April 1890.

2. *Ibid.*

3. *My Apprenticeship*.

4. BWD, Whitsun 1890.

5. 11 June 1890, Passfield Papers.

6. 16 June 1890, Passfield Papers.

7. 22 June 1890, Passfield Papers.

8. BWD, 27 July 1890.

9. 29 July 1890, Passfield Papers.

10. Passfield Papers (undated).
11. Shaw to William Archer, 17 Aug. 1890.
12. 29 July 1890, Passfield Papers.
13. Passfield Papers (undated).
14. Passfield Papers (undated).
15. BWD, 26 Aug. 1890.
16. 23 Aug. 1890, Passfield Papers.
17. 26 Aug. 1890, Passfield Papers.
18. BWD, 7 Sept. 1890.
19. Passfield Papers (undated).
20. 17 Sept. 1890, Passfield Papers.
21. Report on the Lancashire Campaign, 4 Nov. 1890.
22. 21–26 Sept. 1890, Passfield Papers.
23. 6 Oct. 1896.
24. 8–10 Oct. 1890, Passfield Papers.
25. Passfield Papers (undated).
26. 11 Oct. 1890, Passfield Papers.
27. Passfield Papers (undated).
28. Passfield Papers.
29. *Ibid.*
30. Webb, S., *Socialism in England* (Baltimore: American Economic Association, 1889).
31. Shaw, G. B., *et al.*, *Dr. Annie Besant: Fifty Years in Public Work* (London, 1924).
32. 16 Dec. 1890.
33. Passfield Papers (undated).
34. 5 Dec. 1890, Passfield Papers.
35. BWD, 12 Dec. 1890.

10. EXIT BEATRICE POTTER
1. Policy document of 20 Dec. 1890, Fabian Papers.
2. *Ibid.*
3. Wallas Papers, BLPES.
4. BWD, 1 Dec. 1890.
5. Passfield Papers (undated).
6. BWD, 4 Jan. 1891.
7. BWD, 22 Jan. 1891.
8. 27 Jan. 1891, Passfield Papers.
9. 2 Feb. 1891, *ibid.*
10. 23 Feb. 1891, *ibid.*
11. 13 March 1891, *ibid.*
12. 6 April 1891, *ibid.*
13. *My Apprenticeship.*

14. BWD, 22 May 1891.
15. *Ibid.*
16. *Ibid.*
17. BWD, 31 May 1891.
18. *Ibid.*
19. BWD, 22 June 1891.
20. BWD, 7 July 1891.
21. Passfield Papers (undated).
22. BWD, 14 Aug. 1891.
23. 25 July 1891, Haldane Papers.
24. Passfield Papers (undated).
25. BWD, October 1891.
26. Kate Courtney's diary, BLPES.
27. BWD, 22 May 1893.
28. Passfield Papers (undated).
29. Haldane Papers.
30. 9 Dec. 1891, Passfield Papers.
31. F. W. Galton's unpublished MS autobiography in BLPES.
32. 14 Nov. 1891, Passfield Papers.
33. 11 Dec. 1891, *ibid.*
34. Fabian Papers.
35. 12 Dec. 1891, Passfield Papers.
36. Wallas Papers.
37. *The Speaker*, 3 Oct. 1891.
38. Quoted in McBriar, A. M., *Fabian Socialism and English Politics, 1884–1914* (Cambridge, 1962).
39. 24 March 1892, Passfield Papers.
40. BWD, 21 Jan. 1892.
41. BWD, 4 May 1892.
42. 11 May 1892, Passfield Papers.
43. Fabian Tract No. 41.
44. Fabian Papers.
45. Magnus, P., *Gladstone* (London, 1954).
46. Passfield Papers (undated).
47. Passfield Papers (undated).
48. 6 July 1892, Passfield Papers.
49. Pease, E., *The History of the Fabian Society* (London, 1913).
50. Kate Courtney's diary, BLPES.
51. BWD, 23 July 1892.

11. THE QUINTESSENCE OF SHAW
1. *Collected Letters.*
2. Sonnenschein and Joynes quoted in

Henderson, A., *George Bernard Shaw* (New York, 1956).

3. See Henderson, A., *op. cit.*, and Walency, Maurice, *The Cart and the Trumpet: The Plays of George Bernard Shaw* (New York, 1973).

4. Archer, W., *English Dramatists of To-Day* (London, 1882).

5. See Shaw's preface to *Widowers' Houses,* Independent Theatre Series, ed. J. T. Grein (London, 1893).

6. To Charles Charrington, 28 Jan. 1890.

7. Lees, Edith, *Stories and Essays* (London, 1914).

8. *Clarion*, 1 June 1906.

9. 15 Sept. 1891, Passfield Papers.

10. See the letters from Ibsen in August 1890 quoted in Laurvik, J. N., and Morrison, M., *The Letters of Henrik Ibsen* (New York, 1905).

11. Weintraub, S. (ed.), *Shaw: An Autobiography* (London, 1970).

12. 31 March 1891.

13. On Grein, see Orme, Michael (Alice A. Grein), *J. T. Grein* (London, 1936).

14. See Meisel, Martin, *Shaw and the Nineteenth Century Theatre* (Princeton, 1963).

15. To C. Charrington, 14 Dec. 1892.

16. Dickinson, G. Lowes, *Autobiography* (London, 1973).

17. Archer, W., review of *Widowers' Houses,* in *The World*, 4 May 1893.

18. Meisel, M., *op. cit.*

19. Shaw, G. B., preface to *Plays Unpleasant* (London, 1898).

12. ENTHUSIASTS

1. A file of *Seed-Time* is in the Fabian Papers. This 1890 article is signed "A Fabian" and titled "Individualism in Masquerade."

2. *Seed-Time*, July 1896.

3. *Ibid.*, July 1889.

4. Carpenter's papers are in the Sheffield Reference Library.

5. "The Simple Life," article by Henry Binns in *Seed-Time*, 1894.

6. Lees, Edith, *Attainment* (London, 1909).

7. Binns, Henry, *op. cit.*

8. Weir, L. Macneil, *The Tragedy of Ramsay MacDonald* (London, 1938); and Elton, Lord, *The Life of James Ramsay MacDonald* (London, 1939). See also the forthcoming biography of MacDonald by David Marquand.

9. *Labour Leader*, 23 Dec. 1904.

10. The correspondence is in the Fabian Papers.

11. *Clarion*, 25 April 1896.

12. On Blatchford, see Thompson, Laurence, *Robert Blatchford* (London, 1951).

13. *Ibid.*

14. *Ibid.*

15. *Ibid.*

16. *Ibid.*

17. On John Trevor, see Pierson, Stanley, *Marxism and the Origins of British Socialism* (Ithaca, 1973), and Trevor, J., *My Quest for God* (Manchester, 1897).

18. Trevor, J., *My Quest for God.*

19. Herford, C. H., *Philip Henry Wicksteed* (London, 1931).

20. 25 Jan. 1892, Passfield Papers.

21. McMillan, Margaret, *The Life of Rachel McMillan* (London, 1927).

22. Thompson, L., *op. cit.*

13. POSTULATE, PERMEATE, PERORATE

1. *Our Partnership.*

2. Passfield Papers.

3. *Our Partnership.*

4. Quoted in Irvine, William, *The Universe of G.B.S.* (New York, 1949).

5. Ervine, St. John, *Bernard Shaw* (London, 1956).

6. BWD, 10 July 1894.

7. *Ibid.*

8. Letter to Pease, 18 April 1892, Passfield Papers.
9. BWD, 1 Dec. 1892.
10. Quoted in Pelling, H., *The Origins of the Labour Party* (London, 1954).
11. See *Workman's Times*, 26 Nov. 1892; also, Fabian Society Minutes for 17 and 28 Oct. 1892.
12. See Shaw's extended account in *Workman's Times*, 28 Jan. 1893.
13. Shaw later wrote a long description of this episode to Walter Crane on 15 Dec. 1895.
14. Shaw attributed the phrase to Wallas when writing to William P. Johnson on 24 April 1893.
15. BWD, 30 July 1893.
16. BWD, 17 Sept. 1893.
17. *Ibid.*
18. Shaw diary.
19. Preface to *Mrs. Warren's Profession*.
20. BWD, 12 Oct. 1893.
21. *Ibid.*
22. Wallas Papers.
23. BWD, Christmas Day 1893.
24. Fabian Papers.
25. The Massingham and Haldane letters are in the Passfield Papers.
26. BWD, 25 Dec. 1893.
27. BWD, 12 March 1894.
28. BWD, 24 Dec. 1893.
29. BWD, 12 March 1894.
30. *Ibid.*
31. Hughes, Emrys, *Keir Hardie* (London, 1956).

14. PROFESSIONALS

1. 13 Feb. 1893.
2. 17 April 1894.
3. Yeats, W. B., *Autobiographies* (London, 1961).
4. To Elisabeth Marbury. Quoted in Henderson, A., *George Bernard Shaw* (New York, 1956).
5. 23 April 1894.
6. Quoted in Henderson, A., *op. cit.*

7. 2 July 1894, *Collected Letters*.
8. 14 April 1895. Quoted in *Collected Letters*.
9. 5 May 1894, Passfield Papers.
10. In Cole, M., *The Webbs and Their Work* (London, 1949).
11. The method is described in an appendix to *My Apprenticeship*.
12. BWD, 25 July 1894.
13. *Ibid.*
14. The Hutchinson Papers are in the BLPES. An extended summary is given in Caine, Sidney, *The History of the Foundation of the London School of Economics and Political Science* (London, 1963).
15. BWD, September 1894.
16. 28 Sept. 1894. Quoted in Caine, S., *op. cit.*
17. The Haldane opinion is given in Caine, S., *op. cit.*
18. *Labour Leader*, 28 July 1894.
19. BWD, 23 Jan. 1895.
20. BWD, 27 May 1895.
21. BWD, 8 July 1895.
22. On the Liberal crisis see Emy, H. V., *Liberals, Radicals and Social Politics, 1893–1914* (Cambridge, 1973), and Hamer, D. A., *Liberal Politics in the Age of Gladstone and Rosebery* (Oxford, 1972).
23. Samuel, H., *Memoirs* (London, 1945).
24. 18 July 1895, Lloyd Papers.
25. BWD, 10 July 1895.
26. BWD, 5 Jan. 1896.
27. Samuel, H., *op. cit.*
28. 13 April 1895.
29. Strachey, Amy, *St. Loe Strachey: His Life and His Paper* (London, 1930).
30. Bertha Newcombe to Ashley Dukes, quoted in *Collected Letters*.
31. 24 Aug. 1895.
32. *Ibid.*
33. *Ibid.*
34. 16 Sept. 1895.
35. Preface to *Man of Destiny*.
36. 9 March 1896.

15. NEW ALLIANCES

1. BWD, Whitsun 1896.
2. BWD, 5 Jan. 1896.
3. Passfield Papers.
4. Hutchinson Papers, BLPES.
5. BWD, Whitsun 1896.
6. BWD, 29 July 1897.
7. 22 Jan. 1896.
8. Passfield Papers.
9. BWD, 18 April 1896.
10. Quoted in Fremantle, Anne, *This Little Band of Prophets* (London, 1960).
11. BWD, 18 April 1896.
12. The letters are in the Fabian Papers.
13. 25 Jan. 1897, Samuel Papers.
14. *Ethical World*, 8 Oct. 1896. On the mood of depression that led to several breakdowns and suicides, see also *Labour Leader*, 27 Aug. 1898; Wallis, Lena, *Life and Letters of Carolyn Martin* (London, 1898); and Shaw, G. B., "The Illusions of Socialism," in Carpenter, E. (ed.), *Forecasts of the Coming Century* (Manchester, 1897).
15. 21 Nov. 1899, Passfield Papers.
16. *Labour Prophet*, February 1895.

14. Ellen Terry to Shaw, 6 Nov. 1896.
15. Shaw to Charlotte Payne-Townshend, 9 Nov. 1896.
16. 10 Nov. 1896.
17. 17 Nov. 1896.
18. Wallas Papers, BLPES.
19. 18 March 1897.
20. BWD, 9 March 1897.
21. BWD, 1 May 1897.
22. BWD, 8 May 1897.
23. BWD, 3 May 1897.
24. BWD, 28 June 1897.
25. 29 April 1897.
26. To Ellen Terry, 28 May 1897.
27. BWD, 15 July 1897.
28. Fabian Papers.
29. BWD, 21 Jan. 1898.
30. BWD, 27 Sept. 1897.
31. 4 April 1896.
32. To Ellen Terry, 30 Nov. 1896.
33. Fabian Papers.
34. BWD, 16 Sept. 1896.
35. BWD, January 1898.
36. BWD, 11 Jan. 1898.
37. BWD, March 1898.
38. BWD, 15 June 1897.
39. BWD, 11 Jan. 1898.
40. 3 Dec. 1897.
41. 18 Jan. 1898.
42. BWD, March 1898.

16. THE IRISH LADY

1. BWD, 16 Sept. 1896.
2. Charlotte Shaw to T. E. Lawrence, 17 May 1927; see also Dunbar, Janet, *Mrs. G.B.S.* (New York, 1963).
3. Fabian Papers.
4. BWD, 14 Aug. 1896.
5. Russell, Bertrand, *Portraits from Memory* (London, 1956).
6. 10 July 1906, in Archer, C., *William Archer* (London, 1931).
7. BWD, 16 Sept. 1896.
8. 27 Oct. 1896.
9. 2 and 4 Nov. 1896.
10. 4 Nov. 1896.
11. 7 Nov. 1896.
12. 2 Nov. 1896.
13. 5 Nov. 1896.

17. FRESH STARTS

1. Shannon, D. (ed.), *Beatrice Webb's American Diary* (Madison, 1963). On this journey see also *Visit to New Zealand in 1898* (Beatrice Webb's diary with entries by Sidney Webb) (Wellington, 1959); Austin, A. G., *The Webbs' Australian Diary, 1898* (Melbourne, 1964); and a draft chapter omitted from *Our Partnership*, "Round the English Speaking World, 1898," BLPES.
2. Beatrice Webb to Kate Courtney, 1 Nov. 1898, Passfield Papers.
3. Shaw to Sidney Webb, 11 April 1898.

4. *American Diary.*
5. 26 April 1898, Passfield Papers.
6. *American Diary.*
7. *Ibid.*
8. 6 April 1898, Passfield Papers.
9. *American Diary.*
10. *Ibid.*
11. *Ibid.*
12. *Ibid.*
13. *Ibid.*
14. 26 April 1898, Passfield Papers.
15. 29 April 1898, *ibid.*
16. *Ibid.*
17. *American Diary.*
18. 5 June 1898, Passfield Papers.
19. *American Diary.*
20. *Ibid.*
21. *Ibid.*
22. *Visit to New Zealand.*
23. To Kate Courtney, 24 Aug. 1898, Passfield Papers.
24. *Australian Diary.*
25. To Kate Courtney, 7 Nov. 1898, Passfield Papers.
26. 16 Oct. 1898, Fabian Papers.
27. Interview in the *Echo,* 30 Dec. 1898.
28. See Tsuzuki, C., *The Life of Eleanor Marx* (Oxford, 1967).
29. 11 April 1898.
30. 13 April 1898.
31. 19 April 1898.
32. 22 April 1898.
33. Charlotte Shaw Papers, British Museum.
34. Fabian Papers.
35. See Dunbar, Janet, *Mrs. G.B.S.* (New York, 1963).
36. 21 June 1898.
37. *Ibid.*
38. 26 May 1898.
39. *The Star,* 2 June 1898.
40. 21 June 1898.
41. 28 July 1898.
42. 18 Oct. 1898.
43. 7 May 1898, Passfield Papers.
44. Passfield Papers.
45. *Ibid.*
46. BWD, January 1899.
47. Fabian Papers.
48. Quoted in Dunbar, J., *op. cit.*
49. BWD.

18. JOE'S WAR

1. 24 Jan. 1899.
2. 8 Aug. 1899.
3. 24 Aug. 1899.
4. 30 Oct. 1899.
5. *Labour Leader,* 10 Dec. 1898.
6. *Clarion,* 28 Oct. 1899.
7. BWD, 10 Oct. 1899.
8. *Our Partnership.*
9. Fabian Papers.
10. 17 Oct. 1899, Fabian Papers.
11. 9 April 1900, Passfield Papers.
12. Fabian Papers.
13. *Ibid.*
14. *Ibid.* Reprinted in full in McBriar, A. M., *Fabian Socialism and English Politics, 1884–1914* (Cambridge, 1962).
15. To George Samuel, *c.* 23–24 Dec. 1899.
16. 8 March 1899.
17. Shaw to members of the Fabian Society, 11 April 1900, *Collected Letters.*
18. See Pelling, Henry, *The Origins of the Labour Party* (London, 1954); Pelling, Henry, *Labour and Politics, 1900–1906* (London, 1958); and Reid, J. H. S., *The Origins of the British Labour Party* (Minneapolis, 1955).
19. On the LRC conference, see Pelling, Henry, *op. cit.*
20. To J. M. Strudwick, 4 Sept. 1900.

19. MEN AND SUPERMEN

1. BWD, March 1898.
2. BWD, 31 Jan. 1900.
3. BWD, 15 Dec. 1900.
4. BWD, 7 Oct. 1900.
5. BWD, 19 July 1900.
6. Passfield Papers.

7. Quoted in Caine, Sidney, *The History of the Foundation of the London School of Economics and Political Science* (London, 1963).
8. BWD, 1 Jan. 1901.
9. BWD, 9 Feb. 1901.
10. BWD, 4 July 1900.
11. BWD, 22 March 1901.
12. BWD, 2 Jan. 1901.
13. Russell, B., *Portraits from Memory* (London, 1956).
14. BWD, 1 July 1901.
15. BWD, 28 Feb. 1902.
16. *Ibid.*
17. BWD, 2 April 1901.
18. BWD, 22 March 1901.
19. BWD, 8 March 1901.
20. Passfield Papers.
21. BWD, 15 Jan. 1901.
22. *Ibid.*
23. BWD, 9 Dec. 1901.
24. BWD, 9 July 1901.
25. See Wilson, John, *CB: The Life of Campbell-Bannerman* (London, 1973).
26. BWD, 28 July 1901.
27. *Collected Letters.*
28. 30 July 1901, *Collected Letters.*
29. BWD, 28 July 1901.
30. Passfield Papers.
31. 23 Sept. 1901, Passfield Papers.
32. BWD, 25 Feb. 1902.
33. *Ibid.*
34. *Ibid.*
35. BWD, 19 March 1902.
36. *Ibid.*
37. 26 Sept. 1903, Russell Papers, McMaster University.
38. See Semmel, Bernard, *Imperialism and Social Reform* (London, 1960), and Searle, C. R., *The Quest for National Efficiency* (Oxford, 1971).
39. Wells Archive.
40. BWD, 16 Jan. 1903.
41. Ensor Papers.
42. 27 Jan. 1900.
43. 3 and 8 Aug. 1899.
44. 6 May 1903.
45. 2 Aug. 1903.
46. BWD, 16 Jan. 1903.
47. 2 Sept. 1903.
48. 6 March 1903.

20. WIREPULLERS

1. Passfield Papers.
2. BWD, 25 Feb. 1903.
3. BWD, 20 June 1904.
4. 10 Jan. 1904, Passfield Papers.
5. Fabian Papers.
6. 30 May 1903, Fabian Papers.
7. BWD, 15 June 1903.
8. Burns Papers.
9. Fabian Papers.
10. *Collected Letters.*
11. Passfield Papers.
12. *Ibid.*
13. 22 Jan. 1904, Fabian Papers.
14. BWD, 15 June 1904.
15. Gardiner, A. G., *Pillars of Society* (London, 1914).
16. 2 Nov. 1902, Passfield Papers.
17. BWD, 24 July 1903.
18. 26 July 1903, Passfield Papers.
19. BWD, 8 July 1903.
20. BWD, 7 March 1904.
21. BWD, 6 Dec. 1903.
22. BWD, 7 March 1904.
23. 14 March 1904.
24. 8 July 1900.
25. 25 Dec. 1900.
26. See Purdom, C. B., *Harley Granville Barker* (London, 1955).
27. Purdom, C. B., *The Shaw-Barker Letters* (London, 1956).
28. 5 Oct. 1904, quoted in *Collected Letters.*
29. To Ada Rehan, 5 July 1904.
30. McCarthy, Lillah, *Myself and Friends* (London, 1933).
31. 5 March 1905.
32. 24 Dec. 1905.
33. BWD, 29 Nov. 1905.
34. BWD, 2 Dec. 1905.
35. BWD, 14 Oct. 1905.
36. Quoted in Pelling, H., *Labour and Politics, 1900–1906* (London, 1958).

37. BWD, 2 Dec. 1905.
38. *Clarion*, 2 Feb. 1906.

23. Wells Archive.
24. 4 July 1905.

21. MODERN UTOPIANS

1. Rowntree, S., *Poverty* (London, 1901); see also Bruce M., *The Rise of the Welfare State* (London, 1973); Williams, G., *The Coming of the Welfare State* (London, 1967); Fraser, D., *The Evolution of the British Welfare State* (London, 1973), which includes bibliography.
2. Mowat, C. L., *The Charity Organisation Society* (London, 1961).
3. Report of the Royal Commission on the Poor Laws and Relief of Distress, 1901, Vol. I, Appendix.
4. BWD, 2 Dec. 1905.
5. BWD, 15 Dec. 1905.
6. BWD, 15 June 1906.
7. BWD, 29 May 1906.
8. Wells, H. G., "The Faults of the Fabian," reprinted as an appendix in Hynes, S., *The Edwardian Frame of Mind* (London, 1968).
9. BWD, December 1901.
10. Wells Archive.
11. *Ibid.*
12. See MacKenzie, Norman and Jeanne, *The Time Traveller: A Biography of H. G. Wells* (London, 1973), for an extended study of Wells, especially his relations with the Fabian Society, and for bibliography.
13. *Ibid.*
14. Wells, H. G., *Experiment in Autobiography* (London, 1934).
15. Chesterton, A. E. C., *The Chestertons* (London, 1941).
16. Wells Archive.
17. 26 March 1904.
18. Wells Archive.
19. BWD, 17 April 1905.
20. Olivier, M., *Sydney Olivier* (London, 1948).
21. Ford, F. M., *Mightier than the Sword* (London, 1938).
22. 5 June 1905.

22. NEW WORLDS FOR OLD

1. "The Faults of the Fabian," in Hynes, S., *The Edwardian Frame of Mind* (London, 1968).
2. Wells Archive.
3. 18 Feb. 1906, Wells Archive.
4. BWD, 1 March 1906.
5. Wells Archive.
6. 25 Nov. 1906.
7. 24 March 1906.
8. Wells Archive.
9. BWD, 20 March 1906.
10. BWD, 2 July 1906.
11. 4 Sept. 1906, Wells Archive.
12. 6 Sept. 1906, *ibid.*
13. 3 Sept. 1906, *ibid.*
14. 13 June 1906, *ibid.*
15. Wells Archive.
16. 14 Sept. 1906.
17. *Ibid.*
18. *The Times Literary Supplement*, 14 Sept. 1906.
19. Fabian Papers.
20. BWD, 18 Oct. 1906.
21. Wells Archive (n.d.).
22. To S. McClure, 11 Nov. 1906, *ibid.*
23. 4 Dec. 1906.
24. 1 Sept. 1906.
25. 10 Dec. 1906.
26. 12 Dec. 1906, Wells Archive.
27. Wells Archive.
28. Fabian Papers.
29. BWD, 15 Dec. 1906.
30. Letter of 4 Jan. 1907, *Fabian News*, February 1907.
31. *The Christian Commonwealth*, 19 May 1909.
32. Wells Archive.
33. Ensor Papers.
34. Wells Archive.
35. 24 Jan. 1907, Passfield Papers.
36. Undated letter, Wells Archive.
37. BWD, 10 April 1907.
38. BWD, 12 Nov. 1907.
39. BWD, 18 Feb. 1907.

40. Betty Balfour to Beatrice Webb, 11 Sept. 1906, Passfield Papers.
41. To Mary Playne, June 1907, Passfield Papers.
42. Young, Kenneth, *Arthur James Balfour* (London, 1963).
43. BWD, 18 March 1907.
44. To Mary Playne, Passfield Papers.
45. Letter to G. C. Cotterill, 12 Dec. 1907, in *The Letters of Rupert Brooke*, ed. Geoffrey Keynes (London, 1968).
46. Dalton, Hugh, *Call Back Yesterday* (London, 1953).
47. Fabian Papers.
48. Gill, Eric, *Letters* (London, 1947).
49. Mairet, P., *A. K. Orage* (London, 1936); Martin, Wallace, *The New Age Under Orage* (Manchester, 1967).
50. 9 June 1907, Wells Archive.
51. *Fabian News*, April 1907.
52. 12 June 1907, Wells Archive.
53. Wells Archive.
54. *Ibid.*
55. 14 Aug. 1907.
56. Wells Archive.
57. Purdom, C. B., *The Shaw–Barker Letters* (London, 1936).
58. Undated letter, December 1907.
59. *Ibid.*
60. See Archer, William, "Fabianism and the Drama," *New Age*, 3 Oct. 1908.
61. *Labour Leader*, March 1908.
62. 10 March 1908, Wells Archive.
63. 9 March 1908, *ibid.*
64. Wells Archive.
65. *Ibid.*
66. *Ibid.*
67. 25 April 1908, *ibid.*
68. Fabian Papers.

23. LUXURIOUS PERVERSITY
1. BWD, 22 Feb. 1908.
2. BWD, 13 Jan. 1908.
3. BWD, 2 Feb. 1908.
4. BWD, 3 May 1908.
5. 12 Dec. 1907, Bodleian.
6. BWD, n.d. (early April 1908).
7. Letter to Asquith, 14 March 1908, quoted in Churchill, Randolph S., *Winston S. Churchill*, Vol. II (London, 1967).
8. BWD, 8 July 1908.
9. BWD, 11 March 1908.
10. BWD, 15 May 1908.
11. BWD, 10 Feb. 1908.
12. BWD, 11 March 1908.
13. BWD, 19 May 1908.
14. BWD, 27 July 1908.
15. BWD, 29 Oct. 1908.
16. 6 July 1908, Passfield Papers.
17. Passfield Papers.
18. BWD, 15 Nov. 1908.
19. July 1908, Passfield Papers.
20. BWD, 18 Feb. 1909.
21. *Ibid.*
22. 12 Aug. 1908, Fabian Papers.
23. BWD, 17 Jan. 1909.
24. In Shaw, *Collected Letters*.
25. Shaw to Trebitsch, 29 June 1908.
26. 22 April 1908.
27. Undated letter, Wells Archive. See MacKenzie, N. and J., *The Time Traveller* (London, 1973) for relevant letters and an extended account.
28. Letter to Pease, 16 Sept. 1908, Wells Archive.
29. Letter to Cazenove, 18 May 1908, *ibid.*
30. BWD, 15 Sept. 1908.
31. BWD, August 1909.
32. 27 Feb. 1909, Fabian Papers.
33. To Trebitsch, 29 June 1908.
34. 19 Aug. 1908, in Purdom, E. B., *The Shaw–Barker Letters* (London, 1956).
35. *Fabian News*, June 1909.
36. BWD, 15 May 1909.
37. *Ibid.*
38. BWD, 22 July 1909.
39. BWD, 23 July 1909.
40. BWD, 22 July 1909.
41. Passfield Papers.

42. BWD, 27 Sept. 1909.
43. BWD, 3 Oct. 1909.
44. BWD, 8 Jan. 1910.
45. August 1910, Passfield Papers.
46. 22 Dec. 1910, *ibid.*
47. BWD, 24 May 1910.
48. BWD, 19 Aug. 1910.
49. 18 Dec. 1910, Passfield Papers.
50. 5 Sept. 1910, in *The Letters of Rupert Brooke*, ed. Geoffrey Keynes (London, 1968).
51. BWD, 4 Sept. 1910.
52. Undated letter, Wells Archive.
53. Wells Archive.
54. Passfield Papers.
55. 30 Sept. 1909.
56. 11 Sept. 1909, Passfield Papers.
57. BWD, 4 Oct. 1909.
58. *Spectator*, 20 Nov. 1909.
59. See MacKenzie, N. and J., *op. cit.*
60. "My Lucky Moment," *The View*, 29 April 1911.
61. BWD, 5 Nov. 1910.
62. BWD, 13 March 1910.
63. Ervine, C. St. John, (ed.), *Ellen Terry and Bernard Shaw* (London, 1931).
64. BWD, 27 Dec. 1909.

24. HEARTBREAK HOUSE
1. BWD, 10 Dec. 1910.
2. BWD, 30 Nov. 1910.
3. BWD letter to Betty Balfour, 22 Dec. 1910, Passfield Papers.
4. BWD, 7 March 1911. Cf. *The Crusade* for details of the campaign.
5. BWD, 19 Oct. 1910. The relevant letters are in the diary MS.
6. BWD, 5 Nov. 1910.
7. BWD, 9 Oct. 1910.
8. 22 March 1911, Passfield Papers.
9. 27 March 1910, Fabian Papers.
10. 13 Oct. 1910, Shaw Papers.
11. 5 Dec. 1911, Fabian Papers.
12. *Fabian News*, August 1912.
13. Shaw to Pease, 3 March 1911. There is a copy in the Ensor Papers.

14. 6 March 1911, Shaw Papers.
15. See materials in the Ensor Papers.
16. 20 Oct. 1911, Passfield Papers.
17. *New Age*, 14 April 1910.
18. Quoted in Muggeridge, Kitty, and Adam, Ruth, *Beatrice Webb* (London, 1967).
19. Cole, Margaret, *The Life of G. D. H. Cole* (London, 1971).
20. BWD, 2 May 1914.
21. BWD, 16 April 1912.
22. *Ibid.*
23. 20 Sept. 1911, Passfield Papers.
24. 30 Nov. 1911, *ibid.*
25. BWD, 5 Sept. 1911.
26. BWD, 1 Dec. 1912.
27. BWD, 11 Oct. 1912.
28. 12 Dec. 1912, Lansbury Papers.
29. Fabian Papers.
30. *Ibid.*
31. Passfield Papers.
32. See Hyams, Edward, *The New Statesman* (London, 1963).
33. BWD, 13 Jan. 1913.
34. BWD, 21 April 1911.
35. 3 Oct. 1909.
36. McCarthy, Lilliah, *My Life and Friends* (London, 1933).
37. *Ellen Terry and Bernard Shaw: A Correspondence* (London, 1931).
38. See Dent, Alan, *Mrs. Patrick Campbell* (London, 1961).
39. Purdom, E. D. (ed.), *The Shaw-Barker Letters* (London, 1956).
40. *Bernard Shaw and Mrs. Patrick Campbell: Their Correspondence* (London, 1952) and for subsequent quotations.
41. Campbell, Mrs. Patrick, *My Life and Some Letters* (London, n.d.).
42. *Ibid.*
43. *Ibid.*
44. 12 April 1914, Shaw Papers.
45. Dent, Alan, *op. cit.*
46. Campbell, Mrs. Patrick, *op. cit.*
47. BWD, 12 July 1913.
48. BWD, 2 Jan. 1914.
49. Shaw Papers.
50. BWD, 3 May 1914.

51. BWD, Aug. 1918 (inserted in 1914 entry).
52. BWD, late 1915.

EPILOGUE

1. For the later years of the Webbs see the manuscript of BWD and the two volumes of extracts by Cole, Margaret (London, 1952, 1956); Muggeridge, K., and Adam, R., *Beatrice Webb;* Hamilton, M. A., *Sidney and Beatrice Webb* (London, 1933); and Cole, Margaret (ed.), *The Webbs and Their Work* (London, 1949).
2. BWD, 10 Jan. 1918.
3. BWD, 6 July 1916.
4. Muggeridge, K., and Adam, R., *op. cit.*
5. BWD, 17 Nov. 1922.
6. BWD, 13 Feb. 1923.
7. BWD, 8 Jan. 1924.
8. BWD, 5 Dec. 1925.
9. *Ibid.*
10. The letter of 14 Aug. 1914 is inserted in the BWD MS.
11. BWD, 28 Nov. 1929.
12. BWD, 14 Dec. 1929.
13. Epilogue to *Our Partnership.*
14. BWD, 10 Sept. 1931.
15. BWD, 4 Jan. 1932.
16. *Ibid.*
17. Cole, Margaret (ed.), *The Webbs and Their Work.*
18. "Sixty Years of Fabianism," appendix to 1962 edition of *Fabian Essays.*
19. *Ibid.*
20. Olivier, M., *Sydney Olivier* (London, 1948): letters of 28 Aug. 1942 and 10 Oct. 1942.
21. 29 Jan. 1934, Shaw Papers.
22. Passfield Papers.
23. Shaw Papers.
24. BWD, 16 July 1935.

INDEX